P9-CJF-503

Voice over IP Fundamentals, Second Edition

Jonathan Davidson
James Peters
Manoj Bhatia
Satish Kalidindi
Sudipto Mukherjee

Cisco Press

800 East 96th Street
Indianapolis, IN 46240 USA

ii

Voice over IP Fundamentals, Second Edition

Jonathan Davidson, James Peters, Manoj Bhatia, Satish Kalidindi, and Sudipto Mukherjee

Copyright© 2007 Cisco Systems, Inc.

Published by:
Cisco Press
800 East 96th Street
Indianapolis, IN 46240 USA

All rights reserved. No part of this book may be reproduced or transmitted in any form or by any means, electronic or mechanical, including photocopying, recording, or by any information storage and retrieval system, without written permission from the publisher, except for the inclusion of brief quotations in a review.

Printed in the United States of America 1 2 3 4 5 6 7 8 9 0

First Printing   July   2006

Library of Congress Cataloging-in-Publication Number: 2005934132

ISBN: 1-58705-257-1

Warning and Disclaimer

This book is designed to provide information about the fundamentals of Voice over IP (VoIP). Every effort has been made to make this book as complete and as accurate as possible, but no warranty or fitness is implied.

The information is provided on an "as is" basis. The authors, Cisco Press, and Cisco Systems, Inc. shall have neither liability nor responsibility to any person or entity with respect to any loss or damages arising from the information contained in this book or from the use of the discs or programs that may accompany it.

The opinions expressed in this book belong to the author and are not necessarily those of Cisco Systems, Inc.

Feedback Information

At Cisco Press, our goal is to create in-depth technical books of the highest quality and value. Each book is crafted with care and precision, undergoing rigorous development that involves the unique expertise of members from the professional technical community.

Readers' feedback is a natural continuation of this process. If you have any comments regarding how we could improve the quality of this book, or otherwise alter it to better suit your needs, you can contact us through email at feedback@ciscopress.com. Please make sure to include the book title and ISBN in your message.

We greatly appreciate your assistance.

Trademark Acknowledgments

All terms mentioned in this book that are known to be trademarks or service marks have been appropriately capitalized. Cisco Press or Cisco Systems, Inc., cannot attest to the accuracy of this information. Use of a term in this book should not be regarded as affecting the validity of any trademark or service mark.

Publisher	Paul Boger
Cisco Representative	Anthony Wolfenden
Cisco Press Program Manager	Jeff Brady
Acquisitions Editor	Elizabeth Peterson
Production Manager	Patrick Kanouse
Senior Development Editor	Christopher A. Cleveland
Project Editor	Tonya Simpson
Copy Editor	Karen Gill
Technical Editors	Brian Gracely, Jesse Herrera, Brion Washington
Editorial Assistant	Vanessa Evans
Book Designer	Louisa Adair
Cover Designer	Louisa Adair
Composition	Mark Shirar
Indexer	Tim Wright

CISCO SYSTEMS

Corporate Headquarters
Cisco Systems, Inc.
170 West Tasman Drive
San Jose, CA 95134-1706
USA
www.cisco.com
Tel: 408 526-4000
 800 553-NETS (6387)
Fax: 408 526-4100

European Headquarters
Cisco Systems International BV
Haarlerbergpark
Haarlerbergweg 13-19
1101 CH Amsterdam
The Netherlands
www-europe.cisco.com
Tel: 31 0 20 357 1000
Fax: 31 0 20 357 1100

Americas Headquarters
Cisco Systems, Inc.
170 West Tasman Drive
San Jose, CA 95134-1706
USA
www.cisco.com
Tel: 408 526-7660
Fax: 408 527-0883

Asia Pacific Headquarters
Cisco Systems, Inc.
Capital Tower
168 Robinson Road
#22-01 to #29-01
Singapore 068912
www.cisco.com
Tel: +65 6317 7777
Fax: +65 6317 7799

Cisco Systems has more than 200 offices in the following countries and regions. Addresses, phone numbers, and fax numbers are listed on the
Cisco.com Web site at www.cisco.com/go/offices.

Argentina • Australia • Austria • Belgium • Brazil • Bulgaria • Canada • Chile • China PRC • Colombia • Costa Rica • Croatia • Czech Republic
Denmark • Dubai, UAE • Finland • France • Germany • Greece • Hong Kong SAR • Hungary • India • Indonesia • Ireland • Israel • Italy
Japan • Korea • Luxembourg • Malaysia • Mexico • The Netherlands • New Zealand • Norway • Peru • Philippines • Poland • Portugal
Puerto Rico • Romania • Russia • Saudi Arabia • Scotland • Singapore • Slovakia • Slovenia • South Africa • Spain • Sweden
Switzerland • Taiwan • Thailand • Turkey • Ukraine • United Kingdom • United States • Venezuela • Vietnam • Zimbabwe

Copyright © 2003 Cisco Systems, Inc. All rights reserved. CCIP, CCSP, the Cisco Arrow logo, the Cisco *Powered* Network mark, the Cisco Systems Verified logo, Cisco Unity, Follow Me Browsing, FormShare, iQ Net Readiness Scorecard, Networking Academy, and ScriptShare are trademarks of Cisco Systems, Inc.; Changing the Way We Work, Live, Play, and Learn, The Fastest Way to Increase Your Internet Quotient, and iQuick Study are service marks of Cisco Systems, Inc.; and Aironet, ASIST, BPX, Catalyst, CCDA, CCDP, CCIE, CCNA, CCNP, Cisco, the Cisco Certified Internetwork Expert logo, Cisco IOS, the Cisco IOS logo, Cisco Press, Cisco Systems, Cisco Systems Capital, the Cisco Systems logo, Empowering the Internet Generation, Enterprise/Solver, EtherChannel, EtherSwitch, Fast Step, GigaStack, Internet Quotient, IOS, IP/TV, iQ Expertise, the iQ logo, LightStream, MGX, MICA, the Networkers logo, Network Registrar, *Packet*, PIX, Post-Routing, Pre-Routing, RateMUX, Registrar, SlideCast, SMARTnet, StrataView Plus, Stratm, SwitchProbe, TeleRouter, TransPath, and VCO are registered trademarks of Cisco Systems, Inc. and/or its affiliates in the U.S. and certain other countries.

All other trademarks mentioned in this document or Web site are the property of their respective owners. The use of the word partner does not imply a partnership relationship between Cisco and any other company. (0303R)

Printed in the USA

About the Authors

Jonathan Davidson, CCIE No. 2560, is the Director of SP Solution Engineering in Integrated Network Systems Engineering. He has coauthored *Voice over IP Fundamentals* and edited *Deploying Cisco Voice over IP*. He has been with Cisco for 10 years in postsales support, marketing, and engineering divisions.

James Peters is the Director of Product Marketing in the Carrier Core and Multiservice Business Unit at Cisco Systems. He coauthored the first edition of *Voice over IP Fundamentals* and is currently authoring a book on multiservice networking. James has more than 20 years experience in building and designing Internet-based voice and data networks, and product development.

Manoj Bhatia is a Business Development Manager for Partner Programs at IP Communications Business Unit (IPCBU) for Cisco Systems, Inc. He was among the first to start the software development for SIP technology on Cisco VoIP gateways and IOS-based routers. His past projects include technical marketing for VoIP products such as media gateways, call agents, and SIP-based residential voice solutions. Prior to Cisco, Manoj worked in Nortel Networks and Summa Four (now Cisco) and has 14+ years of experience in telephony protocols such as SS7, call control, and VoIP technologies.

Satish Kalidindi is a Software Engineer with Cisco Systems. He has more than six years experience working on development and deployment of VoIP technologies. He has been involved with various products, including IOS gateways and Cisco CallManager. More recently he has been involved with security features on CCM. He is a graduate of Purdue University with an M.S. in engineering.

Sudipto Mukherjee is a Software Development Engineer with Cisco Systems. He has product development and deployment experience for a variety of telecommunication devices for wireline, wireless, and VoIP networks. More recently at Cisco he has been working on SIP gateway development. Sudipto has a bachelors of engineering degree in electronics communication engineering from GS Institute of Technology, Indore, and a masters degree in electronics design and technology from Indian Institute of Science, Bangalore.

About the Technical Reviewers

Brian Gracely, CCIE No. 3077, is a Technical Leader for Cisco/Linksys Small Business Systems Business Unit. He is responsible for the overall solution architecture of the Linksys One solution, which targets converged networking for small businesses. He has been with Cisco for 10 years and has worked in a number of design, engineering, marketing, and support positions. He was a coauthor of the first edition of *Voice over IP Fundamentals*.

Jesse J. Herrera is a Senior Systems Analyst for a Fortune 100 company located in Houston, Texas. Mr. Herrera holds a bachelor of science in computer science from the University of Arizona and a master of science in telecommunications management from Southern Methodist University. Responsibilities have included design and implementation of enterprise network architectures, including capacity planning, performance monitoring, and network integration services. Recent activities include wireless and virtual private network initiatives and support of electronic business services.

Brion S. Washington, CCNA, has more than 10 years internetworking experience, with the last 4 years dedicated to VoIP. He is studying now for his second R/S lab attempt and for the CCVP certification. He lives in the Midwest, where he works as a network consultant.

Acknowledgments

Jonathan Davidson:

I'd like to give special recognition to John Kane for working so diligently and patiently while we put together this second edition. I also would like to thank Manoj Bhatia, Satish Kalidindi, and Sudipto Mukherjee for making this second edition possible.

I also would like to once again thank my children, Megan and Ethan, for putting up with a dad always typing on his laptop. You two are the best.

Manoj Bhatia:

I would like to thank the Cisco press team, my coauthors and reviewers, and Chris Losack, my manager, for encouraging me in this effort.

I also would like to thank my wife Anu, and my kids, Dhvani and Rhythm, for keeping up with me during long-haul hours of research and typing for the topics. I hope they are much more aware of the buzzword VoIP, as they are the true users of VoIP now and in the years to come!

Satish Kalidindi:

I would like to acknowledge John Kane and the editorial team at Cisco Press for their concerted efforts and encouragement. Thanks to reviewers and my coauthors for their diligent work.

Thanks also to my wife Valli, for bearing with me over many long nights.

Sudipto Mukherjee:

I thank my coauthors, reviewers, and my manager, Kimberly Quinn, for providing support and encouragement. Special thanks to the Cisco Press team for its patience and understanding as the material came together.

I thank my parents for their encouragement and support.

I thank my wife Chandrima, and children, Shreyasi and Joydeep, for their love and support while I worked on this book.

Contents at a Glance

Contents

Icons Used in This Book

Communication Server — PC — PC with Software — Sun Workstation — Macintosh — Access Server — ISDN/Frame Relay Switch

Token Ring — Terminal — File Server — Web Server — Cisco Works Workstation — ATM Switch — Modem

Printer — Laptop — IBM Mainframe — Front End Processor — Cluster Controller — Multilayer Switch

Gateway — Router — Bridge — Hub — DSU/CSU — FDDI — Catalyst Switch

Network Cloud — Line: Ethernet — Line: Serial — Line: Switched Serial

Command Syntax Conventions

The conventions used to present command syntax in this book are the same conventions used in the IOS Command Reference. The Command Reference describes these conventions as follows:

- **Boldface** indicates commands and keywords that are entered literally as shown. In actual configuration examples and output (not general command syntax), boldface indicates commands that are manually input by the user (such as a **show** command).

- *Italics* indicate arguments for which you supply actual values.

- Vertical bars (|) separate alternative, mutually exclusive elements.

- Square brackets [ ] indicate optional elements.

- Braces { } indicate a required choice.

- Braces within brackets [{ }] indicate a required choice within an optional element.

Introduction

In the first edition of this book, which was completed in 1999, there was a struggle happening between the "new-world service providers" and the existing "monolithic providers and corporations." We all know the ending to this particular story. Most of the new-world companies and service providers went out of business, and their assets were liquidated or consumed by the monolithic service providers.

The fallout from the bubble burst had an impact on Voice over IP (VoIP) as well. Was VoIP going to be an additional victim of the technologies and startups that were attached to the new way of doing business? You don't have to look into a crystal ball to determine the outcome. The marketplace has decided. VoIP, and in general, "IP communications," is and will continue to be the de facto mechanism for communications for the foreseeable future.

In a recent report by the Telecommunications Industry Association (TIA), residential VoIP consumers more than tripled in 2005. The TIA also predicted a compounded annual growth rate of more than 40% through 2009. This would account for more than 18 million consumer VoIP connections. This shows that packet voice is not only growing rapidly, it is here to stay. This is just one example in the consumer space of the adoption of this technology. The adoption in small, midsize, and large businesses has also been tremendous.

Legacy TDM PBXs are being replaced at a rapid pace by feature-rich enterprise business communication tools. It is not just about a cheaper way to transmit voice, but rather an entirely new way of communicating with your peers and associates.

The original version of this book has had a rather long shelf life. My original coauthor James Peters and I designed the book to focus on the basic fundamentals that would allow for this to be a reference for many years. Although the marketplace may change week to week and month to month, once the basic foundational technologies are over their initial hyper growth, they usually level off to a steady technical growth driven by new applications.

The original *Voice over IP Fundamentals* is a dinosaur in technical book lifespan, but many of its original tenets hold true. One goal for the update of this book was to refresh all the technology elements that have changed over the past six years. For example, Session Initiation Protocol (SIP) was just being finalized in 1999, and yet today it is the cornerstone for many new applications (mobile phone "push to talk" and the IMS architecture). A second key goal of the refresh, and just as important, is to discuss the new applications for these fundamental technologies and how they impact their users.

Purpose of This Book

What is VoIP and in what ways does it apply to you? VoIP provides the capability to break up your voice into small pieces (known as samples) and place them in an IP packet. Voice and data networking on their own are complex technologies, and there are many books written on each subject. This book explains how a basic telephony infrastructure is built and works today, major concepts concerning voice and data networking, transmission of voice over data, and IP signaling protocols used to interwork with current telephony systems. It also answers the following key questions:

- What is IP?
- How is voice signaled in telephone networks today?
- What are the various IP signaling protocols, and which one is best for which types of networks?
- What is quality of service (QoS) and how does one ensure good voice quality in a network?

In addition to covering these concepts, this book also explains the basics of VoIP so that a network administrator, software engineer, or someone simply interested in the technology has the foundation of information needed to understand VoIP networks.

This book is meant to accomplish the following goals:

- Provide an introduction to the basics of enterprise and public telephony networking
- Introduce IP networking concepts
- Provide a solid explanation of how voice is transported over IP networks
- Cover the various caveats of converging voice and data networks
- Provide detailed reference information on various Public Switched Telephone Network (PSTN) and IP signaling protocols

Although this book contains plenty of technical information and suggestions for ways you can build a VoIP network, it is not a design and implementation guide in that it doesn't provide detailed deployment information.

Who Should Read This Book?

Even though this book is written for anyone seeking to understand how to use IP to transport voice, its target audience comprises both voice and data networking experts. In the past, voice and data gurus did not have to know or understand each other's roles. In this world of time-division multiplexing (TDM) and IP convergence, however, it is important to understand how these technologies work. This book explains the details so that voice experts can begin to understand data networking, and vice versa.

The book layout generates yet another audience: Those who have limited data and voice networking knowledge but are technically savvy will be able to understand the basics of both voice and data networking along with how the two converge.

Despite its discussions of voice and data networking, this book is really about VoIP, and the protocols that affect VoIP are explained in great detail. This makes this book a reference guide for those designing, building, deploying, or even writing software for VoIP networks.

Readers familiar with IP networking might want to skip Chapter 6, "IP Tutorial." Similarly, voice-networking experts might want to skip Chapter 3, "Basic Telephony Signaling."

Chapter Organization

Chapter 1, "Overview of the PSTN and Comparisons to Voice over IP," contrasts the similarities and differences between traditional TDM networks and networks running packetized voice.

Chapter 2, "Enterprise Telephony Today," Chapter 3, Chapter 4, "Signaling System 7," and Chapter 5, "PSTN Services," cover enterprise telephony, the basics of PSTN signaling, Signaling System 7 (SS7), and other PSTN services. These chapters provide the background information needed by data networking professionals who are just stepping into the voice realm. They also act as a good primer for those in specific voice areas who want to brush up on various other voice-networking protocols.

Chapter 6 is an introduction into the world of IP. Basic subnetting and the Open Systems Interconnection (OSI) reference model are covered, and comparisons between Transmission Control Protocol (TCP) and User Datagram Protocol (UDP) are provided.

Chapter 7, "VoIP: An In-Depth Analysis," and Chapter 8, "Quality of Service," go into great detail on VoIP and how all the functional components fit together to form a solution. They include discussions of jitter, latency, packet loss, codecs, QoS tools, mean opinion scores (MOS), and the caveats to consider when implementing packet voice networks.

Chapter 9, "Billing and Mediation Services," reviews the importance of billing in a connectionless IP environment. Without a required physical location and the capability to connect from anywhere, new business models are built requiring us to rethink how billing and mediation takes place in the Voice over IP network.

Chapter 10, "Voice Security," discusses the common types of threats that are inherent in a packet voice environment.

Chapter 11, "H.323," Chapter 12, "SIP," and Chapter 13, "Gateway Control Protocols," cover the various signaling protocols and their potential uses. These chapters enable implementers to understand the network components and signaling required to set up calls, tear down calls, and offer services.

Chapter 14, "PSTN and VoIP Interworking," and Chapter 15, "Service Provider VoIP Applications and Services," cover the functional components of using Cisco gateways to deploy a VoIP network. These chapters include configuration details and sample case studies.

Chapter 16, "Enterprise Voice over IP Applications and Services," covers the architectural and functional components required to deploy an enterprise voice network using gateways. This chapter also discusses how VoIP technology can boost enterprise productivity using collaborative applications such as web conferencing and presence-aware services.

Features and Text Conventions

Text design and content features used in this book are intended to make the complexities of VoIP clearer and more accessible.

Key terms are italicized the first time they are used and defined. In addition, key terms are spelled out and followed with their acronym in parentheses, where applicable.

Note boxes point out areas of special concern or interest that might not fit precisely into the discussion at hand but are worth considering. Sometimes, these boxes contain extraneous information in the form of tips, and sometimes they appear in the form of cautions to help you avoid certain pitfalls.

Chapter summaries provide a chance for you to review and reflect upon the information discussed in each chapter. You might also use these summaries to determine whether a particular chapter is appropriate for you to read in full.

References to further information, including many Requests for Comments (RFCs), are included at the end of many chapters. Although not all the references are cited directly in each chapter, all were useful to us as we prepared this book.

Timeliness

As of the writing of this book, the baseline technologies have been well-defined. However, the use of these technologies and which architectural mechanisms to use for application deployment and development are still in their infancy. Many applications have been developed and successfully deployed; however, the network is just beginning its migration into a rapid application development framework. In the first writing of this book, the legality of VoIP in many developing countries was tenuous or unknown. This has greatly changed, and in most places VoIP is legal and prospering. This book is still a basic guide for the new VoIP technologist. Keep in mind that these technologies will continue to evolve to support new applications. I would recommend continuing your learning by reviewing the appropriate signaling drafts from the Internet Engineering Task Force (IETF; http://www.ietf.org) and the International Telecommunication Union (ITU; http://www.itu.int/).

The Road Ahead...

VoIP has already drastically changed the way we communicate with each other on a daily basis. Right now, it is highly likely that you have already talked to someone over an IP network. As VoIP allows data networks and voice networks to converge, you will continue to see new applications, such as presence-based voice, that will drive new means of communication and collaboration. We hope you enjoy reading this book as much as we enjoyed writing it!

Part I: PSTN

CHAPTER 1

Overview of the PSTN and Comparisons to Voice over IP

The Public Switched Telephone Network (PSTN) has been evolving ever since Alexander Graham Bell made the first voice transmission over wire in 1876. But, before explaining the present state of the PSTN and what's in store for the future, it is important that you understand PSTN history and its basics. As such, this chapter discusses the beginnings of the PSTN and explains why the PSTN exists in its current state.

This chapter also covers PSTN basics, components, and services to give you a good introduction to how the PSTN operates today. Finally, it discusses where the PSTN could be improved and ways in which it and other voice networks are evolving to the point at which they combine data, video, and voice.

The Beginning of the PSTN

The first voice transmission, sent by Alexander Graham Bell, was accomplished in 1876 through what is called a *ring-down* circuit. A ring-down circuit means that there was no dialing of numbers, Instead, a physical wire connected two devices. Basically, one person picked up the phone and another person was on the other end (no ringing was involved).

Over time, this simple design evolved from a one-way voice transmission, by which only one user could speak, to a bi-directional voice transmission, whereby both users could speak. Moving the voices across the wire required a carbon microphone, a battery, an electromagnet, and an iron diaphragm.

It also required a physical cable between each location that the user wanted to call. The concept of dialing a number to reach a destination, however, did not exist at this time.

To further illustrate the beginnings of the PSTN, see the basic four-telephone network shown in Figure 1-1. As you can see, a physical cable exists between each location.

Figure 1-1   *Basic Four-Phone Network*

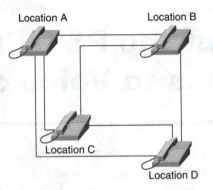

Place a physical cable between every household requiring access to a telephone, however, and you'll see that such a setup is neither cost-effective nor feasible (see Figure 1-2). To determine how many lines you need to your house, think about everyone you call as a value of N and use the following equation: $N \times (N-1)/2$. As such, if you want to call 10 people, you need 45 pairs of lines running into your house.

Figure 1-2   *Physical Cable Between All Telephone Users*

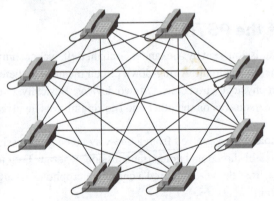

Due to the cost concerns and the impossibility of running a physical cable between everyone on Earth who wanted access to a telephone, another mechanism was developed that could map any phone to another phone. With this device, called a *switch*, the telephone users needed only one cable to the centralized switch office, instead of seven.

At first, a telephone operator acted as the switch. This operator asked callers where they wanted to dial and then manually connected the two voice paths. Figure 1-3 shows how the four-phone network example would look today with a centralized operator to switch the calls.

Figure 1-3   *Centralized Operator: The Human Switch*

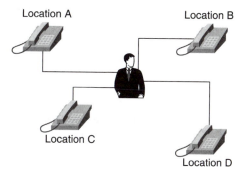

Now, skip ahead 100 years or so—the human switch is replaced by electronic switches. At this point, you can learn how the modern PSTN network is built.

Understanding PSTN Basics

Although it is difficult to explain every component of the PSTN, this section explains the most important pieces that make the PSTN work. The following sections discuss how your voice is transmitted across a digital network, basic circuit-switching concepts, and why your phone number follows E.164 numbering format.

> **NOTE**   E.164 is an ITU-T recommendation that defines the international public telecommunication numbering plan used in the PSTN and some other data networks. It also defines the format of telephone numbers. E.164 numbers can have a maximum of 15 digits and are usually written with a + prefix. For international dialing, an appropriate international call prefix may be used.

Analog and Digital Signaling

Everything you hear, including human speech, is in analog form. Until several decades ago, the telephony network was based on an analog infrastructure as well.

Although analog communication is ideal for human interaction, it is neither robust nor efficient at recovering from line noise. (*Line noise* is normally caused by the introduction of static into a voice network by nearby electrical appliances or radio transmitters.) Telephone lines are very sensitive to inductance or voltage produced by these nearby electric circuits and lines. In the early telephony network, analog transmission was passed through amplifiers to boost the signal. But, this practice amplified not just the voice, but the line noise as well. This line noise resulted in an often unusable connection.

NOTE When making a long-distance call, any μ-law to a-law conversion is the responsibility of the μ-law country.

Local Loops, Trunks, and Interswitch Communication

The telephone infrastructure starts with a simple pair of copper wires running to your home. This physical cabling is known as a *local loop*. The local loop physically connects your home telephone to the central office switch (also known as a *Class 5 switch* or *end office switch*). The communication path between the central office switch and your home is known as the *phone line*, and it normally runs over the local loop.

The communication path between several central office switches is known as a *trunk*. Just as it is not cost-effective to place a physical wire between your house and every other house you want to call, it is also not cost-effective to place a physical wire between every central office switch. You can see in Figure 1-7 that a meshed telephone network is not as scalable as one with a hierarchy of switches.

Figure 1-7 *Meshed Network Versus Hierarchical Network*

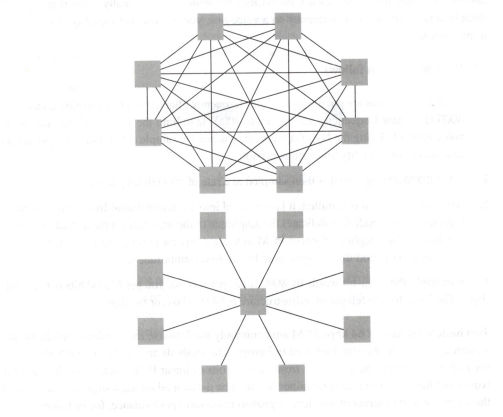

Switches are currently deployed in hierarchies. End office switches (or central office switches) interconnect through trunks to *tandem switches* (also referred to as Class 4 switches). Higher-layer tandem switches connect local tandem switches. Figure 1-8 shows a typical model of switching hierarchy.

Figure 1-8 *Circuit-Switching Hierarchy*

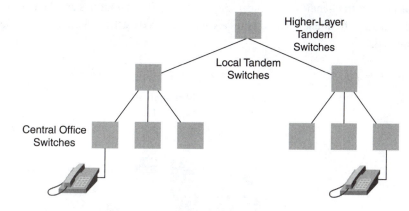

Central office switches often directly connect to each other. Where the direct connections occur between central office switches depends to a great extent on call patterns. If enough traffic occurs between two central office switches, a dedicated circuit is placed between the two switches to offload those calls from the local tandem switches. Some portions of the PSTN use as many as five levels of switching hierarchy.

Now that you know how and why the PSTN is broken into a hierarchy of switches, you need to understand how they are physically connected, and how the network communicates.

PSTN Signaling

Generally, two types of signaling methods run over various transmission media. The signaling methods are broken into the following groups:

- User-to-network signaling—This is how an end user communicates with the PSTN.

- Network-to-network signaling—This is generally how the switches in the PSTN intercommunicate.

User-to-Network Signaling

Generally, when using *twisted copper pair* as the transport, a user connects to the PSTN through analog, Integrated Services Digital Network (ISDN), or through a T1 carrier.

The most common signaling method for user-to-network analog communication is *Dual Tone Multi-Frequency (DTMF)*. DTMF is known as in-band signaling because the tones are carried through the voice path. Figure 1-9 shows how a DTMF keypad is set up.

The DTMF keypad is laid out in a 4×4 matrix, with each row representing a low frequency and each column representing a high frequency. A single key press such as **0** will send a sinusoidal tone of the two frequencies: 941 and 1336 hertz (Hz). The two tones are the reason for calling it dual-tone multifrequency. These tones are then decoded by the switch to determine which key was pressed.

Figure 1-9 *DTMF Keypad*

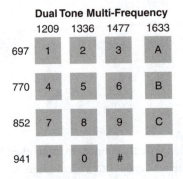

When you pick up your telephone handset and press the digits (as shown in Figure 1-9), the tone that passes from your phone to the central office switch to which you are connected tells the switch what number you want to call.

ISDN uses another method of signaling known as *out-of-band*. With this method, the signaling is transported on a channel separate from the voice. The channel on which the voice, data, fax is carried is called a *bearer* (or B channel) and is 64kbps. The channel on which the signal is carried is called a data or a control channel (D channel).

Basic Rate Interface (BRI) service is the entry level and offers two 64-kbps B channels and one 16-kbps D channel (2B+D). It is intended to meet the needs of most individual users and small offices.

Primary Rate Interface (PRI) service is a more scalable form of the BRI service. A PRI offers twenty three 64-kbps B channels and one 64-kbps D channel (23B+D). PRI is intended for larger enterprises with higher voice, data, or fax traffic. Figure 1-10 shows a BRI that consists of two B channels and one D channel.

Figure 1-10 *BRI*

Out-of-band signaling offers many benefits, including the following:

- Signaling is multiplexed (consolidated) into a common channel.

- Glare is reduced (glare occurs when two people on the same circuit seize opposite ends of that circuit at the same time).

- A lower post dialing delay.

- Additional features, such as higher bandwidth, are realized.

- Because setup messages are not subject to the same line noise as DTMF tones, call completion is greatly increased.

In-band signaling suffers from a few problems, the largest of which is the possibility for *lost tones*. This occurs when signaling is carried across the voice path and it is a common reason why you can sometimes experience problems remotely accessing your voice mail.

Network-to-Network Signaling

Network-to-network communication is normally carried across the following transmission media:

- T1/E1 carrier over twisted pair

  T1 is a 1.544-Mbps digital transmission link normally used in North America and Japan.

  E1 is a 2.048-Mbps digital transmission link normally used in Europe.

- T3/E3, T4 carrier over coaxial cable

  T3 carries 28 T1s or 672 64-kbps connections and is 44.736 Mbps.

  E3 carries 16 E1s or 512 64-kbps connections and is 34.368 Mbps.

  T4 handles 168 T1 circuits or 4032 4-kbps connections and is 274.176 Mbps.

- T3, T4 carrier over a microwave link

- Synchronous Optical Network (SONET) across fiber media

  SONET is normally deployed in OC-3, OC-12, and OC-48 rates, which are 155.52 Mbps, 622.08 Mbps, and 2.488 Gbps, respectively.

Network-to-network signaling types include in-band signaling methods such as Multi-Frequency (MF) and Robbed Bit Signaling (RBS). These signaling types can also be used to carry network signaling methods.

Digital carrier systems (T1, T3) use A and B bits to indicate on/off hook supervision. The A/B bits are set to emulate Single Frequency (SF) tones (SF typically uses the presence or absence of a signal to signal A/B bit transitions). These bits might be *robbed* from the information channel or multiplexed in a common channel (the latter occurs mainly in Europe). More information on these signaling types is found in Chapter 3, "Basic Telephony Signaling."

MF is similar to DTMF, but it utilizes a different set of frequencies. As with DTMF, MF tones are sent in-band. But, instead of signaling from a home to an end office switch, MF signals from switch to switch.

Network-to-network signaling also uses an out-of-band signaling method known as *Signaling System 7* (SS7) (or C7 in European countries). This section covers some of the benefits of SS7, however SS7 is covered in depth in Chapter 4, "Signaling System 7."

> **NOTE**   SS7 is beneficial because it is an out-of-band signaling method and it interconnects to the Intelligent Network (IN). Connection to the IN enables the PSTN to offer Custom Local Area Signaling Services (CLASS) services.

SS7 is a method of sending messages between switches for basic call control and for CLASS. These CLASS services still rely on the end-office switches and the SS7 network. SS7 is also used to connect switches and databases for network-based services (for example, 800-number services and Local Number Portability [LNP]).

Some of the benefits of moving to an SS7 network are as follows:

- Reduced post-dialing delay

   There is no need to transmit DTMF tones on each hop of the PSTN. The SS7 network transmits all the digits in an initial setup message that includes the entire calling and called number. When using in-band signaling, each MF tone normally takes 50 ms to transmit. This means you have at least a .5-second post-dialing delay per PSTN hop. This number is based on 11-digit dialing (11 MF tones × 50 ms = 550 ms).

- Increased call completion

   SS7 is a packet-based, out-of-band signaling protocol, compared to the DTMF or MF in-band signaling types. Single packets containing all the necessary information (phone numbers, services, and so on) are transmitted faster than tones generated one at a time across an in-band network.

■ Connection to the IN

This connection provides new applications and services transparently across multiple vendors' switching equipment as well as the capability to create new services and applications more quickly.

To further explain the PSTN, visualize a call from my house to my Grandma's house 10 miles away. This call traverses an end office switch, the SS7 network (signaling only), and a second end office switch. Figure 1-11 displays the call flow from my house to Grandma's.

Figure 1-11 *PSTN Call Flow to Grandma's House*

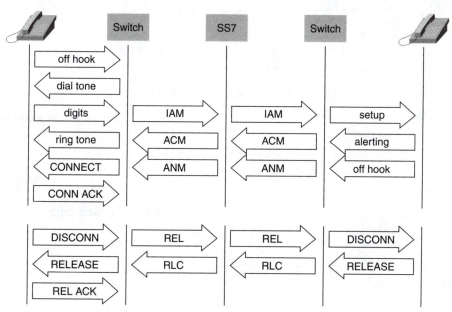

To better explain the diagram in Figure 1-11, let's walk through the flow of the call:

1. I pick up the phone and send an off-hook indication to the end office switch.

2. The switch sends back a dial tone.

3. I dial the digits to call Grandma's house (they are sent in-band through DTMF).

4. The switch interprets the digits and sends an Initial Address Message (IAM, or setup message) to the SS7 network.

5. The SS7 network reads the incoming IAM and sends a new IAM to Grandma's switch.

6. Grandma's switch sends a setup message to Grandma's phone (it rings her phone).

7. An alerting message (alerting is the same as the phone ringing) is sent from Grandma's switch (not from her phone) back to the SS7 network through an Address Complete Message (ACM).

8. The SS7 network reads the incoming ACM and generates an ACM to my switch.

9. I can hear a ringing sound and know that Grandma's phone is ringing. (The ringing is not synchronized; your local switch normally generates the ringing when the ACM is received from the SS7 network.)

10. Grandma picks up her phone, sending an off-hook indication to her switch.

11. Grandma's switch sends an ANswer Message (ANM) that is read by the SS7, and a new ANM is generated to my switch.

12. A connect message is sent to my phone (only if it's an ISDN phone) and a connect acknowledgment is sent back (again, only if it's an ISDN phone). (If it is not an ISDN phone, then on-hook or off-hook representations signal the end office switch.)

13. I can now talk to Grandma until I hang up the phone (on-hook indication).

14. When I hang up, my on-hook is interpreted as a disconnect, which is further translated into a RELEASE (REL) message from the SS7 side. In response to a RELEASE, Grandma's switch side releases the call resources and responds with an acknowledgement in the form of a RELEASE Complete (or RLC). When the switch on my side releases the resources as well, the call disconnect is complete.

If Grandma's phone was busy, I could use an IN feature by which I could camp on her line and have the PSTN call me back after she got off the phone.

Now that you have a basic understanding of how the PSTN functions, the next section discusses services and applications that are common in the PSTN.

If you want more information on PSTN signaling types, see Chapter 3 and Chapter 4.

PSTN Services and Applications

As with almost every industry, it is usually better and easier to acquire additional business from current customers than it is to go out and get new customers. The PSTN is no different. Local Exchange Carriers (LECs) have been increasing the features they offer to create a higher revenue stream per consumer.

Numerous services are now available, for example, which were not available just a few years ago. These services come in two common flavors: *custom calling* features and CLASS features.

Custom calling features rely upon the end office switch, not the entire PSTN, to carry information from circuit-switch to circuit-switch. CLASS features, however, require SS7 connectivity to carry these features from end to end in the PSTN.

The following list includes a few of the popular custom calling features commonly found in the PSTN today:

- Call waiting—Notifies customers who already placed a call that they are receiving an incoming call.

- Call forwarding—Enables a subscriber to forward incoming calls to a different destination.

- Three-way calling—Enables conference calling.

With the deployment of the SS7 network, advanced features can now be carried end to end. A few of the CLASS features are mentioned in the following list:

- Display—Displays the calling party's directory number, or Automatic Number Identification (ANI).

- Call blocking—Blocks specific incoming numbers so that callers are greeted with a message saying the call is not accepted.

- Calling line ID blocking—Blocks the outgoing directory number from being shown on someone else's display. (This does not work when calling 800-numbers or certain other numbers.)

- Automatic callback—Enables you to put a hold on the last number dialed if a busy signal is received and then automatically place the call to the initiator's line once the destination is free. This is sometimes also called *camp on*.

- Call return (*69)—Enables users to quickly reply to missed calls.

A majority of these features are possible due to the use of SS7 and the IN. Many inter-exchange carriers (IXCs) also offer business features, such as the following:

- Circuit-switched long distance—Basic long-distance services (normally at a steeply discounted rate).

- Calling cards—Pre-paid and post-paid calling cards. You dial a number, enter a password, and then call your destination.

- 800/888/877 numbers—The calling party is not charged for the call; Rather, the party called is charged (normally at a premium rate).

- Virtual Private Networks (VPNs)—The telephone company manages a private dialing plan. This can greatly reduce the number of internal Information Service (IS) telecommunications personnel.

- Private leased lines—Private leased lines from 56 kbps to OC-48s enable both data and voice to traverse different networks. The most popular speed by far in North America is T1.

- Virtual circuits (Frame Relay or Asynchronous Transfer Mode [ATM])—The telephone carrier (IXC or LEC) switches your packets. It does this packet by packet (or cell by cell in ATM), not based upon a dedicated circuit.

This list of IXC business features is merely a sampling of the more popular features and applications available in the PSTN. Although the PSTN is evolving and consumers are using more of its features, the basic user experience has remained somewhat consistent since the inception of digital networking for telephony communications.

PSTN Numbering Plans

One feature that slowly changed over time is the dial plan. The addition of second lines for Internet access, cell phones, and fax machines has created a relative shortage of phone numbers. The next section delves into how the PSTN dial plan is put together and what you can expect over the next few years.

In some places in the United States, it is necessary to dial 1+10 digits for even a local call. This will become more and more prevalent as more devices require telephone numbers. The need to dial 1+10 digits for a local number is normally due to an *overlay*. An overlay can result in next-door neighbors having different area codes. An overlay is when a region with an existing area code has another area code "overlayed." This offers the existing customers the benefits of not having to switch area codes, but forces everyone in that region to dial 10 digits to call anywhere.

Some areas do not require the use of 1+ but use the 10 digits. For example, in Houston, the use of 1+ will render an automated reply that it is not necessary to dial 1. However, all 10 other digits are required.

Essentially, two numbering plans are used with the PSTN: the North American Numbering Plan (NANP) and the International Telecommunication Union Telecommunication Standardization Sector (ITU-T; formerly CCITT) International Numbering Plan. They are discussed in the following sections.

NANP

NANP is an 11-digit dialing plan that contains three parts: the Numbering Plan Area (NPA, also referring to as area code), Central Office Code (NXX), and Station Number. This plan is often referred to as NPA-NXX-XXXX.

NPA codes use the following format:

NXX, where N is a value between 2–9 and X is a value between 0–9.

NANP is also referred to as 1+10. This means that when a 1 is the first number dialed, it will be proceeded by a 10-digit NPA-NXX-XXXX number. This enables the end office switch to determine whether it should expect a 7- or 10-digit telephone number.

Your LEC keeps track of what long-distance provider you use in a static table on the end office switch. Each long-distance carrier has a code. This long-distance code is assigned by the North American Numbering Plan Association (NANPA) and is added to the number you call so that it is routed to the proper long-distance network carrier (or IXC).

NOTE   Popular today, carrier-selection numbers are used to have a "secondary" long-distance carrier. Dial-around numbers allow you to choose a long-distance carrier call by call by adding 7 digits to each outgoing call. Much advertising has been done to have telephony users specify 10+XX+XXX to not use their primary carrier.

The reason for carrier selection is simple. You don't have to switch and can use different LD carriers based upon the time of day, week, location called, type of call, or personal preference.

ITU-T International Numbering Plan

ITU-T Recommendation E.164 specifies that a Country Code (CC), National Destination Code (NDC), and Subscriber Number (SN) be used to route a call to a specific subscriber.

The CC consists of one, two, or three digits. The first digit (1–9) defines world numbering zones. A list of all the defined CCs is found in ITU-T Recommendation E.164 Annex A.

NDC and SN vary in length based on the needs of the country. Neither one has more than 15 digits.

Many other recommendations and specifications for international number plans are found in the E. recommendations from the ITU-T.

Although dial plans might not seem extremely important at the moment, they are crucial to the successful deployment and implementation of Voice over IP (VoIP) or traditional circuit-switched networks.

Regardless of which dialing plan is used in your country, you can expect to see changes in the ways you can dial as well as whom you dial.

Drivers Behind the Convergence Between Voice and Data Networking

Understanding PSTN basics includes knowing why the existing PSTN does not fit all the needs of its builders or users. After you understand where today's PSTN is lacking, you will know where to look to find a solution. This section sets the stage for why the voice and data networks are merging into a signal network.

Drawbacks to the PSTN

Although the PSTN is effective and does a good job at what it was built to do (that is, switch voice calls), many business drivers are striving to change it to a new network, whereby voice is an application on top of a data network. This is happening for several reasons:

■ Data has overtaken voice as the primary traffic on many networks built for voice.

Data is now running on top of networks that were built to carry voice efficiently. Data has different characteristics, however, such as a variable use of bandwidth and a need for higher bandwidth.

Soon, voice networks will run on top of networks built with a data-centric approach. Traffic will then be differentiated based upon application instead of physical circuits. New technologies (such as Fast Ethernet, Gigabit Ethernet, and Optical Networking) will be used to deploy the high-speed networks that are needed to carry all this additional data.

■ The PSTN cannot create and deploy features quickly enough.

With increased competition due to deregulation in many telecommunications markets, LECs are looking for ways to keep their existing clientele. The primary method of keeping customers is by enticing them through new services and applications.

The PSTN is built on an infrastructure whereby only the vendors of the equipment develop the applications for that equipment. This means you have one-stop shopping for all your needs. It is very difficult for one company to meet all the needs of a customer. A more open infrastructure, by which many vendors can provide applications, enables more creative solutions and applications to be developed. It is also not possible with the current architecture to enable many vendors to write new applications for the PSTN. Imagine where the world would be today if vendors, such as Microsoft, did not want other vendors to write applications for its software.

- Data/Voice/Video (D/V/V) cannot converge on the PSTN as currently built.

    With only an analog line to most homes, you cannot have data access (Internet access), phone access, and video access across one 56-kbps modem. High-speed broadband access, such as digital subscriber line (DSL), cable, or wireless, is needed to enable this convergence. After the last bandwidth issues are resolved, the convergence can happen to the home. In the backbone of the PSTN, the convergence has already started.

- The architecture built for voice is not flexible enough to carry data.

    Because the bearer channels (B channels and T1 circuits), call-control (SS7 and Q.931), and service logic (applications) are tightly bound in one closed platform, it is not possible to make minor changes that might improve audio quality.

It is also important to note that circuit-switched calls require a permanent 64-kbps dedicated circuit between the two telephones. Whether the caller or the person called is talking, the 64-kbps connection cannot be used by any other party. This means that the telephone company cannot use this bandwidth for any other purpose and must bill the parties for consuming its resources.

Data networking, on the other hand, has the capability to use bandwidth only when it is required. This difference, although seemingly small, is a major benefit of packet-based voice networking.

Packet Telephony Network Drivers

The previous section discussed political drivers for competition in the PSTN. This section explains why a carrier might choose to develop a packet telephony network in lieu of a traditional circuit-switching network.

The integration of D/V/V is more than just a change in infrastructure. D/V/V integration also enables new features to be developed more quickly and opens up application development to thousands of Independent Software Vendors (ISVs). You can compare this integration of D/V/V to the change from mainframe computers, for which very few vendors developed applications, to client/servers, for which multiple vendors developed applications for distributed systems.

Figure 1-12 shows how the circuit-switching model is breaking into a new model by which open standards exist between all three layers. A packet infrastructure will carry the actual voice (media), the call-control layer will be separate from the media layer, and open APIs (Application Programming Interfaces) will enable new services to be created by ISVs.

Figure 1-12 *Circuit Switching Versus Packet Switching*

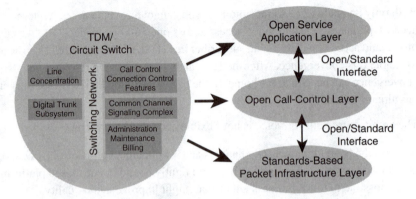

Figure 1-12 is an over-simplification of the changes that are actually happening. To further discuss these changes, you need to take a closer look at each of the three layers.

Standards-Based Packet Infrastructure Layer

The packet infrastructure replaces the circuit-switching infrastructure in this new model. This infrastructure most likely will be IP, although this model also works if ATM is the underlying transport and IP rides across the top. IP is so attractive as the packet infrastructure because of its ubiquitous nature and the fact that it is the de facto application interface. This means that software applications running over IP do not have to be known. IP simply transports the data end to end, with no real interest in the payload.

> **NOTE** To provide the proper prioritization on a *congested* IP network, the IP network must have some knowledge of the applications.

Real-time Transport Protocol (RTP) is utilized in addition to a User Datagram Protocol (UDP)/IP header to provide *timestamping*. RTP runs atop UDP and IP and is commonly noted as RTP/UDP/IP. RTP is currently the cornerstone for carrying real-time traffic across IP networks. (Microsoft Netmeeting, for instance, utilizes RTP to carry audio and video communications.) To date, all VoIP signaling protocols utilize RTP/UDP/IP as their transport mechanism for voice traffic. Often, RTP packet flows are known as *RTP streams*. This nomenclature is used to describe the audio path.

In IP networks, it is common and normal for packet loss to occur. In fact, Transmission Control Protocol/Internet Protocol (TCP/IP) was built to utilize packet loss as a means of controlling the flow of packets. In TCP/IP, if a packet is lost, it is retransmitted. In most real-time applications, retransmission of a packet is worse than receiving a packet due to the time-sensitive nature of the information.

The ITU-T recommends a one-way delay of no more than 150 ms. In a Cisco VoIP network, the unidirectional delay might be 120 ms (currently, 65 ms to 85 ms of that 120-ms delay is derived from two Cisco VoIP gateways when using G.729). If the receiving station must request that a packet be re-transmitted, the delay will be too large, and large gaps and breaks in the conversation will occur.

> **NOTE**   The RTP stream is also often referred to as the *media stream*. Therefore, you can use IP in conjunction with UDP and RTP to replace a traditional 64-kbps voice circuit.

RTP has a field that stamps the exact time the packet was sent (in relation to the entire RTP stream). This information is known as *RTP timestamps* and is used by the device terminating/receiving the audio flow. The receiving device uses the RTP timestamps to determine when a packet was expected, whether the packet was in order, and whether it was received when expected. All this information helps the receiving station determine how to tune its own settings to mask any potential network problems such as delay, jitter, and packet loss.

> **NOTE**   *Jitter* is the variation of interpacket arrival time, or the difference between when a packet is supposed to be received and when it is actually received.

One of the main benefits of IP is the fact that properly built IP networks are *self-healing*. This means that because dynamic routing protocols are used and multiple possible destinations exist, a network can re-converge based upon the best route. It also means that it is possible for your voice (packetized in IP) to take multiple paths to the same destination. Currently you cannot nail up a single path between two destinations. Each individual packet takes the best path between sender and receiver.

The fact that the packet layer is based upon open standards enables multiple vendors to provide solutions that are interoperable. These open standards enable increased competition at this packet layer. The ITU-T, Internet Engineering Task Force (IETF), European Telecommunication Standards Institute (ETSI), and EIA-TIA are only a few of the standards bodies you might be familiar with.

One key component of having a standards-based packet infrastructure is the ability to have open standards to layers at the call-control layer. Referring to Figure 1-12, these open standards are provided by protocols such as SIP, H.323, SGCP, MGCP, MEGACO, and so on, which have open defined interfaces and are widely deployed into the packet infrastructure. One of the jobs of the call-control protocol is to tell the RTP streams where to terminate and where to begin. Call-control accomplishes this task by translating between IP addresses and phone numbering plans.

Open Call-Control Layer

Call-control, in a nutshell, is the process of making a routing decision about where a call needs to go and somehow making the call happen. In the PSTN today, these decisions are carried out by SS7 and are made by Service Control Points (SCPs). Chapter 7, "VoIP: An In-Depth Analysis," discusses how the different VoIP protocols work and how they solve different network design issues.

In this new model of separating the bearers (RTP streams) from the call-control layer and separating the call-control layer from the services, it is necessary to make sure that standards-based protocols are used. Data networking is unique in the fact that multiple protocols can co-exist in a network and you can tailor them to the particular needs of the network.

Many different IP routing protocols exist, for example, and each is specifically designed for a certain type of network. Some of these include the Router Information Protocol (RIP), Interior Gateway Routing Protocol (IGRP), Enhanced Interior Gateway Routing Protocol (EIGRP), Intermediary System to Intermediary System (IS-IS), Open Shortest Path First (OSPF), and Border Gateway Protocol (BGP). Each protocol solves a similar problem—routing updates. Each routing problem is slightly different, however, and requires a different tool. In this case, the tool is a routing protocol, which solves each problem.

You can say the same of VoIP call-control protocols. They all solve a similar problem—phone numbering to IP address translation; however, they might all be used for slightly different purposes.

Many VoIP call-control protocols are being developed, most notably SIP, which continues to take the IP communications world by storm. For the last few years, SIP-based architectures offered more intelligence to the endpoints and have grown substantially in offering VoIP services. They have led to changes in the network that assumed centralized call control using session controllers and *softswitches* that use other protocols like H.323, MGCP, and H.248/MEGACO. Each protocol was developed to fix a certain problem and serve a particular purpose. For the short term, at least, many protocols will be used, and there will be a hybrid network for a while addressing the needs of different network topologies.

VoIP Call-Control Protocols

As of this writing, the main VoIP call-control protocols are SIP, H.323, MGCP, and H.248/MEGACO. Another very popular extension of VoIP telephony is the Peer to Peer (P2P) VoIP IP Telephony Model as used by Skype; however, it is still not endorsed as a standard. The current standards on protocols are defined as follows:

■ H.323 is the ITU-T recommendation with the largest installed base, simply because it has been around the longest and no other protocol choices existed before H.323. Chapter 11, "H.323," discusses this protocol in detail.

■ MGCP has its roots in earlier protocols such as SGCP, and IPDC was developed starting in 1998 to reduce the cost of endpoints (gateways) by having the intelligent call-control occur in a centralized platform (or gateway controller). Chapter 13, "Gateway Control Protocols," covers this in more detail.

■ ITU's H.248, also known as the MEGACO protocol, is the international standard for media gateway control. It is a standard published jointly by the ITU and the IETF. It is primarily used to separate the call control logic from the media processing logic in a gateway. The device that handles the call control function is referred to as a Media Gateway Controller (MGC) and the device that handles the media is referred to as a Media Gateway.

■ SIP is being developed as a media-based protocol that will enable end devices (endpoints or gateways) to be more intelligent, and enable enhanced services down at the call-control layer. Chapter 12, "Session Initiation Protocol," covers SIP in detail.

> **NOTE**   Peer to Peer (P2P) VoIP is still in its infancy and is actively promoted as another technology option for VoIP. P2P networking is the utilization of the relatively powerful computers (personal computers) that exist at the edge of the Internet for more than just client-based computing tasks. The modern PC has a very powerful architecture that can perform VoIP and audio/video conferencing besides performing common computing tasks such as e-mail and Web browsing. The modern PC can easily act as both a client and a server (a peer) for many types of applications. Microsoft and Skype are two vendors that are testing and deploying VoIP as a service over a P2P network.

To briefly explain the various differences between these call-control protocols, let's take a look at how they signal endpoints.

H.323

H.323 is an ITU-T recommendation that specifies how multimedia traffic is carried over packet networks. H.323 utilizes existing standards (Q.931, for example) to accomplish its goals. H.323 is a rather complex protocol that was not created for simple development of applications. Rather, it was created to enable multimedia applications to run over "unreliable" data networks. Voice traffic is only one of the applications for H.323. Most of the initial work in this area focused on multimedia applications, with video and data-sharing a major part of the protocol.

Applications require significant work if they are to be scalable with H.323; for example, to accomplish a call transfer requires a separate specification (H.450.2). SGCP and MGCP, on the other hand, can accomplish a call transfer with a simple command, known as a modify connection (MDCX), to the gateway or endpoint. This simple example represents the different approaches built into the protocol design itself—one tailored to large deployment for simple applications

(MGCP), and the other tailored to more complicated applications but showing limitations in its scalability (H.323).

To further demonstrate the complexity of H.323, Figure 1-13 shows a call-flow between two H.323 endpoints.

Figure 1-13 *H.323 Call-Flow*

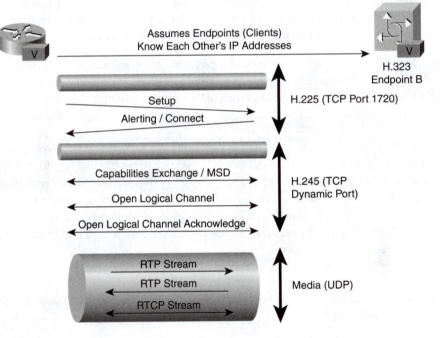

Figure 1-13 illustrates the most basic H.323 call-flow. In most cases, more steps are needed because gatekeepers are involved.

To better explain Figure 1-13, let's step through the call-flow:

1. Endpoint A sends a setup message to Endpoint B on TCP Port 1720.

2. Endpoint B replies to the setup message with an alerting message and a port number to start H.245 negotiation.

3. H.245 negotiation includes codec types (G.729 and G.723.1), port numbers for the RTP streams, and notification of other capabilities the endpoints have.

4.   Logical channels for the UDP stream are then negotiated, opened, and acknowledged.

5.   Voice is then carried over RTP streams.

6.   Real Time Transport Control Protocol is used to transmit information about the RTP stream to both endpoints.

This call-flow is based on H.323 v1. H.323 v2, however, enables H.245 negotiation to be tunneled in the H.225 setup message. This is known as *fast-start*, and it cuts down on the number of roundtrips required to set up an H.323 call. It does not, however, make the protocol any less complex. More detailed analysis of H.323 is found in Chapter 10.

MGCP (Evolution from SGCP and IPDC)

SGCP and MGCP were developed to enable a central device, known as a Media Gateway Controller (MGC) or *softswitch,* to control endpoints or Media Gateways (MGs). You can develop applications through the use of standard-based APIs that interface with the MGCs and offer additional functionality (such as call waiting and CLASS features) and applications.

The Cisco version of this technology is better known in the field as two unique products: Cisco PGW2200 and Cisco BTS10200. Cisco PGW2200, the call agent described here, further consists of many different elements such as Cisco Media Gateway Controller (MGC) software, Cisco Signaling Link Terminals (SLT), LAN switch for IP interconnectivity of Cisco PGW2200 elements, and so on. In this scenario, the entire IP network acts like one large virtual switch, with the PGW controlling all the MGs.

Figure 1-14 shows how a typical network design works with a virtual switch running MGCP.

Figure 1-14   *Cisco PGW2200: Packet Tandem*

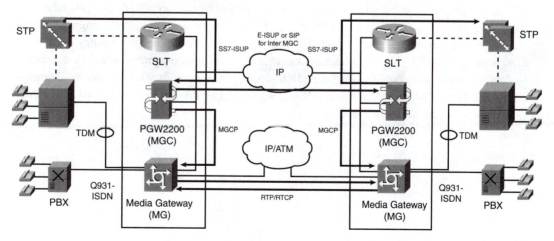

Figure 1-14 also shows how the legacy PSTN and enterprise networks are connected to gateways or endpoints that enable access into the new packet network. This packet gateway receives direction from the Call Agent (PGW2200), which can communicate with the SS7 network and the IN and can tell the gateways or endpoints how and when to set up the call.

To understand Figure 1-14 in greater detail, all the various components must be described. The existing PSTN/SS7 network is connected to the Switching Transfer Point (STP), which also is connected to the MGC or Call Agent. This connection is where the signaling (SS7) links terminate and is called the Signaling Link Terminal (SLT), as shown in the figure. The SLT provides the SS7 interface for the PGW and forms an integral component of any MGC that provides SS7 interface.

The PSTN/SS7 network is also connected to an MG, which is a signal-less trunk that is often known as an *Inter-Machine Trunk* or IMT. The MG is where the 64-kbps voice trunks are converted into packets and placed onto the IP network.

The MGCs or Call Agents (PGW200, in this case) also intercommunicate. There is no common protocol mandated by standards bodies to achieve this, however. Based on the current state of the industry, however, it appears that a variant of SIP or ISDN User Part (ISUP) over IP—a portion of SS7 running on top of IP—will be the primary protocol. The MGCs have a connection to the IN (described earlier in this chapter) to provide CLASS services. The MGCs receive signals from the SS7 network and tell the MGs when to set up IP connections and with which other MGs they should set them up.

The PGW2200, a typical MGC in this case, communicates with the other PGW via the Extended variant of ISUP called E-ISUP. It also separates the D channel from the B channels and forwards the D channel information to the MGC through IP. This mechanism is called *signaling* backhaul and is done via a set of protocol adaptations developed by *sigtran*. SIGTRAN (Signaling Transport) is a working group within the IETF standards organization. These protocols address the functional and performance requirements for the transport of PSTN signaling over IP networks. SIGTRAN helps in identifying what and how signaling protocols can be transported, translated, and/or terminated between IP nodes and other nodes, such as Signaling Gateways (SG), Media Gateway Controllers (MGC), Signaling End Points (SEP) and IP-based databases or Service Control Points (IP-SCP).

SIP

SIP is best described by RFC 3261, which states that it is an application-layer control (signaling) protocol for creating, modifying, and terminating sessions with one or more participants. However, there are numerous additional RFCs developed by the IETF community that complement the core RFC to offer new features with SIP as a protocol for session control in VoIP, as well as PacketCable Multimedia (PCMM), Wireless and Enterprise telephony-based networks.

SIP invitations used to create sessions carry session descriptions that allow participants to agree on a set of compatible media types. SIP makes use of elements called proxy servers to help route requests to the user's current location, authenticate and authorize users for services, implement provider call-routing policies, and provide features to users. SIP also provides a registration function that allows users to upload their current locations for use by proxy servers. SIP runs on top of several different transport protocols.

A lot of implementations of SIP are currently running, although many vendors and customers are interested in using SIP in conjunction with H.323 or MGCP in a hybrid model to allow peering to other nodes in the network to deploy enhanced services.

See Chapter 12 for more detailed information on SIP.

H.248/MEGACO

The Media Gateway Control Protocol (MEGACO) is a result of joint efforts of the IETF and the ITU-T Study Group 16. The protocol definition of this protocol is common text with ITU-T Recommendation H.248.

MGCP/MEGACO exploded H.323's gatekeeper model and removed the signaling control from the gateway, putting it in a media gateway controller (MGC) or *softswitch*. This device would control multiple "media gateways." Effectively, this was a decomposition of the H.323 architecture into SS7 equivalents, creating signaling intelligence that could act as a peer to the SS7 entities.

In the MGCP/MEGACO architecture, the intelligence is unbundled from the media. It is a master-slave protocol where the master has absolute control and the slave simply executes commands. The master is the media gateway controller, or softswitch (or call agent) and the slave is the media gateway (this can be a VoIP gateway, a Digital Subscriber Line Access Multiplexer (DSLAM), Multiprotocol Label Switching (MPLS) router, IP phone, and so on). This is in contrast to the peer-to-peer nature of SIP and other models like that of Skype, where a client can directly establish a session with another client.

MEGACO instructs the media gateway to connect streams coming from outside a packet network on to a packet stream such as RTP. The softswitch issues commands to send and receive media from addresses, to generate tones, and to modify configuration. The architecture, however, requires SIP as the protocol for communication between media gateway controllers (MGC). The key components of MEGACO are as follows:

■   Signaling Gateway (SG)

■   Media Gateway Control (MGC)

■   Media Gateway (MG)

Open Service Application Layer

By far the most interesting layer of any networking protocol is the application layer. Without good applications, the network infrastructure is built for naught. When moving to a new infrastructure, it is not necessary to carry over all the features that are on the old infrastructure. Only the features or applications that customers need are required.

When building a network that has open interfaces from the packet layer to the call-control layer and from the call-control layer to the application layer, vendors no longer have to develop applications. Now, they can simply write to these standard APIs and have access to a whole new infrastructure. When a new packet infrastructure is built, opportunities for new applications become widely available.

Legacy applications such as call-centers for enterprise networks, and standard PSTN applications such as call waiting and call forwarding, must be ported onto a new infrastructure without the end user realizing that the change occurred. After these legacy applications are ported, literally thousands of new enhanced applications can be specifically developed for packet infrastructures. These include (but are not limited to) Internet call waiting, push to talk, find me-follow me, and unified messaging. These applications are discussed in Chapter 6, "Voice over IP Benefits and Applications."

New PSTN Network Infrastructure Model

As discussed in the previous sections, the new infrastructure will focus on the ability to separate the old stagnant infrastructure into a model by which multiple vendors can develop applications and features quickly for the consumer. Figure 1-15 shows how Cisco Systems wants to carry this model forward.

Figure 1-15 clearly shows the relationship between all three layers as well as the relationship between these layers and the components that would be used in a live network. Carriers will enjoy this method, as it means they won't be locked into a single solution for any of their layers. They will be able to mix and match all three layers to offer the services, functionality, and time-to-market that they need.

Some carriers might be hesitant to utilize more than one equipment vendor to cut down on their integration timeframe, but many service providers will partner with a minimum of two vendors to ensure competition.

The reality of Figure 1-15 is that the bearers, connection plane, or media transport will be either IP gateways or ATM gateways, or a combination of both. Multiple vendors will be in this space initially, but most likely, they will consolidate to three to five major players.

Figure 1-15 *Elements of Packet Telephony*

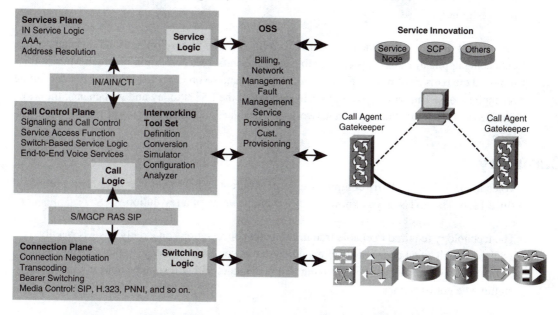

> **NOTE** A common trend in the manufacturing and carrier arena is *consolidation*. The consolidation of manufacturers is one reason for the dramatic reduction in the number of players in this space.

The call-control plane is an extremely important piece of the new PSTN network infrastructure model, as it must gracefully coexist with both the connection plane and the service (application) layers. Many vendors are building technology extensions to SIP and MGCP for enhanced services.

In fact, the authors are working with approximately 15 vendors to ensure compatibility from the connection plane into the call-control and service/application plane.

Many vendors will continue to be in the call-control plane, as service providers will more than likely use several vendors for this key technology, depending upon what service they decide to deploy. The onus on the Call Agent vendors will be to ensure compatibility from one Call Agent to another. Call Agent interoperability is one of the components that could keep service providers from using large-scale, packet-based voice networks.

The service or application plane is where the innovation in the network will happen. One major issue affecting the service plane is its reliance upon softswitch vendors to open APIs that are useful enough to develop services. For this reason, you will see many application vendors attempting to develop Call Agent technology until APIs into the top Call Agent vendors are fully open and service-friendly.

The service plane is where thousands of ISVs will converge to develop new and revenue-enhancing applications. This is comparable to the client/server revolution in which Microsoft removed the barriers of having to code video drivers, and so on, and enabled ISVs to concentrate on applications. This same revolution is happening in the PSTN today and will change the way services and telephony/multimedia networks are designed, built, and deployed.

Summary

Voice in the PSTN is a fairly complex weave of different technologies that have been evolving since 1876. The PSTN as you know it today is on the verge of a revolution.

The technology required to enable true multimedia conversations on a daily basis is readily available. Such a feat does not require a computer as you know it today. Rather, the telephone/communications infrastructure is moving to a new model and will soon be able to carry these multimedia conversations.

The remaining piece of the puzzle is the bandwidth necessary to complete these multimedia conversations. This is being accomplished in the bandwidth wars currently being fought by the DSL and cable providers. In the end, consumers will be the ultimate winners, in that they will have access to technology that will eliminate distance barriers and communication barriers, and will truly revolutionize the way things are currently done.

CHAPTER 2

Enterprise Telephony Today

Enterprise Telephony (ET) is a business telephone system that provides basic business features, such as call hold, three-way calling, call transfer, and call forwarding. ET shares many similarities with the Public Switched Telephone Network (PSTN), but there are many key differences. This chapter details both the similarities and differences between these two networks, the ways in which they interoperate, and typical ET network designs.

Similarities Between PSTN and ET

The PSTN and ET are similar in the following ways:

- Circuit Switching—Both networks are based on the time-division multiplexing (TDM) switching of 64-kbps circuits.

- Common Infrastructure Model—Bearer channels, call-control, and service planes are contained in one platform. These features are described in Chapter 1, "Overview of the PSTN and Comparisons to Voice over IP."

- Local Loop—Phones can plug "directly" into the switch and receive a dial tone, place and receive phone calls, and so on.

- Services Offered—Both networks can provide basic services such as call hold, three-way calling, call transfer, and call forwarding.

Both networks switch 64-kbps circuits; however, the scale is orders of magnitude different. The PSTN uses a Class 5 switch that can support hundreds of thousands of local loops. The ET equivalent to a Class 5 switch, the Private Branch eXchange (PBX), supports from five to several thousand local loops.

The primary task of a Class 5 switch is to provide residential telephony, but it also offers a few basic business features, such as call waiting and call return. A PBX, however, usually offers more features, including call hold, three-way calling or conferencing, call transfer, auto-attendant, voice mail, and many others.

Differences Between PSTN and ET

PSTN and ET are different from each other in the way they treat signaling and in the types of advanced features they offer.

Signaling Treatment

Although the PSTN uses signaling interfaces developed by industry bodies, PBX manufacturers often create proprietary protocols to enable their PBXs to intercommunicate and carry additional features transparently throughout the ET voice network.

Chapter 1 discusses how the PSTN uses Signaling System 7 (SS7), ISDN, and in-band signaling as its primary signaling links. These are well-documented standards that have been evolving for many years. Although these signaling protocols cannot solve all signaling problems today, anyone can develop software to interface with the PSTN network.

> **NOTE**   This software and hardware must be *homologated* in each country to which it is connected to the network. Homologation is a process in which each country certifies any equipment that connects with its PSTN. Depending on the country, this may even require re-homologation when new software updates come out for the device to be connected.

Many PBXs in ET use CAS and PRI for signaling with the PSTN. In many cases, computer telephony integration (CTI) links are also used to enable a third-party computer application to control some of the PBX's operations. Most PBX vendors, however, implement a proprietary signaling mechanism. This forces enterprise networks to consolidate on one brand of PBX. Although this can be good for the manufacturer, the enterprise business customer is now locked into one vendor for their voice transport, services, and applications.

Additionally, many PBX vendors use proprietary signaling to offer advanced features to proprietary handsets. This also forces the Enterprise customer to utilize one vendor's handsets to maintain compatibility with the PBX.

> **NOTE**   Many vendors are starting to implement standards-based signaling protocols that enable interoperability between different vendors' PBXs. A list of these protocols is as follows:
>
> - Q Signaling (QSIG)—This is an open standard designed to enable multiple vendors to agree on supplementary services, dial plans, and much more. (The "Q" comes from the International Telecommunication Union Telecommunication Standardization Sector [ITU-T] Q.xxx set of standards.)
>
> - Digital Private Network Signaling System (DPNSS)—This is a British standard designed to enable cross-vendor or multivendor interoperability between PBXs. This standard was rolled into QSIG.

Advanced Features

Providing advanced features is also an important differentiation between ET and PSTN. Business requirements for telephone networks are much greater than the average home user. Enterprise customers have the need for high-use, feature-rich systems that enable applications such as the following:

- Inbound and outbound call centers—ET networks with this feature usually contain a CTI link that enables new applications—for instance, a screen pops up on the representative's computer screen that gives the representative the caller-ID information, as well as other information about that caller (buying patterns, shipping address, and so on).

- Financial Enterprise Telephony—ET networks with this feature often include a network known as *hoot-n-holler*, in which one person speaks and many people listen. This is common in stock brokerage.

ET customers can use the PSTN to service basic PBX needs, but the legacy PSTN does not typically have advanced applications such as call centers. Also, using the PSTN is usually less cost effective than using ET.

Common ET and PSTN Interworking

Although ET is feature-rich and pervasive in the Enterprise space, it must interconnect with the PSTN in order to place calls outside the local business. This inter-working can be as simple as an analog line from the PSTN or a leased line between two PBXs. It can also be as complex as an Asynchronous Transfer Mode (ATM) connection using an inter-exchange carrier's (IXC's) public ATM network. This section covers the various methods and network designs commonly used in most ET networks.

There are five methods that businesses can choose, each of which uses slightly different components. These methods include the following:

- Simple business line—This method involves using a line directly from the PSTN as a business line. This line is similar to a residential line, however the business customer is normally charged a higher monthly rate. This simple business line is usually used for very small businesses that do not need many telephony features. This service is provided and managed by the Local Exchange Carrier (LEC) or Challenger LEC (CLEC).

- PBX—A Private Branch Exchange (PBX) provides many features (such as hold, transfer, park, and so on) that business customers require. The PBX switch often connects to the PSTN through a T1 or E1 circuit. These systems often integrate voice mail, local lines, and PSTN trunks.

■ Key-system—This is a smaller version of a PBX and is generally used in offices of fewer than 50 people. The key-system often has less functionality, a fully integrated voicemail system, and multiple "presences" on the key-system phones in lieu of the capability to transfer a call.

■ Centrex line—Provided and managed by the LEC or CLEC, this line offers additional services similar to a PBX, but an additional monthly charge is involved. These services include transfer, three-way calling, and a closed user-dialing plan.

■ Virtual Private Networks (VPNs)—With a VPN, the PSTN contains a private dial plan for the enterprise customer. LECs, CLECs, and IXCs can provide VPNs. However, local PBX can provide additional features.

These methods are broken into two groups: those that the PSTN provides and manages, and those that are privately owned and merely need to interconnect with the PSTN. Each category is discussed in the following sections.

ET Networks Provided by PSTN

If a business has little capital resources for an internal department to manage the telephone network, it often looks to a PSTN carrier or a Value-Added Reseller (VAR) to provide telephony services. While the Incumbent or Challenger PSTN carrier will provide the personnel as well as the equipment and transport service, a VAR will install the PBX equipment and provide the management services necessary to connect to the PSTN. An Enterprise business might use PSTN because it is not cost effective for the internal Information Technology (IT) department to efficiently manage the entire network. The three PSTN-provided telephony networks include the following:

■ A simple business line

■ A Centrex line

■ A VPN

Simple Business Line

The most basic of these methods is a simple business line. This service is usually used by small businesses of one or two people who do not need additional phone services.

A landscaping company with one owner and one employee, for example, does not need more than one telephone line with an answering machine attached. Such a company does not need features such as call hold or call transfer. A simple business line is similar to a residential line, but it usually has a higher monthly fee than a residential line. The local carrier charges more for this additional fee due to the additional costs of that business subscriber on the local carrier.

Centrex Line

As a business begins to grow, it typically requires additional services, such as call transfer, call hold, and call waiting. The business can purchase a key-system or PBX, which starts at around U.S. $2000, or it can simply pay a few extra dollars every month (U.S. $20–$30) to the PSTN for additional services.

These services enable the PSTN to offer features in a Closed User Group (CUG). A *CUG* describes a situation where all the phones within the business become a virtual switch and can dial one another with only four or five digits, transfer calls, and put callers on hold. This service offers more functionality than a simple business line, but it usually becomes cost-prohibitive to implement as the company grows.

VPN

Another option available to business users is a VPN. VPNs offer enterprise customers the benefits of a private network (CUG) without the administration or equipment hassles of a large *tie-line* network (a tie-line is simply a permanent circuit between two points).

A VPN enables an enterprise customer to dial a specific number, which then directs the PSTN to treat the customer as a CUG. Say, for example, that a large retail corporation with offices throughout the U.S. does not want to have key-systems or PBXs in each of its 3000 stores. That would be a large network to manage and administer.

This retail corporation decides to contract with a long-distance (IXC) company to provide a VPN for all 3000 of its retail stores. Each store has its own four-digit store ID, assigned by the company, which is used for inter-company business. Therefore, the store ID is a good way to uniquely identify each branch of the retail operation. Figure 2-1 shows a graphical representation of the potential network and call-flow.

Figure 2-1 *Virtual Private Network*

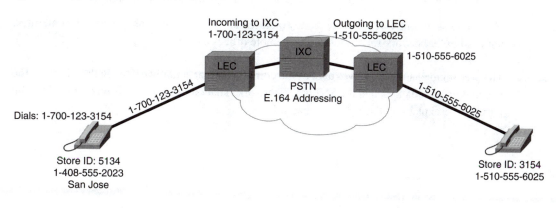

The IXC gives the retail store a phone number to dial—1-700-123-3154. The IXC informs the LEC to hand off the call to the IXC so that the IXC knows which dial plan applies to the incoming number. (The last four digits of the dialed number correspond to the store ID.)

The store ID for the store in San Jose, California, for example, is 5134. Store 5134 is running low on toasters and needs to call the nearby store in Fremont (Store 3154). The old method was to look at a lengthy table and place a long-distance call from the 1-408 (San Jose) area code to the 1-510 (Fremont) area code. Today, Store 5134 only needs to know the ID of the Fremont store and can dial 1-700-123-3154 to reach that store.

The IXC translates the 1-700-123-3154 number to the "real" telephone number assigned by the local LEC, but this is completely transparent to the retail store clerks. (As a side note, the Fremont store had the toasters and sent them over right away.)

By referring to Figure 2-1, you can step through the call in more detail:

1. The user in San Jose dials 1-700-123-3154.

2. The LEC receives the dialed digits.

3. The LEC switch sends those digits to the IXC.

4. The IXC receives the digits 1-700-123-3154, knows this is a VPN, and translates the digits to 1-510-555-6025, which is the true phone number for the Fremont retail store.

5. The IXC sends the call to the local LEC as 1-510-555-6025 because that is what the LEC can understand. If the IXC had sent 1-700, the LEC would route the call back to the IXC.

6. The LEC receives the call from the IXC.

7. The LEC looks up the particular local line for 555-6025 and routes the call to that local loop.

8. The retail store receives the call, not knowing that it was routed through the VPN.

VPN enables the enterprise to save money on internal IS costs as well as provides the enterprise with a simpler network for all 3000 of its remote offices to use.

The preceding example removes a lot of the complexity that actually exists. In the example, the call lookup would happen in the SS7 or C7 network. That complexity has been removed for the purposes of explaining the VPN at a macro layer.

Private ET Networks

By far, the most popular option for ET is for the business to purchase their own key-system or PBX to provide local telephone access to their employees. This method provides many benefits, including the following:

- No recurring charges—Owning a PBX costs less per month than purchasing Centrex services from the PSTN.

- Control over adds, moves, and changes—There is no need to contact the PSTN carrier to add new lines, move a phone, or change subscriber information.

PBX Networks

Figure 2-2 shows the relationship between having individual lines from the PSTN, or using a PBX to lower the number of lines (trunks) from the PSTN. Because most users of the telephone system are not calling externally at the same time (depending upon the business type), cost savings on PSTN trunks are realized.

Figure 2-2   *PSTN Compared to a PBX or Key-System*

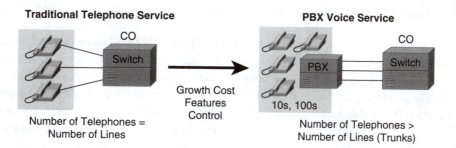

Another advantage to enterprise customers who have their own circuit-switch (PBX) is the control such a setup offers. If you need to add a new user, change a feature, or move a user to a different location, there is no need to contact the PSTN carrier.

The PBX adds another level of complexity. The enterprise customer must now deal with the additional burden of configuring and maintaining call routing on the PBX. Figure 2-3 shows a sample block diagram of a user now dialing outside the PBX to the PSTN.

Figure 2-3   *PSTN Call Through a PBX*

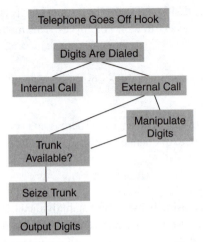

Figure 2-3 details how a PBX makes a basic call-routing decision regarding when to route the call to the PSTN or to an internal phone extension. This process can be hidden from the user (all calls starting with a "1" use an outbound trunk, for example), or the user can be "trained" (forcing the user to dial "9" for an outbound trunk, for instance) to assist the PBX to choose the proper path.

In many cases, the user decides to route the call to the PSTN based on an "escape" digit (this is usually "9" in the U.S. and "0" in Europe). Other times, the user is unaware that the call is routed over the PSTN. As an example, consider a five-digit dialing plan for a company that has locations over a large geographical area. Each PBX can be programmed to translate that five-digit number to a 1+10 (ITU-T Recommendation E.164) number and route the call over the PSTN, as shown in Figure 2-4. This 1+10 number also can be referenced as an E.164 number, as it follows that ITU-T recommendation.

Figure 2-4   *Number Translation Through a PBX*

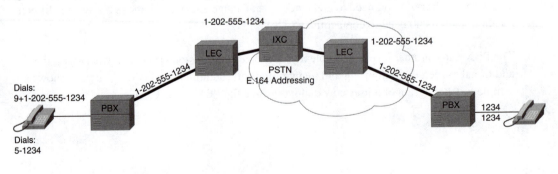
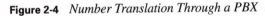

In Figure 2-4, the following occurs:

1.   A user dials 5-1234 (the equivalent of dialing 9+1+202+555+1234), which the local PBX translates to 1-202-555-1234 and sends to the LEC switch.

2.   The LEC passes the 1+10 number to the IXC, which passes it to another LEC.

3.   The LEC in area code 202 passes the entire 10-digit number to the remote PBX.

4.   The remote PBX modifies the incoming number from 202-555-1234 to a four-digit number and rings the appropriate line (1234).

This process of digit manipulation enables the PBX user to dial the least amount of digits possible. This not only saves users time, but it also makes it easier for users to remember frequently used extensions.

Tie-Lines for PBX Interconnection

If a business has two sites and they have a large call volume between them, the business usually purchases a tie-line. Recall that a *tie-line* is simply a permanent circuit between two points (T1, E1, fractional T1/E1, or some other transport). For this scenario to be cost-effective, it must cost less to run a call between site A and site B over the tie-line than it does to send a call over a permanent PSTN.

Figure 2-5 shows two sites (one in San Jose, California, and one in Dallas, Texas), with a T1 circuit between them.

Figure 2-5   *Tie-Line Between San Jose and Dallas*

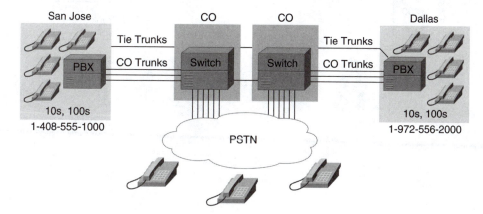

This tie-line still uses the PSTN, but the business pays a flat rate for the dedicated use of the circuit between San Jose and Dallas.

The PBX uses a preprogrammed Automatic Route Selection (ARS) table to determine which trunk should be used. Referring back to Figure 2-5, the PBX is configured to use the tie-line between San Jose and Dallas. If that tie-line becomes full, the PBX uses the PSTN or Central Office (CO) trunks as overflow to the PSTN.

To determine whether having a tie-line is cost-effective, a careful analysis of the call volume and cost between San Jose and Dallas as compared to the cost of the T1 circuit must be performed. Figure 2-6 shows that the break-even point for a tie-line is reached when there are 30–35 hours worth of calls between San Jose and Dallas each month. (This is sample data; typically, an Erlang analysis would be done to determine the amount of trunk lines needed.) Anything over the 30–35 hours of calls between these two sites becomes additional savings, as long as the traffic is balanced so that it might all traverse the dedicated T1 circuit.

Tie-lines are another way in which ET network designers can route their traffic. The routing of call traffic is a very complex issue that requires a myriad of experience and knowledge. Entire books cover the subject of call-traffic modeling. Chapter 15, "Service Provider Voice over IP Applications and Services," covers traffic analysis in more detail.

Figure 2-6 *Tie-Line Costs Compared to PSTN Costs*

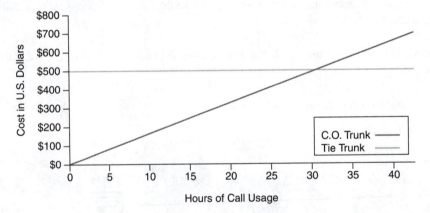

Summary

ET users have requirements that are different from those of the average user on the PSTN. Therefore, ET users have equipment and networks built specifically for those needs. As telecommunications moves to open standards, the alternatives to enterprise customers will grow exponentially.

These alternatives—including packet-based networks for voice and data, integrated access, and much more—will change the way least-cost routing and trunking/busy hour calculations are achieved.

CHAPTER **3**

Basic Telephony Signaling

Many corporations find it advantageous to operate their own voice networks, and they do so by connecting dedicated links between Private Branch eXchanges (PBXs) for inter-office communication, or by using Virtual Private Networks (VPNs) for voice. Originally, PBXs were connected to the Public Switched Telephone Network (PSTN) for voice services, or they were interconnected using analog tie-lines to transfer voice. When the need for more voice trunks and the technology matured, analog tie-lines were replaced with higher-speed digital facilities capable of accessing sophisticated and feature-rich networks. This chapter analyzes the signaling techniques that traverse analog and digital facilities in corporate and interexchange networks.

This chapter also discusses channel-associated signaling (CAS) systems, such as Bell System MF, Consultative Committee for International Telegraph and Telephone (CCITT) No. 5, R1, and R2, and it reviews how these CAS systems operate.

It also describes access protocols, such as Integrated Services Digital Network (ISDN), Q Signaling (QSIG), and Digital Private Network Signaling System (DPNSS). These protocols deliver PBX signaling through a network to distant PBXs. Private ISDN networks use the PSTN for connectivity and services. QSIG is an inter-PBX signaling system similar to ISDN that enables corporate PBXs to connect, thus creating a private voice network. DPNSS is an ISDN-type protocol that enables PBX connectivity; however, it is not as widely used as ISDN and QSIG.

Signaling Overview

Before covering signaling methods and standards, it's important to discuss some basic concepts. These basic concepts are applied in the individual signaling methods further along in the chapter.

Analog and Digital Signaling

Originally, PBXs were connected by simple analog lines that enabled the transmission of voice-band information. Analog systems are not as common today as they used to be, however, and in many cases, they have been replaced by higher-speed digital facilities that cost less than their analog counterparts.

Digital signaling is the most common type of telephony signaling used in today's corporate and service provider networks. In digital networks, many forms of signaling techniques are used.

One form is robbed-bit signaling. With this method, a bit is "robbed" from designated frames to use for signaling purposes. Robbed-bit signaling inserts the signaling information into the digital voice stream without affecting voice quality. This signaling technique is discussed in more detail in the "CAS" section later in this chapter. In addition to CAS, other digital protocols include R1, R2, ISDN, QSIG, and DPNSS.

Direct Current Signaling

This form of signaling relies on direct current (DC) to signal the end switch or office. DC signaling indicates transition state changes by toggling on or off the flow of DC. These end office switches use current detectors to identify changes in state. DC signaling is used in the following two signaling arrangements:

- Subscriber Loop—This is a simple form of DC signaling between the subscriber and the local end office. When a subscriber goes off-hook, DC (-48V) flows across the line or loop between the telephone and the local end office switch. Line cards in the local office are equipped with current detectors to determine when a connection is being requested. When a subscriber goes on-hook, the capacitor in the telephone blocks the flow of current.

  Similarly to off-hook, the change in DC signals to the end office switch that the call was terminated. In this case, the same pair of wires is used to provide the voice and signaling path.

- recEive and transMit (E&M)—This trunking arrangement uses a form of DC signaling to indicate state changes on trunks or tie-lines. With E&M, two leads—one called "E" and the other called "M"—are dedicated to signaling. You can detect the toggling of E&M leads by applying either ground (earth) or a voltage potential (magneto). This form of signaling is covered in the "E&M Signaling" section later in this chapter.

DC signaling has some limitations. Signaling is limited to the number of states you can represent by DC, for instance. Also, when you use the same pair of wires for voice and signaling, the lines or trunks are kept busy even when the two subscribers are not connected.

In-Band and Out-of-Band Signaling

In-band signaling uses tones in place of DC. These tones are transmitted over the same facility as voice and, therefore, are within the 0–4kHz voice band. The tones include Single Frequency, Multi-Frequency (MF), and Dual-Tone Multi-Frequency (DTMF), described here:

- Single Frequency—This tone is used for interoffice trunks and has two possible states: on-hook or idle, and off-hook or busy. The Single Frequency tone is based on a single frequency of 2600 Hz and is used to identify a change in state. Therefore, no tone is present when a connection or circuit is up. When either party hangs up, however, a 2600 Hz tone is sent over the circuit, notifying all interoffice exchanges of the disconnect.

  At one time, the Single Frequency tone was used to gain fraudulent long-distance services from service providers. The perpetrator attached a "blue box" to the subscriber line and used it to fool interoffice exchanges into interpreting the 2600 Hz tone as a clear-forward signal. The interoffice switch then accepted the called party number and believed that the local switch would charge for the call. Access to the interoffice switch was accomplished by dialing 0 and fooling the interoffice switch before the operator answered. Service providers eventually curbed this activity by implementing certain protective measures.

- MF—This tone is used by interoffice trunks to indicate events, such as seizure, release, answer, and acknowledge, and to transmit information, such as the calling party number. MF signaling uses a combination of pulses specified by frequencies to signal across a network. These frequencies are system-specified and are covered in more detail in the "CAS," "R1," and "R2" sections later in this chapter. MF signaling uses the same facilities as the voice path and, therefore, is less efficient than common channel signaling (CCS) systems, such as Signaling System 7 (SS7).

- DTMF—This form of addressing is used to transmit telephone number digits from the subscriber to the local office. With the development of DTMF came the replacement of transistor oscillators in telephones with keypads and dual-tone oscillators. DTMF tones identify the numbers 0 through to 9 and the "*" and "#" symbols. When a subscriber presses one of these keys, the oscillator sends two simultaneous tones. Digits are represented by a particular combination of frequencies: one from the low group (697, 770, 852, and 941 Hz) and one from the high group (1290, 1336, 1447, and 1633 Hz). Sixteen possible combinations exist; however, only 12 are implemented on the keypad.

Loop-Start and Ground-Start Signaling

The two most common methods for end-loop signaling are loop-start and ground-start signaling.

■ Loop-Start Signaling—This is the simplest and least intelligent of the two signaling protocols. It also is the most common form of subscriber loop signaling. This protocol basically works in the same way as the telephone and the local end office, whereby the creation of a loop initiates a call and the closure of a loop terminates a call. Loop-start signaling is not common for PBX signaling and has one significant drawback, in that glare can occur. *Glare* occurs when two endpoints try to seize the line at the same time, and it often results in two people being connected unknowingly. The person picking up the phone thinks he has a dial tone, but unbeknownst to him he is connected to someone who called him.

■ Ground-Start Signaling—This signaling protocol differs from loop-start signaling, in that it provides positive recognition of connects and disconnects. Current-detection mechanisms are used at each end of the trunk, enabling end office switches to agree on which end is seizing the trunk before it is seized. This form of signaling minimizes the effect of glare and costs the same as loop-start signaling. As such, it is the preferred signaling method for PBXs.

CAS and CCS

CAS exists in many networks today. CAS systems carry signaling information from the trunk in the trunk itself. CAS systems were originally developed by different equipment vendors and, therefore, exist in many versions or variants. Today's telecommunication networks require more efficient means for signaling, however, so they are moving to common channel-type systems, such as CCS.

CCS uses a common link to carry signaling information for a number of trunks. This form of signaling is cheaper, has faster connect times, and is more flexible than CAS. The first generation of CCS is known as SS6; the second generation, SS7, is the basis of Chapter 4, "Signaling System 7."

E&M Signaling

E&M is a common trunk-signaling technique used on telephony switches and PBXs. The signaling and voice trunks in E&M are separated. In E&M, voice is transmitted over either two or four-wire circuits, with six methods for signaling. E&M signaling methods are referred to as Types I, II, III, IV, and V; they also are known by the British Telecom (BT) standard, SSDC5.

The remainder of this section focuses on four-wire E&M Types I through V. E&M lead conditions for off-hook and on-hook for Types I through V are summarized in Table 3-1.

Table 3-1   *E&M Signaling*

Type	M Lead		E Lead	
	Off-Hook	**On-Hook**	**Off-Hook**	**On-Hook**
I	Battery	Ground	Ground	Open
II	Battery	Open	Ground	Open
III	Loop current	Ground	Ground	Open
IV	Ground	Open	Ground	Open
V	Ground	Open	Ground	Open

Type I

With the Type I interface, the trunk equipment generates the E signal to the PBX by grounding the E lead (shown in Figure 3-1). The PBX detects the E signal by sensing the increase in current through a resistive load. Similarly, the PBX generates the M signal by sourcing a current to the trunk equipment, which detects it through a resistive load. The numbers 7, 2, 6, and 3 are the pinouts used on an RJ-48c connector.

Figure 3-1   *E&M Type I*

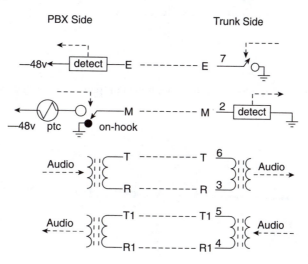

Type II

E&M Type II has two additional leads over Type I: signal battery (SB) and signal ground (SG). In this method, the E lead is paired up with the SG lead, and the M lead is paired up with the SB lead. An on-hook at the PBX end is indicated when the E and M leads are open. Alternatively, an off-hook is indicated when the E lead is grounded and the M lead is providing battery (see Figure 3-2).

Figure 3-2   *E&M Type II*

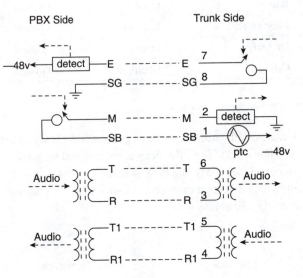

Type III

E&M Type III is used mostly in older telephone company switching centers. Figure 3-3 shows the Type III setup.

Figure 3-3 *E&M Type III*

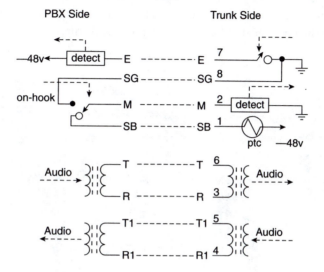

Type IV

E&M Type IV is similar to E&M Type II; however, from the PBX side, an on-hook occurs when the E and M leads are open, and an off-hook occurs when both leads are at ground (see Figure 3-4).

Figure 3-4 *E&M Type IV*

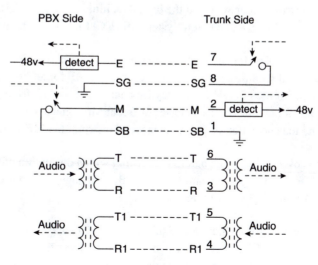

Type V

Under E&M Type V, both the PBX and the switching endpoint supply battery (see Figure 3-5). At the PBX, battery is supplied on the E lead, and at the endpoint it is supplied on the M lead. Type V is the most common method of E&M signaling outside North America.

Figure 3-5   *E&M Type V*

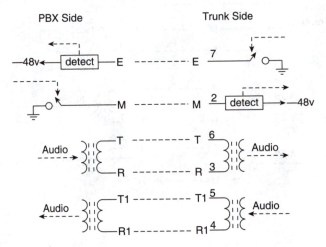

CAS

CAS exists in many varieties that operate over various analog and digital facilities. The analog facilities are either two- or four-wire and the digital facilities are either North American T1 or European E1. This section discusses Bell System MF, CCITT No. 5, R1, and R2 CAS systems.

The main areas of discussion for each CAS system are supervision signaling and address signaling over analog and digital facilities. Bell System uses in-band MF for address signaling. For supervision signaling it uses Single Frequency for analog and a/b bits for digital trunks. CCITT No. 5 was designed for analog trunks and uses different MF signals for supervision and address signaling. In-band tone detection is used to detect and interpret the MF signals.

It is important to cover a few points before proceeding with a discussion of CAS systems. When a call is placed from Exchange A toward Exchange B, Exchange A is considered the outgoing exchange and Exchange B the incoming exchange.

One-way trunks are trunks on which only Exchange A or Exchange B can initiate a call. Exchanges A and B can initiate a call over two-way trunks. Double seizures can occur over two-way trunks when both exchanges try to seize the trunk at the same time, however. When this occurs, mechanisms such as timers are used to detect and resolve such events.

Three groups of signals are present in channel-associated interexchange signaling systems:

- Supervision Signals—These signals represent events that occur on a trunk and can be specific to the CAS variant. Signals include seizure, wink, and answer; they also are referred to as *line signals*.

- Address Signals—These signals typically represent the digits dialed or called party number and, in some instances, other information. In this chapter, address signals are based on MF signaling and can be system- or variant-specific.

- Tones and Announcements—These include tones such as ringing and busy tones and announcements such as, "The number you have dialed is no longer in service."

One more concept to cover before moving forward is that of service circuits. *Service circuits* are used in most exchanges to send and receive address signals and tones, as well as to play announcements. These circuits are typically system-specific; the processor connects a path from the trunk to the appropriate service circuit inside the switch. The pools of service circuits are temporarily used to send and receive tones or to play announcements.

Bell System MF Signaling

This section introduces the MF signaling systems developed by Bell System in the 1950s. The Bell System is still used today in local networks in the United States and is nearly identical to the R1 signaling system discussed later in this chapter.

With Bell System MF signaling, which you can use on one-way or two-way trunks, supervision and address signaling are signaled link-by-link. Supervision signaling is accomplished through a Single Frequency tone for analog facilities and through robbed-bit signaling for digital facilities. Address information is sent through MF tones.

Supervision Signaling

Supervision signals are continuously sent by endpoint exchanges indicating the state of the trunk. This is known as *continuous two-state signaling*. States can be different at each endpoint of the trunk. MF signaling is used to indicate on-hook and off-hook states, as listed in Table 3-2.

Table 3-2   *Supervision Signals*

Direction	Signal Type	Transition
Forward	Seizure	On-hook to off-hook
Forward	Clear-forward	Off-hook to on-hook
Backward	Answer	On-hook to off-hook
Backward	Clear-back	Off-hook to on-hook
Backward	Proceed-to-send (wink)	Off-hook pulse, 120-290 ms

Supervision signals operate slightly differently for analog and digital trunks.

Analog Trunks

A Single Frequency 2600 Hz tone is used to indicate trunk state between exchanges over analog facilities. This tone is applied in-band over the trunk and is turned off when a call is in progress or established. Therefore, the state is on-hook or idle when the tone is present and off-hook or in use when the tone is absent. The supervision signals for the Single Frequency method are illustrated in Figure 3-6.

Figure 3-6 *Forward and Backward Supervision Signals for a Call*

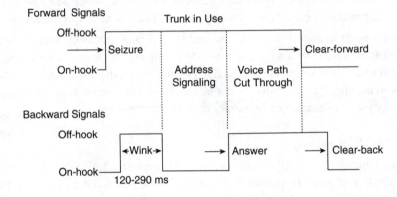

In Figure 3-6, assume that Switch A sends the forward signals and Switch B sends the backward signals. Switch A sends a forward seizure or off-hook signal to Switch B on a chosen trunk. Then, Switch B sends a backward wink or proceed-to-send to Switch A and waits for address signaling or dialed digits. After the digits are sent and the call is answered, Switch B sends a backward answer or off-hook to Switch A, enabling an end-to-end voice path.

In this case, the calling party hangs up first and a clear-forward is sent from Switch A to Switch B. When the called party hangs up, a clear-back signal is sent by Switch B.

Two important aspects of this signaling method need to be discussed:

■ First, Bell System MF does not have backward signaling for connections that fail during setup. Therefore, the exchange where the call failed must connect an announcement server indicating to the calling party that a problem occurred.

   The signaling system then relies on the calling party to release or drop the call so that clear-forward procedures can be initiated.

■ Second, no release guard-type signal exists, and timers are used after trunks are released. Therefore, after an exchange releases a trunk, it initiates a timer for approximately 1 second. After this timer expires, the exchange assumes that the trunk was released at the other end and is available for use.

Digital Trunks

The digital trunks most commonly used today are either T1 or E1 facilities (as described in the "Physical Layer—MTP L1" section of Chapter 4). With digital trunks, bits are robbed from specific frames and are used for signaling purposes. This discussion focuses on T1 digital trunks.

T1 has two types of framing formats: Super Frame (SF) and Extended Superframe (ESF). The least significant bits are robbed from frames 6 and 12 for SF and frames 6, 12, 18, and 24 for ESF. These bits are referred to as the Sa and Sb bits for SF, and the Sa, Sb, Sc, and Sd bits for ESF. Robbing these bits has a negligible effect on voice quality.

The SF signaling bits—Sa and Sb—are equal to each other and provide two-state, continuous supervision signaling. Bit values of zero are used to indicate on-hook, and bit values of 1 are used to indicate off-hook.

Address Signaling

Address signaling is used to indicate the called and calling number as well as to identify the start and end of the address information. In the Bell System MF method, address signals are a combination of two voice-band frequencies chosen from six different frequencies, as illustrated in Table 3-3.

Table 3-3   *Bell System MF Address Signals*

Signal	Frequencies in Hz
Digit 1	700 and 900
Digit 2	700 and 1100
Digit 3	900 and 1100
Digit 4	700 and 1300
Digit 5	900 and 1300
Digit 6	1100 and 1300
Digit 7	700 and 1500
Digit 8	900 and 1500
Digit 9	1100 and 1500
Digit 0	1300 and 1500
KP (start)	1100 and 1700
ST (end)	1500 and 1700

The address signaling sequence is initiated with a KP or start-of-pulsing signal and terminated with an ST or end-of-pulsing signal. Two important timing intervals exist:
The KP signal's duration is from 90 to 110 ms, and the ST signal's duration is from 61 to 75 ms. The silent interval between signals also is from 61 to 75 ms. Figure 3-7 demonstrates supervision and address signaling sequences.

Figure 3-7 *Supervision and Address Signaling Sequences*

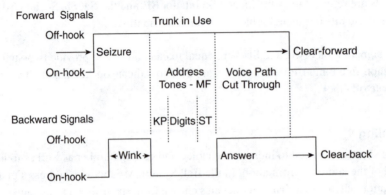

Address signaling uses two other key information digits. The codes in this information (or I bits) indicate the calling number or Automatic Number ID (ANI), as well as operator services (see Table 3-4).

Table 3-4   *Address Signaling Codes*

I-Codes	Information
I = 00	Calling number is available.
I = 02	Calling number is not available.
I = 06	Hotel room identification required.
I = 10	Test call.

The information codes are sent after the KP signal and before the called party number.
I codes 02 and 06 identify that operator assistance is required to proceed with these calls.

CCITT No. 5 Signaling

The CCITT adopted the CCITT No. 5 signaling system in the 1960s for use in international networks. This signaling system is still used today, usually on long international trunks and, in some cases, over transoceanic and satellite links. This signaling system was designed to operate over analog trunks equipped with Time Assignment Speech Interpolation (TASI). TASI is similar to voice activity detection (VAD), in that it enables unused bandwidth (silences or pauses in speech) to be used for other phone conversations. Link-by-link and in-band signaling are used for both supervision and address signaling.

Supervision Signaling

Supervision signaling is accomplished by two frequencies, sent either individually or in combination. CCITT No. 5 uses compelled supervision signaling, whereby the signaling tone is left on until an acknowledgment is received.

The two in-band frequencies are f1, which equals 2400 Hz, and f2, which equals 2600 Hz. The combination of f1 and f2 produces a composite signal; these signals and frequencies are listed in Table 3-5.

Table 3-5   *CCITT No. 5 Supervision Signals*

Direction	Signal Type	Frequency
Forward	Seizure	f1
Backward	Proceed-to-send	f2
Backward	Answer	f1
Forward	Acknowledgment	f1
Backward	Clear-back	f2
Forward	Acknowledgment	f1
Forward	Clear-forward	f1 and f2
Backward	Release-guard	f1 and f2
Backward	Busy-flash	f2
Forward	Acknowledgment	f1
Forward	Forward-transfer	f2

Three new signals are introduced in Table 3-5: Release-guard, Busy-flash, and Forward-transfer.

- Release-guard—This signal is used by the incoming exchange to acknowledge a clear-forward from the outgoing exchange. It also indicates to the outgoing exchange that the trunk is now available for an incoming call.

- Busy-flash—This signal is used by the incoming exchange to indicate to the outgoing exchange that call setup cannot be extended toward the destination.

- Forward-transfer—This signal is used on calls for operator services.

Address Signaling

In CCITT No. 5, address signaling is based on the combination of two frequencies, as illustrated in Table 3-6. The address signaling sequence starts with KP1 for national numbers and KP2 for international numbers. Codes 11 and 12 are used to connect international operator services.

Table 3-6 *CCITT No. 5 Address Signals*

Signal	Frequencies in Hz
Digit 1	700 and 900
Digit 2	700 and 1100
Digit 3	900 and 1100
Digit 4	700 and 1300
Digit 5	900 and 1300
Digit 6	1100 and 1300
Digit 7	700 and 1500
Digit 8	900 and 1500
Digit 9	1100 and 1500
Digit 0	1300 and 1500
Code 11	700 and 1700
Code 12	900 and 1700
KP1	1100 and 1700
KP2	1300 and 1700
ST	1500 and 1700

R1

The CAS system known as R1 is available in the International Telecommunication Union Telecommunication Standardization Sector (ITU-T) Q.310 to Q.332 specifications. This signaling system is almost identical to Bell System MF signaling and, therefore, is not further discussed.

R2

R2 signaling is a CAS system developed in the 1960s that is still in use today in Europe, Latin America, Australia, and Asia. Originally known as multi-frequency code (MFC) signaling, R2 signaling exists in several country versions or variants and in an international version called CCITT-R2.

R2 signaling operates over two- or four-wire analog and digital trunks and does not operate over TASI-equipped trunks or satellite links. R2 signaling is more suitable for relatively short international trunks. One of the differentiating aspects of this system compared to R1 is its register or inter-register signaling.

This section focuses on supervision and inter-register signaling for CCITT-R2 and National R2 signaling systems.

Supervision Signaling on Analog Trunks

For the purposes of supervision signaling on analog trunks, this section covers operation over four-wire trunks. The transmission path is divided into two parts: a 300- to 3400 Hz voice-band and a 3825Hz narrow-band for signaling. In this method, filters separate the signaling tone from the voice path. This is considered out-of-band signaling, even though signaling is over the same facility.

CCITT-R2 uses the tone-on-idle signaling supervision method; National R2 uses pulse signaling.

CCITT-R2

This method is commonly used on one-way trunks, is tone-on-idle, and provides two-state signaling. The forward and backward signals and transition states are similar to Bell System MF signaling and are illustrated in Table 3-7.

Table 3-7   *CCITT-R2 Supervision Signals*

Direction	Signal Type	Transition
Forward	Seizure	Tone-on to tone-off
Forward	Clear-forward	Tone-off to tone-on
Backward	Answer	Tone-on to tone-off
Backward	Clear-back	Tone-off to tone-on
Backward	Release-guard	Tone-off to tone-on
Backward	Blocking	Tone-on to tone-off

National R2

National R2 signaling has many country variants. Most versions of National R2 use pulse out-of-band supervision signals, however. Examples of National R2 supervision signals are illustrated in Table 3-8.

Table 3-8 *Examples of National R2 Supervision Signals*

Direction	Signal Type	Pulse Duration in ms
Forward	Seizure	150
Forward	Clear-forward	600
Backward	Answer	150
Backward	Clear-back	600
Backward	Release-guard	600
Backward	Blocking	Continuous

Supervision Signaling on Digital Trunks

R2 signaling operates over E1 digital facilities (described in the "Physical Layer—MTP L1" section of Chapter 4). E1 has 32 time-slots, numbered TS0 to TS31, whereby TS1–TS15 and TS17–TS31 are used to carry voice encoded with pulse code modulation (PCM), or to carry 64 kbps data.

Sixteen consecutive frames are in the SF format, and they are numbered 0 to 15. TS16 in frame 0 is used for SF alignment, and TS16 in the remaining frames (1–15) is used for trunk signaling. Four status bits are used from TS16 for signaling. They are called a, b, c, and d.

In the case of CCITT-R2 signaling, only the a and b bits are used. The c and d bits are set to 0 and 1, respectively. An idle state is denoted when a and b are equal to 1 and 0. Signaling is continuous. For two-way trunks, the supervision roles for forward and backward signaling vary on a call-by-call basis. Table 3-9 illustrates the R2 supervision signal, transition, and direction used on digital trunks.

Table 3-9 *R2 Supervision Signaling on Digital Trunks*

Direction	Signal Type	Transition
Forward	Seizure	a,b: 1,0 to 0,0
Forward	Clear-forward	a,b: 0,0 to 1,0
Backward	Seizure acknowledgment	a,b: 1,0 to 1,1
Backward	Answer	a,b: 1,1 to 0,1

Table 3-9   *R2 Supervision Signaling on Digital Trunks (Continued)*

Direction	Signal Type	Transition
Backward	Clear-back	a,b: 0,1 to 1,1
Backward	Release-guard	a,b: 0,1 to 1,0

Inter-Register Signaling

The concept of address signaling in R2 is slightly different from that used in the other CAS systems previously discussed. In the case of R2, the exchanges are considered registers, and the signaling between these exchanges is called inter-register signaling. *Inter-register signaling* uses forward and backward in-band MF signals to transfer called and calling party numbers as well as the calling party category.

In this case, signaling is compelled because the registers in the outgoing and incoming exchanges hold the signal until an acknowledgment is received. The signals consist of two voice-band frequencies and are listed in Table 3-10.

Table 3-10   *CCITT-R2 and National R2 Inter-Register Signal Frequencies*

Signal	Forward Frequency in Hz	Backward Frequency in Hz
Digit 1	1380 and 1500	1140 and 1020
Digit 2	1380 and 1620	1140 and 900
Digit 3	1500 and 1620	1020 and 900
Digit 4	1380 and 1740	1140 and 780
Digit 5	1500 and 1740	1020 and 780
Digit 6	1620 and 1740	900 and 780
Digit 7	1380 and 1860	1140 and 660
Digit 8	1500 and 1860	1020 and 660
Digit 9	1620 and 1860	900 and 660
Digit 0	1740 and 1860	780 and 660
Not used	1380 and 1980	1140 and 540
Not used	1500 and 1980	1020 and 540
Not used	1620 and 1980	900 and 540
Not used	1740 and 1980	780 and 540
End of #	1860 and 1980	660 and 540

Groups for Inter-Register Signaling

In R2 signaling, the forward and backward signals can have different meanings depending on which group is used. Three groups of forward signals and two groups of backward signals exist. The forward groups are I, II, and III, and the backward groups are A and B.

- Group I—These forward signals represent the called party number or dialed digits.

- Group II—These forward signals identify the calling party category.

- Group III—These forward signals represent the digits of the calling party number.

- Group A—These backward signals indicate if the signaling ended or if a particular forward signal is required.

- Group B—These backward signals are sent by the terminating switch to acknowledge a forward signal, or to provide call charging and called party information.

The following inter-register group sequence rules are used to identify the signal's group:

- The initial signal received by the incoming exchange is a Group I signal.

- Outgoing exchanges consider backward signals as Group A signals.

- Group A signals received by outgoing exchanges are used to identify whether the next signal is a Group B signal.

- Group B signals always indicate an end-of-signaling sequence.

Feature Support

The end-to-end information and status that National R2 signaling provides enable support for several features. These features include free calls, called party hold, malicious call tracing, and release on failed connections.

ISDN

ISDN has been available to the public since the 1980s. International Telecommunication Union (ITU; formerly CCITT) I series recommendations define the international standards for ISDN. This subscriber or user-based interface protocol provides single access to multiple services.

ISDN signaling is compatible with SS7 and inter-works with the ISDN User Part (ISUP) protocol. This inter-working enables ISDN subscribers to access the same services and intelligence as they can on the SS7 network. ISDN also enables PBXs to connect over the PSTN and create VPNs. This is accomplished by delivering PBX signaling over the network to distant PBXs.

The ISDN suite defines the specifications for access to the network. The following list outlines some ISDN functions and capabilities:

- ISDN provides circuit-based (voice and data) communications and packet-based communications to its users.

- Many new services can be extended to users.

- ISDN includes two access methods: Basic Rate Interface (BRI) and Primary Rate Interface (PRI).

- ISDN includes single access for PSTN, Direct-Inward-Dial (DID), Direct-Outward-Dial (DOD), 800, Foreign Exchange (FX), tie-lines, packet-switched data, circuit-switched data, and dedicated data.

- ISDN is capable of adding additional channels for high-speed data communications.

- ISDN is capable of transmitting voice and data on the same facility.

- ISDN uses separate channels for signaling.

- ISDN signaling is compatible with SS7.

- ISDN enables the creation of VPNs.

ISDN Services

The following communication services are available in circuit-switched ISDN networks:

- Bearer Services—Three types of bearer services are available for a call. They include speech, 3.1 kHz audio (for modem data), and 64 kbps digital data.

  Bearer services are specified by the calling user in the call setup message and are transferred over the network to the called user. The exchanges within the network also use this information when selecting the appropriate outgoing trunk. In the case of speech, exchanges can use analog or digital trunks for interconnection, whereas 64 kbps digital data requires digital trunks.

- Teleservice—This service enables the calling user to specify the type of data service for 3.1 kHz audio and 64 kbps digital data. The teleservice information (fax, telex, and so on) is transmitted transparently across the network to the called user. The called user processes the information to select the appropriate terminal equipment (TE) function to terminate the incoming call.

■ Supplementary Services—The ISDN service offering also provides many supplementary services. These services also are typically found on PBXs and virtual private voice networks. The following are examples of supplementary services: calling line identification (caller ID), closed users groups, call waiting, user-to-user signaling, advice of charge, call forward, and call hold. When a user requests these services, supplementary service messages are sent to the network to invoke the requested processes. In the case of user-to-user signaling, the two ISDN users send signaling information transparently during the call setup and teardown parts of the call.

ISDN Access Interfaces

Before discussing ISDN access methods, it is important to cover the concept of B and D channels:

■ B Channel—The B channel is a 64 kbps channel that carries user information streams. No signaling information is carried in the B channel. B-channel user streams include speech encoded at 64 kbps according to ITU G.711, data at or less than 64 kbps, and voice encoded at lower bit rates.

■ D Channel—The D channel is used primarily to carry signaling for circuit switching by ISDN networks. D-channel bit rates are different depending on the access method. The D channel also is capable of transmitting user packet data up to 9.6 kbps.

Two types of access methods exist for ISDN:

■ BRI

■ PRI

BRI

BRI delivers two bi-directional 64 kbps B channels and one bi-directional 16 kbps D channel over standard two-wire telephone lines. Basic rate ISDN service typically is used for residential and small office, home office (SOHO) applications. Each B channel can transmit speech or data; the D channel transmits the signaling or call control messages.

The configuration and reference points for BRI are specified in Figure 3-8.

Figure 3-8 *ISDN BRI Reference Points*

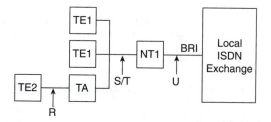

The reference configuration for ISDN is defined in the ITU specification I.411. The reference points specify the transmission medium, interface, and connectors (if used).

- U Reference Point—The U reference point specifies the transmission characteristics of the local loop. For BRI, this two-wire interface operates at 160 kbps (2B + D + 16 kbps for overhead) over standard copper-twisted wires.

- S/T Reference Point—For basic rate access, this interface provides a four-wire connection to ISDN-compatible terminals or terminal adapters. The interface operates at 144 kbps (2B + D) between the ISDN device and the network termination device. You can connect up to eight ISDN devices to the S/T interface.

- R Reference Point—The R reference point provides connection for non-ISDN devices. Such devices connect to the terminal adapter using interfaces such as RS-232 and V.35.

This reference configuration also specifies the set of functions required to access ISDN networks:

— Network Termination 1 (NT1)—Outside the United States, NT1 is on the network side of the defined user-network interface and is considered part of the service provider network. NT1s terminate the two-wire local loop and provide four-wire S/T bus for ISDN terminal equipment (TE).

— TE1—TE1s are ISDN-compatible devices that connect directly to the S/T connector on the NT1.

— TE2—TE2s are non-ISDN compatible devices that require terminal adapter (TA) interconnection.

— TA—TAs provide an ISDN-compliant interface to NT1s and standard interfaces for TE2s. These standard interfaces include RS-232, V.35, RS-449, and X.21.

PRI

PRI corresponds to two primary rates: 1.544 Mbps (T1) and 2.048 Mbps (E1). PRIs typically are used in medium to large business applications. PRI is comprised of B channels and one 64 kbps D channel. The interface structure for T1 is 23B + D (North America and Japan). The interface structure for E1 is 30B + D (Europe).

The configuration and references for PRI are specified in Figure 3-9.

Figure 3-9   *ISDN PRI Reference Points*

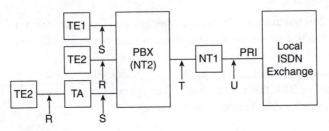

The configuration and reference points for PRI are similar to those for BRI. The differences between the two reference models are discussed here.

- U Reference Point—For PRI, the U interface is four-wire and operates at either T1 (1.544 Mbps) or E1 (2.048 Mbps) PRI rates.

- T Reference Point—For PRI, the T interface provides access to the Network Termination 2 (NT2) device.

- NT2—PBX equipment can provide such NT2 functions as Layer 2 (L2) and Layer 3 (L3) protocol handling as well as multiplexing, switching, interface termination, and maintenance. NT2s also can provide connections to ISDN-compatible TE1s and non-ISDN compatible TE2s.

ISDN L2 and L3 Protocols

ISDN user-network interface L2 and L3 specifications also are referred to as Digital Subscriber Signaling System No. 1 (DSS1). L2 provides error-free and secure connections for two endpoints across the ISDN reference configuration. L3 provides the mechanism for call establishment, control, and access to services. The L2 protocol for ISDN is Q.920/921, and the L3 protocol is Q.930/931. Q.932 enables general procedures for accessing and controlling supplementary services.

The specifications for L2 are referred to as Link Access Procedures on the D channel (LAPD). This protocol provides the reliable transfer of frames between the local exchange and the TE. The specifications for Q.920 and Q.921 are extensive and are available from the Q series of ITU recommendations.

The specifications for L3 define the messages that pass between the local exchange and the TE. These messages are used for call setup, call supervision, call teardown, and supplementary services. The next section discusses the specifics of ISDN messaging.

Q.931 Call Control Messages

The message structure and signaling elements of Q.931 are used in ISDN networks to provide call control capabilities. Q.931 messages are sent from the network to the user and from the user to the network. They are referred to as user-network and network-user messages, as illustrated in Tables 3-11 and 3-12.

Some of the most important Q.931 messages are listed in Table 3-11. The message type field in the general format of the Q.931 message is used to determine the type of message being sent.

Table 3-11   *Q.931 Messages and Type Codes*

Q.931 Message Type	Message Type Value
Setup message (SETUP)	00000101
Setup acknowledgment message (SETACK)	00001101
Call proceeding message (CALPRC)	00000010
Progress message (PROG)	00001111
Alerting message (ALERT)	00000011
Connect message (CONN)	00000101
Connect acknowledgment message (CONACK)	00000111
Disconnect message (DISC)	01000101
Release message (RLSE)	01001101
Release complete message (RLCOM)	01011010
Information message (INFO)	01111011

Source: ITU-T Q.931 3/93

The information or signaling elements of each message type are listed in Table 3-12. Table 3-12 also indicates the mandatory (M) and optional (O) fields for each network-to-user message.

Table 3-12 *User to Network—Information Elements in Q.931 Messages*

Information Elements	SETUP	CALPC	ALERT	CONN	CONAK	DISC	RLSE	RLCOM	INFO
Bearer Capability	M								
Called party number	M								
Calling party number	O								
Called party subaddress	O								
Calling party subaddress	O								
Cause						M	O	O	
Channel identification	O	M	O	O					
High-layer compatibility	O								
Keypad	O								M
Low-layer compatibility	O								
Transit network selection	O								
User-to-user information	O		O	O		O	O	O	

Table 3-13 indicates the mandatory (M) and optional (O) fields for each network-to-user message.

Table 3-13   *Network to User—Information Elements in Q.931 Messages*

Signaling Elements	SETUP	SETACK	CALPC	PROG	ALET	CONN	CONAK	DISC	RLSE	RLCOM	INFO
Bearer Capability	M										
Called party number	M										
Calling party number	O										
Called party subaddress	O										
Calling party subaddress	O										
Cause				O				M	O	O	
Channel identification	M	M	O								
High-layer compatibility	OO										
Low-layer compatibility	O										
Progress indicator	O	O		M	O	O					
Signal	M	O		O	M	O	O	O	O	O	O
User-to-user information	O	O			O			O	O	O	

Basic ISDN Call

This section outlines a typical ISDN call between two users served by the same local exchange. The signaling sequence between User A (TE-A), the local exchange, and User B (TE-B) is illustrated in Figure 3-10.

Figure 3-10 *Basic ISDN Call*

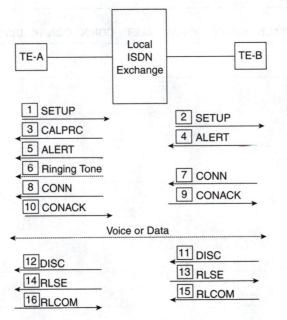

Call Setup

TE-A initiates the call by sending a SETUP message to TE-B. The SETUP message contains the complete called party number (also known as the en-bloc signal). The local exchange then sends a SETUP message to TE-B and includes in the message the B-channel assignment.

> **NOTE** Overlap signaling occurs when digits are sent one by one in separate messages.

At this point, the local exchange sends a CALPRC message to TE-A indicating that the call setup started. If TE-B accepts the incoming call, an ALERT message is returned. The local exchange then sends an ALERT to TE-A, and if this is a speech call, a ringing tone is applied to the B channel.

When TE-B answers the call, a CONN message is sent to the exchange where the B channels are connected; a CONN message also is sent to TE-A. The local exchange acknowledges TE-B's CONN with a CONACK; TE-A also can acknowledge the CONN with a CONACK.

Call Disconnect

Consider the example in which TE-B is the first to initiate a disconnect. TE-B sends a DISC, and the local exchange then sends a DISC to TE-A.

At this point, the local exchange clears the B channel to TE-B and sends an RLSE message to TE-B. Next, TE-B releases the endpoint B channel and sends an RLCOM message. The same release procedure also occurs between TE-A and the local exchange.

QSIG

QSIG is a peer-to-peer signaling system used in corporate voice networking. Internationally, QSIG is known as Private Signaling System No. 1 (PSS1). This open standard is based on the ITU-T Q.9XX series of recommendations for basic service and supplementary services. Therefore, as well as providing inter-PBX communications, QSIG is compatible with public and private ISDN.

QSIG also has one important mechanism known as Generic Functional Procedures (QSIG GF). This mechanism provides a standard method for transporting features transparently across a network.

The following are attributes of the QSIG global signaling system:

- It is a standards-based protocol enabling the interconnection of multivendor equipment.

- It enables inter-PBX basic, feature transparency, and supplementary services.

- It is interoperable with public and private ISDNs.

- It operates in any network configuration (star, mesh, and so on) and is compatible with many PBX-type interfaces.

- It does not impose restrictions on private numbering plans.

QSIG is an important signaling system. The remainder of this section covers the following key aspects of QSIG:

- Services

- Architecture and Reference Points

- Protocol Stack

- Basic Call Setup and Teardown

QSIG Services

QSIG supports a suite of services and features for corporate PBX networks. The three main service groups include basic services, generic functional procedures, and supplementary services.

■ Basic service (QSIG BC)—This service provides the capabilities to set up, manage, and tear down a call. Similar to an ISDN bearer service, basic services include speech, 3.1 kHz audio, and 64 kbps unrestricted.

■ QSIG GF—This is a standardized method for transporting nonstandard features, thus providing feature transparency. This mechanism enables the exchange of signaling information for the control of supplementary and additional network features over a corporate network.

■ Supplementary services—This category includes services and additional network features (ANFs). Supplementary services and ANFs include call completion, call forward, call diversion, call transfer, call waiting, caller ID, and advice of charge.

QSIG Architecture and Reference Points

It is necessary to extend the ISDN reference model to include PBX-to-PBX signaling for corporate networks. To accommodate these two new reference points, "Q" and "C" were identified by the standard, as illustrated in Figure 3-11.

The Q reference point defines the logical signaling between PBXes, and the C reference point identifies the physical interconnection. A corporate network can have dedicated analog or digital channels, or it can have VPN switched connections. Typically, it is assumed that a T1 or E1 digital interface is used to connect to the network. QSIG end-to-end signaling is maintained from PBX to PBX, and ISDN and ISUP inter-working is critical for end-to-end signaling in the ISDN network. As mentioned previously, QSIG is compatible with ISDN; these reference points also are noted in Figure 3-11.

The T reference point defines access to the NT2 device for ISDN PRI. The C reference point is the physical interconnection point to the PBX. It is compatible with many interfaces, including two- and four-wire analog, BRI, PRI, and radio and satellite links. The Q reference point specifies the logical signaling point between two PBXs. This reference point is used to specify signaling-system and related protocols.

Figure 3-11 *Reference Model for Corporate Networks*

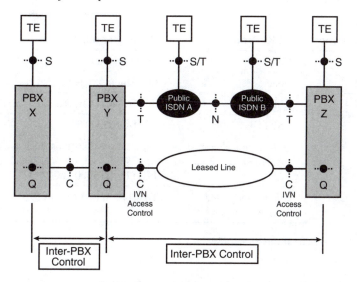

QSIG Protocol Stack

The QSIG protocol stack specifies a signaling system at reference point Q and is illustrated in Table 3-14. QSIG has an identical structure to that of ISDN, and at L1 and L2, these protocols can be the same. They differ at L3, however, where QSIG is split into the following three sublayers:

■   QSIG BC—With this symmetrical protocol, the interfaces and messages for the user and network sides are identical. The messages and sequences of this protocol are more easily understood and demonstrated in the example at the end of this section.

■   QSIG GF—This protocol specifies the control entities for supplementary services and ANFs. This protocol does not have the capability to control these services, but it does provide the generic layer capabilities to enable them. The protocol provides a connection-oriented and connectionless mechanism between the application entities of different PBXs.

■   QSIG Supplementary Service and ANF Protocols—These define the procedures for individual or specific services and features. These services and ANFs are defined and detailed in separate specifications. Such organizations as the European Computer Manufacturers Association (ECMA) and the European Telecommunication Standards Institute (ETSI) are developing these protocol standards.

Table 3-14 *QSIG Protocol Stack*

OSI Reference	QSIG Protocol	QSIG Standard
L1	None	Based on interface being used
L2	None	Identical to ISDN L2 (LAPD)
L3	QSIG BC	ECMA 142/143; ETS300* 171/172
	QSIG GF	ECMA 165; ETS300 239
	QSIG protocols for supplementary services	Separate specifications, such as call forward (ECMA 173/174, ETS300 256/257) and call transfer (ECMA 177/178, ETS300 260/261)
L4–L7	Application-based service elements	Transparent to the network

*ETS300 is an ETSI-based standard.

QSIG Basic Call Setup and Teardown Example

The QSIG BC protocol provides the basic capabilities for call setup and teardown. This protocol extends the ISDN access protocol for use in a corporate network or private ISDN. QSIG BC is a symmetrical protocol whereby both the network and user sides of the interface are identical. The message sequence for a basic call is demonstrated in Figure 3-12. The QSIG BC messages are functionally similar to the messages discussed in the "ISDN" section of this chapter.

Figure 3-12 *QSIG BC Message Sequence*

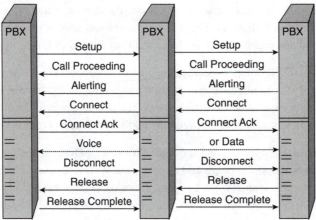

DPNSS

BT and a group of PBX vendors developed DPNSS in the 1980s. They designed this open standard to provide digital private networks at a time when ISDN and QSIG standards were still being defined.

DPNSS has rich services and feature sets and provided the basis for much of the work on the QSIG protocols. Also, interoperability between DPNSS and the QSIG signaling system is specified as part of the inter-working of both protocols.

The ISDN and QSIG protocols became more popular since they were developed, and DPNSS is not as widely used in today's private networks. DPNSS specifications are available from BT Plc and are defined in the following four documents:

- BTNR 188—DPNSS1

- BTNR 188-T—DPNSS1 testing schedule

- BTNR 189—Inter-working between DPNSS1 and other signaling systems

- BTNR 189-I—Inter-working between DPNSS1 and ISDN signaling systems

Summary

The signaling systems discussed in this chapter are wide in scope and exist in many versions. It will take some time before Voice over IP (VoIP) systems fully support all these protocols and their variations. Also, standards bodies such as the Internet Engineering Task Force (IETF) are drafting proposals on ways you can inter-work or backhaul these protocols where appropriate.

As standards are accepted and implemented, the inter-working of telephony signaling systems and VoIP systems will become more like "business as usual."

Signaling System 7

Signaling System 7 (SS7) is a common-channel signaling standard developed in the late 1970s by the International Telecommunication Union Telecommunication Standardization Sector (ITU-T), formerly known as the Consultative Committee for International Telegraph and Telephone (CCITT). SS7 was derived from SS6, which was developed in the late 1960s and was the first generation of common-channel signaling. SS7 was initially designed for telephony call-control applications. SS7 applications have greatly expanded since they were first developed, however, and today's SS7 functionality includes database queries, transactions, network operations, and Integrated Services Digital Network (ISDN).

The SS7 network provides the intelligence to the existing PSTN. SS7 is used to perform out-of-band signaling in the Public Switched Telephone Network (PSTN). SS7 signaling enhances the PSTN by handling call establishment, exchange of information, routing, operations, billing, and support for Intelligent Network (IN) services.

While VoIP networks have continued to rapidly grow over the past 10 years, the SS7 protocol is important to Voice over IP (VoIP) and the way it interworks with the PSTN. As long as users of VoIP networks need to connect to users of the legacy PSTN, it is critical that the translation points (gateways) between these two networks be fairly seamless and efficient to the carriers. Although all communication might move to VoIP sometime in the future, it is important to provide a smooth migration and preserve some of the usability to which end users and carriers have become accustomed.

Although SS7 often is considered an edge technology when integrated with VoIP networks, this chapter will focus on how SS7 works from a legacy perspective. Once you clearly understand this perspective, it is not complicated to see how SS7 can be integrated at the edge of a VoIP network.

SS7's objective was to provide a worldwide standard for telephony network signaling. This did not occur, and many national variants were developed, such as the American National Standards Institute (ANSI) and Bell Communications Research (Bellcore) standards used in North America as well as the European Telecommunication Standards Institute (ETSI) standards used in Europe.

This chapter focuses on the ITU-T-defined standards for SS7 and covers the following aspects:

- SS7 Network Elements and Links

- SS7 Protocol Suite and Messages

- SS7 Examples and Call-flows

SS7 Network Architecture

The SS7 network is used to switch information messages to set up, manage, and release telephone calls as well as to maintain the signaling network. SS7 network nodes are equipped with SS7 functionality and features to become SS7 signaling points or elements. SS7 is a common-channel signaling network, in that all signaling information is carried on a common signaling plane. The signaling planes and the voice circuit planes are logically separated.

SS7 networks consist of three signaling elements—Service Switching Point (SSP), Signal Transfer Point (STP), and Service Control Point (SCP)—and several link types, as illustrated in Figure 4-1. This section covers the signaling elements and signaling links in more detail.

Figure 4-1 *SS7 Network Architecture*

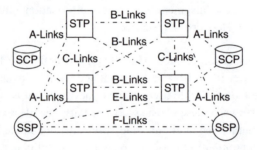

Signaling Elements

Signaling elements—which also are referred to as *signaling points, endpoints, exchanges, switches,* or *nodes*— separate the voice network from the signaling network. All signaling elements are identified by a numerical *point code*, which acts as a routing address in SS7. Each signaling message contains the source and destination point code address. Signaling elements route signaling messages and provide access to the SS7 network and to databases.

Figure 4-2 shows the three types of signaling elements in the SS7 network.

Figure 4-2 *Signaling Elements/Endpoints*

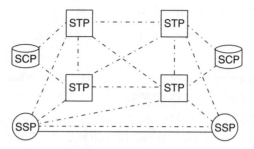

- SSPs are end office or tandem switches that connect voice circuits and perform the necessary signaling functions to originate and terminate calls.

- The STP routes all the signaling messages in the SS7 network.

- The SCP provides access to databases for additional routing information used in call processing. Also, the SCP is the key element for delivering IN applications on the telephony network.

The following sections explore the three signaling elements of the SS7 network in more detail.

SSP

SSPs are telephone switches that are provisioned with SS7 capabilities. End office SSPs originate and terminate calls, and core network switches (STPs) provide tandem or transit calls. The SSP provides circuit-based signaling messages to other SSPs for the purposes of connecting, disconnecting, and managing voice calls. Non-circuit based messages are used to query databases when the dialed number is insufficient to complete the call.

End office SSPs connect directly to users on their subscriber interfaces. The protocols used can vary from analog to digital and can be based on ISDN Primary Rate Interface (PRI) or channel-associated switching (CAS). The end office is in charge of translating subscriber protocol requests into SS7 messages to establish calls.

The SSP uses the dialed number to complete the call, unless, for example, it is an 800, 8xx, 9xx, or Local Number Portability exchange (or is ported NXX). In the latter case, a query is sent to an SCP requesting the routing information (number) necessary to complete the call.

The following steps help explain the functions an SSP uses to complete a call. In this case, assume that the originating and destination SSPs are directly attached, as illustrated in Figure 4-2:

1. The SSP uses the called number from the calling party or routing number from the database query to begin circuit connection signaling messages.

2. Then the SSP uses its routing table to determine the trunk group and circuit needed to connect the call.

3. At this point, a signaling setup message is sent to the destination SSP requesting a connection on the circuit specified by the originating SSP.

4. The destination SSP responds with an acknowledgment granting permission to connect to the specified trunk and proceeds to connect the call to the final destination.

STP

STPs, as illustrated in Figure 4-2, are an integral part of the SS7 architecture providing access to the network. STPs route or switch all the signaling messages in the network based on the routing information and destination point code address contained in the message.

The STP provides the logical connectivity between SSPs without requiring direct SSP-to-SSP links. STPs are configured in pairs and are mated to provide redundancy and higher availability. These mated STPs perform identical functions and are considered the home STPs for the directly connected SSP or SCP. The STP also is capable of performing global title translation, which is discussed later in this section.

Circuit-based messages are created on the SSP. Then, they are packetized in SS7 packets and sent from the SSP. Usually they contain requests to connect or disconnect a call. These packets are forwarded to the destination SSP where the call is terminated. It is the STP network's job to properly route such packets to the destination.

Non-circuit based messages that originate from an SSP are database queries requesting additional information needed to complete the call. It is the STP network's job to properly route packets between the SSP and the database interface known as the SCP. These packets are routed to the destination SCP and are addressed to the appropriate subsystem database. The SCP is the interface to the database that provides the routing number required to complete the call.

STPs also measure traffic and usage. Traffic measurements provide statistics such as network events and message types, and usage measurements provide statistics on the access and number of messages per message type. This information is used by the carrier's network planning teams to look at overall system capacity and future planning.

Global Title Translation

In addition to performing basic SS7 packet routing, STPs are capable of performing gateway services such as *global title translation*. This function is used to centralize the SCP and database selection versus distributing all possible destination selections to hundreds or thousands of distributed switches. If the SSP is unaware of the destination SCP address, it can send the database query to its local STP. The STP then performs global title translation and re-addresses the destination of the database query to the appropriate SCP.

Global title translation centralizes the selection of the correct database by enabling queries to be addressed directly to the STP. SSPs, therefore, do not have the burden of maintaining every potential destination database address. The term *global title translation* is taken from the term *global title digits*, which is another term for *dialed digits*.

The STP looks at the global dialed digits and through its own translation table to resolve the following:

■ The point code address of the appropriate SCP for the database

■ The subsystem number of the database

The STP also can perform an intermediate global title translation by using its translation table to find another STP. The intermediate STP then routes the message to the other STP to perform the final global title translation.

STP Hierarchy

STP hierarchy defines network interconnection and separates capabilities into specific areas of functionality. STP implementation can occur in multiple levels, such as:

■ Local Signal Transfer Point

■ Regional Signal Transfer Point

■ National Signal Transfer Point

■ International Signal Transfer Point

■ Gateway Signal Transfer Point

The local, regional, and national STPs transfer standards-based SS7 messages within the same network. These STPs usually are not capable of converting or handling messages in different formats or versions.

International STPs provide international connectivity where the same International Telecommunication Union (ITU) standards are deployed in both networks.

Gateway STPs can provide the following:

- Protocol conversion from national versions to the ITU standard

- Network-to-network interconnection points

- Network security features such as screening, which is used to examine all incoming and outgoing messages to ensure authorization

You can deploy and install STP functions on separate dedicated devices or incorporate them with other SSP functions onto a single end office or *tandem switch*. Integrating SSP and STP functions is particularly common in Europe and Australia. This is why fully associated SS7 or CCS7 (CCS7 is the ITU-T version of SS7) networks are prevalent in those areas. *Fully associated SS7* occurs when the same transmission channel carries the bearer's information and the signaling information.

SCP

The SCP, as shown in Figure 4-2, provides the interface to the database where additional routing information is stored for non-circuit based messages. Service-provider SCPs do not house the required information; they do, however, provide the interface to the system's database. The interface between the SCP and the database system is accomplished by a standard protocol, which is typically X.25. The SCP provides the conversion between the SS7 and the X.25 protocol. If X.25 is not the database access protocol, the SCP still provides the capability for communication through the use of primitives.

The database stores information related to its application and is addressed by a subsystem number, which is unique for each database. The subsystem number is known at the SSP level; the request originated within the PSTN contains that identifier. The subsystem number identifies the database where the information is stored and is used by the SCP to respond to the request.

The following databases are the most common in the SS7 network:

- 800 Database—Provides the routing information for special numbers, such as 800, 877, 888, 900, and 976 numbers. The 800 database responds to the special number queries with the corresponding routing number. In the case of 800, 888, and 900 numbers, the routing number is the actual telephone number at the terminating end.

- Line Information Database (LIDB)—Provides subscriber or user information such as screening and barring, calling-card services including card validation and personal identification number (PIN) authentication, and billing. The billing features of this database determine ways you can bill collect calls, calling-card calls, and third-party services.

- Local Number Portability Database (LNPDB)—Provides the 10-digit Location Routing Number (LRN) of the switch that serves the dialed-party number. The LRN is used to route the call through the network, and the dialed-party number is used to complete the call at the terminating SSP.

- Home Location Register (HLR)—Used in cellular networks to store information such as current cellular phone location, billing, and cellular subscriber information.

- Visitor Location Register (VLR)—Used in cellular networks to store information on subscribers roaming outside the home network. The VLR uses this information to communicate to the HLR database to identify the subscriber's location when roaming.

Signaling Links

All signaling points in the SS7 network are connected by signaling links. These full-duplex links simultaneously transmit and receive SS7 messages over the network link. The signaling links are typically 56- and 64 kbps data network facilities, either on standalone lines or extracted on channelized facilities such as structured T1/E1 trunks.

This section covers the following topics:

- Signaling Modes

- Signaling Links and Linksets

- Signaling Routes

- Signaling Link Performance

Signaling Modes

The SS7 network has three modes of signaling:

- Associated Signaling

- Nonassociated Signaling

- Quasi-associated Signaling

Associated signaling, illustrated in Figure 4-3, is the simplest form of signaling, in that the signaling and voice paths are directly connected between the two signaling endpoints. This is not common in North America because end office switches would require direct connections to all other end office switches; however, associated signaling is common in Europe, where the signaling path is actually derived within the E1 trunk facilities.

Figure 4-3   *Associated Signaling*

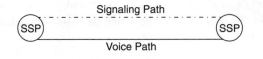

Nonassociated signaling uses a separate logical path for signaling and voice. As illustrated in Figure 4-4, the signaling messages travel through multiple endpoints before reaching the final destination. Alternatively, the voice path can have a direct path to the destination end office switch. Nonassociated signaling is the most common form of signaling in the SS7 network.

Figure 4-4   *Nonassociated Signaling*

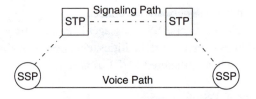

Quasi-associated signaling, shown in Figure 4-5, uses a separate logical path for signaling through the minimal number of transfer points to reach the final destination. The benefit of quasi-associated signaling is that network delay is minimized due to the low number of transfer points between the origin and destination. The quasi-associated method is more costly than the nonassociated method, however, because signaling links need to be backhauled to a small number of STPs.

Figure 4-5   *Quasi-Associated Signaling*

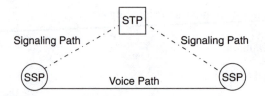

Signaling Links and Linksets

The *signaling links* in the SS7 network are identified by the function provided to the corresponding endpoints, as illustrated in Figure 4-6.

Figure 4-6 *Signaling Links*

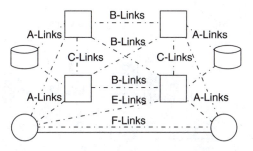

The following list outlines the six types of links present in the SS7 network:

- A-links are interconnects between signaling endpoints and STPs, as illustrated in Figure 4-6. The signaling endpoints are SSPs or SCPs, and each has at least two A-links that connect to the "home" STP pair. It is possible to have only one A-link to an STP; however, this is not common practice. These links provide access to the network for the purposes of transmitting and receiving signaling messages. The STP routes the A-link signaling messages received from the originating SSP or SCP toward the destination.

- Bridge Links (B-links) are interconnects between two mated pairs of STPs, as illustrated in Figure 4-6. These mated STPs are peers operating at the same hierarchical level and are interconnected through a quad of B-links. B-links carry signaling messages from the origin to the intended destination.

- Cross Links (C-links) interconnect an STP with its mate, as illustrated in Figure 4-6. The STP pairs perform identical functions and are mated to provide redundancy in the network. C-links are used only when failure or congestion occurs, causing these links to become the only available path to the network. Under normal conditions, these links carry only management traffic.

- Diagonal Links (D-links) are used to interconnect mated STP pairs of one hierarchical level to mated STP pairs of another hierarchical level, as illustrated in Figure 4-7. The D-links are connected in a quad-like fashion similar to B-links. These links provide the same function as B-links; the distinction between B- and D-links is arbitrary.

Figure 4-7   *D-Links Interconnect Mated STPs on Different Hierarchical Levels*

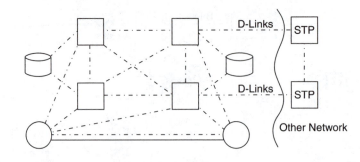

■ Extended Links (E-links) are used to interconnect an SSP to an alternate STP, as illustrated in Figure 4-6. The SSP also is connected to the home STP pair through A-links; however, if more reliability is required, you can implement E-links. This is not common practice, however, because the SSPs have dual A-links to redundant mated STP pairs. These links are used only if failure or congestion occurs in the home STPs.

■ F-links are used to directly interconnect two signaling endpoints, as illustrated in Figure 4-6. These links are used when STPs are not available or when high traffic volumes exist. This is the only link type whose signaling traffic is allowed to follow the same path as the voice circuits. The signaling messages between the two signaling endpoints are associated only with the voice circuits directly connected between the two signaling endpoints. This method is not commonly used in North America; it is common in Europe, however.

Signaling links are grouped together into *linksets* when the links are connected to the same endpoint. Signaling endpoints provide load sharing across all the links in a linkset. *Combined linksets* are used when connecting to mated STP pairs with different point code addresses. In this case, links are assigned to different linksets and are configured as a single combined linkset.

Load sharing across combined linksets occurs when signaling endpoints re-address the messages to adjacent point codes. You can configure alternate linksets to provide redundant paths, increasing reliability over other signaling links such as E- and F-links, as described later in this section.

Signaling Routes

Signaling endpoints have statically predefined routes for destination endpoints. The route is made up of linksets; linksets can be part of more than one route. Groups of routes are called *routesets* and are defined in routing tables to provide alternate routes when the current route is unavailable.

Signaling Link Performance

The availability of signaling in the SS7 network is critical to connect and serve telephone network users. Signaling links provide signaling transmission and access to the SS7 network and, therefore, must be available at all times. If congestion or failure occurs in the network, the links and STP pairs must handle the additional traffic. The STP mated pairs and linkset configurations provide the necessary load sharing and redundancy required to maintain SS7 network reliability.

SS7 Protocol Overview

The SS7 protocol stack and levels differ slightly from the Open Systems Interconnection (OSI) reference model discussed in Chapter 6, "IP Tutorial." A comparison between SS7 protocol levels and the layers of the OSI model is illustrated in Figure 4-8. As you can see, the SS7 protocol has only four levels, and the OSI model has seven. SS7 Levels 1–3 (L1–L3) are identical to OSI L1–L3, and SS7 Level 4 (L4) corresponds to OSI L4–Level 7 (L7).

Figure 4-8 *SS7 Protocol Stack Versus the OSI Model*

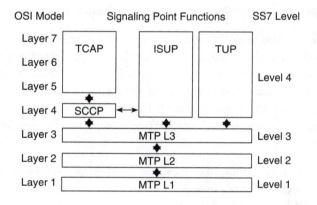

The following sections cover the suite of SS7 protocols identified in Figure 4-8:

- Message Transfer Part (MTP) L1, L2, and L3 provide the transport protocols for all other SS7 protocols. MTP functionality includes network interface specifications, reliable transfer of information, and message handling and routing.

- Signaling Connection Control Part (SCCP) provides end-to-end addressing and routing for L4 protocols such as transaction capabilities application part (TCAP).

- Telephone User Part (TUP) primarily is a link-by-link signaling system used to connect telephone or speech calls as well as facsimile calls.

■ ISDN User Part (ISUP) is a circuit-based protocol used to establish and maintain connections for voice and data calls.

■ TCAP provides access to remote databases for routing information and enables features in remote network entities.

Physical Layer—MTP L1

The physical layer (L1) of the MTP defines the physical and electrical characteristics of the signaling link. Also called MTP1, this SS7 protocol layer is virtually identical to OSI L1 and does not specify any particular interface. The following list provides some examples of possible MTP1 network interfaces available in networks today:

■ T1—The standard in North America, Australia, Hong Kong, and Japan for digital transmission of voice, data, and images. T1 (also known as *DS1*) signals transmit over two pairs of twisted wires with a capacity of 1.544 Mbps. The T1 link has 24 full duplex channels or digital signal level 0s (DS-0s), each consisting of 64 kbps. The payload yields a total of 1.536 Mbps, with the remaining 8 kbps used for framing the T1 link.

■ DS-0—The standard speed for digitizing one voice conversation using pulse code modulation (PCM). Each of the 24 individual DS-0 channels is sampled at a rate of 8000 times per second, producing an 8-bit value (1 bit every 125 ms). The 24-channel, 8-bit values are multiplexed into a serial bit stream using time-division multiplexing (TDM) to generate a 192-bit frame. One of the 8kbps framing bits is added as the 193rd bit. The result is a T1 signal consisting of 8000 frames per second, whereby each frame contains one framing bit and 24 channels of 8-bit samples.

■ E1—The standard in South America, Europe, and Mexico for digital transmission of voice, data, and images. E1 signals transmit over two pairs of twisted wire with a capacity of 2.048 Mbps. The E1 link has 32 full duplex channels, each consisting of 64 kbps, which yields a total of 2.048 Mbps.

E1 is made up of 30 DS-0s (identical to the DS-0s found in T1) for voice and data, plus one channel for signaling and one channel for framing.

■ 56/64 kbps—The 56- and 64 kbps channels in T1 and E1 systems are DS-0s. The 56- and 64 kbps interface rates are the most commonly used physical interfaces in the SS7 network.

■ V.35—The ITU standard for interfacing between a digital service unit (DSU) and a packet/data device. The V.35 interface has defined pin and electrical configurations for a 37-pin connector.

Data Layer—MTP L2

The data layer (L2) of the SS7 protocol is MTP L2, also called MTP2. The MTP2 protocol is used to create reliable point-to-point links between endpoints in a network. MTP2 does not run across the network and, therefore, is not concerned with the final destination of the message. MTP2 has the following mechanisms:

- Error Detection and Correction—Used to maintain data integrity during transmission. The error detection mechanism in MTP2 is provided by cyclic redundancy check (CRC)-16. If CRC-16 detects errors, MTP2 must request a retransmission.

- Sequencing of Packets—Used to identify lost messages during transmission. If lost messages are detected, MTP2 must request a retransmission. Most protocols have a unique message structure to indicate retransmissions. The message structure in SS7 enables the identification of retransmissions in any message. Retransmission requests can be accompanied with the user data of the next message. The user data in a retransmission message can be from another L4 application (that is, SCCP, ISUP, TUP, or TCAP).

- Link Status Indicators—Used to maintain and monitor signaling links as well as monitor remote processor outages.

The MTP2 protocol uses packets called *signal units* to transmit SS7 messages. The signal units are used in the SS7 network to perform error detection, indicate link status, and transfer information messages. Three types of signal units provide MTP2's data layer functions:

- Fill-in Signal Unit (FISU)—Provides link error detection in the SS7 network. As its name signifies, the FISU packets fill in when no traffic is being sent on the network. This enables you to monitor the link at all times, even when no traffic is on the network.

- Link Status Signal Unit (LSSU)—Provides link status on the link between two directly connected signaling elements.

- Message Signal Unit (MSU)—Provides the structure to carry the information messages in the SS7 network. These information messages carry the payload for higher-level messages such as SCCP, TUP, ISUP, and TCAP.

The following sections further discuss these signal units and the role they play in the SS7 network.

FISU

FISUs constantly are transmitted on the signaling links when the LSSU and MSUs are not present. FISUs are sent only between signaling points and are not sent across the SS7 network. The FISU provides error-detection capabilities to the signaling points at both ends of the link. This enables the signaling points to perform error detection to verify link integrity and maintain reliability in the SS7 network.

If the signaling endpoints receive an FISU with errors, the signal unit is discarded. Retransmission of FISUs is not required, as these signal units do not provide any L4 or user information. FISU fields are illustrated in Figure 4-9.

Figure 4-9   *Fill-In Signal Unit Fields*

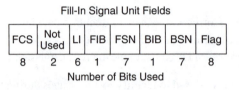

The following list describes the FISU fields (these also are common to the LSSU and MSU):

- The frame check sequence (FCS) is the most important field in the FISU. You use this field to verify the integrity of the link between two adjacent signaling elements. MTP Layer 3 (MTP3) uses the bits in the FCS field to determine whether any errors occurred in the FISU, the LSSU, and the MSU. These bits perform error detection using the CRC-16 mechanism. The originating endpoint calculates FCS bit values using the CRC-16 equation. It applies the CRC-16 equation on the user data of the message and places the value in the FCS field. The receiving endpoint applies the CRC-16 equation on the received user data and compares the result with the value in the FCS field.

- The Length Indicator (LI) field identifies the type of signal unit. In the case of the FISU, the LI is set to a value of zero. The LI value is 1 or 2 for an LSSU and from 3 to 63 for an MSU.

- The Forward Indicator Bits (FIBs) and Backward Indicator Bits (BIBs) are used for retransmissions. Under normal conditions (no link errors), the FIB and BIB have the same value. As illustrated in Figure 4-9, the field length is 1 bit; therefore, only two values are possible: 0 or 1.

  In the case of a rejected signal unit, the BIB value is toggled and an FISU is sent back. Toggling the BIB value causes the BIB and FIB to be unequal, which indicates a negative acknowledgment. The *negative acknowledgment* signifies a request for retransmission. When the originator retransmits the signal unit, the FIB is set to equal the BIB until the next retransmission is required.

- The Forward Sequence Number (FSN) and Backward Sequence Number (BSN) are used to acknowledge the link status and MSUs. Acknowledgments are accomplished by sending an FISU with the BSN value equal to the FSN value of the last signal unit. In the case of retransmissions, the BSN values are examined to determine which signaling units need to be retransmitted.

- The Flag field is used to indicate the beginning of a signal unit by implying the end of the previous signal unit. These signal units are separated on the signaling link by the binary value of the flag octet, which is set to 01111110.

LSSU

LSSUs provide link status information over the signaling links between two adjacent signaling endpoints. You use this information to maintain link alignment and to identify a processor outage at the remote endpoint. The LSSU contains the L2 interface link status and L3 status of the transmitting endpoint. LSSUs maintain reliability because these endpoints are not synchronized and, instead, run independently of each other. The LSSU identifies the status of the remote endpoint link interfaces and processors. If the endpoints receive an LSSU with errors, the signal unit is discarded. Retransmission of LSSUs is not required, as these signal units do not provide any information.

The LSSU has the same fields as the FISU, with the addition of the Status field, as illustrated in Figure 4-10. The Status field in the LSSU relays the link status information between endpoints. LSSUs are not transmitted across the network and only are carried on links between two adjacent endpoints.

Figure 4-10 *LSSU Fields*

FCS	SF	Not Used	LI	FIB	FSN	BIB	BSN	Flag
8	8 or 16	2	6	1	7	1	7	8

Number of Bits Used

MTP3 uses the L2 information the LSSU provides to track the status of the link and of the remote endpoint processor, both of which are responsible for maintaining link alignment. You use the link alignment procedures to correct a misalignment or problem on the link.

The following list describes fields that are unique to the LSSU:

- The LI field determines the type of signal unit. In the case of the LSSU, the LI is set to a value of 1 or 2. The LI value is 0 for an FISU and from 3 to 63 for an MSU.

- The Status field carries the information regarding the status of the link between endpoints. This field is either 1 octet (8 bits) or 2 octets (16 bits) and provides status on the link on which it is carried. In the Status field, only 3 bits are actually used to identify link status; the remaining bits are set to zero.

The SF identifies the following indicators:

- Status Indicator Busy (SIB)—Identifies L2 congestion at the transmitting endpoint. Receiving an SIB causes the receiving end to stop sending MSUs and start sending FISUs.

- Status Indicator Processor Outage (SIPO)—Identifies that the transmitting endpoint can't communicate with the upper-level protocols. Processor failures or other endpoint component failures can cause this to occur. Receiving an SIPO causes the receiving end to stop sending MSUs and start sending FISUs.

- Status Indicator Out-of-Alignment (SIO)—Identifies that a link failed and alignment procedures need to be initiated.

- Status Indicator Out-of-Service (SIOS)—Identifies that the transmitting endpoint cannot send or receive any MSUs. An SIOS is used when the problem is not related to a processor failure. Receiving an SIOS causes the receiving end to stop sending MSUs and start sending FISUs.

- Status Indicator Normal (SIN) and Status Indicator Emergency (SIE)—Identify that the transmitting endpoint initiated alignment procedures. The FISU packets are continually transmitted until the link alignment procedure is complete and MSUs are again transmitted on the link.

MSU

The MSU provides the structure for transmitting circuit- and non-circuit based messages in the SS7 network. You use circuit-based messages to set up, manage, and release telephone calls. Non-circuit based messages refer to queries for additional routing information and network management data. MSUs originate from MTP3 or from an MTP3 user. MTP3 users include SCCP, ISUP, TUP, and TCAP. These user messages are transferred between two peer L4 protocols in signaling endpoints.

In the case of ISUP, the two endpoints transfer ISUP messages over the SS7 network. An MSU with a routing label carries the ISUP information. The routing label contains the point code addresses of the originating endpoint and destination endpoint.

The originating endpoint passes the ISUP information to MTP3. MTP3 expands the MTP3 message and passes the message to MTP2. MTP2 expands the MTP3 message in an MSU. At this point, the MSU is passed to MTP1 for transmission across the signaling link. The destination endpoint receives the MTP1 message and MTP2 extracts the MTP3 message. The L4 protocol or user data is identified and the message is passed to the ISUP process of the destination endpoint.

The MSU has the same fields as the FISU, with the addition of the SIO and SIF, as illustrated in Figure 4-11.

Figure 4-11 *MSU Fields*

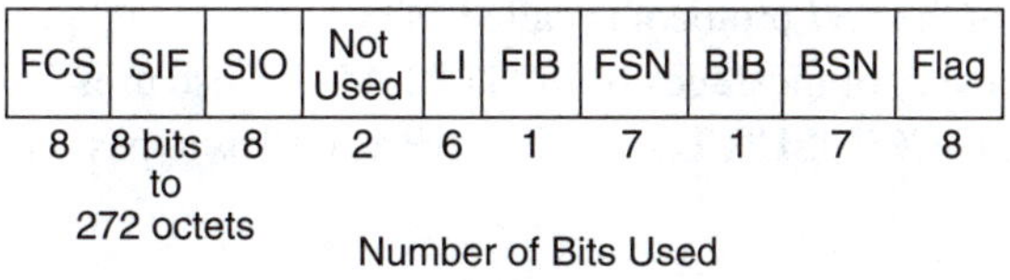

FCS	SIF	SIO	Not Used	LI	FIB	FSN	BIB	BSN	Flag
8	8 bits to 272 octets	8	2	6	1	7	1	7	8

Number of Bits Used

The new MSU fields are defined as follows:

■ The SIO identifies the protocol type, such as SCCP, ISUP, TUP, and TCAP, present in the MSU. It also identifies the version of the SS7 protocol. The SIO is an 8-bit (1-octet) value that is broken into two parts: a 4-bit subservice field and a 4-bit service indicator field.

The 4-bit subservice field identifies the protocol version (national or international) and the MSU priority. The MSU priority bits have four possible options, ranging from a lowest-priority value of 0 to a highest-priority value of 3.

The 4-bit service indicator specifies the MTP3 user or L4 protocol, as indicated in Table 4-1.

Table 4-1 *Service Indicator*

MTP User	Service Indicator Value
Signaling Network Management (SNM) Message	0
Maintenance (MTN) Regular Message	1
Maintenance Special (MTNS) Message	2
SCCP	3
TUP	4
ISUP	5
Data User Part (DUP)—circuit-based messages	6
DUP—facility messages	7

■ The Service Information Field (SIF) contains the routing label and control information from upper-level protocols (that is, SCCP, ISUP, TUP, TCAP, or network management). It has a maximum length of 272 octets. Routing labels route the MSU through the network to its final destination and are discussed in the next section. The remaining part of the SIF carries the user message or control data of the higher-level protocols.

Network Layer—MTP3

The network layer of the SS7 protocol is called MTP3. The MTP3 protocol routes SS7 messages and relies on the delivery of messages from MTP2. MTP3 also uses primitives to communicate to L4 protocols such as SCCP, ISUP, TUP, and TCAP as well as to pass and receive information from MTP2.

The MTP3 protocol is divided into two main functions:

■ Signaling Message Handling (SMH)—Routes SS7 messages during normal conditions.

■ SNM—Reroutes link traffic during network failure conditions.

This section first analyzes the message format of the MTP3 layer and then studies the SMH and SNM processes and functions.

Message Format

The MTP3 message consists of the SIO and SIF. As previously discussed, the SIO identifies the user or protocol type (SCCP, TUP, ISUP, or TCAP) and the version of the SS7 protocol (national or international). The SIF is divided into two parts: the routing label, and the user or L4 message. The user message contains the control information of the upper-level protocols, which are discussed in more detail in the SCCP, ISUP, and TCAP sections of this chapter.

The signaling endpoint MTP3 processes use the routing label (RL) to determine the destination address. The RL contains the Destination Point Code (DPC), Originating Point Code (OPC), and Signaling Link Selector (SLS) fields, as illustrated in Figure 4-12.

Figure 4-12 *MTP3 Message Format*

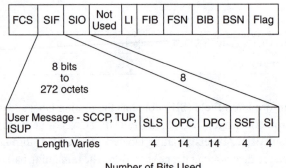

The following list describes the fields in the RL:

- The DPC identifies the point code or address of the destination endpoint and has an address space of 14 bits.

- The OPC identifies the point code or address of the originating endpoint and has an address space of 14 bits.

NOTE   You can provision signaling endpoints with more than one point code address.

- The SLS value identifies the signaling link to which the message is to be routed. MTP users or L4 protocols (SCCP, ISUP, TUP, and TCAP) assign the 4-bit SLS value to each outgoing message. Signaling endpoints use these pre-assigned values to route messages over the appropriate links.

SMH

The SMH function routes SS7 messages during normal conditions. SMH identifies whether the destination address is the receiving endpoint or whether the message needs to be routed. If the destination address is the receiving endpoint, SMH also identifies the user application (SCCP, ISUP, TUP, or TCAP). If the message needs to be forwarded, SMH identifies the link to which the message is to be forwarded.

The SMH is divided into three processes:

- SMH Message Discrimination—Determines the SS7 message's destination endpoint address. Message discrimination reads the DPC from the routing label in the SIF of the MSU. If it is addressed to the receiving node, message discrimination passes the message to the message distribution function. If it is not addressed to the receiving node, message discrimination passes the message to the message routing function.

- SMH Message Distribution—Identifies the user and delivers the user information (SCCP, TUP, ISUP, TCAP, or network management) in the SS7 message to the upper-level protocol. As previously mentioned, the message distribution process is invoked only when the message is addressed to the receiving endpoint or to itself. The Service Indicator value in the Service Indicator octet field of the MSU determines the user of the message.

If the user of the message is unavailable for processing, the User Part Unavailable (UPU) message is sent back to the transmitting endpoint. UPU messages sent by the network management process include a cause code that identifies one of the following problems:

— User part function is not provisioned.

— User part function is out of service.

— User part function is unavailable for unknown reasons.

■ SMH Message Routing—Interfaces with MTP2 to route messages over the network. The SMH routing process routes messages to the appropriate signaling links. The SMH routing process receives messages from the message discrimination and L4 applications. Message discrimination passes messages to the routing process when the message is destined for another signaling point. Higher-level applications pass messages to the routing process to transport the outgoing messages.

Routing Overview

Service Provider personnel statically maintain signaling endpoint routing tables. The routing table identifies the links, linksets, primary routes, and alternate routes for each DPC. All links in the linkset share the traffic load equally. When a particular destination has more than one linkset, the linksets involved share the traffic load equally.

Priority codes identify primary and alternate routes. The direct, most-direct, or fewest-hop-count route (or link) is always the first choice as the outgoing link. The routes are chosen based on link type (A- to F-links) and signaling endpoint type (SSP, STP, or SCP). An F-link between two SSPs, for example, is the first route choice for messages between these two endpoints. A most-direct-route example is an E-link; if available, this link is the second choice for messages between the (E-link-attached) SSP and the destination SSP.

The SNM function reroutes traffic in the SS7 network. The SMH handles the following during network link failures:

■ Linkset rerouting

■ Alternate link rerouting

■ Traffic flow rerouting to specific endpoints

The SNM process handles the rerouting of traffic through alternate links or linksets during network link failures. The SNM process also controls the flow of traffic to specific endpoints during network link failures.

SNM is divided into three functions:

- Link Management—Monitors and controls the individual links of the signaling endpoint. Link management manages the link interfaces of the signaling endpoint as opposed to the end-to-end link. The link management function is divided into three parts—Link Activation, Link Restoration, and Link Deactivation—described here:

  — The Link Activation process uses the LSSU to inform the adjacent endpoint of the link status. Signaling Link Test Messages (SLTMs) activate links between endpoints. The SLTM acknowledgment (SLTA) restores the link to service and enables traffic to flow over the link.

  — The Link Restoration process uses the LSSU to inform the adjacent endpoint of L3 alignment activities. When the alignment procedures are complete, the link activation process is initiated.

  — The Link Deactivation process places links into alignment procedures when links are failed or in error. Link deactivation uses local MTP2 information and remote information provided by the LSSU to initiate alignment procedures. Link deactivation triggers traffic management procedures when link failures or errors are detected.

- Route Management—Exchanges routing information and status between signaling endpoints. Routing problems are transmitted using transfer messages to redirect traffic during network failure conditions. This enables the other signaling endpoints to choose alternate routes.

  You can use several types of transfer messages for normal and cluster routing management. The functionality and capabilities of these messages are outside the context of this book. The following is a list of the transfer messages used when failures are identified:

  — Transfer Prohibited

  — Transfer Allowed

  — Transfer Restricted

  — Transfer Controlled

  — Signaling Route Set and Congestion Test

  — Cluster Router Set Test

- Traffic Management—Used to reroute or divert traffic and control congestion during network failure conditions. The traffic management process receives link availability information from SNM Link Management and is advised of routing problems to particular destinations from SNM Route Management. Traffic management also has the capability of advising SMH and the upper-layer protocols of failure conditions. Traffic management uses the following:

— An interface to SMH to reroute or divert messages over an alternate route

— Primitives to advise the upper-level protocols about the status of signaling links

— MSU to transmit messages to SNM peer processes in other signaling points

— Commands to MTP2 for signaling links

SNM Message Structure

SNM messages transmit and receive network management information between signaling endpoints. SNM uses MTP3 messages (similar to L4 applications) and transmits information in the User Message (UM) field of the MSU. The SNM routing label is illustrated in Figure 4-13.

Figure 4-13 *SNM User—MTP3 Message*

User Message - SNM	SLS	OPC	DPC	SSF	SI=0000
Length Varies	4	14	14	4	4

Number of Bits Used

The SI field equals 0000, denoting that the user of this message is network management. The SLS is replaced with the Signaling Link Code (SLC) parameter. The SLC parameter provides the status information of a particular link. If the message does not pertain to any particular link, SLC is set to 0.

Congestion Control

MTP2 monitors the level of messages queued in buffers (both output and retransmission) and alerts SNM in case of congestion.

Onset of congestion messages are sent to SNM when the threshold value for the buffers is exceeded. The SNM process considers all destinations across the link to be congested.

Now consider congestion from the signaling endpoint and STP perspective:

■ Signaling endpoints (SSP, SCP) receive congestion information from MTP2 *onset of congestion* indications. Excessive higher-layer messages can cause congestion over signal endpoint (SSP and SCP) links. In this case, SNM sends status messages to applications indicating which DPCs are affected. The application should reduce outgoing messages for a period of time. SNM continues to send the *congestion* status message until MTP2 receives the *end of congestion* indication. At this point, SNM stops sending the status messages, and after the timeout period, user applications resume normal activity.

■ If the STP SNM process receives an *onset of congestion* alert concerning a particular link, it considers that the route to its adjacent node is congested. When messages are received for the affected node, the STP SNM process sends a Transfer Controlled (TFC) message to the SNM of the transmitting endpoint. The STP indicates the affected node in the TFC message. This enables the signaling endpoint to choose an alternate route to the affected node. When the SNM process receives the *end of congestion* indication, it stops sending the status indications to the transmitting endpoint.

Rerouting

The SNM rerouting process reroutes traffic around an affected node without causing congestion or losing messages. STPs use this process when the route to a specific endpoint is unavailable. SNM uses the Transfer Prohibited (TFP) message to advise all directly connected nodes of the lost route to the specific endpoint. This enables the other STPs to choose an alternate route to the affected node. When the links are restored, Transfer Allowed (TFA) messages alert the directly connected nodes that normal routing procedures can resume.

Changeover and Changeback

You use changeover procedures when signaling links become unavailable and messages need to be diverted over alternate links. You use changeback procedures when the signaling links become available and normal routing needs to be re-established. Changeover and changeback procedures require SNM actions from both signaling points to maintain sequence and minimize loss.

You initiate the changeover procedure using the *changeover order* (COO) message between the signaling points. The COO message indicates the affected link in the SLC field of the MSU. The SMH function does not select the signaling link identified in the SLC field as the outgoing link. SMH selects an alternate route to reach the adjacent signaling point.

When the receiving point receives the COO message, it selects an alternate route and sends a *changeover acknowledgment* (COA) to the transmitting signaling point. The COO and COA messages contain the FSNs of the last message accepted on the unavailable link. Both signaling points retrieve the messages in the output buffers of the unavailable link and move these messages to the output of the alternate link. At this point, all waiting messages are sent in sequence and without loss, completing the changeover procedure.

You use the changeback procedure when the affected link becomes available. Either signaling point can initiate changeback procedures. SNM advises the SMH process that the messages destined for the alternate link should be stored in the *changeback buffer* (CBB) instead. The *changeback declaration* (CBD) is then sent to the adjacent signaling point identifying that the link is now available. The receiving signaling point responds with a *changeback acknowledgment* (CBA). When the signaling point receives the CBA, SNM advises SMH to send the buffered messages out the primary link and resume normal routing procedures.

SCCP

The SCCP provides network services on top of MTP3: The combination of those two layers is called the Network Service Part (NSP) of SS7. TCAP typically uses SCCP services to access databases in the SS7 network. As illustrated in Figure 4-8, the SCCP provides service interfaces to TCAP and ISUP. SCCP routing services enable the STP to perform Global Title Translation (GTT) by determining the DPC and subsystem number of the destination database.

The following SCCP features are covered in the next few sections:

■ Connection-Oriented Services

■ Connectionless Services and Messages

■ SCCP Management Functions

Connection-Oriented Services

SCCP supports connection-oriented services for TCAP and ISUP, however none of these services is used today. As such, this section does not cover SCCP connection-oriented capabilities, messages, or services.

Connectionless Services and Messages

SCCP provides the transport layer for the connectionless services of TCAP (discussed in the section entitled "Transaction Capabilities Applications Part [TCAP]"). TCAP-based services include 800, 888, 900, calling card, and mobile applications. Together, SCCP and MTP3 transfer non-circuit based messages used in these services. The SCCP also enables the STP to perform GTT on behalf of the end office exchange. The end office exchange views the 800 number as a functional address or, in other words, as a global title address. Because global title addresses are not routed, the SCCP in the end office exchange routes query messages to its home STP.

In this section, connectionless services are based on end office exchanges querying a database to obtain the routing number for an 800 number. The following is an example of how this works in the network.

Together, SCCP and MTP3 transport TCAP 800-based queries to centralized databases. The connectionless messages passed between the SCCP and MTP are called *Unitdata Messages (UDTs)* and *Unitdata Service Messages (UDTSs)*.

The SCCP sends a UDT to transfer subsystem information, and it sends a UDT to perform the GTT function. UDTs also are used to query and receive responses from databases. Table 4-2 lists parameters used in the UDT message.

Table 4-2   *UDT Parameters*

Parameter	Type	Length (Octets)
Message Type	M	1
Protocol Class (PRC)	M	1
Called Party Address (CDA)	M	3 minimum
Calling Party Address (CGA)	M	3 minimum
Subsystem Data	M	Variable

Source: ITU-T Q.713 (7/96)

A UDTS is sent to the originating SCCP advising that the receiving SCCP was unable to deliver the UDT to its destination. The return cause parameter indicates why the UDT is being returned. Table 4-3 lists parameters used in the UDTS.

Table 4-3   *UDTS*

Parameter	Type	Length (Octets)
Message Type	M	1
Return Cause	M	1
CDA	M	3 minimum
CGA	M	3 minimum
Subsystem Data	M	Variable

Source: ITU-T Q.713 (7/96)

SCCP Connectionless Example

This example demonstrates ways you can use SCCP services and messages in a typical 800 call:

1. When the end office switch receives a call setup for an 800 number, it launches a query to a database. TCAP passes the calling and called address parameters to SCCP, which then fills the appropriate fields in the UDT and sets the routing indicator bit indicating that a GTT is required. The SCCP addresses the query to the home STP and passes the message to MTP. MTP in the end office switch creates the MSU and forwards the message to the STP.

2. The SCCP function in the STP receives the query and, using its translation tables, re-addresses the message with the Subsystem Number of the database. The SSN includes the DPC and the database subsystem address. The MTP in the STP then forwards the query to the SCP serving the database.

3. The SCCP in the SCP passes the message to TCAP, which queries the database. The database translates the functional number into the routing number and passes the information to the SCCP, which sets the DPC and sends the response back to the originating end office. The SCCP also sets the routing indicator bit indicating to MTP that the routing should be based on the DPC.

SCCP Management Functions

SCCP management functions maintain the transfer of SCCP messages during failure conditions, including network and subsystem failures. SCCP management processes alert SCCP users, such as TCAP or ISUP, during these failure conditions. SCCP management has interfaces to MTP, SCCP connectionless control, and the subsystems (SCCP users). SCCP management uses the unit data connectionless message format.

The SCCP management function is divided into three groups:

-   Signaling Point Status—Relies on MTP services. MTP pause, resume, and status information is sent to the SCCP management process.

-   Subsystem Status—Each subsystem provides information directly to the SCCP management process. This enables SCCP management to maintain the status of each subsystem.

-   Traffic Management—Consists of rerouting messages from one subsystem to another duplicate subsystem. This ensures that services are not lost when one subsystem fails.

TUP

TUP was the first SS7 user part defined when all calls were considered voice calls. TUP supports physical circuit connections but is unable to handle the virtual connections and bearer circuits used in today's digital networks. North America was first to implement ISUP as opposed to TUP. The

ISUP protocol was defined to inter-work with ISDN and offers increased capabilities and services over TUP. For this reason, this chapter focuses on ISUP rather than TUP.

ISUP

ISUP connects, manages, and disconnects all voice and data calls in the PSTN. ISUP sets up and tears down the circuits used to connect PSTN voice and data subscribers. The subscribers include ISDN, analog, and ISDN-to-analog users. ISUP also is used in cellular or mobile networks for trunking connections. ISUP is widely implemented in North America and is preferred over TUP . Internationally, ISUP also is widely adopted, although several national variations exist. ISUP offers increased capabilities and services over TUP. The broadband ISUP (BISUP) signaling protocol for broadband network services is not covered in this book.

ISUP information is transferred in MTP3 messages similar to the other L4 protocols. The ISUP section covers the following topics:

- ISUP Services—Basic and Supplementary

- End-to-end Signaling—Pass-along and SCCP

- Call Setup and Teardown

- ISUP Message Format

- ISUP Call Control Messages

The "SS7 Examples" section later in this chapter provides basic call setup and teardown examples that include ISUP messages.

ISUP Services

ISUP services provide the capability to reach an endpoint destination in the PSTN. The two types of ISUP services are:

- ISUP Basic Service—Provides the setup, management, and teardown of voice and data calls in the PSTN.

- ISUP Supplementary Services—Services used to support voice and data connections such as caller ID and call forward. The end office exchanges have access to databases where subscriptions to these services are stored.

End-to-End Signaling

End-to-end signaling procedures establish, maintain, and release connections. They also enable signaling endpoints to exchange information using the Information Request (INR) and Information (INF) messages, which are detailed in the "ISUP Call Control Messages" section later in this chapter.

The originating and terminating endpoints exchange signaling capabilities using call indicators. The originating end office indicates its signaling capabilities in the forward call indicators field of the Initial Address Message (IAM). The terminating end office indicates its capabilities in the backward call indicators field of the Address Completion Message (ACM), ANswer Message (ANM), or Call Progress (CPG) message.

ISUP uses two methods for passing end-to-end signaling: the pass-along method and the SCCP method.

In the pass-along method, signaling information travels from the originating switch to each intermediate switch until it reaches the terminating end office. The initial setup information uses the same path used for all subsequent information relating to this circuit.

The SCCP method is an alternative to the pass-along method. In this case, ISUP uses the SCCP to route signaling information through the network. The signaling path does not have to be the same for messages related to a particular circuit. SCCP enables ISUP messages to be routed directly from the originating to the terminating end office.

Call Setup and Teardown

ISUP capabilities are more easily understood after you understand the basics of setting up and releasing calls in the SS7 network. For the purposes of this exercise, assume that the call is destined for a remote end office, ISUP signaling is available end to end, only one intermediate switch is available, and the dialed digits do not require queries from a database.

The following describes a basic call setup and teardown in the SS7 network:

1. The subscriber initiates an off-hook, and the local end office sends the caller a dial tone. The caller dials the desired digits, and the local end office collects the digits dialed.

2. The local end office determines how to connect the call based on its routing tables. The routing tables identify the circuits available to establish an end-to-end connection. The originating office creates and sends an IAM to the switch that provides the first connection (the pass-along method) and indicates the circuit to be used.

3. When it receives the IAM, the intermediate switch responds by sending an ACM to the originating switch. The ACM is a confirmation that the intermediate switch reserved the same circuit that the originating end office designated in the IAM. The ACM also alerts the originating office to provide a ringback tone to the calling party.

4. While sending the ACM, the intermediate switch prepares to set up the next connection by creating an IAM containing the called and calling information provided by the originating end office. The intermediate switch forwards the IAM to the terminating office using its routing tables.

5. Upon receipt of the IAM, the terminating switch determines whether the called party is busy.

    If the called party is not busy. the terminating switch responds by sending an ACM to the intermediate switch. Following the ACM, the terminating switch signals the subscriber's (called party) line by ringing the telephone. When the called party answers the call, the terminating office cuts through the voice path and sends an ANM along the same path to the intermediate switch.

6. The intermediate switch in turn cuts through the voice path and sends an ANM to the originating switch. Now the originating switch can connect the voice path and enable the conversation to begin.

7. For this example, the called party goes on-hook first and initiates the release procedures at the terminating exchange. The terminating exchange immediately sends a SUSPEND (SUS) message to the intermediate switch, and in turn, the intermediate switch sends an SUS message to the originating switch.

8. When the calling party goes on-hook, the originating switch sends a Release (REL) message toward the terminating switch using the same path as the other signaling messages. The intermediate and terminating switches acknowledge the release with a RELEASE COMPLETE (RLC) message. The RLC message also signifies that each circuit returned to an idle state.

ISUP Message Format

The message type value in the ISUP message indicates the type of message carried in the MSU and is illustrated in Figure 4-14. The circuit identification code (CIC) identifies the circuit being set up or released.

Figure 4-14 *ISUP Message*

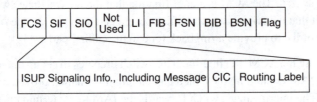

ISUP Call Control Messages

Table 4-4 identifies the most important ISUP call control signaling messages. All ISUP signaling messages contain the ISUP message type parameter.

Table 4-4 *ISUP Messages and Message Types*

ISUP Signaling Message	Message Type Value
IAM	00000001
ACM	00000110
ANM	00001001
REL Message	00001100
RLC Message	00010000
Continuity Test (COT)	00000101
CPG Message	00101100
SUS Message	00001101
Resume (RES) Message	00001110
Forward Transfer (FOT) Message	00001000
INR Message	00000011
INF Message	00000100

Source: ITU-T Q.763 (9/97)

The ISUP call control message formats, including signaling parameters, optional and mandatory fields, and field lengths, are listed in Appendix A, "ISUP Messages/Types Formats."

Each ISUP call control message is explained as follows:

■ IAM is the first message used to initiate a call setup. The IAM typically contains the complete called number, also called the *en-bloc address signal*. An o*verlap address signal* occurs when the called number is sent in more than one message.

- ACM is a backward message the terminating end office sends to indicate that the end office is ringing the called subscriber. Tandem offices also can send an ACM to signify that an outgoing trunk was seized where ISUP signaling is not supported. The terminating switch sends a *backward message*, whereas the originating switch sends a *forward message*. ANM is a backward message the terminating end office sends to indicate that the called subscriber answered.

- REL is a forward or backward message requesting an immediate release of a connection. The forward and backward nature of the REL message is based on the ability of the called and calling users to initiate a release. You also use the REL message when the tandem or terminating end office cannot set up a call.

- RLC is a forward or backward message indicating that the exchange released the trunk at its end.

- COT is a forward message used to perform a continuity test on an outgoing trunk.

- CPG is a backward message used to report an occurrence, such as an alert, during call setup. The CPG message is sent only after an ACM.

- SUS is a backward message used to suspend a call while its connections are kept intact.

- RES is a message used to resume a suspended call. The SUS and RES messages share the same message format and parameters.

- FOT is a message an outgoing operator uses to request the assistance of an incoming operator.

- INR is a message used to obtain additional call-related information. Usually, the terminating end office sends this message to the originating end office.

- INF is a message used to provide the information requested in the INR.

TCAP

TCAP provides the transaction capabilities carried out by non-circuit based messages used to access remote databases and invoke remote feature capabilities in network elements.

TCAP was first used for 800-number translation. TCAP messages carry the instructions SCPs use to query databases for specific information. TCAP also provides the mechanism to carry the queries and responses from switch to switch. TCAP uses SCCP and MTP protocols to route messages end-to-end. This is different from ISUP, which passes messages from switch to switch. The TCAP protocol provides the means for an application in one signaling point to communicate to an application in another signaling point.

The database information is used for 800, 888, and 900 service, Local Number Portability (LNP), subscriber service such as LIDB, and Mobile Home/Visitor records.

The Intelligent Network (IN) also uses TCAP to invoke features in remote end offices. IN relies on TCAP's services to enable one signaling endpoint to access features in a remote signaling endpoint. IN features such as automatic callback are made possible by TCAP invoke messages that inform the local exchange that the destination party is now available.

The following sections analyze TCAP interfaces, messages, message types, and components. The end of this chapter includes an example of an 800 query using the TCAP protocol.

TCAP Interfaces

TCAP, as illustrated in Figure 4-15, uses SCCP and MTP to route transaction messages in the SS7 network. You use TCAP messages to communicate from one signaling point (Exchange X) to another signaling point (Exchange Y).

Figure 4-15 *TCAP Interfaces and Message Path*

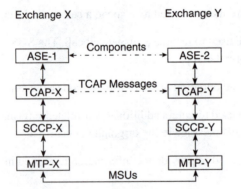

An Application Service Element (ASE) invokes operations at one end, and an ASE executes them at the other end. The ASEs are dedicated to an application, and they peer between remote entities. In the case of an 800 call, Exchange X ASE-1 is the local exchange querying Exchange Y ASE-2, the SCP, for the routing number corresponding to the 800 number.

TCAP messages are contained inside the SCCP portion of the MSU. TCAP messages are comprised of a transaction portion and a component portion.

Transaction Portion of TCAP

The transaction portion of the TCAP message provides the necessary information for the signaling point to route the component to the appropriate destination. The ASEs at both the originating and receiving signaling points are identified with a unique transaction ID. The transaction portion also contains a package type identifier indicating the following message types:

- Unidirectional—Used to transfer components in one direction. The receiver is not required to reply to a unidirectional message.

- Begin or Query—Used to initiate a TCAP transaction. The Begin message initiates an 800 query.

- Continue—Sent after a Begin or Continue message. These messages continue the TCAP transaction.

- End or Response—Used to terminate the TCAP transaction. This message is sent after the Begin or Continue message. The End message contains the response to an 800 query.

- Abort—Used when a problem occurs during a transaction. This message terminates the transaction.

Component Portion of TCAP

The component portion of TCAP can include a request to perform an 800 query. The component information is the communication between peer ASEs and contains either the request operation or the results of an operation. Components specific to TCAP include:

- Invoke—Used to request a specific operation. Begin messages always include at least one Invoke. The Continue and End messages also can include Invokes.

- Return Result (Last)—Used to return the results of the Invoke operation. This message signifies the successful completion and last component of the response.

- Return Result (Not Last)—Used to return a portion of the result requested by the Invoke operation.

- Return Error—Indicates that a requested operation failed. The Return Error component also is the final response to the Invoke operation.

- Reject—Indicates that the received component was deemed incorrect. The Reject component also is the final response to the Received component.

SS7 Examples

This section provides some detailed examples of ways you can use SS7 in the PSTN. The examples cover signaling endpoint activity, messages used, and sequencing of events. Each example provides a different look at ways you can use SS7 and covers general in-progress operations. Protocols such as ISUP and TCAP are discussed, including key messages and order of messaging. The two examples examined are as follows:

- Basic Call Setup and Teardown

- 800 Database Query

Basic Call Setup and Teardown Example

This example demonstrates the steps involved in basic call setup and teardown. The example also shows ways you can use the ISUP protocol to connect and disconnect calls in the SS7 network. Figure 4-16 provides the network topology for this example.

Figure 4-16 *Network for Call Setup and Teardown*

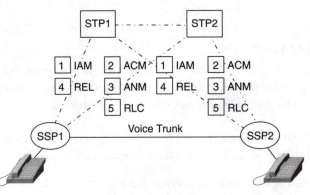

In this example, the analog subscriber connected to SSP1 places a call to the analog subscriber connected to SSP2. The following steps occur when the subscriber on SSP1 places the call:

1. When the subscriber goes off-hook, call processing is initiated in SSP1. Call processing causes SSP1 to enter the *originating call* state and move to the *collecting information* state. SSP1 collects the information or dialed digits from the subscriber.

2. After all the digits are collected, the call enters the *analyzing information* state. SSP1 analyzes the dialed digits and determines that the call needs to be sent to SSP2. The call then enters the *selecting route* state, and SSP1 locates an available trunk in the trunk group to SSP2.

3. After SSP1 selects an idle trunk, it creates an IAM addressed to SSP2. The IAM identifies the originating exchange (SSP1), destination exchange (SSP2), called and calling number, and trunk selected. SSP1 sends the IAM (1) out one of the A-links toward the destination.

4. When STP1 receives the IAM, it reads the routing label and routes the IAM to SSP2. The IAM is received and SSP2 determines that it's the serving center. At this point, SSP2 verifies that the called number is idle and returns an ACM (2) to SSP1. At the same time, SSP2 connects the trunk back to SSP1, applies a ringing tone on the trunk, and rings the subscriber line of the called number. When STP2 receives the ACM, it reads the routing label and routes the ACM to SSP1. The ACM indicates that the IAM was received and that SSP2 is the terminating exchange.

5. STP1 receives the ACM and connects the subscriber line of the calling party to the trunk. At this point, the calling subscriber can hear the ringing tone. When the called subscriber answers the call, SSP2 creates and sends an ANM (3) to SSP1. STP2 receives the ANM, reads the routing label, and routes the ANM to SSP1. SSP1 simply verifies that the subscriber and the trunk are connected.

6. If the calling party hangs up the call first, SSP1 creates an REL message (4) addressed to SSP2. The REL message identifies the trunk associated with the call. SSP1 then routes the REL message toward SSP2, where STP1 reads the routing label and routes the REL to SSP2.

7. When SSP2 receives the REL message, it disconnects the trunk from the subscriber line and returns the trunk to an idle state. SSP2 then creates an RLC (5) message, identifying the trunk used for the call. SSP2 addresses the RLC message to SSP1 and routes it toward SSP1. STP2 receives the RLC message, reads the routing label, and routes the message to SSP1. When it receives the RLC message, SSP1 idles the trunk identified in it.

800 Database Query Example

This example demonstrates the steps involved in making an 800 query. The example also shows ways you can use the TCAP protocol for transactions in the SS7 network. Figure 4-17 provides the network topology for this example.

Figure 4-17 *Network for 800 Database Query Example*

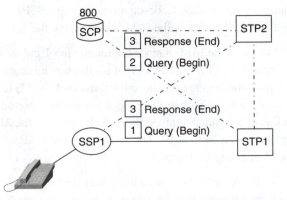

In this example, the analog subscriber connected to SSP1 places an 800 call. The following steps occur when the subscriber on SSP1 places the 800 call:

1. When the subscriber goes off-hook, call processing is initiated in SSP1. Call processing causes SSP1 to enter the *originating call* state and move to the *collecting information* state. SSP1 collects the information or dialed digits from the subscriber.

2. After all the digits are collected, the call enters the *analyzing information* state. SSP1 analyzes the dialed digits and determines that the 800 number is not routable. At this point, the call enters the *wait* state, and the SSP1-TCAP orders the (800) ASE to initiate a transaction with the (800) SCP.

3. SSP1 creates the 800 Query or Begin (1) message that contains the Invoke component requesting the routing number for the specified 800 number. SSP1 then forwards the Query or Begin message to one of its home STPs.

4. STP1 receives the message and determines that it is an 800 query. Next, STP1 selects the appropriate database to process the transaction. STP1 re-addresses the Query or Begin message (2) to the (800) SCP point code (DPC) and the (800) database subsystem number (SSN). STP1 then routes the Query or Begin message to the (800) SCP.

5. When the SCP receives the 800 Query or Begin message, it extracts the request and passes the information to the (800) ASE to execute the database translation. The SCP creates a Response or End message (3) that includes the routing number in the Return Results (Last) component portion of the message. The SCP addresses the message to SSP1 and forwards the message to STP2.

6. When STP2 receives the Response or End message, it reads the routing label and routes the message to SSP1. SSP1 receives the information in the Response message indicating the routing number for the 800 query. At this point, the call enters the *selecting route* state and repeats the same steps as indicated in the "Basic Call Setup and Teardown Example" section of this chapter.

List of SS7 Specifications

The ITU-T standards for SS7 are found in the Q series documents. Table 4-5 lists ITU-T specifications and related Q series document numbers.

Table 4-5   *ITU-T SS7 Specifications*

Title	Doc. Number
Introduction to CCITT Signaling System No. 7	Q.700
Message Transfer Part (MTP)	Q.701–Q.709
Simplified Message Transfer Part	Q.710
Signaling Connection Control Part (SCCP)	Q.711–Q.719
Telephone User Part (TUP)	Q.720–Q.729
Data User Part (DUP)	Q.740–Q.749
Signaling System No. 7 Management	Q.750–Q.759
ISDN User Part (ISUP)	Q.760–Q.769
Transaction Capabilities Application Part (TCAP)	Q.770–Q.779
Intelligent Network (IN)	Q.1200–Q.1999

Summary

SS7/C7 is a complex and important part of the PSTN architecture today. For packet voice to truly be an option for service providers, packet telephony and the SS7 network must integrate.

This chapter covered in detail the four layers of SS7. It also covered the detailed message flows of a common call in SS7.

The details in this chapter can help those who are deploying SS7 and packet voice networks to better understand how SS7 works. Also, this chapter shows how many details must be covered for packet telephony and the PSTN to successfully integrate. Some of the key areas in which VoIP must inter-work with SS7 include:

■ Physical link interconnection of MTP1

■ Signal unit termination and acknowledgments of MTP2

■ L4 user data extraction from MSUs (for ISUP and TCAP)

■ L4 protocol support for call completion- and transaction-based services (ISUP and TCAP, respectively)

These key areas must be addressed for VoIP networks to fit seamlessly into or interface to the PSTN.

CHAPTER 5

PSTN Services

Today's Public Switched Telephone Network (PSTN) offers many different services, each with a desirable suite of features and functionality. Service providers (SPs) can offer competitive services, differentiate themselves, and generate revenue from these offerings. Many of these services are not currently available in packet voice networks. However, much work is being done to determine the best and most scalable way to add these and many new services and functions to packet voice networks.

From an external point of view—or in terms of what the end user can use—the current generation of digital switching systems offers similar, if not identical, functionality. This makes it difficult for SPs to differentiate among the offerings. Traditionally, most of the value-added software used with advanced services is bundled with the switch itself.

This chapter explains how the PSTN offers services to consumers and business customers. It discusses ways corporations use different applications to drive their business and bottom-line profits, the main features of these applications, and how enterprise and PSTN networks work together. The following services are discussed:

- Plain old telephone service (POTS)

- Business services, including virtual private networks (VPNs), Centrex, and call-center services

- SP services, including database and operator services

Plain Old Telephone Service

Standard telephony service is commonly referred to as plain old telephone service (POTS). This service provides a dial tone to rotary and touch-tone telephones, as well as access to national and international carriers. Standard dialing devices such as 500-type telephones (rotary), 2500-type telephones (touch-tone), facsimiles, and modems are compatible with POTS.

POTS evolved internationally to include the emergency number services and operator services. The following additional features and services are now almost universally available to POTS subscribers:

- Custom calling features

- Custom Local Area Signaling Service (CLASS) features

- Voice mail

Each feature is discussed in more detail in the following sections.

Custom Calling Features

The services available from custom calling features have been popular since they were introduced in the PSTN. Although you can activate and use each function individually, SPs usually combine features in a single package for simplicity and convenience.

The providers enable and control custom calling features from within end office switches directly. Signaling System 7 (SS7) messaging and service enablers are not required to operate these features. The following list describes some common custom calling features:

- Call forwarding—Enables calls to follow as the subscriber moves from one location to another

- Call waiting—Indicates an incoming call when the subscriber is already involved in a call

- Three-way calling—Enables subscribers to conference a third party in on a conversation

- Speed dialing—Provides a convenient way for subscribers to store frequently used numbers (this is often provided via the memory of the end-user phone)

- Added number—Enables subscribers to add a second line that they can identify by a distinctive ring and call-waiting tones

CLASS Features

CLASS is a popular suite of features available to subscribers. CLASS features provide subscribers with a powerful and convenient tool to control incoming and outgoing calls. Telecordia, formerly known as Bell Communications Research (Bellcore), defined the CLASS standard, which added to the custom calling feature foundation. With CLASS, users interact with the switch software from their own telephone sets and give instructions on which services they want. SS7 messages and functions are then invoked and sent within the network to perform the requested operations.

The following list describes some common CLASS features:

- Customer-originated trace—Enables the subscriber to dial a code after he or she receives a harassing call, which notifies the local law enforcement agency.

- Automatic callback—Used when the subscriber receives a busy signal. This feature notifies the subscriber when the called party line is free by placing the call. (This feature is also referred to as *camp on.*)

- Automatic recall—Enables the subscriber to easily return a missed call.

- Display features—Requires a display telephone to display the calling name and calling number.

- Calling number blocking—Enables the called party to hide his or her identity when dialing subscribers who have CLASS display capabilities.

- Call screening—Enables subscribers to accept, reject, or forward calls based on a list of received calling numbers.

Voice Mail

PSTN-based voice mail enables SPs to offer an alternative to answering machines. This is attractive because subscribers do not need to purchase or operate any additional equipment. Another benefit of network-based voice mail is that voice messaging is still available even if the called party's line is busy. Network-based voice mail also enables the subscriber to retrieve their voice mail from remote locations. The two main voice mail services available to residential and small-business users are

- Voice messaging—Enables subscribers to store and play recorded greetings and receive, review, and distribute messages from outside users

- Fax messaging—Enables subscribers to receive faxes and view them at a later time

Business Services

Business services are important to SPs because they represent a large portion of SP's revenue base. Corporate environments require an extensive array of communication services to support their businesses. The following services are described in this section:

- Virtual Private Voice Networks

- Centrex services

- Call center services

Virtual Private Voice Networks

Virtual Private Voice Networks cost-effectively interconnect corporate voice traffic between multiple locations over the PSTN. The alternative to Virtual Private Voice Networks is dedicated tie-lines between locations. Because multiple locations are not typically served by the same exchange, however, Virtual Private Voice Networks are a far more economical solution in such scenarios.

SPs offer cost-competitive Virtual Private Voice Network services by maximizing the private use of public infrastructure. Therefore, public network facilities are somewhat balanced by corporate use during weekdays and residential use during nights and weekends.

Virtual Private Voice Network customers access the public network by interconnecting private network facilities, such as T1 circuits. SS7 facilities, messaging, and inter-working enable VPNs across the public infrastructure. SS7 capabilities also enable corporate and PBX features to be carried transparently across the network. Another benefit of deploying a voice-capable network is to ease the process of adding new and multiple sites to an existing Virtual Private Voice Network. With Virutal Private Voice Networks, this is as easy as adding a new connection to the network and provisioning the appropriate translations and dialing plans. With tie-lines, on the other hand, new end-to-end connections are required between the new location and each existing location, resulting in higher costs to the customer.

Public switching systems identify, process, and route calls based on different protocols and dialing plans. The identity of each Virtual Private Voice Network is made possible by customer-group ID numbers that are maintained and transmitted across the public network through SS7. You use this capability to distinguish and route public calls from private intra-network calls. The customer group identity and other information is inserted in ISDN User Part (ISUP) messages for transmission across the public network.

Dialing plans ensure proper handling of full North American Numbering Plan (NANP) 10-digit station routing and 7-digit on-net to on-net, on-net to off-net, and off-net to on-net routing. The call processing, routing, and dialing capabilities provide uniform dialing plans and access to users at remote locations.

> **NOTE** Dedicated Access Lines (DALs) connect to the public network. DALs provide both public and private routing of calls and connect through various signaling protocols. These include ISDN, channel-associated signaling (CAS), QSIG (Q Signaling), and Digital Private Network Signaling System (DPNSS), which are detailed in Chapter 3.

Centrex Services

Centrex enables SPs to offer smaller businesses voice and data services similar to those found in larger and more costly private solutions. Centrex services can be delivered by public switching infrastructure and do not require costly customer premise equipment.

The Centrex software loaded in the switch can create a virtual private business network. Centrex services are comparable to on-premise systems and provide call handling, distribution, accounting, and data networking between sites. You can access Centrex services in the following ways:

- POTS—You can designate and use these lines as Centrex lines.

- Feature lines—Equipped with fully featured telephones, these lines can provide additional features and functionality over standard POTS lines, ISDN circuits, or Switched 56/64 circuits.

Centrex offers many features to subscribers. The following list explains some of Centrex's services and capabilities:

- Call handling—Includes call waiting, call forwarding, call park, hunt grouping, and voice mail

- Convenience features—Include automatic dial, speed dialing, ring again, and calling line identification (caller-ID)

- Custom dialing plans—Provide customized plans for each customer group and enable abbreviated dialing for internally placed calls

- Management—Can track and control various aspects of a business' service

- Security—Includes line restrictions, employee authorization codes, virtual access to private networks, and detailed call records to track unusual activity

Call Center Services

Call centers have large volumes of incoming calls and need to be able to efficiently handle and distribute these calls among multiple agents. The distribution method needs to be intelligent enough to route calls to answering positions that are occupied with the appropriate personnel. Reservation centers, courier companies, and government agencies all need call center-type services. The following implementations are the most commonly used in call centers:

- Automatic call distribution (ACD)— Efficiently routes incoming calls to multiple answering stations. ACDs also enable call centers to track usage patterns as well as traffic and agent performance. ACD systems provide many specific features, such as queuing of customer calls, answer in order of arrival, and agent routing based on most idle. ACD systems are located in the central office or at the customer site. In central offices, SPs deliver the service over public lines such as Primary Rate Interface (PRI). If the ACD is located at the customer site, it is typically connected to the public network using trunks.

- Switch-Computer Applications Interface (SCAI)—Enables SP switches to communicate to the call center computer for appropriate call routing and handling. In the SCAI method, call center computers store and coordinate incoming and outgoing calls and provide the switch with appropriate routing information. SCAI services include providing information on the calling party as the call is passed to the agent. These services can also interconnect calling parties to an Interactive Voice Response (IVR) system to collect more information before routing the call to the appropriate answering position.

Service Provider Services

Service provider (SP) services are internal functions provided in the background to support PSTN users. They include number translation, routing, calling services, and special assistance. The following SP services are discussed in this section:

- Database services

- Operator services

Database Services

Databases enable SPs to maintain, access, and translate information used to support special service and access numbers. These information databases are centrally located and accessible to all end offices. Databases hold subscriber calling and called information that is used in inter-exchange call processing. Databases in the United States frequently provide the following services:

- 800 number services—Enable SPs to offer the called party, typically businesses, bulk usage rates for high levels of incoming calls. Translation from these service numbers to the actual number is provided by SP 800-database access.

- 900 number services—Typically used for providing information, contest call-in numbers, and public opinion polls. The dialed 900 number is translated into the actual number by accessing the database. Unlike 800 services, 900 services imply that the calling party pays to access the service.

- Calling card services—Enable subscribers to access long-distance services from almost any type of PSTN access. Databases provide access and billing by authenticating subscriber account codes and personal identification numbers (PINs), as well as recognize dialed access codes for routing to the long-distance service or requested carrier.

- Authorization services—Establish access to VPN services and provide security against fraud. Activation and validation are enabled through five- to seven-digit authorization codes.

Operator Services

Operator services have changed tremendously in the past few years. The main driver of this change was the advancement of technology in automated systems, speech recognition and recording, online information databases, and SS7 service-invoking capabilities.

Today, central office switching systems can handle most of the calls that once required operator intervention. This enables operators to focus on special-need and value-added types of revenue-generating services. The typical operator services available today are as follows:

- Toll and assistance—Even in today's PSTN, operator intervention is required to complete some long-distance (toll) calls and provide general assistance. The reasons for using toll operators include accounting for coin usage in public payphones, alternative billing needs such as called party charging, and controlling guest bills for hotels. By simply dialing 0, hotel guests can reach a hotel operator who can provide room rate information, can accurately transfer calls, and can provide valuable emergency assistance.

- Directory assistance—Directory services are available by dialing a three-digit national code or an area-specific code. Directory assistance operators can search for telephone numbers based on directory listings. After the operator finds a match, he or she transfers the call to an audio response unit that quotes the number to the customer. The database search engines available to SPs are extensive and provide effective and timely responses for requesting subscribers.

- Billing services—Operator intervention is still required for about 20 percent of long-distance calls in the U.S. The bulk of this intervention is for collect calls, third-party billing, calling cards, and credit card services. The remaining 80 percent of long-distance calls are handled by automated systems, speech recognition, recording technology, and databases all linked together through an underlying SS7 network.

Summary

Plain old telephone service will not be plain for much longer. With broadband (DSL, cable, wireless) access to the home, voice will simply be another application in everyone's home. The available features listed in the previous list are just the tip of the iceberg. This chapter discussed enhanced services, where the PSTN operators make a hefty portion of their revenue.

The PSTN offers many valuable services to subscribers and is critical to the operation of small, medium, and large businesses. These subscribers and businesses are, however, increasingly relying on the power and value of data networking and the Internet. To this end, the PSTN services discussed in this chapter as well as new voice services will, over time, be delivered over data networks and the Internet.

Part II: Voice over IP Technology

CHAPTER 6

IP Tutorial

Many of the benefits of voice over IP (VoIP) are derived from the use of Internet Protocol (IP) as the transport mechanism. To truly understand these benefits, you must first understand what IP actually means. What are the behavioral characteristics of IP, and what does an IP packet look like? These questions, and a few others, are answered in this chapter.

Before you can understand what IP can do for you and ways you can run applications through IP, you must first become familiar with the Open Systems Interconnection (OSI) reference model and how it applies to IP.

OSI Reference Model

The International Organization for Standardization (ISO) developed the OSI reference model in the early 1980s. OSI is now the de facto standard for developing protocols that enable computers to communicate. Although not every protocol follows this model, most new protocols use this layered approach. In addition, when starting to learn about networking, most instructors will begin with this model to simplify understanding.

The OSI reference model breaks up the problem of intermachine communication into seven layers. Each layer is concerned only with talking to its corresponding layer on the other machine (see Figure 6-1). This means that Layer 5 has to worry only about talking to Layer 5 on the receiving machine, and not what the actual physical medium might be.

In addition, each layer of the OSI reference model provides services to the layer above it (Layer 5 to Layer 6, Layer 6 to Layer 7, and so on) and requests certain services from the layer directly below it (5 to 4, 4 to 3, and so on).

This layered approach enables each layer to handle small pieces of information, make any necessary changes to the data, and add the necessary functions for that layer before passing the data along to the next layer. Data becomes less human-like and more computer-like the further down the OSI reference model it traverses, until it becomes 1s and 0s (electrical impulses) at the physical layer. Figure 6-1 shows the OSI reference model.

The focus of this chapter is to discuss the seven layers (application, presentation, session, transport, network, data link, and physical). Understanding these layers allows you to understand how IP routing works and how IP is transported across various media residing at Layer 1.

The Internet Protocol suite (see Figure 6-1) maps to the corresponding OSI layers. From the IP Suite figure, you can see how applications (FTP or email) run atop protocols such as TCP before they are transmitted across some Layer 1 transport mechanism.

Figure 6-1   *OSI Reference Model*

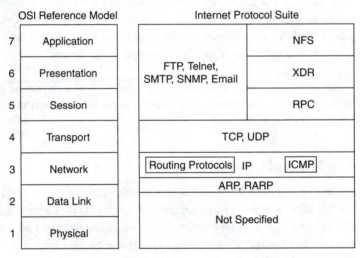

The Application Layer

Most users are familiar with the application layer. Some well-known applications include the following:

- E-mail

- Web browsing

- Word processing

The Presentation Layer

The presentation layer ensures that information sent by the application layer of one system is readable by the application layer of another system. If necessary, the presentation layer translates between multiple data formats by using a common data representation format.

The presentation layer concerns itself not only with the format and representation of actual user data, but also with data structures used by programs. Therefore, in addition to actual data format transformation (if necessary), the presentation layer negotiates data transfer syntax for the application layer.

Common examples include

- Encryption
- Compression
- ASCII EBCDIC

The Session Layer

As its name implies, the session layer establishes, manages, and terminates sessions between applications. Sessions consist of dialogue between two or more presentation entities (recall that the session layer provides its services to the presentation layer).

The session layer synchronizes dialogue between presentation layer entities and manages their data exchange. In addition to basic regulation of conversations (sessions), the session layer offers provisions for data expedition and exception reporting of session-layer, presentation-layer, and application-layer problems.

The Transport Layer

The transport layer is responsible for ensuring reliable data transport on an internetwork. This is accomplished through flow control, error checking (checksum), end-to-end acknowledgments, retransmissions, and data sequencing.

Some transport layers, such as Transmission Control Protocol (TCP), have mechanisms for handling congestion. TCP adjusts its retransmission timer, for example, when congestion or packet loss occurs within a network. TCP slows down the amount of traffic it sends when congestion is present. Congestion is determined through the lack of acknowledgments received from the destination node.

The Network Layer

The network layer provides for the logical addressing which enables two disparate systems on different logical networks to determine a possible path to communicate. The network layer is the layer in which routing protocols reside.

On the Internet today, IP addressing is by far the most common addressing scheme in use. Routing protocols such as Enhanced Interior Gateway Routing Protocol (Enhanced IGRP, or EIGRP),

Open Shortest Path First (OSPF), Border Gateway Protocol (BGP), Intermediary System to Intermediary System (IS-IS), and many others are used to determine the optimal routes between two logical subnetworks (subnets).

> **NOTE**   You can switch IP traffic outside its own subnetwork only if you use an IP router.

Traditional routers route IP packets based on their network layer address.

Key functions of the network layer include the following:

- Packet formatting, addressing networks and hosts, address resolution, and routing

- Creating and maintaining routing tables

The Data Link Layer

The data link layer provides reliable transport across a physical link. The link layer has its own addressing scheme. This addressing scheme is concerned with physical connectivity and can transport frames based upon the data link layer address.

Traditional Ethernet switches switch network traffic based upon the data link layer (Layer 2) address. Switching traffic based on a Layer 2 address is generally known as *bridging*. In fact, an Ethernet switch is nothing more than a high-speed bridge with multiple interfaces.

The Physical Layer

The physical layer is concerned with creating 1s and 0s on the physical medium with electrical impulses/voltage changes. Common physical layer communication specifications include the following:

- EIA/TIA-232—Electrical Industries Association/Telecommunications Industry Association specification used for communicating between computing devices. This interface is often used for connecting computers to modems, and might use different physical connectors.

- V.35—International Telecommunication Union Telecommunication Standardization Sector (ITU-T) signaling mechanism that defines signaling rates from 19.2 Kbps to 1.544 Mbps. This physical interface is a 34-pin connector and also is known as a Winchester Block.

- RS-449—Specification used for synchronous wide area communication. The physical connector uses 37 pins and is capable of significantly longer runs than EIA/TIA-232.

- 802.3—One of the most widely utilized physical mediums is Ethernet. Currently, Ethernet speeds are deployed from 10Mbps to 1000Mbps.

Internet Protocol

IP itself is a connectionless protocol that resides at Layer 3 (the network layer), which means that no reliability mechanisms, flow control, sequencing, or acknowledgments are present. Other protocols, such as TCP, can sit on top of IP (Layer 4, session) and can add flow control, sequencing, and other features.

Given IP's relative position in the OSI reference model, it doesn't have to deal with common data link issues such as Ethernet, Asynchronous Transfer Mode (ATM), Frame Relay, and Token Ring, or with physical issues such as Synchronous Optical Network (SONET), copper, and fiber. This makes IP virtually ubiquitous.

You can offer IP services into a home or business through many potential physical media (for instance, wireless, broadband, or baseband). This doesn't mean that when a network is designed one can ignore the lower two layers. It simply means that the physical media are independent of any *applications* you put on IP.

IP is considered a *bursty* protocol, which means that the applications residing above IP experience long periods of silence, followed by a need for a large portion of bandwidth. A good example of this is e-mail. If you set your mail package to download e-mail every 20 minutes, about 20 minutes of relative silence exist during which very little or no bandwidth is needed. While email is simply one application, other applications running over IP follow similar burst tendencies (banking applications, video, voice over IP).

One of the major benefits of IP is the ability to write an application *once* and have it delivered through an assorted type of media *anywhere*, regardless of whether this occurs through a digital subscriber line (DSL) connection in your home or a T1 line in your business.

An IP packet can be addressed in three general ways: through unicast, multicast, or broadcast mechanisms. Briefly explained, these three mechanisms provide the means for every IP packet to be labeled with a destination address, each in its unique way:

- Unicast is fairly simple, in that it identifies one specific host address and only that node is supposed to send the packet to the higher layers of the OSI reference model.

- Broadcast packets are sent to all users on a local subnetwork. Broadcasts can traverse bridges and switches, but they are not passed through routers (unless they are specially configured to do so).

- Multicast packets use a special addressing range that enables a group of users on different subnetworks to receive the same flow. This enables the sender to send only one packet that several disparate hosts can receive.

Unicast, broadcast, and multicast packets each have a significant purpose. Unicast packets enable two stations to communicate with each other, regardless of physical location. Broadcast packets are used to communicate with everyone on a subnetwork simultaneously. Multicast packets enable applications, such as videoconferencing, that have one transmitter and multiple receivers.

Regardless of the type of IP packet used, data link layer addressing is always needed.

Data Link Layer Addresses

The two types of addresses are data link layer and network layer addresses. Data link layer addresses—also known as Media Access Control (MAC) addresses and physical layer addresses—are unique to every device. In a local-area network (LAN), for instance, each device has a MAC address which identifies itself on the LAN. This enables computers to know who is sending what message. If you look at an Ethernet frame, the first 12 bytes are the destination and source MAC addresses.

If you use an Ethernet LAN switch, the traffic is routed through the switch based on the data link layer address (the MAC address). If you use a repeater or hub to connect the devices to the LAN, the packet is forwarded to all ports, regardless of the MAC address. This is because forwarding through a hub is based upon the *physical* layer and not the data link layer.

When traffic is routed based on the MAC layer address, it is generally referred to as being *switched* or *bridged*. Before routing became prominent in the late 1980s, many companies developed bridges to connect two disparate networks. This enabled a simple and inexpensive method of connecting two networks at the data link layer. Because these bridges did not look at the network layer address, however, unwanted traffic such as broadcasts and multicasts could be transmitted across the bridge, which consumed a large amount of bandwidth.

Most LANs in the 1980s and early 1990s used a hub to connect their Ethernet workstations. This device was known as a *repeater* and replicated the Layer 1 information only. So, if a corporation had an eight-port hub and one of the eight ports received a packet, the packet would be repeated (exactly, errors and all) to the other seven ports.

In the early 1990s, companies began developing LAN switches, which were basically a combination of a hub and bridge. In this scenario, the LAN switch learned which Layer 2 addresses were attached to each of its physical interfaces and forwarded traffic based on the Layer 2 address. If the switch did not have a list of a particular destination Layer 2 address in its switching table, or if the packet were a broadcast packet, the packet was repeated to all other interfaces on the switch.

This transition to network switches enabled networks to make better use of the available bandwidth. This saving in bandwidth was accomplished by preventing unnecessary IP packets from being transmitted on a physical port where the receiving device did not reside.

Now that you understand MAC addresses and how networks use them to route packets, it is time to discuss how networks use IP addressing to further route those packets.

IP Addressing

Understanding IP addressing is a fundamental building block in constructing IP networks.

As previously noted, many protocols exist, each with their own unique addressing scheme.

Network layer addressing is typically hierarchical. For example, in the North American Public Switched Telephone Network (PSTN) each Numbering Plan Area (NPA) includes a region, with a prefix (Nxx) denoting a sub-region and station identifier (xxxx) denoting the actual phone.

> **NOTE**   The North American PSTN hierarchical dial-plan is managed by the North American Numbering Plan Association (NANPA). The PSTN is both hierarchical and geographically defined. IP addressing is hierarchical, but not necessarily geographically defined.

Network layer addressing lies at Layer 3 of the OSI model. This enables a group of computers to be given similar logical addresses. Logical addressing is similar to determining a person's address by looking at his or her country, state, postal code, city, and street address.

Routers forward traffic based on the Layer 3 or network layer address. IP addressing supports five network classes. The first bits in the destination IP address indicate the network class, as follows:

- Class A networks are intended mainly for use with a few large networks because they provide only 7 bits for the network address field and 24 bits for the host field (networks available = 126, hosts available = 16,777,214).

- Class B networks allocate 14 bits for the network address field and 16 bits for the host address field. This address class offers a good compromise between network and host address space (networks available = 16,384, hosts available = 65,534).

- Class C networks allocate 21 bits for the network address field. They provide only 8 bits for the host field, however, so the number of hosts per network can be a limiting factor (networks available = 2,097,152, hosts available = 254).

■ Class D addresses are reserved for multicast groups, as described formally in RFC 1112. In class D addresses, the four highest-order bits are set to 1, 1, 1, and 0 (networks available = 268,435,456, hosts available = N/A).

■ Class E addresses also are defined by IP but are reserved for future use. In class E addresses, the four highest-order bits are set to 1, and the fifth bit is always 0 (networks available = N/A, hosts available = N/A).

IP addresses are written in dotted decimal format—for example, 121.10.3.116. Figure 6-2 shows the address formats for class A, B, and C IP networks. An easy way to think of class addressing is that the more networks you have, the fewer hosts you can have on that network.

Figure 6-2 *Class A, B, and C Address Formats*

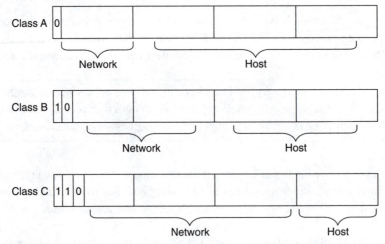

You can also divide IP networks into smaller units called *subnets*. Subnets provide extra flexibility for network administrators. Assume, for example, that a network is assigned a class B address, and all the nodes on the network currently conform to a class B address format. Then assume that the dotted decimal representation of this network's address is 128.10.0.0 with a subnet mask of 255.255.0.0 (all 0s in the host field of an address specify the entire network).

Rather than change all the addresses to some other basic network number, the administrator can subdivide the network using subnetting. He can do this by borrowing bits from the host portion of the address and using them as a subnet field, as shown in Figure 6-3.

Figure 6-3 *Subnetting a Class B Address*

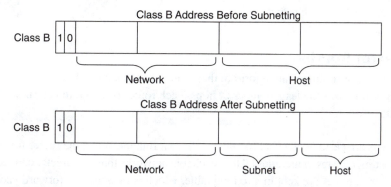

Although this section discusses the makeup of IP addressing, it does not explain how a router knows where to send an IP packet. This is discussed in the next section.

Routing Protocols

IP is a routed protocol. A routed protocol is a packet that carries data. It is different from a routing protocol, in that the latter updates routers to let them know which path a packet should traverse.

Various routing protocols are used in IP internetworks today. This book does not cover routing protocols in depth. For more information on routing protocols, see the reference list of Cisco Press books covering the subject at the end of this chapter.

> **NOTE**   It is important to note that with routing protocols, a well-engineered data network is self-healing and redundant, thus increasing the reliability of the network. A network that is self-healing allows for the applications which reside on that network to have minimal downtime. In the case of voice over IP as the application, self-healing networks allow for critical real-time traffic to continue to be received and understood.

IP networks today use two main types of dynamic routing protocols: distance-vector routing and link-state routing.

Simply explained, *distance-vector* routing is concerned with how many hops (routers) are traversed, whereas link-state routing is concerned mainly with the state of the interfaces the router supports (in other words, whether they are up or down; hence, the name *link state*).

Within these two routing protocols are interior and exterior routing protocols. Interior routing protocols are usually used to update routers under the control of one administrative authority (autonomous system). Exterior routing protocols are usually used to enable networks in different autonomous systems to pass routing updates. A good example of an exterior routing protocol is the use of BGP on the Internet.

Distance-Vector Routing

Distance-vector routing is an algorithm that routers use to enable them to choose the best route. This algorithm uses the least number of hops (each router is a hop) to determine the best path to the destination.

Broadcasts are periodically sent to update adjacent routers. When the router first starts broadcasting updates, it includes all the reachable networks that are directly connected. The routes received by a router are kept in a routing table, which is then used to forward packets.

This method is bandwidth-intensive because the entire routing update is sent out periodically (usually every 30 seconds).

Link-State Routing

Link-state routing differs from distance-vector routing in that the former transmits routing updates only when the state of an interface changes. Link-state routers maintain a topology table that is used to construct a common picture of the network. This means that routing traffic updates are sent, bandwidth is consumed, and topology tables are updated only when an interface goes up or down.

BGP

BGP performs interdomain routing in Transmission Control Protocol/Internet Protocol (TCP/IP) networks. BGP is an Exterior Gateway Protocol (EGP), which means that it performs routing between multiple autonomous systems and exchanges routing and reachability information with other BGP systems.

BGP was developed to replace its predecessor, the now obsolete EGP, as the standard exterior gateway routing protocol used in the global Internet. BGP solves serious problems with EGP and scales to Internet growth more efficiently.

IS-IS

IS-IS is an OSI link-state hierarchical routing protocol. It floods the network with link-state information to build a complete, consistent picture of network topology.

To simplify router design and operation, IS-IS distinguishes between Level 1 and Level 2 Intermediate Systems (ISs):

■   Level 1 ISs communicate with other Level 1 ISs in the same area.

■   Level 2 ISs route between Level 1 areas and form an intradomain routing backbone.

Hierarchical routing simplifies backbone design because Level 1 ISs only need to know how to get to the nearest Level 2 IS. The backbone routing protocol also can change without impacting the intra-area routing protocol.

OSPF

OSPF is a link-state, Interior Gateway Protocol (IGP). It was designed to operate in TCP/IP networks and to address the shortcomings of the Router Information Protocol (RIP).

OSPF is derived from a number of sources, including the shortest path first (SPF) algorithm developed by Bolt, Beranek, and Newman, Inc. (BBN), an early version of the OSI IS-IS routing protocol, and other research efforts.

IGRP

IGRP is a robust protocol for routing within an autonomous system having arbitrarily complex topology and consisting of media with diverse bandwidth and delay characteristics.

Cisco Systems developed IGRP in the mid-1980s. It is a distance-vector interior gateway protocol that uses a combination of metrics to make routing decisions.

EIGRP

EIGRP is an enhanced version of the IGRP developed by Cisco Systems.

EIGRP uses the same distance-vector algorithm and distance information as IGRP. EIGRP's convergence properties and operating efficiency are significantly better than those of IGRP.

EIGRP is a distance-vector interior gateway protocol that has the following features:

■   It uses a combination of metrics to make routing decisions.

■   It uses the Diffusing Update Algorithm (DUAL) to enable routes to converge quickly.

■   It sends partial routing-table updates.

■   It implements a neighbor discovery mechanism.

RIP

RIP is a distance-vector protocol that uses hop count as its metric. RIP is an Interior Gateway Protocol (IGP); it performs routing within a single autonomous system.

All these various routing protocols are used in different networks based upon their advantages and disadvantages. This book does not discuss in depth when to choose one over the other, but it is important to understand the basics about each protocol to further understand ways you can assemble IP networks.

It also is important to understand the different transport mechanisms that give IP different characteristics. These transport mechanisms are discussed next.

IP Transport Mechanisms

TCP and User Datagram Protocol (UDP) have different characteristics that various applications can use. If reliability is more important than delay, for instance, you can use TCP/IP to guarantee packet delivery. By contrast, UDP/IP does not utilize packet re-transmissions. This can lower reliability, but in some cases a late retransmission is of no use.

To compare various transport layer protocols, you must first understand what makes up an IP packet. Figure 6-4 shows the fields of the IP packet.

Figure 6-4 *IP Packet Fields*

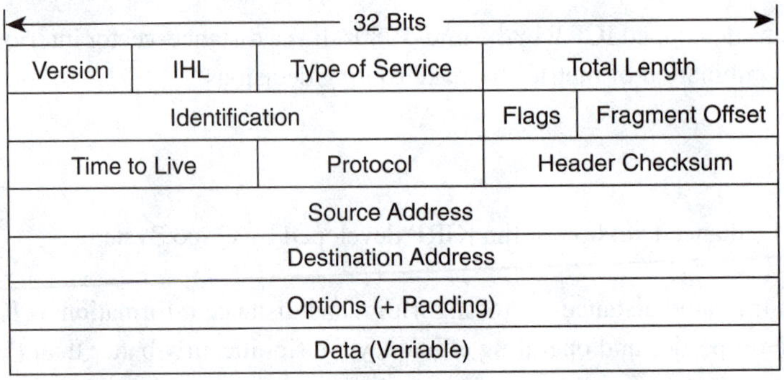

← 32 Bits →					
Version	IHL	Type of Service	Total Length		
Identification			Flags	Fragment Offset	
Time to Live		Protocol	Header Checksum		
Source Address					
Destination Address					
Options (+ Padding)					
Data (Variable)					

IP packet fields are defined as follows:

■ Version—indicates whether IPv4 or IPv6 is being used.

■ IP header length (IHL)—Indicates the datagram header length in 32-bit words.

■ Type of service—Specifies how a particular upper-layer protocol wants the current datagram to be handled. You can assign packets various quality of service (QoS) levels based on this field.

- Total length—Specifies the length of the entire IP packet, including data and header, in bytes.

- Identification—Contains an integer that identifies the current datagram. This field is used to help piece together datagram fragments.

- Flags—A 3-bit field of which the low-order 2 bits control fragmentation. The high-order bit in this field is not used. One bit specifies whether you can fragment the packet; the second bit specifies whether the packet is the last fragment in a series of fragmented packets.

- Time To Live—Maintains a counter that gradually decrements down to zero, at which point the datagram is discarded. This keeps packets from looping endlessly.

- Protocol—Indicates which upper-layer protocol receives incoming packets after IP processing is complete.

- Header checksum—Used to verify that the header is not corrupted.

- Source address—The sending address.

- Destination address—The address to receive the datagram.

- Options—Enables IP to support various options, such as security.

- Data—Contains application data as well as upper-layer protocol information.

TCP

TCP provides full-duplex, acknowledged, and flow-controlled service to upper-layer protocols. It moves data in a continuous, unstructured byte stream where bytes are identified by sequence numbers.

To maximize throughput, TCP enables each station to send multiple packets before an acknowledgment arrives. After the sender receives an acknowledgment for an outstanding packet, the sender slides the packet window along the byte stream and sends another packet. This flow control mechanism is known as a *sliding window*.

TCP can support numerous simultaneous upper-layer conversations. The port numbers in a TCP header identify an upper-layer conversation. Many well-known TCP ports are reserved for File Transfer Protocol (FTP), World Wide Web (WWW), Telnet, and so on.

Within the signaling portion of VoIP, TCP can be used to ensure the reliability of the setup of a call. Due to the methods by which TCP operates, it is not feasible to use TCP as the mechanism to carry the actual voice media (RTP) in a VoIP call. With VoIP, packet loss is less important than latency. Currently, H.323 uses TCP, while SIP and MGCP use UDP (SIP also supports TCP as a transport mechanism).

The TCP packet fields are as follows:

- Source port and destination port—Identifies the points at which upper-layer source and destination processes receive TCP services.

- Sequence number—Usually specifies the number assigned to the first byte of data in the current message. Under certain circumstances, it also can be used to identify an initial sequence number to be used in the upcoming transmission.

- Acknowledgment number—Contains the sequence number of the next byte of data the sender of the packet expects to receive.

- Data offset—Indicates the number of 32-bit words in the TCP header.

- Reserved—Reserved for future use.

- Flags—Carry a variety of control information.

- Window—Specifies the size of the sender's receive window (that is, buffer space available for incoming data).

- Checksum—Indicates whether the header and data were damaged in transit.

- Urgent pointer—Points to the first urgent data byte in the packet.

- Options—Specifies various TCP options.

- Data—Contains upper-layer information.

UDP

UDP is a much simpler protocol than TCP and is useful in situations where the reliability mechanisms of TCP are unnecessary. UDP also is connectionless and has a smaller header, which translates to minimal overhead.

The UDP header has only four fields: source port, destination port, length, and UDP checksum. The source and destination port fields serve the same functions as they do in the TCP header. The length field specifies the length of the UDP header and data, and the checksum field enables packet integrity checking. The UDP checksum is optional.

UDP is used in VoIP to carry the actual voice traffic (the *bearer channels*). TCP is not used because flow control and retransmission of voice audio packets are unnecessary. Because UDP is used to carry the audio stream, it continues to transmit, regardless of whether you are experiencing 5 percent packet loss or 50 percent packet loss.

If TCP were utilized for VoIP, the latency incurred waiting for acknowledgments and retransmissions would render voice quality unacceptable. With VoIP and other real-time applications, controlling latency is more important than ensuring the reliable delivery of each packet.

TCP is used, on the other hand, for call setup in most VoIP signaling protocols. See Chapter 11, "H.323," Chapter 12, "Session Initiation Protocol," and Chapter 13, "Gateway Control Protocols," for details on VoIP call signaling.

Summary

IP is one of the most ubiquitous protocols for machine-to-machine communication. It enables usually disparate applications and networks to communicate in new ways.

This chapter touched on the basics of IP. Armed with this information, you should now begin to see some of the possibilities of VoIP, as well as many other IP-based applications.

For more detailed information on IP, consult one of the following Cisco Press books dedicated to this topic:

■ *IP Routing Primer*, by Robert Wright, CCIE. ISBN: 1-57870-108-2.

■ *Routing TCP/IP*, Volume I *(CCIE Professional Development)*, by Jeff Doyle, CCIE. ISBN: 1-57870-041-8.

References

New Requests For Comments (RFCs) rendered some of the following protocols obsolete. This list will help you start researching IP:

RFC 761—Transmission Control Protocol
RFC 768—User Datagram Protocol
RFC 791—Internet Protocol
RFC 1058—Routing Information Protocol
RFC 1131—Open Shortest Path First
RFC 1518—An Architecture for IP Address Allocation with CIDR
RFC 1583—Open Shortest Path First 2
RFC 1654—Border Gateway Protocol 4
RFC 1723—Routing Information Protocol 2
RFC 1771—Border Gateway Protocol 4 (latest version)
RFC 1883—Internet Protocol, Version 6 (IPv6)

CHAPTER 7

VoIP: An In-Depth Analysis

To create a proper network design, it is important to know all the caveats and inner workings of networking technology. This chapter explains many of the issues facing Voice over IP (VoIP) and ways in which Cisco addresses these issues.

Communications via the Public Switched Telephone Network (PSTN) has its own set of problems, which are covered in Chapter 1, "Overview of the PSTN and Comparisons to Voice over IP," and Chapter 2, "Enterprise Telephony Today." VoIP technology has many similar issues and a whole batch of additional ones. This chapter details these various issues and explains how they can affect packet networks.

The following issues are covered in this chapter:

- Delay/latency

- Jitter

- Pulse Code Modulation (PCM)

- Voice compression

- Echo

- Packet loss

- Voice activity detection

- Digital-to-analog conversion

- Tandem encoding

- Transport protocols

- Dial-plan design

Delay/Latency

VoIP *delay* or *latency* is characterized as the amount of time it takes for speech to exit the speaker's mouth and reach the listener's ear.

Three types of delay are inherent in today's telephony networks: *propagation delay*, *serialization delay*, and *handling delay*. Propagation delay is caused by the length a signal must travel via light in fiber or electrical impulse in copper-based networks. Handling delay—also called processing delay—defines many different causes of delay (actual packetization, compression, and packet switching) and is caused by devices that forward the frame through the network.

Serialization delay is the amount of time it takes to actually place a bit or byte onto an interface. Serialization delay is not covered in depth in this book because its influence on delay is relatively minimal.

Propagation Delay

Light travels through a vacuum at a speed of 186,000 miles per second, and electrons travel through copper or fiber at approximately 125,000 miles per second. A fiber network stretching halfway around the world (13,000 miles) induces a one-way delay of about 70 milliseconds (70 ms). Although this delay is almost imperceptible to the human ear, propagation delays in conjunction with handling delays can cause noticeable speech degradation.

Handling Delay

As mentioned previously, devices that forward the frame through the network cause handling delay. Handling delays can impact traditional phone networks, but these delays are a larger issue in packetized environments. The following paragraphs discuss the different handling delays and how they affect voice quality.

In the Cisco IOS VoIP product, the Digital Signal Processor (DSP) generates a speech sample every 10 ms when using G.729. Two of these speech samples (both with 10 ms of delay) are then placed within one packet. The packet delay is, therefore, 20 ms. An initial look-ahead of 5 ms occurs when using G.729, giving an initial delay of 25 ms for the first speech frame.

Vendors can decide how many speech samples they want to send in one packet. Because G.729 uses 10 ms speech samples, each increase in samples per frame raises the delay by 10 ms. In fact, Cisco IOS enables users to choose how many samples to put into each frame.

Cisco gave DSP much of the responsibility for framing and forming packets to keep router/gateway overhead low. The Real-Time Transport Protocol (RTP) header, for example, is placed on the frame in the DSP instead of giving the router that task.

Queuing Delay

A packet-based network experiences delay for other reasons. Two of these are the time necessary to move the actual packet to the output queue (packet switching) and queuing delay.

When packets are held in a queue because of congestion on an outbound interface, the result is *queuing delay*. Queuing delay occurs when more packets are sent out than the interface can handle at a given interval.

The actual queuing delay of the output queue is another cause of delay. You should keep this factor to less than 10 ms whenever you can by using whatever queuing methods are optimal for your network. This subject is covered in greater detail in Chapter 8, "Quality of Service."

The International Telecommunication Union Telecommunication Standardization Sector (ITU-T) G.114 recommendation specifies that for good voice quality, no more than 150 ms of one-way, end-to-end delay should occur, as shown in Figure 7-1. With the Cisco VoIP implementation, *two* routers with minimal network delay (back to back) use only about 60 ms of end-to-end delay. This leaves up to 90 ms of network delay to move the IP packet from source to destination.

Figure 7-1 *End-to-End Delay*

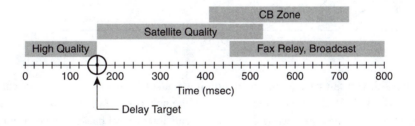

As shown in Figure 7-1, some forms of delay are longer, although accepted, because no other alternatives exist. In satellite transmission, for example, it takes approximately 250 ms for a transmission to reach the satellite, and another 250 ms for it to come back down to Earth. This results in a total delay of 500 ms. Although the ITU-T recommendation notes that this is outside the acceptable range of voice quality, many conversations occur every day over satellite links. As such, voice quality is often defined as what users will accept and use.

In an unmanaged, congested network, queuing delay can add up to two seconds of delay (or result in the packet being dropped). This lengthy period of delay is unacceptable in almost any voice network. Queuing delay is only one component of end-to-end delay. Another way end-to-end delay is affected is through jitter.

Jitter

Simply stated, *jitter* is the variation of packet interarrival time. Jitter is one issue that exists only in packet-based networks. While in a packet voice environment, the sender is expected to reliably transmit voice packets at a regular interval (for example, send one frame every 20 ms). These voice packets can be delayed throughout the packet network and not arrive at that same regular interval at the receiving station (for example, they might not be received every 20 ms; see Figure 7-2). The difference between when the packet is expected and when it is actually received is *jitter*.

Figure 7-2 *Variation of Packet Arrival Time (Jitter)*

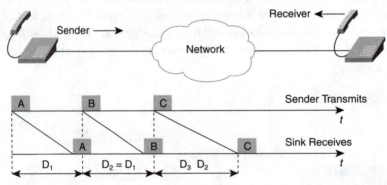

In Figure 7-2, you can see that the amount of time it takes for packets A and B to send and receive is equal (D1=D2). Packet C encounters delay in the network, however, and is received *after* it is expected. This is why a *jitter buffer*, which conceals interarrival packet delay variation, is necessary. Voice packets in IP networks have highly variable packet-interarrival intervals. Recommended practice is to count the number of packets that arrive late and create a ratio of these packets to the number of packets that are successfully processed. You can then use this ratio to adjust the jitter buffer to target a predetermined, allowable late-packet ratio. This adaptation of jitter buffer sizing is effective in compensating for delays.

Note that jitter and total delay are *not* the same thing, although having plenty of jitter in a packet network can increase the amount of total delay in the network. This is because the more jitter you have, the larger your jitter buffer needs to be to compensate for the unpredictable nature of the packet network.

Most DSPs do not have infinite jitter buffers to handle excessive network delays. Sometimes it is better to just drop packets or have fixed-length buffers instead of creating unwanted delays in the jitter buffers. If your data network is engineered well and you take the proper precautions, jitter is usually not a major problem and the jitter buffer does not significantly contribute to the total end-to-end delay.

RTP timestamps are used within Cisco IOS Software to determine what level of jitter, if any, exists within the network.

The jitter buffer found within Cisco IOS Software is considered a dynamic queue. This queue can grow or shrink exponentially depending on the interarrival time of the RTP packets.

Although many vendors choose to use static jitter buffers, Cisco found that a well-engineered dynamic jitter buffer is the best mechanism to use for packet-based voice networks. Static jitter buffers force the jitter buffer to be either too large or too small, thereby causing the audio quality to suffer, due to either lost packets or excessive delay. The Cisco jitter buffer dynamically increases or decreases based upon the interarrival delay variation of the last few packets.

Pulse Code Modulation

Although analog communication is ideal for human communication, analog transmission is neither robust nor efficient at recovering from line noise. In the early telephony network, when analog transmission was passed through amplifiers to boost the signal, not only was the voice boosted but the line noise was amplified, as well. This line noise resulted in an often-unusable connection.

It is much easier for digital samples, which are comprised of 1 and 0 bits, to be separated from line noise. Therefore, when analog signals are regenerated as digital samples, a clean sound is maintained. When the benefits of this digital representation became evident, the telephony network migrated to pulse code modulation (PCM).

What Is PCM?

As covered in Chapter 1, PCM converts analog sound into digital form by sampling the analog sound 8000 times per second and converting each sample into a numeric code. The Nyquist theorem states that if you sample an analog signal at twice the rate of the highest frequency of interest, you can accurately reconstruct that signal back into its analog form. Because most speech content is below 4000 Hz (4 kHz), a sampling rate of 8000 times per second (125 microseconds between samples) is required.

A Sampling Example for Satellite Networks

Satellite networks have an inherent delay of around 500 ms. This includes 250 ms for the trip up to the satellite, and another 250 ms for the trip back to Earth. In this type of network, packet loss is highly controlled due to the expense of bandwidth. Also, if some type of voice application is already running through the satellite, the users of this service are accustomed to a quality of voice that has excessive delays.

Cisco IOS, by default, sends two 10-ms G.729 speech frames in every packet. Although this is acceptable for most applications, this might not be the best method for utilizing the expensive bandwidth on a satellite link. The simple explanation for wasting bandwidth is that a header exists for every packet. The more speech frames you put into a packet, the fewer headers you require.

If you take the satellite example and use four 10-ms G.729 speech frames per packet, you can cut by half the number of headers you use. Table 7-1 clearly shows the difference between the various frames per packet. With only a 20-byte increase in packet size (20 extra bytes equals two 10 ms G.729 samples), you carry twice as much speech with the packet.

Table 7-1 *Frames per Packet (G.729)*

G.729 Samples per Frame	IP/RTP/UDP Header	Bandwidth Consumed	Latency[*]
Default (two samples per frame)	40 bytes	24,000 bps	25 ms
Satellite (four samples per frame)	40 bytes	16,000 bps	45 ms
Low Latency (one sample per frame)	40 bytes	40,000 bps	15 ms

* Compression and packetization delay only

To reduce the overall IP/RTP/UDP overhead introduced by the 54-byte header, multiple voice samples can be packed into a single Ethernet frame to transmit. Although this can increase the voice delay, increasing this count can improve the overall voice quality, especially when the bandwidth is constrained.

How many voice samples to be sent per frame depends on what codec you choose and the balance between bandwidth utilization and impact of packet loss. The bigger this value, the higher the bandwidth utilization because more voice samples are packed into the payload field of a UDP/RTP packet and thus the network header overhead would be lower. The impact of a packet loss on perceived voice quality will be bigger, however. Table 7-2 lists the values for some of the commonly used codec types.

Table 7-2 *Voice Samples per Frame for VoIP Codecs*

Codec Type	Voice Samples per Frame (Default)	Voice Samples per Frame (Maximum)
PCMU/PCMA	2	10
G.723	1	32
G.726-32	2	20
G.729	2	64
G.728	4	64

Voice Compression

Two basic variations of 64 Kbps PCM are commonly used: μ-law and a-law. The methods are similar in that they both use logarithmic compression to achieve 12 to 13 bits of linear PCM quality in 8 bits, but they are different in relatively minor compression details (μ-law has a slight advantage in low-level, signal-to-noise ratio performance). Usage is historically along country and regional boundaries, with North America using μ-law and Europe and other countries using a-law modulation. It is important to note that when making a long-distance call, any required μ-law to a-law conversion is the responsibility of the μ-law country.

Another compression method used often is *adaptive differential pulse code modulation (ADPCM)*. A commonly used instance of ADPCM is ITU-T G.726, which encodes using 4-bit samples, giving a transmission rate of 32 Kbps. Unlike PCM, the 4 bits do not directly encode the amplitude of speech, but they do encode the differences in amplitude, as well as the rate of change of that amplitude, employing some rudimentary linear prediction.

PCM and ADPCM are examples of *waveform* codecs—compression techniques that exploit redundant characteristics of the waveform itself. New compression techniques were developed over the past 10 to 15 years that further exploit knowledge of the source characteristics of speech generation. These techniques employ signal processing procedures that compress speech by sending only simplified parametric information about the original speech excitation and vocal tract shaping, requiring less bandwidth to transmit that information.

These techniques can be grouped together generally as *source* codecs and include variations such as *linear predictive coding (LPC)*, *code excited linear prediction compression (CELP)*, and *multipulse, multilevel quantization (MP-MLQ)*.

Voice Coding Standards

The ITU-T standardizes CELP, MP-MLQ PCM, and ADPCM coding schemes in its G-series recommendations. The most popular voice coding standards for telephony and packet voice include:

- G.711—Describes the 64 Kbps PCM voice coding technique outlined earlier; G.711-encoded voice is already in the correct format for digital voice delivery in the public phone network or through Private Branch eXchanges (PBXs).

- G.726—Describes ADPCM coding at 40, 32, 24, and 16 Kbps; you also can interchange ADPCM voice between packet voice and public phone or PBX networks, provided that the latter has ADPCM capability.

- G.728—Describes a 16 Kbps low-delay variation of CELP voice compression.

- G.729—Describes CELP compression that enables voice to be coded into 8 Kbps streams; two variations of this standard (G.729 and G.729 Annex A) differ largely in computational complexity, and both generally provide speech quality as good as that of 32 Kbps ADPCM.

- G.723.1—Describes a compression technique that you can use to compress speech or other audio signal components of multimedia service at a low bit rate, as part of the overall H.324 family of standards. Two bit rates are associated with this coder: 5.3 and 6.3 Kbps. The higher bit rate is based on MP-MLQ technology and provides greater quality. The lower bit rate is based on CELP, provides good quality, and affords system designers with additional flexibility.

- iLBC (Internet Low Bitrate Codec)—A free speech codec suitable for robust voice communication over IP. The codec is designed for narrow band speech and results in a payload bit rate of 13.33 kbps with an encoding frame length of 30 ms and 15.20 kbps with an encoding length of 20 ms. The iLBC codec enables graceful speech quality degradation in the case of lost frames, which occurs in connection with lost or delayed IP packets. The basic quality is higher than G.729A, with high robustness to packet loss. The PacketCable consortium and many vendors have adopted iLBC as a preferred codec. It is also being used by many PC-to-Phone applications, such as Skype, Google Talk, Yahoo! Messenger with Voice, and MSN Messenger.

Mean Opinion Score

You can test voice quality in two ways: subjectively and objectively. Humans perform subjective voice testing, whereas computers—which are less likely to be "fooled" by compression schemes that can "trick" the human ear—perform objective voice testing.

Codecs are developed and tuned based on subjective measurements of voice quality. Standard objective quality measurements, such as total harmonic distortion and signal-to-noise ratios, do not correlate well to a human's perception of voice quality, which in the end is usually the goal of most voice compression techniques.

A common subjective benchmark for quantifying the performance of the speech codec is the *mean opinion score (MOS)*. MOS tests are given to a group of listeners. Because voice quality and sound in general are subjective to listeners, it is important to get a wide range of listeners and sample material when conducting a MOS test. The listeners give each sample of speech material a rating of 1 (bad) to 5 (excellent). The scores are then averaged to get the mean opinion score.

MOS testing also is used to compare how well a particular codec works under varying circumstances, including differing background noise levels, multiple encodes and decodes, and so on. You can then use this data to compare against other codecs.

MOS scoring for several ITU-T codecs is listed in Table 7-3. This table shows the relationship between several low-bit rate coders and standard PCM.

Table 7-3   *ITU-T Codec MOS Scoring*

Compression Method	Bit Rate (Kbps)	Sample Size (ms)	MOS Score
G.711 PCM	64	0.125	4.1
G.726 ADPCM	32	0.125	3.85
G.728 Low Delay Code Excited Linear Predictive (LD-CELP)	15	0.625	3.61
G.729 Conjugate Structure Algebraic Code Excited Linear Predictive (CS-ACELP)	8	10	3.92
G.729a CS-ACELP	8	10	3.7
G.723.1 MP-MLQ	6.3	30	3.9
G.723.1 ACELP	5.3	30	3.65
iLBC Freeware	15.2	20	3.9
	13.3	30	

Source: Cisco Labs

For iLBC codec - Research Paper - "COMPARISONS OF FEC AND CODEC ROBUSTNESS ON VOIP QUALITY AND BANDWIDTH EFFICIENCY" - WENYU JIANG AND HENNING SCHULZRINNE. Columbia University, Department of Computer Science, USA.

Perceptual Speech Quality Measurement

Although MOS scoring is a subjective method of determining voice quality, it is not the only method for doing so. The ITU-T put forth recommendation P.861, which covers ways you can objectively determine voice quality using Perceptual Speech Quality Measurement (PSQM).

PSQM has many drawbacks when used with voice codecs (vocoders). One drawback is that what the "machine" or PSQM hears is not what the human ear perceives. In layman's terms, a person can trick the human ear into perceiving a higher-quality voice, but a computer cannot be tricked. Also, PSQM was developed to "hear" impairments caused by compression and decompression and not packet loss or jitter.

Echo

Echo is an amusing phenomenon to experience while visiting the Grand Canyon, but echo on a phone conversation can range from slightly annoying to unbearable, making conversation unintelligible.

Hearing your own voice in the receiver while you are talking is common and reassuring to the speaker. Hearing your own voice in the receiver after a delay of more than about 25 ms, however, can cause interruptions and can break the cadence in a conversation.

In a traditional toll network, echo is normally caused by a mismatch in impedance from the four-wire network switch conversion to the two-wire local loop (as shown in Figure 7-3). Echo, in the standard Public Switched Telephone Network (PSTN), is regulated with echo cancellers and a tight control on impedance mismatches at the common reflection points, as depicted in Figure 7-3.

Echo has two drawbacks: It can be loud, and it can be long. The louder and longer the echo, of course, the more annoying the echo becomes.

Figure 7-3   *Echo Caused by Impedance Mismatch*

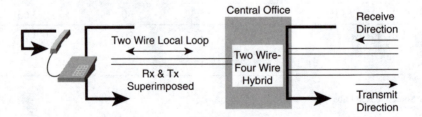

Telephony networks in those parts of the world where analog voice is primarily used employ echo suppressors, which remove echo by capping the impedance on a circuit. This is not the best mechanism to use to remove echo and, in fact, causes other problems. You cannot use Integrated Services Digital Network (ISDN) on a line that has an echo suppressor, for instance, because the echo suppressor cuts off the frequency range that ISDN uses.

In today's packet-based networks, you can build echo cancellers into low-bit-rate codecs and operate them on each DSP. In some manufacturers' implementations, echo cancellation is done in software; this practice drastically reduces the benefits of echo cancellation. Cisco VoIP, however, does all its echo cancellation on its DSP.

To understand how echo cancellers work, it is best to first understand where the echo comes from.

In this example, assume that user A is talking to user B. The speech of user A to user B is called G. When G hits an impedance mismatch or other echo-causing environments, it bounces back to user A. User A can then hear the delay several milliseconds after user A actually speaks.

To remove the echo from the line, the device user A is talking through (router A) keeps an inverse image of user A's speech for a certain amount of time. This is called *inverse speech (–G)*. This echo canceller listens for the sound coming from user B and subtracts the –G to remove any echo.

Echo cancellers are limited by the total amount of time they wait for the reflected speech to be received, a phenomenon known as *echo tail*. Cisco has configurable echo tails of 16, 24, 32, 64, and 128 ms.

It is important to configure the appropriate amount of echo cancellation when initially installing VoIP equipment. If you don't configure enough echo cancellation, callers will hear echo during the phone call. If you configure too much echo cancellation, it will take longer for the echo canceller to converge and eliminate the echo.

Packet Loss

Packet loss in data networks is both common and expected. Many data protocols, in fact, use packet loss so that they know the condition of the network and can reduce the number of packets they are sending.

When putting critical traffic on data networks, it is important to control the amount of packet loss in that network.

Cisco Systems has been putting business-critical, time-sensitive traffic on data networks for many years, starting with Systems Network Architecture (SNA) traffic in the early 1990s. With protocols such as SNA that do *not* tolerate packet loss well, you need to build a well-engineered network that can prioritize the time-sensitive data ahead of data that can handle delay and packet loss.

When putting voice on data networks, it is important to build a network that can successfully transport voice in a reliable and timely manner. Also, it is helpful when you can use a mechanism to make the voice somewhat resistant to periodic packet loss.

Cisco Systems developed many quality of service (QoS) tools that enable administrators to classify and manage traffic through a data network. If a data network is well engineered, you can keep packet loss to a minimum.

Cisco Systems' VoIP implementation enables the voice router to respond to periodic packet loss. If a voice packet is not received when expected (the expected time is variable), it is assumed to be lost and the last packet received is replayed, as shown in Figure 7-4. Because the packet lost is only 20 ms of speech, the average listener does not notice the difference in voice quality.

Figure 7-4   *Packet Loss with G.729*

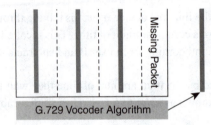

Using Cisco's G.729 implementation for VoIP, let's say that each of the lines in Figure 7-4 represents a packet. Packets 1, 2, and 3 reach the destination, but packet 4 is lost somewhere in transmission. The receiving station waits for a period of time (per its jitter buffer) and then runs a *concealment strategy*.

This concealment strategy replays the last packet received (in this case, packet 3), so the listener does not hear gaps of silence. Because the lost speech is only 20 ms, the listener most likely does not hear the difference. You can accomplish this concealment strategy only if one packet is lost. If multiple consecutive packets are lost, the concealment strategy is run only once until another packet is received.

Because of the concealment strategy of G.729, as a rule of thumb G.729 is tolerant to about five percent packet loss averaged across an entire call.

Voice Activity Detection

In normal voice conversations, someone speaks and someone else listens. Today's toll networks contain a bi-directional, 64,000 bit per second (bps) channel, regardless of whether anyone is speaking. This means that in a normal conversation, at least 50 percent of the total bandwidth is wasted. The amount of wasted bandwidth can actually be much higher if you take a statistical sampling of the breaks and pauses in a person's normal speech patterns.

When using VoIP, you can utilize this "wasted" bandwidth for other purposes when voice activity detection (VAD) is enabled. As shown in Figure 7-5, VAD works by detecting the magnitude of speech in decibels (dB) and deciding when to cut off the voice from being framed.

Figure 7-5   *Voice Activity Detection*

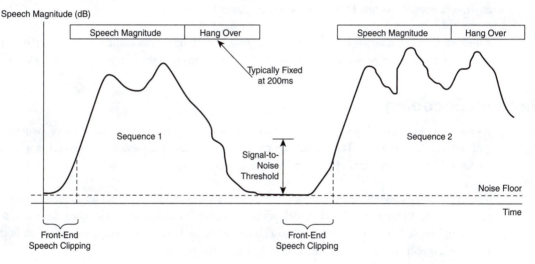

Typically, when the VAD detects a drop-off of speech amplitude, it waits a fixed amount of time before it stops putting speech frames in packets. This fixed amount of time is known as *hangover* and is typically 200 ms.

With any technology, tradeoffs are made. VAD experiences certain inherent problems in determining when speech ends and begins, and in distinguishing speech from background noise. This means that if you are in a noisy room, VAD is unable to distinguish between speech and background noise. This also is known as the *signal-to-noise threshold* (refer to Figure 7-5). In these scenarios, VAD disables itself at the beginning of the call.

Another inherent problem with VAD is detecting when speech begins. Typically the beginning of a sentence is cut off or clipped (refer to Figure 7-5). This phenomenon is known as *front-end speech clipping*. Usually, the person listening to the speech does not notice front-end speech clipping.

Digital-to-Analog Conversion

Digital to analog (D/A) conversion issues also currently plague toll networks. Although almost all the telephony backbone networks in first-world countries today are digital, sometimes multiple D/A conversions occur.

Each time a conversion occurs from digital to analog and back, the speech or waveform becomes less "true." Although today's toll networks can handle at least seven D/A conversions before voice quality is affected, compressed speech is less robust in the face of these conversions.

It is important to note that D/A conversion must be tightly managed in a compressed speech environment. When using G.729, just two conversions from D/A cause the MOS score to decrease rapidly. The only way to manage D/A conversion is to have the network designer design VoIP environments with as few D/A conversions as possible.

Although D/A conversions affect all voice networks, VoIP networks using a PCM codec (G.711) are just as resilient to problems caused by D/A conversions as today's telephony networks are.

Tandem Encoding

As covered in Chapter 1, all circuit-switched networks today work on the premise of switching calls at the data link layer. The circuit switches are organized in a hierarchical model in which switches higher in the hierarchy are called *tandem switches*.

Tandem switches do not actually terminate any local loops; rather, they act as a *higher-layer* circuit switch. In the hierarchical model, several layers of tandem circuit switches can exist, as shown in Figure 7-6. This enables end-to-end connectivity for anyone with a phone, without the need for a direct connection between every home on the planet.

Figure 7-6   *Tandem Switching Hierarchy*

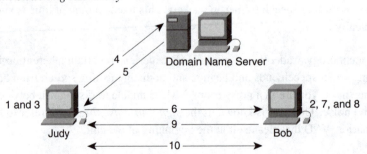

Typically, a voice call that passes through the two TDM switches and one tandem switch does not incur degradation in voice quality because these circuit switches use 64 Kbps channels.

If the TDM switches compress voice and the tandem switch must decompress and recompress the voice, the voice quality can be drastically affected. Although compression and recompression are not common in the PSTN today, you must plan for it and design around it in packet networks.

Voice degradation occurs when you have more than one compression/decompression cycle for each phone call. Figure 7-7 provides an example of when this scenario might occur.

Figure 7-7   *VoIP Tandem Encoding*

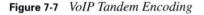
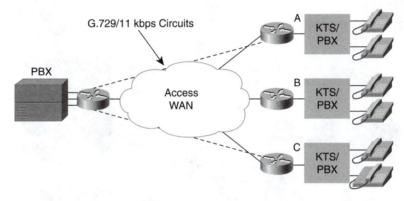

Figure 7-7 depicts three VoIP routers connected and acting as tie-lines between one central-site PBX and three remote-branch PBXs. The network is designed to put all the dial-plan information in the central-site PBX. This is common in many enterprise networks to keep the administration of the dial plan centralized.

A drawback to tandem encoding when used with VoIP is that, if a telephony user at branch B wants to call a user at branch C, two VoIP ports at central site A must be utilized. Also, two compression/decompression cycles exist, which means that voice quality will degrade.

Different codecs react differently to tandem encoding. G.729 can handle two compression/decompression cycles, while G.723.1 is less resilient to multiple compression cycles.

Assume, for example, that a user at remote site B wants to call a user at remote site C. The call goes through PBX B, is compressed and packetized at VoIP router B, and is sent to the central site VoIP router A, which decompresses the call and sends it to PBX A. PBX A circuit-switches the call back to its VoIP router (router A), which compresses and packetizes the call, and sends it to the remote site C, where it is then decompressed and sent to PBX C. This process is known as *tandem-compression*; you should avoid it in all networks where compression exists.

It is easy to avoid tandem compression. This customer simplified the router configuration at the expense of voice quality. Cisco IOS has other mechanisms that can simplify management of dial plans and still keep the highest voice quality possible.

One possible method is to use a Cisco IOS Multimedia Conference Manager (for instance, H.323 Gatekeeper). Another mechanism is to use one of Cisco's management applications, such as Cisco Voice Manager, to assist in configuring and maintaining dial plans on all your routers.

Taking the same example of three PBXs connected through three VoIP routers, but configuring the VoIP routers differently, simplifies the call-flow and avoids tandem encoding, as shown in Figure 7-8.

Figure 7-8 *VoIP Without Tandem Encoding*

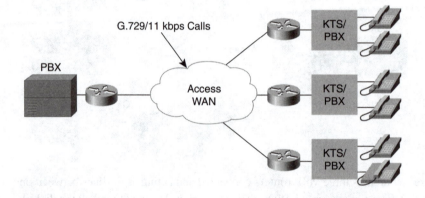

You can see one of IP's strengths in Figure 7-8: a tie-line does not have to be leased from the telephone company to complete calls between two PBXs. If a data network connects the sites, VoIP can ride across that network.

The dial plan is moved from the central-site PBX to each of the VoIP routers. This enables each VoIP device to make a call-routing decision and removes the need for tie-lines. The major benefit of this change is the removal of needless compression/decompression cycles.

Transport Protocols

As explained in Chapter 6, "IP Tutorial," two main types of traffic ride upon Internet Protocol (IP): User Datagram Protocol (UDP) and Transmission Control Protocol (TCP). In general, you use TCP when you need a reliable connection and UDP when you need simplicity and reliability is not your chief concern.

Due to the time-sensitive nature of voice traffic, UDP/IP was the logical choice to carry voice. More information was needed on a packet-by-packet basis than UDP offered, however. So, for real-time or delay-sensitive traffic, the Internet Engineering Task Force (IETF) adopted RTP. VoIP rides on top of RTP, which rides on top of UDP. Therefore, VoIP is carried with an RTP/UDP/IP packet header.

RTP

RTP is the standard for transmitting delay-sensitive traffic across packet-based networks. RTP rides on top of UDP and IP. RTP gives receiving stations information that is not in the connectionless UDP/IP streams. As shown in Figure 7-9, two important bits of information are sequence number and timestamp. RTP uses the sequence information to determine whether the packets are arriving in order, and it uses the time-stamping information to determine the interarrival packet time (jitter).

Figure 7-9   *Real-Time Transport Header*

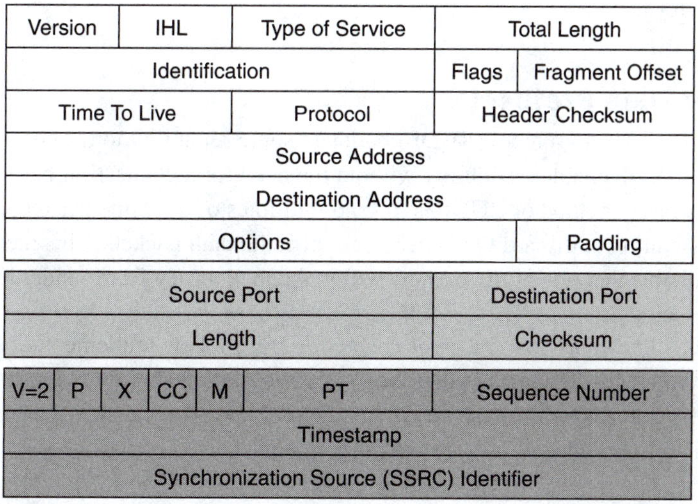

Version	IHL	Type of Service	Total Length	
Identification			Flags	Fragment Offset
Time To Live		Protocol	Header Checksum	
Source Address				
Destination Address				
Options			Padding	
Source Port			Destination Port	
Length			Checksum	
V=2 P X CC M		PT	Sequence Number	
Timestamp				
Synchronization Source (SSRC) Identifier				

You can use RTP for media on demand, as well as for interactive services such as Internet telephony. RTP (refer to Figure 7-9) consists of a data part and a control part, the latter called RTP Control Protocol (RTCP).

The data part of RTP is a thin protocol that provides support for applications with real-time properties, such as continuous media (for example, audio and video), including timing reconstruction, loss detection, and content identification.

RTCP provides support for real-time conferencing of groups of any size within an Internet. This support includes source identification and support for gateways, such as audio and video bridges as well as multicast-to-unicast translators. It also offers QoS feedback from receivers to the multicast group, as well as support for the synchronization of different media streams.

Another new proposal defined in RFC 3611, RTP Control Protocol Extended Reports (RTCP XR), provides a rich set of data for VoIP management. The data for these extended reports can be provided by technology such as VQmon embedded into VoIP phones or gateways and sent periodically during the call to provide real-time feedback on voice quality. The reports generated present a very useful set of VoIP metrics data on network packet loss, RTP round trip delay, and so on.

Using RTP is important for real-time traffic, but a few drawbacks exist. The IP/RTP/UDP headers are 20, 8, and 12 bytes, respectively. This adds up to a 40-byte header, which is twice as big as the payload when using G.729 with two speech samples (20 ms). You can compress this large header to 2 or 4 bytes by using RTP Header Compression (CRTP). CRTP is covered in depth in Chapter 8.

Reliable User Data Protocol

Reliable User Data Protocol (RUDP) builds in some reliability to the connectionless UDP protocol. RUDP enables reliability without the need for a connection-based protocol such as TCP. The basic method of RUDP is to send multiples of the same packet and enable the receiving station to discard the unnecessary or redundant packets. This mechanism makes it more probable that one of the packets will make the journey from sender to receiver.

This also is known as *forward error correction* (FEC). Few implementations of FEC exist due to bandwidth considerations (a doubling or tripling of the amount of bandwidth used). Customers that have almost unlimited bandwidth, however, consider FEC a worthwhile mechanism to enhance reliability and voice quality.

Cisco currently utilizes RUDP in its PGW2200 product, which enables Signaling System 7 (SS7) to Q.931 over IP conversion. The Q.931 over IP is transmitted over RUDP.

Dial-Plan Design

One of the areas that causes the largest amount of headaches when designing an Enterprise Telephony (ET) network is the *dial plan*. The causes of these head pains might be due to the complex issues of integrating disparate networks. Many of these disparate networks were not designed for integration.

A good data example of joining disparate networks is when two companies merge. In such a scenario, the companies' data networks (IP addressing, ordering applications, and inventory database) must be joined. It is highly improbable that both companies used the same methodologies when implementing their data networks, so problems can arise.

The same problems can occur in telephony networks. If two companies merge, their phone systems (voice mail, billing, supplementary features, and dial-plan addressing) might be incompatible with each other.

These dial-plan issues also can occur when a company decides to institute a corporate dial plan. Consider Company X, for example. Company X grew drastically in the last three years and now operates 30 sites throughout the world, with its headquarters in Dallas. Company X currently dials through the PSTN to all its 29 remote sites. Company X wants to simplify the dialing plan to all its remote sites to enable better employee communication and ease of use.

Company X currently has a large PBX at its headquarters and smaller PBX systems at its remote sites. Several alternatives are available to this company:

- Purchase leased lines between headquarters and all remote sites.

- Purchase a telephony Virtual Private Network (VPN) from the telephone company and dial an access code from anywhere to access the VPN.

- Take advantage of the existing data infrastructure and put voice on the data network.

Regardless of which option Company X chooses, it must face dial-plan design, network management, and cost issues.

Without getting into great detail, most companies must decide on their dial-plan design based on the following issues:

- Plans for growth

- Cost of leased circuits or VPNs

- Cost of additional equipment for packet voice

- Number overlap (when more than one site has the same phone number)

- Call-flows (the call patterns from each site)

- Busy hour (the time of day when the highest number of calls are offered on a circuit)

Depending on the size of the company, the dial plan can stretch from two digits to seven or eight digits. It is important that you not force yourself down a particular path until you address the previous issues.

Company X plans on sustaining 20–30 percent growth and decides on a seven-digit dial plan based on its growth patterns. This choice also cuts down on the number overlap that might be present.

Company X will have a three-digit site code, and four digits for the actual subscriber line. It made this decision because it does not believe it will have more than 999 branch offices.

> **NOTE** For companies that have hundreds of branch offices, it is common to have more site codes and fewer subscriber lines. If a company has several hundred branch offices and needs thousands of subscriber lines, it must use more digits (that is, it must use an eight- or nine-digit dial plan).

End Office Switch Call-Flow Versus IP Phone Call

To simplify a TDM or end office switch call-flow and an IP call-flow, this section looks at ways you can call your next-door neighbor using both the PSTN and the Internet. Figure 7-10 shows a basic call-flow in the PSTN today. Compare this to an IP phone call-flow and notice the similarities of necessary call setup.

Figure 7-10 *Calling My Neighbor with Today's PSTN*

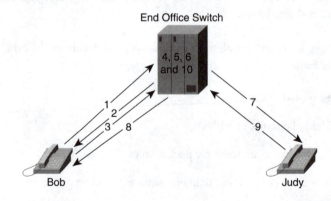

In this example, Bob calls his neighbor Judy. They are both subscribers on the local end office switch, and therefore, no SS7 is needed. The following steps occur:

1. Bob picks up his handset (off hook).

2. The local end office switch gives Bob a dial tone.

3. Bob dials Judy's seven-digit phone number.

4. The end office switch collects and analyzes the seven-digit number to determine the destination of the phone call. The end office switch knows that someone from Bob's house is placing the call because of the specific port that it dedicated to Bob.

5. The switch analyzes the seven-digit called number to determine whether the number is a local number that the switch can serve.

NOTE   If the same end office switch does not service Judy, Bob's end office switch looks in its routing tables to determine how to connect this call. It can add prefix digits to make the number appear as a fully qualified E.164 number when contacting Judy.

6. The switch determines Judy's specific subscriber line.

7. The end office switch then signals Judy's circuit by ringing Judy's phone.

8. A voice path back to Bob is cut through so that Bob can hear the ring-back tone the end office switch is sending. The ring-back tone is sent to Bob so that he knows Judy's phone is ringing. (The ringing of Judy's phone and the ring-back tone that Bob hears need not be synchronized.)

9. Judy picks up her phone (off hook).

10. The end office switch cuts through the voice path from Bob to Judy. This is a 64 Kbps, full-duplex DS-0 (Digital Service, Level 0) in the end office switching fabric to enable voice transmission.

Figure 7-11 demonstrates the call-flow necessary to complete an Internet phone call using a PC application.

Figure 7-11 *Calling with an Internet-Phone Application*

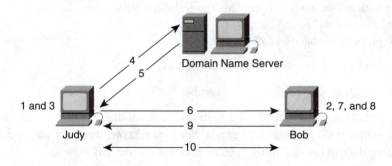

Both Bob and Judy need to be on the Internet or have some other IP network between their homes to talk to each other. Assuming this IP network exists or that both neighbors have a connection to the Internet, you can then follow this possible call-flow:

1. Judy launches her Internet phone (I-phone) application, which is H.323-compatible.

2. Bob already has his I-phone application launched.

3. Judy knows that Bob's Internet "name," or Domain Name System (DNS) entry, is bob@nextdoorneighbor.com, so she puts that into the "who to call" section in her I-phone application and presses Return.

4. The I-phone application converts Bob.nextdoorneighbor.com to a DNS host name and goes to a DNS server that is statically configured in Judy's machine to resolve the DNS name and get an actual IP address.

5. The DNS machine passes back Bob's IP address.

6. Judy's I-phone application takes Bob's IP address and sends an H.225 message to Bob.

7. The H.225 message signals Bob's PC to begin ringing.

8. Bob clicks on the Accept button, which tells his I-phone application to send back an H.225 connect message.

9. Judy's I-phone application then begins H.245 negotiation with Bob's PC.

10. H.245 negotiation finishes and logical channels are opened. Bob and Judy can now speak to one another through a packet-based network.

The example does not show all the steps and omits some details that a service provider needs to deploy a VoIP network. Because IP is a ubiquitous protocol, as mentioned in Chapter 6, when a call is packetized, it could be destined to your next-door neighbor or to a relative in Norway.

Summary

This chapter brought up many of the issues surrounding VoIP. Many of these issues, such as compression/decompression of the speech frame and propagation delay, are inherent to VoIP, and you can't do much to minimize these effects on VoIP networks.

With careful planning and solid network design, however, you can control and possibly avoid many problematic issues. Some of these issues are jitter, overall latency, handling delay, sampling rates, tandem encodings, and dial-plan design.

References

The following Requests For Comments (RFCs) will help you to continue researching VoIP:

RFC 1889—RTP: A Transport Protocol for Real-Time Applications
RFC 2327—SDP: Session Description Protocol
RFC 2326—RTSP: Real-Time Streaming Protocol
ITU-T Recommendation H.323
ITU-T G. specifications for codecs
ITU-T G.113 Voice Quality Specification
ITU-T P.861 Perceptual Speech Quality Measure(ment), PSQM
iLBC Codec—http://www.ilbcfreeware.org/
RFC 3550—Real Time Transport Control Protocol
RFC 3611—RTCP Extended Reports

CHAPTER 8

Quality of Service

Quality of service (QoS) is an often-used and misused term that has a variety of meanings. In this book, QoS refers to both Integrated Services (IntServ) and Differentiated Services (DiffServ). Although the two mechanisms greatly differ, the basic goal of IntServ and DiffServ is to achieve the bandwidth and latency needed for a particular application.

DiffServ is typically used on large networks to classify the appropriate level of QoS a particular stream or group of traffic from an individual or corporation requires. This is done via setting the Type of Service (ToS) field or DiffServ Code Point (DSCP).

IntServ is typically used to ensure that the specific flow of traffic is going to receive the appropriate level of QoS across the entire network before sending that traffic. This is typically achieved using the Resource ReSerVation Protocol (RSVP).

Various tools are available to achieve the necessary QoS for a given user and application. This chapter discusses these tools, when to use them, and potential drawbacks associated with some of them.

It is important to note that the tools for implementing these services are not as important as the end result achieved. In other words, do not focus on one QoS tool to solve all your QoS problems. Instead, look at the network as a whole to determine which tools, if any, belong in which portions of your network.

Keep in mind that the more granular your approach to queuing and controlling your network, the more administrative overhead the Information Technology (IT) department will endure. This increases the possibility that the entire network will slow down due to a miscalculation.

QoS Network Toolkit

In a well-engineered network, you must be careful to separate functions that occur on the edges of a network from functions that occur in the core or backbone of a network. It is important to separate edge and backbone functions to achieve the best QoS possible.

Cisco offers many tools for implementing QoS. In some scenarios, you can use none of these QoS tools and still achieve the QoS you need for your applications. In general, though, each network has individual problems that you can solve using one or more of Cisco's QoS tools.

This chapter discusses the following tools associated with the edge of a network:

■ Additional bandwidth

■ Compressed Real-Time Transport Protocol (cRTP)

■ Queuing

— Weighted Fair Queuing (WFQ)

— Custom Queuing (CQ)

— Priority Queuing (PQ)

— Class-Based Weighted Fair Queuing (CB-WFQ)

— Priority Queuing—Class-Based Weighted Fair Queuing

■ Packet classification

— IP Precedence/ToS/DiffServ

— Policy routing

— Resource Reservation Protocol (RSVP)

■ Shaping traffic flows and policing

— Generic Traffic Shaping (GTS)

— Frame Relay Traffic Shaping (FRTS)

— Committed Access Rate (CAR)

■ Fragmentation

— Multi-Class Multilink Point-to-Point Protocol (MCML PPP)

— Frame Relay Forum 12 (FRF.12)

— MTU

— IP Maximum Transmission Unit (IP MTU)

This chapter also discusses the following issues associated with the backbone of a network tools:

■ High-speed queuing

— Weighted Random Early Drop/Detect (WRED)

— Distributed Weighted Fair Queuing (DWFQ)

Voice over IP (VoIP) comes with its own set of problems. As discussed in Chapter 7, "VoIP: An In-Depth Analysis," QoS can help solve some of these problems—namely, packet loss, jitter, and handling delay. (Serialization delay, or the time it takes to transmit bits onto a physical interface, is not covered in this book.)

Some of the problems QoS *cannot* solve are propagation delay (no solution to the speed-of-light problem exists as of the printing of this book), codec delay, sampling delay, and digitization delay.

Voice is a mission-critical application and requires significant planning to ensure that the appropriate service level agreement (SLA) can be met. One of the elements of this planning is to understand the amount of delay that is in your "budget." Some of these elements of delay can be controlled and tuned, while others are simply due to physics. Refer to Figure 8-1 for more details on items that are within your controllable delay budget.

Figure 8-1   *End-to-End Delay Budget*

	Fixed Delay	Variable Delay
Coder Delay G.729 (5 ms Look Ahead)	5 ms	
Coder Delay G.729 (10 ms Per Frame)	20 ms	
Packetization Delay Included in Coder Delay		
Queuing Delay 64 kbps Trunk		6 ms
Serialization Delay 64 kbps Trunk	3 ms	
Propagation Delay (Private Lines)	32 ms	
Network Delay (For Example, Public Frame Relay Svc)		
Dejitter Buffer		2-200 ms
Total - Assuming 50 ms Jitter Buffer	**110 ms**	

The International Telecommunication Union Telecommunication Standardization Sector (ITU-T) G.114 recommendation suggests no more than 150 milliseconds (ms) of end-to-end delay to maintain "good" voice quality. Any customer's definition of "good" might mean more or less delay, so keep in mind that 150 ms is merely a recommendation.

> **NOTE**   "Good" voice quality is relative to the user's experience and expectation. A broader discussion of MOS and how *good* is calculated is included in Chapter 7 of this book.

Edge Functions

Edge functions are generally assigned to Provider Edge (PE) and Customer Edge (CE) equipment. When designing a VoIP network, edge QoS functions that are discussed in this book usually correspond to wide-area networks (WANs) that have less than a T1 or E1 line of bandwidth from the central site. When higher-bandwidth edge links are utilized the QoS mechanisms described in this chapter are typically not necessary.

> **NOTE**   It is becoming increasingly common to deploy QoS mechanisms or "session control" mechanisms that allow for various subscriber policies to be implemented across the network. These work in conjunction with the described QoS mechanisms.

Bandwidth Limitations

The first issue of major concern when designing a VoIP network is bandwidth constraints. Depending upon which codec you use and how many voice samples you want per packet, the amount of bandwidth per call can increase dramatically. For an explanation of packet sizes and bandwidth consumed, see Table 8-1.

Table 8-1   *Codec Type and Sample Size Effects on Bandwidth*

Codec	Bandwidth Consumed	Bandwidth Consumed with cRTP (2-Byte Header)	Sample Latency
G.729 w/ one 10-ms sample/frame	40 kbps	9.6 kbps	15 ms
G.729 w/ four 10-ms samples/frame	16 kbps	8.4 kbps	45 ms
G.729 w/ two 10-ms samples/frame	24 kbps	11.2 kbps	25 ms
G.711 w/ one 10-ms sample/frame	112 kbps	81.6 kbps	10 ms
G.711 w/ two 10-ms samples/frame	96 kbps	80.8 kbps	20 ms

After reviewing this table, you might be asking yourself why 24 kbps of bandwidth is consumed when you're using an 8-kbps codec. This occurs due to a phenomenon called "The IP Tax." The G.729 codec using two 10-ms samples consumes 20 bytes per frame, which works out to 8 kbps. The packet headers that include IP, RTP, and User Datagram Protocol (UDP) add 40 bytes to each frame. This "IP Tax" header is *twice* the amount of the payload.

Using G.729 with two 10-ms samples as an example, without RTP header compression, 24 kbps are consumed in each direction per call. Although this might not be a large amount for T1 (1.544-mbps), E1 (2.048-mbps), or higher circuits, it is a large amount (42 percent) for a 56-kbps circuit.

Also, keep in mind that the bandwidth in Table 8-1 does not include Layer 2 headers (PPP, Frame Relay, and so on). It includes headers from Layer 3 (network layer) and above only. Therefore, the same G.729 call can consume different amounts of bandwidth based upon which data link layer is used (Ethernet, Frame Relay, PPP, and so on).

cRTP

To reduce the large percentage of bandwidth consumed on point-to-point WAN links by a G.729 voice call, you can use cRTP. cRTP enables you to compress the 40-byte IP/RTP/UDP header to 2 to 4 bytes most of the time (see Figure 8-2).

Figure 8-2 *RTP Header Compression*

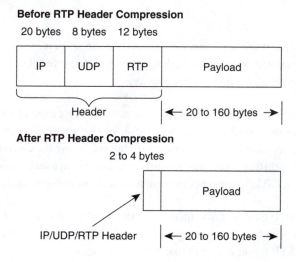

With cRTP, the amount of traffic per VoIP call is reduced from 24 kbps to 11.2 kbps. This is a major improvement for low-bandwidth links. A 56-kbps link, for example, can now carry four G.729 VoIP calls at 11.2 kbps each. Without cRTP, only two G.729 VoIP calls at 24 kbps can be used.

To avoid the unnecessary consumption of available bandwidth, cRTP is used on a link-by-link basis. This compression scheme reduces the IP/RTP/UDP header to 2 bytes when UDP checksums are not used, or 4 bytes when UDP checksums are used.

cRTP uses some of the same techniques as Transmission Control Protocol (TCP) header compression. In TCP header compression, the first factor-of-two reduction in data rate occurs because half of the bytes in the IP and TCP headers remain constant over the life of the connection.

The big gain, however, comes from the fact that the difference from packet to packet is often constant, even though several fields change in every packet. Therefore, the algorithm can simply add 1 to every value received. By maintaining both the uncompressed header and the first-order differences in the session state shared between the compressor and the decompressor, cRTP must communicate only an indication that the second-order difference is zero. In that case, the decompressor can reconstruct the original header without any loss of information, simply by adding the first-order differences to the saved, uncompressed header as each compressed packet is received.

Just as TCP/IP header compression maintains shared state for multiple, simultaneous TCP connections, this IP/RTP/UDP compression must maintain state for multiple session contexts. A *session context* is defined by the combination of the IP source and destination addresses, the UDP source and destination ports, and the RTP synchronization source (SSRC) field. A compressor implementation might use a hash function on these fields to index a table of stored session contexts.

The compressed packet carries a small integer, called the *session context identifier*, or CID, to indicate in which session context that packet should be interpreted. The decompressor can use the CID to index its table of stored session contexts.

cRTP can compress the 40 bytes of header down to 2 to 4 bytes most of the time. As such, about 98 percent of the time the compressed packet will be sent. Periodically, however, an entire uncompressed header must be sent to verify that both sides have the correct state. Sometimes, changes occur in a field that is usually constant—such as the payload type field, for instance. In such cases, the IP/RTP/UDP header cannot be compressed, so an uncompressed header must be sent.

You should use cRTP on any WAN interface where bandwidth is a concern and a high portion of RTP traffic exists. The following configuration tip pertaining to Cisco IOS Software shows ways you can enable cRTP on serial and Frame Relay interfaces:

Example 8-1 *Enabling cRTP on Serial and Frame Relay Interfaces*

```
Leased line
!
interface serial 0
   ip address 192.168.121.18 255.255.255.248
   no ip mroute-cache
   ip rtp header-compression
   encapsulation ppp
!
```
```
Frame Relay
!
interface Serial0/0
   ip 192.168.120.10 255.255.255.0
   encapsulation frame-relay
   no ip route-cache
```

Example 8-1 *Enabling cRTP on Serial and Frame Relay Interfaces (Continued)*

```
 no ip mroute-cache
 frame-relay ip rtp header-compression
!
```

You should not use cRTP on high-speed interfaces, as the disadvantages of doing so outweigh the advantages. "High-speed network" is a relative term: Usually anything higher than T1 or E1 speed does not need cRTP. The "need" for compression is simply a comparison between the costs of the transmission link versus the cost and overhead of the compression. If you are willing to pay the extra cost of time for compression/decompression and the additional hardware costs that might be involved, then compression can work on almost any transmission link.

As with any compression, the CPU incurs extra processing duties to compress the packet. This increases the amount of CPU utilization on the edge device. Therefore, you must weigh the advantages (lower bandwidth requirements) against the disadvantages (higher CPU utilization). An edge device with higher CPU utilization can experience problems running other tasks. As such, it is usually a good rule of thumb to keep CPU utilization at less than 60 to 70 percent to keep your network running smoothly.

Queuing

Queuing in and of itself is a fairly simple concept. The easiest way to think about queuing is to compare it to the highway system. Let's say you are on the New Jersey Turnpike driving at a decent speed. When you approach a tollbooth, you must slow down, stop, and pay the toll. During the time it takes to pay the toll, a backup of cars ensues, creating congestion.

As in the tollbooth line, in queuing the concept of first in, first out (FIFO) exists, which means that if you are the first to get in the line, you are the first to get out of the line. FIFO queuing was the first type of queuing to be used in routers, and it is still useful depending upon the network's topology.

Today's networks, with their variety of applications, protocols, and users, require a way to classify different traffic. Going back to the tollbooth example, a special "lane" is necessary to enable some cars to get bumped forward in line. The New Jersey Turnpike, as well as many other toll roads, has a carpool lane, or a lane that allows you to pay for the toll electronically, for instance.

Likewise, Cisco has several queuing tools that enable a network administrator to specify what type of traffic is "special" or important and to queue the traffic based on that information instead of when a packet arrives. The most popular of these queuing techniques is known as WFQ. If you have a Cisco router, it is highly likely that it is using the WFQ algorithm because it is the default for any router interface less than 2 mbps.

Weighted Fair Queuing

FIFO queuing places all packets it receives in one queue and transmits them as bandwidth becomes available. WFQ, on the other hand, uses multiple queues to separate flows and gives equal amounts of bandwidth to each flow. This prevents one application, such as File Transfer Protocol (FTP), from consuming all available bandwidth.

WFQ ensures that queues do not starve for bandwidth and that traffic gets predictable service. Low-volume data streams receive preferential service, transmitting their entire offered loads in a timely fashion. High-volume traffic streams share the remaining capacity, obtaining equal or proportional bandwidth.

WFQ is similar to time-division multiplexing (TDM), as it divides bandwidth equally among different flows so that no one application is starved. WFQ is superior to TDM, however, simply because when a stream is no longer present, WFQ dynamically adjusts to use the free bandwidth for the flows that are still transmitting.

Fair queuing dynamically identifies data streams or flows based on several factors. These data streams are prioritized based upon the amount of bandwidth that the flow consumes. This algorithm enables bandwidth to be shared fairly, without the use of access lists or other time-consuming administrative tasks. WFQ determines a flow by using the source and destination address, protocol type, socket or port number, and QoS/ToS values.

Fair queuing enables low-bandwidth applications, which make up most of the traffic, to have as much bandwidth as needed, relegating higher-bandwidth traffic to share the remaining traffic in a fair manner. Fair queuing offers reduced jitter and enables efficient sharing of available bandwidth between all applications.

WFQ uses the fast-switching path in Cisco IOS. It is enabled with the **fair-queue** command and is enabled by default on most serial interfaces configured at 2.048 mbps or slower, beginning with Cisco IOS Release 11.0 software.

The weighting in WFQ is currently affected by three mechanisms: IP Precedence, Frame Relay forward explicit congestion notification (FECN), backward explicit congestion notification (BECN), and Discard Eligible (DE) bits.

The IP Precedence field has values between 0 (the default) and 7. As the precedence value increases, the algorithm allocates more bandwidth to that conversation or flow. This enables the flow to transmit more frequently. See the "Packet Classification" section later in this chapter for more information on weighting WFQ.

In a Frame Relay network, FECN and BECN bits usually flag the presence of congestion. When congestion is flagged, the weights the algorithm uses change such that the conversation encountering the congestion transmits less frequently.

To enable WFQ for an interface, use the **fair-queue** interface configuration command. To disable WFQ for an interface, use the "no" form of this command:

```
fair-queue [congestive-discard-threshold [dynamic-queues [reservable-queues]]
```

- *congestive-discard-threshold*—(Optional) Number of messages allowed in each queue. The default is 64 messages, and a new threshold must be a power of 2 in the range 16 to 4096. When a conversation reaches this threshold, new message packets are discarded.

- *dynamic-queues*—(Optional) Number of dynamic queues used for best-effort conversations (that is, a normal conversation not requiring special network services). Values are 16, 32, 64, 128, 256, 512, 1024, 2048, and 4096. The default is 256.

- *reservable-queues*—(Optional) Number of reservable queues used for reserved conversations in the range 0 to 1000. The default is 0. Reservable queues are used for interfaces configured for features such as RSVP.

The network administrator must take care to ensure that the weights in WFQ are properly invoked. This prevents a rogue application from requesting or using a higher priority than he or she intended. How to avoid improperly weighting flows is discussed in the "Packet Classification" section later in this chapter.

WFQ also is not intended to run on interfaces that are clocked higher than 2.048 mbps. For information on queuing on those interfaces, see the " High-Speed Transport" section.

Custom Queuing

Custom queuing (CQ) enables users to specify a percentage of available bandwidth to a particular protocol. You can define up to 16 output queues. Each queue is served sequentially in a round-robin fashion, transmitting a percentage of traffic on each queue before moving on to the next queue.

The router determines how many bytes from each queue should be transmitted, based on the speed of the interface as well as the configured traffic percentage. In other words, another traffic type can use unused bandwidth from queue A until queue A requires its full percentage.

Example 8-2 shows ways you can enable CQ on a serial interface. You must first define the parameters of the queue list and then enable the queue list on the physical interface (in this case, serial 0).

Example 8-2 *Enabling Custom Queuing on a Serial Interface*

```
Interface serial 0
ip address 20.0.0.1 255.0.0.0
custom-queue-list 1
!
queue-list 1 protocol ip 1 list 101
queue-list 1 default 2
queue-list 1 queue 1 byte-count 4000
queue-list 1 queue 2 byte-count 2000
!
access-list 101 permit udp any any range 16380 16480 precedence 5
access-list 101 permit tcp any any eq 1720
```

CQ requires knowledge of port types and traffic types. This equates to a large amount of administrative overhead. But after the administrative overhead is complete, CQ offers a highly granular approach to queuing, which is what some customers prefer.

Priority Queuing

PQ enables the network administrator to configure four traffic priorities—high, normal, medium, and low. Inbound traffic is assigned to one of the four output queues. Traffic in the high-priority queue is serviced until the queue is empty; then, packets in the next priority queue are transmitted.

This queuing arrangement ensures that mission-critical traffic is always given as much bandwidth as it needs; however, it starves other applications to do so.

Therefore, it is important to understand traffic flows when using this queuing mechanism so that applications are not starved of needed bandwidth. PQ is best used when the highest-priority traffic consumes the least amount of line bandwidth.

Example 8-3 demonstrates using an access list (**access-list 101** in this case) to specify particular UDP and TCP port ranges. **priority-list 1** then applies **access-list 101** into the highest queue (the most important queue) for PQ. **priority-list 1** is then invoked on serial 1/1 by the command **priority-group 1**.

Example 8-3 *Using an Access List to Specify UDP/TCP Port Ranges for Traffic Flow*

```
!
interface Serial1/1
  ip address 192.168.121.17 255.255.255.248
```

Example 8-3 *Using an Access List to Specify UDP/TCP Port Ranges for Traffic Flow (Continued)*

```
  encapsulation ppp
  no ip mroute-cache
  priority-group 1
!
access-list 101 permit udp any any range 16384 16484
access-list 101 permit tcp any any eq 1720
priority-list 1 protocol ip high list 101
!
```

PQ enables a network administrator to "starve" applications. An improperly configured PQ can service one queue and completely disregard all other queues. This can, in effect, force some applications to stop working. As long as the system administrator realizes this caveat, PQ can be the proper alternative for some customers.

CB-WFQ (CB=Class Based)

CB-WFQ has all the benefits of WFQ, with the additional functionality of providing granular support for network administrator-defined classes of traffic. CB-WFQ also can run on high-speed interfaces (up to T3).

CB-WFQ enables you to define what constitutes a class based on criteria that exceed the confines of flow. Using CB-WFQ, you can create a specific class for voice traffic. The network administrator defines these classes of traffic through access lists. These classes of traffic determine how packets are grouped in different queues.

The most interesting feature of CB-WFQ is that it enables the network administrator to specify the exact amount of bandwidth to be allocated per class of traffic. CB-WFQ can handle 64 different classes and control bandwidth requirements for each class.

With standard WFQ, weights determine the amount of bandwidth allocated per conversation. It is dependent on how many flows of traffic occur at a given moment.

With CB-WFQ, each class is associated with a separate queue. You can allocate a specific minimum amount of guaranteed bandwidth to the class as a percentage of the link, or in kbps. Other classes can share unused bandwidth in proportion to their assigned weights. When configuring CB-WFQ, you should consider that bandwidth allocation does not necessarily mean the traffic belonging to a class experiences low delay; however, you can skew weights to simulate PQ.

PQ within CB-WFQ (Low Latency Queuing)

PQ within CB-WFQ (LLQ) is a mouthful of an acronym. This queuing mechanism was developed to give absolute priority to voice traffic over all other traffic on an interface.

The LLQ feature brings to CB-WFQ the strict-priority queuing functionality of IP RTP Priority required for delay-sensitive, real-time traffic, such as voice. LLQ enables use of a strict PQ.

Although it is possible to queue various types of traffic to a strict PQ, it is strongly recommended that you direct only voice traffic to this queue. This recommendation is based upon the fact that voice traffic is well behaved and sends packets at regular intervals; other applications transmit at irregular intervals and can ruin an entire network if configured improperly.

With LLQ, you can specify traffic in a broad range of ways to guarantee strict priority delivery. To indicate the voice flow to be queued to the strict PQ, you can use an access list. This is different from IP RTP Priority, which allows for only a specific UDP port range.

Although this mechanism is relatively new to IOS, it has proven to be powerful and it gives voice packets the necessary priority, latency, and jitter required for good-quality voice.

Queuing Summary

Although a one-size-fits-all answer to queuing problems does not exist, many customers today use WFQ to deal with queuing issues. WFQ is simple to deploy, and it requires little additional effort from the network administrator. Setting the weights with WFQ can further enhance its benefits.

Customers who require more granular and strict queuing techniques can use CQ or PQ. Be sure to utilize great caution when enabling these techniques, however, as you might do more harm than good to your network. With PQ or CQ, it is imperative that you know your traffic and your applications.

Many customers who deploy VoIP networks in low-bandwidth environments (less than 768 kbps) use IP RTP Priority or LLQ to prioritize their voice traffic above all other traffic flows.

Packet Classification

To achieve your intended packet delivery, you must know how to properly weight WFQ. This section focuses on different weighting techniques and ways you can use them in various networks to achieve the amount of QoS you require.

IP Precedence

IP Precedence refers to the three bits in the ToS field in an IP header, as shown in Figure 8-3.

Figure 8-3 *IP Header and ToS Field*

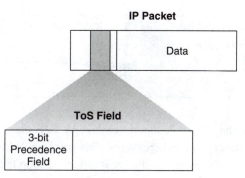

These three bits allow for eight different CoS types (0-7), listed in Table 8-2.

Table 8-2   *ToS (IP Precedence)*

Service Type	Purpose
Routine	Set routine precedence (0)
Priority	Set priority precedence (1)
Immediate	Set immediate precedence (2)
Flash	Set Flash precedence (3)
Flash-override	Set Flash override precedence (4)
Critical	Set critical precedence (5)
Internet	Set internetwork control precedence (6)
Network	Set network control precedence (7)

IP Precedence 6 and 7 are reserved for network information (routing updates, hello packets, and so on). This leaves 6 remaining precedence settings for normal IP traffic flows.

IP Precedence enables a router to group traffic flows based on the eight precedence settings and to queue traffic based upon that information as well as on source address, destination address, and port numbers.

You can consider IP Precedence an in-band QoS mechanism. Extra signaling is not involved, nor does additional packet header overhead exist. Given these benefits, IP Precedence is the QoS mechanism that large-scale networks use most often.

With Cisco IOS, you can set the IP Precedence bits of your IP streams in several ways. With the Cisco VoIP design, you can set the IP Precedence bits based upon the destination phone number (the called number). Setting the precedence in this manner is easy and allows for different types of CoS, depending upon which destination you are calling.

> **NOTE**   To set the IP Precedence using Cisco IOS VoIP, do the following:
>
> ```
> dial-peer voice 650 voip
>   destination-pattern 650
>   ip precedence 5
>   session target RAS
> ```

Cisco IOS also enables any IP traffic that flows through the router to have its precedence bit set based upon an access list or extended access list. This is accomplished through a feature known as *policy routing,* which is covered in the "Policy Routing" section later in this chapter.

IP Precedence Caveats

IP Precedence has no built-in mechanism for refusing incorrect IP Precedence settings. The network administrator needs to take precautions to ensure that the IP Precedence settings in the network remain as they were originally planned. The following example shows the problems that can occur when IP Precedence is not carefully configured.

Company B uses WFQ with VoIP on all its WAN links and uses IP Precedence to prioritize traffic on the network. Company B uses a precedence setting of 5 for VoIP and a precedence setting of 4 for Systems Network Architecture (SNA) traffic. All other traffic is assumed to have a precedence setting of 0 (the lowest precedence).

Although in most applications the precedence is 0, some applications might be modified to request a higher precedence. In this example, a software engineer modifies his gaming application to request a precedence of 7 (the highest setting) so that when he and a co-worker in another office play, they get first priority on the WAN link. This is just an example, but it is possible. Because the gaming application requires a large amount of traffic, the company's VoIP and SNA traffic are not passed.

Creating the workaround for this is easy. You can use Cisco IOS to change to 0 any precedence bits arriving from non-approved hosts, while leaving all other traffic intact.
This is discussed further in the "Policy Routing" section later in this chapter.

Resetting IP Precedence through Policy Routing

To configure the router to reset the IP Precedence bits (which is a good idea on the edge of a network), you must follow several steps. The configuration in Example 8-4 creates **access-list 105** to reset all IP Precedence bits for traffic received from the Ethernet. Only traffic received on the Ethernet interface is sent through the route map. Traffic forwarded out of the Ethernet interface does not proceed through the route map.

Example 8-4 *Using an Access List to Reset IP Precedence Bits*

```
!
interface Ethernet0/0
 ip address 192.168.15.18 255.255.255.0
 ip policy route-map reset-precedence
!
!
access-list 105 permit ip any any
route-map reset-precedence permit 10
  match ip address 105
  set ip precedence routine
```

Policy Routing

With policy-based routing, you can configure a defined policy for traffic flows and not have to rely completely on routing protocols to determine traffic forwarding and routing. Policy routing also enables you to set the IP Precedence field so that the network can utilize different classes of service.

You can base policies on IP addresses, port numbers, protocols, or the size of packets. You can use one of these descriptors to create a simple policy, or you can use all of them to create a complicated policy.

All packets received on an interface with policy-based routing enabled are passed through enhanced packet filters known as *route maps*. The route maps dictate where the packets are forwarded.

You also can mark **route-map** statements as **permit** or **deny**. If the statement is marked **deny**, the packets meeting the match criteria are sent back through the usual forwarding channels (in other words, destination-based routing is performed). Only if the statement is marked **permit** and the packets meet the match criteria are all the set clauses applied.

If the statement is marked **permit** and the packets do not meet the match criteria, those packets also are forwarded through the usual routing channel.

NOTE   Policy routing is specified on the interface that receives the packets, not on the interface that sends the packets.

You can use the IP standard or extended access control lists (ACLs) to establish match criteria, the standard IP access lists to specify the match criteria for source address, and extended access lists to specify the match criteria based upon application, protocol type, ToS, and precedence.

The match clause feature was extended to include matching packet length between specified minimum and maximum values. The network administrator can then use the match length as the criterion that distinguishes between interactive and bulk traffic (bulk traffic usually has larger packet sizes).

The policy routing process proceeds through the route map until a match is found. If no match is found in the route map, or if the route map entry is marked with a **deny** instead of a **permit** statement, normal destination-based routing of the traffic ensues.

NOTE As always, an implicit **deny** statement is at the end of the list of **match** statements.

You must be careful when choosing the type of policies you route, as you can configure certain policies to force Cisco IOS routers to use the process-switching path (a slower method of forwarding packets). If you are careful, you can avoid this. Also, by default, traffic originating from the router is not sent through the policy route. With a special command, you can send internal traffic (routing updates, VoIP, and so on) through the policy route.

RSVP

RSVP enables endpoints to signal the network with the kind of QoS needed for a particular application. This is a great departure from the network blindly assuming what QoS applications require.

Network administrators can use RSVP as *dynamic access lists*. This means that network administrators need not concern themselves with port numbers of IP packet flows because RSVP signals that information during its original request.

RSVP is an out-of-band, end-to-end signaling protocol that requests a certain amount of bandwidth and latency with each network hop that supports RSVP. If a network node (router) does not support RSVP, RSVP moves onto the next hop. A network node has the option to approve or deny the reservation based upon the load of the interface to which the service is requested.

RSVP works much like an ambulance clearing traffic in front of you. You simply follow behind the ambulance. RSVP, or the ambulance driver, tells each stop (tollbooth, policeman, and so on) that the driver behind him in the 1972 yellow AMC Gremlin is important and needs special privileges. Each stop has the right to decide whether the driver in the 1972 yellow AMC Gremlin is important enough to have these special privileges (for instance, not paying tolls, running traffic lights, or, in the case of IP, having bandwidth and latency bounds).

> **NOTE**   In Cisco IOS, each interface for which you want to enable RSVP must be explicitly configured with RSVP. Also, the network administrator must configure the amount of bandwidth allocated to RSVP on that interface.

Applications receive feedback on whether their request for QoS was approved or denied. Some applications transmit their data to anyone, with no QoS concerns; however, some intelligent applications choose not to transmit, or they choose another route. In the case of VoIP, that route could be the Public Switched Telephone Network (PSTN).

It is interesting to note that the requester of the service levels in RSVP is the receiving station and not the transmitting station. This enables RSVP to scale when IP multicast technology is used. (With IP multicast technology, one transmitter sends to multiple receivers.)

RSVP is not a routing protocol and does not currently modify the IP routing table based upon traffic flows or congestion. RSVP simply traverses IP and enables IP routing protocols to choose the most optimal path. This optimal path might not be the most ideal QoS-enabled path. RSVP cannot adjust the routers to modify that behavior, however.

RSVP Syntax

The syntax of RSVP follows:

```
ip rsvp bandwidth
```

To enable RSVP for IP on an interface, use the **ip rsvp bandwidth** interface configuration command. To disable RSVP, use the "no" form of the command:

```
ip rsvp bandwidth [interface-kbps] [single-flow-kbps]
no ip rsvp bandwidth [interface-kbps] [single-flow-kbps]
```

The command options are defined as follows:

- *interface-kbps*—(Optional) Amount of bandwidth (in kbps) on interface to be reserved; the range is 1 to 10,000,000.

- *single-flow-kbps*—(Optional) Amount of bandwidth (in kbps) allocated to a single flow; the range is 1 to 10,000,000.

- *Default*—75 percent of bandwidth available on interface if no bandwidth (in kbps) is specified.

To display RSVP reservations currently in place, use the **show ip rsvp reservation** command:

```
show ip rsvp reservation [type number]
```

The *type number* is optional; it indicates interface type and number.

RSVP Caveats

Although RSVP is an important tool in the QoS arsenal, this protocol does not solve all the necessary problems related to QoS. RSVP has three drawbacks: scalability, admission control, and the time it takes to set up end-to-end reservation.

RSVP has many caveats that keep it from being deployed universally on the Internet. In a worst-case scenario for networks utilizing RSVP, a backbone router must manage several thousand RSVP reservations and queue each flow according to that reservation.

The scalability issues that surround RSVP relegate RSVP toward the edges of the network and force use of other QoS tools for the backbone of the network. In the long term, the Internet Engineering Task Force (IETF) is working on ways to better utilize RSVP and increase the scalability factor.

RSVP works on the total size of the IP packet and does not account for any compression schemes, cyclic redundancy checks (CRCs), or line encapsulation (Frame Relay, PPP, or High-Level Data Link Control [HDLC]).

When using RSVP and G.729 for VoIP, for example, the reservation Cisco IOS software request is 24 kbps, compared to the actual value of ~11 kbps when using cRTP. In other words, on a 56 kbps link, only two 24-kbps reservations are permitted, even though enough bandwidth is available for four 11-kbps VoIP flows.

You can work around this situation by oversubscribing the available bandwidth of the link to enable RSVP to reserve more bandwidth than is actually available. You can use the *bandwidth* statement on a particular interface to make this reservation. This workaround is permitted as long as the network is properly engineered and you can control network flows.

On a 56-kbps link, for example, the bandwidth statement tells the interface that 100 kbps of *bandwidth* actually exists. You can then use RSVP to enable 75 percent of the available bandwidth to be used for RSVP traffic. This scenario enables RSVP to reserve the necessary bandwidth for three VoIP G.729 calls. The inherent danger is evident because if cRTP is not used, the link is oversubscribed.

Traffic Policing

The previous sections covered ways you can queue different flows of traffic and then prioritize those flows. That is an important part of QoS. Sometimes, however, it is necessary to actually regulate or limit the amount of traffic an application is allowed to send across various interfaces or networks.

Cisco has a few tools that enable network administrators to define how much bandwidth an application or even a user can use. These features come in two different flavors: *rate-limiting tools* such as CAR, and *shaping tools* such as GTS or FRTS.

The main difference between these two traffic-regulation tools is that rate-limiting tools drop traffic based upon policing, and shaping tools generally buffer the excess traffic while waiting for the next open interval to transmit the data.

CAR and traffic shaping tools are similar in that they both identify when traffic exceeds the thresholds set by the network administrator.

Often, these two tools are used together. Traffic shaping is used at the edge of the network (customer premises) to make sure the customer is utilizing the bandwidth for business needs.

CAR is often used in service provider networks to ensure that a subscriber does not exceed the amount of bandwidth set by contract with the service provider.

CAR

CAR is a policing mechanism that enables network administrators to set exceed or conform actions. Often you use a conform action to transmit the traffic and an exceed action to drop the packet or to mark it with a lower IP Precedence value.

CAR's rate-limiting mechanism enables a user to

- Control the maximum rate of traffic transmitted or received on an interface

- Give granular control at Layer 3, which enables an IP network to exhibit qualities of a TDM network

You can rate-limit traffic by precedence, Media Access Control (MAC) address, IP addresses, or other parameters. Network administrators also can configure access lists to create even more granular rate-limiting policies.

It is important to note that CAR does not buffer any traffic to smooth out traffic bursts. Therefore, CAR is ideal for high-speed environments, as queuing adds no delay.

To configure CAR and Distributed CAR (DCAR) on Cisco 7000 series routers with RSP7000 or on Cisco 7500 series routers with a VIP2-40 or greater interface processor for all IP traffic, use the following commands, beginning in global configuration mode:

```
rate-limit {input | output} bps burst-normal
burst-max conform-action action exceed-action action
```

The network administrator can specify a basic CAR policy for all IP traffic. See Table 8-3 for a description of conform and exceed action keywords.

For basic CAR and DCAR to be functional, you must define the following criteria:

- Packet direction, incoming or outgoing.

- An average rate, determined by a long-term average of the transmission rate. Traffic that falls under this rate always conforms.

- A normal burst size, which determines how large traffic bursts can be before some traffic is considered to exceed the rate limit.

- An excess burst size.

Traffic that falls between the normal burst size and the excess burst size exceeds the rate limit with a probability that increases as the burst size increases. CAR propagates bursts.
It does not smooth or shape traffic.

Table 8-3 describes the conform and exceed actions.

Table 8-3   **rate-limit** *Command Action Keywords*

Keyword	Description
continue	Evaluates the next **rate-limit** command.
drop	Drops the packet.
set-prec-continue new-prec	Sets the IP Precedence and evaluates the next **rate-limit** command.
set-prec-transmit new-prec	Sets the IP Precedence and transmits the packet.
transmit	Transmits the packet.

You can use CAR and Versatile Interface Processor Distributed CAR (VIP-DCAR) only with IP traffic. Non-IP traffic is not rate-limited.

You can configure CAR or VIP—DCAR on an interface or subinterface. CAR and VIP-DCAR are not supported on the following interfaces, however:

■   Fast EtherChannel

■   Tunnel

■   Primary Rate Interface (PRI)

■   Any interface that does not support Cisco express forwarding (CEF)

Traffic Shaping

Cisco IOS QoS software includes two types of traffic shaping: GTS and FRTS. Both traffic-shaping methods are similar in implementation, although their command-line interfaces differ somewhat and they use different types of queues to contain and shape traffic that is deferred.

If a packet is deferred, GTS uses a WFQ to hold the delayed traffic. FRTS uses either a CQ or a PQ to hold the delayed traffic, depending on what you configured. As of April 1999, FRTS also supports WFQ to hold delayed traffic.

Traffic shaping enables you to control the traffic going out of an interface to match its flow to the speed of the remote, target interface and to ensure that the traffic conforms to policies contracted for it. Thus, you can shape traffic adhering to a particular profile to meet downstream requirements, thereby eliminating bottlenecks in topologies with data-rate mismatches.

You use traffic shaping primarily to

■   Control usage of available bandwidth

■   Establish traffic policies

■   Regulate traffic flow to avoid congestion

You can use traffic shaping in the following situations:

■   You can configure traffic shaping on an interface if you have a network with different access rates. Suppose one end of the link in a Frame Relay network runs at 256 kbps and the other end runs at 128 kbps. Sending packets at 256 kbps could cause the applications using the link to fail.

■   You can configure traffic shaping if you offer a subrate service. In this case, traffic shaping enables you to use the router to partition your T1 or T3 links into smaller channels.

Traffic shaping prevents packet loss. It is especially important to use traffic shaping in Frame Relay networks because the switch cannot determine which packets take precedence and, therefore, which packets should be dropped when congestion occurs.

Moreover, it is of critical importance for VoIP that you control latency. By limiting the amount of traffic and traffic loss in the network, you can smooth out traffic patterns and give priority to real-time traffic.

Differences Between GTS and FRTS

As mentioned, both GTS and FRTS are similar in implementation in that they share the same code and data structures, but they differ in regard to their command-line interfaces and the queue types they use.

Here are two ways in which GTS and FRTS differ:

- FRTS CLI supports shaping based on each data-link connection identifier (DLCI). GTS is configurable per interface or subinterface.

- GTS supports a WFQ shaping queue.

You can configure GTS to behave the same way as FRTS by allocating one DLCI per subinterface and using GTS plus BECN support. The two behave the same, except for the different shaping queues they use.

In versions of software previous to Cisco IOS Software Release 12.04(T), FRTS and WFQ were not compatible. This limitation was removed, and now both FRTS and GTS work with WFQ. This enables network administrators to choose a more granular QoS mechanism (FRTS and WFQ per DLCI).

Traffic Shaping and Queuing

Traffic shaping smoothes traffic by storing traffic above the configured rate in a queue. When a packet arrives at the interface for transmission, the following happens:

- If the queue is empty, the traffic shaper processes the arriving packet.

    If possible, the traffic shaper sends the packet.

    Otherwise, it places the packet in the queue.

- If packets are in the queue, the traffic shaper sends another new packet in the queue.

When packets are in the queue, the traffic shaper removes the number of packets it can transmit from the queue every time interval.

GTS

GTS applies on a per-interface basis and can use access lists to select the traffic to shape. It works with a variety of Layer 2 technologies, including Frame Relay, ATM, Switched Multimegabit Data Service (SMDS), and Ethernet.

On a Frame Relay subinterface, you can set up GTS to adapt dynamically to available bandwidth by integrating BECN signals, or to simply shape to a pre-specified rate. You also can configure GTS on an ATM interface to respond to RSVPs signaled over statically configured ATM permanent virtual circuits (PVCs).

Most media and encapsulation types on the router support GTS. You also can apply GTS to a specific access list on an interface. Figure 8-4 shows how GTS works.

Figure 8-4 *GTS in Action*

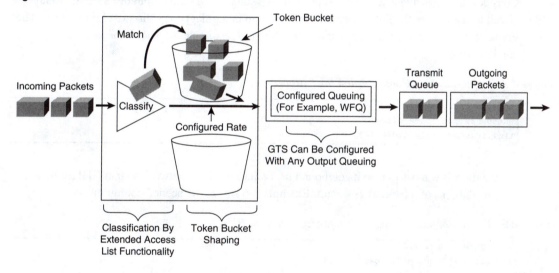

To enable traffic shaping for outbound traffic on an interface, use the **traffic-shape rate** interface configuration command. Use the "no" form of this command to disable traffic shaping on the interface.

```
traffic-shape rate bit-rate [burst-size [excess-burst-size]]
no traffic-shape rate
```

The syntax description follows:

■ *bit-rate*—Bit rate that traffic is shaped to, in bits per second (bps). This is the access bit rate you contract with your service provider, or the service level you intend to maintain.

- *burst-size*—(Optional) Sustained number of bits you can transmit per interval. On Frame Relay interfaces, this is the committed burst size contracted with your service provider; the default is the bit rate divided by 8.

- *excess-burst-size*—(Optional) Maximum number of bits that can exceed the burst size in the first interval in a congestion event. On Frame Relay interfaces, this is the excess burst size contracted with your service provider; the default is equal to the burst size traffic shape group.

To enable traffic shaping based on a specific access list for outbound traffic on an interface, use the **traffic-shape group** interface configuration command. Use the **no** form of this command to disable traffic shaping on the interface for the access list:

```
traffic-shape group access-list bit-rate [burst-size [excess-burst-size]]
no traffic-shape group access-list
```

Consider the following examples. Corporation A wants to limit the output of its Frame Relay circuit to the CIR of the link to prevent packets from being flagged as discard eligible (DE). The Frame Relay circuit is 56 kbps and the CIR is 32 kbps. Example 8-5 shows the needed configuration.

Example 8-5 *Traffic-Shaping Configuration for Corporation A*

```
interface serial 0/0
encapsulation frame-relay
traffic-shape rate 32000 4000 0
```

Corporation B wants to shape its outbound traffic into its WAN network so that FTP traffic uses only 64,000 bps of its 256-kbps circuit. Example 8-6 shows the needed configuration.

Example 8-6 *Traffic-Shaping Configuration for Corporation B*

```
interface serial 0/0
traffic-shape group 101 64000 8000 0
!
access-list 101 permit tcp any eq ftp any
```

FRTS

Like GTS, FRTS smoothes out traffic spikes by buffering excess traffic. FRTS also can eliminate problems caused by different access rates at the ingress and egress of a Frame Relay network. A central-site Frame Relay network, for instance, often has a high-speed (T1 or greater) connection to the network, and a remote site usually has a connection to the frame network less than 384 kbps.

The central-site router can transmit to the remote router at T1 speeds, but the remote router can receive traffic only at 384 kbps or less. This forces the Frame Relay network to buffer the traffic and can add *seconds* to a packet stream. This renders voice unacceptable in almost any network.

FRTS enables the use of FECN and BECN to dynamically transmit more or less bandwidth.

In Frame Relay networks, BECNs and FECNs indicate congestion. You specify BECN and FECN by bits within a Frame Relay frame.

Using information contained in the BECN-tagged packets received from the network, FRTS also can dynamically throttle traffic. With BECN-based throttling, packets are held in the router's buffers to reduce the data flow from the router into the Frame Relay network.

The throttling is done on each virtual circuit (VC) and the transmission rate is adjusted based on the number of BECN-tagged packets received.

Fragmentation

Both propagation and queuing delay are discussed in previous chapters. The reasoning behind the need for fragmentation is simple. Large packets (1500-byte MTUs) take a long time to move across low-bandwidth links (768 kbps and less). Fragmentation breaks larger packets into smaller packets. You can accomplish this at either Layer 2 or Layer 3 of the Open Systems Interconnection (OSI) reference model.

In many data applications, latency caused by low-bandwidth links does not matter to the end user. In real-time applications, however, this can cause many problems (choppy voice quality, missed frames, dropped calls, and so on).

A 1500-byte packet moving across a 56-kbps circuit, for example, takes 214 ms to traverse the circuit. The ITU-T recommendation for uni-directional maximum voice latency is less than 150 ms. Therefore, *one* 56-kbps circuit and *one* 1500-byte packet consume the entire VoIP delay budget. For example:

> Packet size in bytes/sec × 8 = Packet size in bits/sec
> Packet size in bits/sec / Circuit size in bits/sec
> = Time required to transmit packet
> 1500 bytes/sec × 8 = 12000 bits/sec
> 12000 bits/sec / 56000 bits/sec = .214 sec = 214 msec

Fragmentation in itself is not enough to remove the latency problem on low-bandwidth circuits. The router must also be able to queue based upon fragments or smaller packets instead of by the original (prefragmented) packet.

The Cisco Systems VoIP implementation enables users to modify the number of samples per packet. By default with G.729, two 10-ms speech samples are put into one frame. This gives you a packet every 20 ms. This means you need to be able to transmit a VoIP packet out of the router every 20 ms.

This 20-ms distance between each frame can change based upon the number of speech samples you decide to put in each frame. Also, this number is important because it enables you to determine the size of fragmentation needed.

As shown in Figure 8-5, you can determine your fragment size depending on the speed of the link and the samples per frame.

Figure 8-5 *Fixed-Frame Propagation Delay*

Link Speed \ Frame Size	1 Byte	64 Byte	128 Byte	256 Byte	512 Byte	1024 Byte	1500 Byte
56 kbps	143 µs	9 ms	18 ms	36 ms	72 ms	144 ms	214 ms
64 kbps	125 µs	8 ms	16 ms	32 ms	64 ms	128 ms	187 ms
128 kbps	62.5 µs	4 ms	8 ms	16 ms	32 ms	64 ms	93 ms
256 kbps	31 µs	2 ms	4 ms	8 ms	16 ms	32 ms	46 ms
512 kbps	15.5 µs	1 ms	2 ms	4 ms	8 ms	16 ms	23 ms
768 kbps	10 µs	640 µs	1.28 ms	2.56 ms	5.12 ms	10.24 ms	15 ms
1536 kbps	5 µs	320 µs	640 µs	1.28 ms	2.56 ms	5.12 ms	7.5 ms

Blocking

Fragmentation helps to eliminate "blocking" issues. *Blocking* is the amount of time you allow another packet to consume available WAN bandwidth and force other real-time packets to be queued. Blocking directly affects your delay budget. You can use different rules of thumb, but generally, you want to keep the blocking delay at 80 percent of your total voice packet size.

If you have two 10-ms speech samples in one 20-ms packet, for example, you want a maximum blocking delay of approximately 16 ms. Assuming your WAN link is 56 kbps and using Figure 8-5 as an example, you want your packets to be fragmented to about 128 bytes. If you want an exact figure, the algorithm to use to determine your packet fragmentation size is as follows:

WAN bandwidth × blocking delay = fragment size in bits

Utilizing this algorithm to compute the exact delay based on the preceding recommendations:

WAN bandwidth (56 kbps) × blocking delay (16 ms) = 896 bits per second
(112 bytes per second)

MCML PPP

Multi-Class Multilink Point-to-Point Protocol (MCML PPP) allows for the creation of two "bundles." One bundle can be fragmented and interleaved while the second bundle can simply be interleaved, as illustrated in Figure 8-6. This functionality is available starting in Cisco IOS Software Release 12.2(13)T and offers many advantages to using ML PPP.

Figure 8-6   *Multi-Class, Multilink PPP*

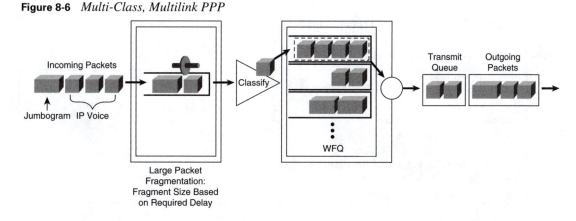

You can use MCML only on interfaces that can run PPP, which immediately rules out a large portion of WAN networks (Frame Relay, ATM, and so on).

MCML specifies only the fragmentation method; it does not specify the queuing technique needed to prioritize the fragments.

FRF.12

FRF.12 is a specification by the Frame Relay Forum Technical Committee, and you can find it at http://www.frforum.com. This specification enables Frame Relay networks to operate in a manner similar to MCML PPP. Because this fragmentation also happens at the link layer, the upper-layer protocols are not aware of the fragmentation.

As with MCML PPP, packets are fragmented at entry to the WAN network and reassembled when the destination router receives them.

FRF.12 also specifies the interworkings between Frame Relay and ATM. This enables packets fragmented by FRF.12 on the Frame Relay side of the circuit to be reassembled on the ATM side of the circuit.

IP MTU and MTU

On WAN interfaces that do not support MCML PPP or FRF.12, you can set the interface or protocol MTU to a lower value, which then forces fragmentation.

The MTU on a serial interface is usually 1500 bytes. With FRF.12 and MCML PPP, you can change the actual packet size sent on the interface without disturbing the actual packet flow. When you lower the MTU or IP MTU size, the packet changes for the duration of that packet's trip.

Example 8-7 shows the IP MTU configuration.

Example 8-7 *Configuring IP MTU*

```
interface Serial0/0
 ip mtu 300
 no ip address
 encapsulation frame-relay
 fair-queue 64 256 1000
!
interface Serial0/0.1 point-to-point
 ip mtu 300
 ip address 40.0.0.7 255.0.0.0
```

Example 8-8 shows the MTU configuration.

Example 8-8 *Configuring MTU*

```
interface Serial0/0
  mtu 300
  no ip address
  ip rsvp bandwidth 1158 1158
  encapsulation frame-relay
fair-queue 64 256 1000
!
interface Serial0/0.1 point-to-point
  mtu 300
  ip address 40.0.0.7 255.0.0.0
```

IP MTU Caveats

Changing the size of the IP packet for its entire life can cause many problems. The receiving station's overall performance is affected, for instance, because it handles many smaller packets more slowly than one big packet. Also, the header of the packet needs to be duplicated for *each* fragment.

Consider one 1500-byte packet that includes a 40-byte header. If you fragment the 1460-byte payload into 100-byte frames, you get 14 packets with 100 bytes and one packet with 60 bytes. You now need to put a 40-byte header back onto each of the 15 packets. In doing so, you increase the header size from 40 bytes to 600 bytes.

Another major problem with IP MTU and MTU sizing is that if the Do Not Fragment (DNF) bit is set on a packet, that packet is discarded. Many applications set this bit to prevent intermediary devices (routers and other network elements) from breaking their packet into many pieces. One reason the DNF bit might be set is to keep the receiving station from being burdened by having to put the fragments back into the proper order.

MTU Caveats

MTU sizing changes the size of *all* packets exiting that interface, including IP, Internetwork Packet eXchange (IPX), AppleTalk, and routing updates. This can be a problem for routing updates, Frame Relay Local Management Interface (LMI) updates, and other protocols that don't support fragmentation.

Edge QoS Wrap-Up

At this point, you should understand the basics of packet classification, fragmentation, queuing, bandwidth, and policing mechanisms. It is important to note that you can use some or many of these mechanisms concurrently in a given environment.

As a rule of thumb, with low bandwidth links you should always use packet classification and queuing mechanisms. Based upon bandwidth constraints and administrative policies, you might need to use compression and fragmentation methods as well.

Backbone Networks

The backbone of the network is completely different than the edge of the network, and you should not treat it with the same QoS mechanisms. Although the classification mechanisms for both might be the same or similar, the queuing, fragmentation, and bandwidth mechanisms are usually either not used or different.

High-Speed Transport

You can define high-speed transport as any interface higher than T1 speed. Although most people refer to digital signal level 3 (DS-3) interfaces and above as high-speed networks, just as with microprocessors what is considered high speed today will be outdated in the future.

It is necessary to focus on different QoS mechanisms with high-speed transports. It is usually not feasible to apply all the same rules and policies on a high-speed interface as you would on a lower-speed interface. This is mainly because the more policies and QoS mechanisms you apply, the longer the router must take to forward a packet. Although this is usually okay on lower-speed interfaces, higher-speed interfaces cannot spend as much time identifying and queuing each packet.

As customers move to higher-speed interfaces (such as OC-48), however, it is important to provide them with options so that they can determine how to properly enable QoS on their networks.

Modified Deficit Round Robin

Cisco 12000 Gigabit Switch Routers (GSRs) are currently the only Cisco IP Routing products that have an IP OC-48 interface. Modified Deficit Round Robin (MDRR) extends Deficit Round Robin (DRR) to provide priority for real-time traffic such as VoIP. Within MDRR, IP packets are mapped to different CoS queues based on precedence bits.

All the queues are serviced in round-robin fashion except for one: the priority queue used to handle voice traffic.

DRR provides queuing similar to WFQ but for higher-speed interfaces from OC-3 to OC-48. MDRR extends the DRR protocol to include a high-priority queue that is treated differently from the other queues associated with service classes.

For each set of CoS queues supported, MDRR includes a low-latency, high-priority (LLHP) queue for VoIP or other real-time traffic. Except for the LLHP queue, MDRR services all queues in round-robin fashion.

This enables service providers or others with a need for high-speed queuing to ensure that VoIP is prioritized above all other traffic.

Congestion Avoidance

As discussed previously, WFQ, PQ, and CQ mechanisms manage existing congestion and prioritize the traffic that is of highest importance.

Congestion avoidance works on a similar problem from a completely different angle. Instead of managing the existing congestion, congestion avoidance works to avoid congestion to begin with. In simplistic terms, you avoid congestion by dropping packets from different flows, which causes applications to slow the amount of traffic being sent. This avoids what is known as *global synchronization*, which occurs when many IP TCP flows begin transmitting and stop transmitting at the same time. This is caused by the lack of QoS in a service provider's backbone.

WRED

Random Early Detection (RED) is a congestion avoidance mechanism (as opposed to a congestion management mechanism) that is potentially useful, especially in high-speed transit networks. Sally Floyd and Van Jacobson proposed it in various papers in the early 1990s.

The theory behind WRED, simply, is that most data transports are somehow sensitive to loss and at least momentarily slow down if some of their traffic gets dropped.

To signal a TCP station to stop transmitting, you simply drop some of the sending station's traffic. WRED is Cisco's implementation of dropping traffic to avoid global synchronization.

WRED combines the capabilities of the RED algorithm with IP Precedence. This combination provides for preferential traffic handling for higher-priority packets. It can selectively discard lower-priority traffic when the interface starts to get congested and provide differentiated performance characteristics for different classes of service.

WRED also is RSVP aware, and it can provide an IS controlled-load QoS service. To fully comprehend how WRED works, you must understand TCP packet loss behavior.

TCP

A stream of data sent on a TCP connection is delivered reliably and in order to the destination. Transmission is made reliable through the use of sequence numbers and acknowledgments. Conceptually, each octet of data is assigned a sequence number. The sequence number of the first octet of data in a segment is the sequence number transmitted with that segment and is called the *segment sequence number.*

Segments also carry an acknowledgment number, which is the sequence number of the next expected data octet of transmissions in the reverse direction. When the TCP transmits a segment, it puts a copy on a retransmission queue and starts a timer; when the acknowledgment for that data is received, the segment is deleted from the queue. If the acknowledgment is not received before the timer runs out, the segment is retransmitted.

An acknowledgment by TCP does not guarantee that the data was delivered to the end user, only that the receiving TCP took the responsibility to do so.

To govern the flow of data into a TCP, you employ a flow control mechanism. The data-receiving TCP reports a window to the sending TCP. This window specifies the number of octets, starting with the acknowledgment number that the data-receiving TCP is currently prepared to receive.

When a user sends a TCP packet and a dropped segment is detected, the user's machine sends the first segment on its awaiting-acknowledge list (to restart the flow of data) and enters a slow-start phase. The user's machine tests the network to find a rate at which it can send without dropping data.

In a network that does not utilize RED, the buffers fill up and packets are tail-dropped. A tail-drop occurs when the router cannot receive packets because its queues are full.

This causes multiple TCP sessions to restart their slow-start mechanism. This scenario eventually causes the network traffic to come in surges as TCP window sizes increase.

The router can use RED to manage the TCP slow-start mechanism to throttle back an individual TCP flow, measure the effect, and then drop packets from more TCP flows, if necessary.

> **NOTE**   To enable WRED, use the following command:
>
> ```
> random-detect [weighting]
> ```
>
> The *weighting* option is optional. Exponential weighting constant in the range 1 to 16 used to determine the rate packets are dropped when congestion occurs; the default is 9.

WRED is useful in high-speed TCP/IP networks to avoid congestion by dropping packets at a controlled rate.

Backbone QoS Wrap-Up

It is important to note that both edge QoS and backbone QoS must work together to achieve the proper QoS for the various applications which might be traversing a network.

As a rule of thumb, it is wise to use high-speed congestion avoidance techniques in the backbone as well as some form of high-speed transmission. You can achieve IP QoS using several different mechanisms. The actual transport mechanism you choose is not as important as verifying that all the tools you need are present to service your applications.

Rules of Thumb for QoS

Before implementing QoS on the edge of a network, ask the following questions:

1. Do you have a low-bandwidth WAN circuit?

   If yes, use cRTP.

   Also, choose a fragmentation method. (FRF.12 is recommended first for Frame Relay networks. MCML PPP is recommended first for all other networks. MTU and IP MTU sizing are *not* recommended.)

2. Does your traffic need to be prioritized on your WAN circuits?

   If yes, use some form of queuing. (CB-WFQ and PQ are recommended.)

3. Have you chosen CB-WFQ?

    If yes, select a method of classifying your traffic flows. IP Precedence is recommended for weighting (usually backbone networks).

4. Do you have a hub-and-spoke Frame Relay network or another need for shaping your traffic flows?

    If yes, select traffic shaping. (GTS is recommended first, followed by FRTS.)

Before implementing QoS on the backbone of a network, ask the following questions:

1. Have you chosen your high-speed networking technology?

2. Have you ensured that the edge QoS is compatible with the backbone QoS or CoS? (IP Precedence is recommended first.)

3. Have you utilized a congestion avoidance mechanism on highly utilized high-speed circuits? These circuits must have a high percentage of loss-tolerable protocols (such as TCP and WRED).

Cisco Labs' QoS Testing

Cisco conducted the following tests to show not only VoIP quality, but also how Cisco QoS tools work under load.

For the testbed, Cisco used a simple network with two Cisco VoIP gateways and one 56-kbps WAN. It completed two tests:

■   Test A consisted of testing with and without QoS enabled while steadily increasing the saturation of the WAN link.

■   Test B consisted of testing with and without QoS enabled while sending traffic across the WAN link in a bursty nature.

When no QoS was used, FIFO queuing was implemented. When QoS was used, MCML PPP, WFQ, and IP Precedence were utilized.

Cisco sent the traffic through two in-house traffic generation tools. It measured latency and voice quality using a voice-quality test tool that utilizes the ITU-T Perceptual Speech Quality (PSQM) recommendation P.861.

When measuring PSQM, the higher the score the worse the voice quality. Table 8-4 shows the results from Test A.

Table 8-4 *Results for Test A*

Bandwidth Saturation (Percent)	Delay (ms)	PSQM	Delay/QoS (ms)	PSQM/ QoS
0	76	1.43	76	1.43
40	233	1.94	106	1.5
60	242	2.1	104	1.43
75	280	7	102	1.51
90	300	9	104	1.51
100	350	10	105	1.51

To better understand the difference QoS can make, see Figure 8-7.

Figure 8-7 *Graph of Test A Results*

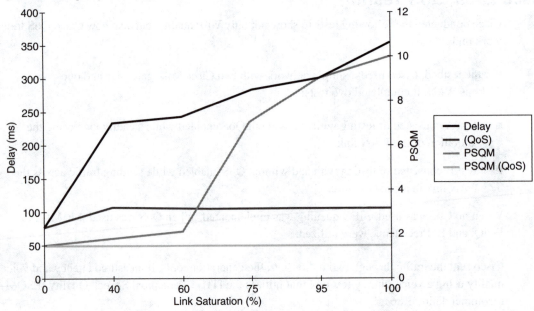

Results for Test B are just as dramatic and appear in Figure 8-8. Cisco IOS Software QoS tools, when implemented properly, can definitely affect the caliber and stability of voice quality.

Figure 8-8   *Graph of Test B Results*

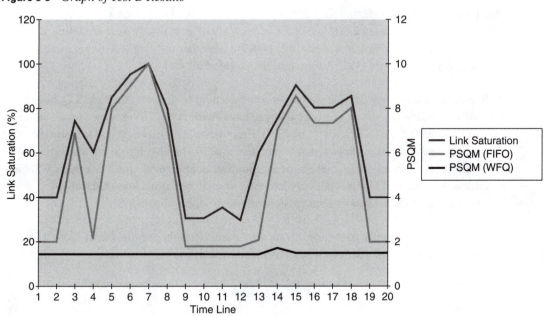

Summary

This chapter covered the broad topic of QoS. The concept of receiving a packet at the instant the sender wants it to be received is complex. Indeed, building a network to run VoIP is complex. Proper QoS is a critical step in ensuring good voice quality.

Cisco offers a variety of tools to enable network administrators to create the proper environment for VoIP. Although it is unlikely that you will use all these tools, it is important to understand how all of them can affect your network.

Cisco has years of experience with prioritizing delay-sensitive traffic over an IP network. This started in the early 1990s when Cisco began developing products to transmit SNA traffic onto IP networks. Even then, due to latency and packet loss concerns, few customers believed SNA could possibly run over an IP network. Today, however, a good portion of SNA traffic is transported over IP networks.

The same thing is happening with voice. As of the first release of this book in 2000 there were many skeptics who did not believe IP could give the proper QoS for such a real-time application. However, over the past six years and with the proper network design and the right tools, it has been proven possible.

This chapter also covered different queuing techniques, such as WFQ, CB-WFQ, LLQ, PQ, and CQ, to give readers an understanding of how these tools evolved over time. Currently it is highly recommended that you use LLQ if you plan to deploy a VoIP network. If you cannot upgrade your IP network to the latest version of code, it is better to use other queuing techniques, such as PQ and CQ, to give you better QoS performance than none at all.

With queuing comes prioritization. Although some queuing techniques, such as LLQ, have built-in prioritization, it is important to ensure that you have all the correct tools turned on. Even if you use LLQ, for instance, you should still enable IP Precedence in case a backbone network uses that tool to prioritize dropped packets. Other components such as bandwidth-saving techniques and backbone tools are part of the arsenal a network administrator has to provide the correct QoS. Each network is different and requires not only attention to detail but also a knowledgeable administrator who knows how to tune the network to provide optimal QoS.

QoS will continue to evolve over time, and in the future, IP might become the de-facto transport method. So, not only will your voice be transmitted over IP, but TDM circuits as well.

CHAPTER 9

Billing and Mediation Services

Billing and mediation services are important in voice over IP (VoIP). They are key factors in helping a service provider or an enterprise vendor understand financial aspects, such as Return on Investment (ROI), when migrating its time-division multiplexing (TDM)-based network to VoIP. The public switched telephone network (PSTN) world offers a simpler billing structure for calls made over the network because the originator and the destination points are static and tied to a physical location. It also expects voice traffic (usage based on minutes of call durations) and data traffic (usage based on a flat fee) to be billed in different ways. VoIP changes this paradigm and allows the endpoints to move. The voice and data traffic are all packets that are transported from one location to another over the network. This raises some issues and requires protocol definitions on whom to bill, where to bill, and what to bill.

Billing Basics

In VoIP, other than a basic call made between two endpoints, you need to consider many service categories where billing requirements differ. It is important to note that the tools for implementing these services can vary. The broad categories of services are as follows:

- Supplementary services:

    — Forking

    — Forwarding

    — Transferring

    — Redirecting

    — Holding

    — Find-me-follow-me

    — Simultaneous ringing

- Service categories:

    — Billed by duration (voice, fax, voice mail recording/playing)

    — Billed by data bytes (modem)

- Billed by page (fax)

- Billed by flat fee (for example, stock quotes)

■ Roaming

- Integration with billing and database services partners

■ Conference calling

- Planned

- Spontaneous

■ Multibox billing

- Conference server

- Voice-mail server

- Translations, SCP-based services

- Unified communications (UC)

- Integration of billing/UC partners

Authentication, Authorization, and Accounting (AAA)

AAA and RADIUS are two foundational blocks for billing services in the IP world. For VoIP, billing and mediation are services that a server requests. The clients are usually the entities that have call control information (for example, Media Gateway Control Protocol [MGCP] Call Agent, Session Initiation Protocol [SIP] Proxy server, and so on), whereas the server is where the processing of billing-related information takes place. Note that the client to the billing server might in turn be a server in the VoIP network for call control to its end users and VoIP clients. The three steps of AAA are as follows:

1. Authentication provides a vehicle to identify a client that requires access to some system and logically precedes authorization. Authentication is done through the exchange of logical keys or certificates between the client and the server.

2. Authorization follows authentication and sets the process of determining whether the client is allowed to perform or request certain tasks or operations. Therefore, authorization is at the heart of policy administration.

3. Accounting is the process of measuring resource consumption, allowing monitoring and reporting of events and usage for various purposes including billing, analysis, and ongoing policy management. VoIP offers innovative accounting models to evolve because of features like mobility, roaming, and inexpensive ways to carry voice traffic over data pipes.

RADIUS

Remote Authentication Dial-In User Service (RADIUS) is a data-communications protocol designed to provide security management and statistics collection in remote computing environments, especially for distributed networks like VoIP. For accounting, it is well understood that centrally stored data is more secure, easier to manage, and scales more smoothly than data scattered throughout the network on multiple devices.

RADIUS operates on the client/server model. A RADIUS *authentication server* provides security services and stores security data, whereas a RADIUS *accounting server* collects and stores statistical data. Typically, a single machine provides both functions; however, the two RADIUS servers can reside on separate machines. Network engineers can configure a RADIUS client to use RADIUS security services, RADIUS accounting services, or both.

A RADIUS client consists of a network access server (NAS), which gives one or more remote users access to network resources. A single RADIUS server can serve hundreds of RADIUS clients and thousands of end users. You can address fault tolerance and redundancy concerns by configuring a RADIUS client to use one or more alternative RADIUS servers.

RADIUS provides three network services, known as authentication, authorization, and accounting (AAA). These services perform the following functions:

- Identify remote users to ensure that they are valid users who can access the network (authentication)

- Define what each user can do by controlling access to network resources (authorization)

- Track the resources that each user consumes for the purpose of billing them for services (accounting)

The following are some other key features of RADIUS:

- Network security—Transactions between the client and RADIUS server are authenticated through the use of a shared secret, which is never sent over the network. In addition, any user passwords are sent encrypted between the client and RADIUS server to eliminate the possibility that someone who is snooping on an unsecured network can determine a user password.

- Protocol extensions—All transactions are composed of variable-length Attribute-Length-Value 3-tuples. You can add new attribute values easily without disturbing existing implementations of the protocol. This property of RADIUS enables vendors to create certain vendor-specific attributes (VSA) that enable network providers to pass valuable information in them.

■ Flexible authentication schemes—The RADIUS server can support a variety of methods to authenticate a user. When it is provided with the username and the original password given by the user, it can support PPP Password Authentication Protocol (PAP) or Challenge Handshake Authentication Protocol (CHAP), UNIX login, and other authentication mechanisms.

Vendor-Specific Attributes (VSA)

Several VoIP protocols are in use today. Each of these protocols has its own set of features and information fields about the session established between two VoIP endpoints. Service providers looking for billing data often have special requests on certain attributes that can be passed to them only if certain additions are being made to the RADIUS accounting requests that are fed to the RADIUS servers. These new additions are mostly protocol specific (for example, H.323 or SIP may call for certain attributes).

Billing Formats

The telephony call control switch collects call detail records (CDR) during the course of the month, depending on how the billing cycle is defined. These CDRs are essentially the standards for every provider to offer billing-related information. If multiple providers are involved in a network, these also serve as tools to reconcile the charges.

Historically, the telephony billing systems were created at a time when most of the telephony industry players had essentially no competition. Now, IP telephony has made the industry unregulated by the FCC and extremely competitive. It has become more critical that the customer management and billing systems used to support IP telephony services can track and manage activities in real time.

VoIP calls are typically billed like PSTN dialed long distance, like cellular phones and prepaid cards with a pool of minutes, or like cable/satellite TV subscriptions as part of a multiservice subscription bundle. In all cases, voice call records are substantiated for billed charges, and all providers use CDRs to settle billing on interdomain calls. Call records are currently being created in several ways, as the sections that follow describe.

Typical Telco Approach

In this approach, the central office (CO) switch is responsible for the generation and exchange of billing records for PSTN-dialed calls. The CO switch produces Automatic Messaging Accounting (AMA) records, which include typical informational elements such as calling number, called number, connect time and date, call duration, and service characteristics. The AMA records are based on formats defined in Telcordia GR-1100-CORE document. They are then fed to a mediation/rating system that applies the tariff and rate basis for each call. The revenue assurance and pricing calculation are done at this step. Mostly, this is owned by the revenue accounting office for the telephony company. The next step is the final post-processing of the data after rate calculations and before being dispatched to the end-user billing system software or to the other carriers for exchange (third-party billing). Figure 9-1 illustrates the billing flow in the typical telco approach.

Figure 9-1 *Basic Billing Flow*

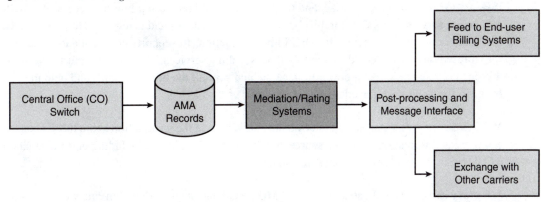

Although Telcordia is responsible for maintaining and updating the telco general requirements (GR) for mostly the U.S. markets, the incumbent telcos (IXCs) and their vendors work out their intercarrier billing and other operational issues in various committees of the Alliance for Telecommunications Industry Solutions (ATIS).

Open Settlements Protocol (OSP)-Based Approach

An alternative to the typical telco way of reconciliation of billing data is the use of Open Settlement Protocol (OSP). The European Telecommunications Standards Institute (ETSI), Telecommunications and Internet Protocol Harmonization Over Networks (TIPHON) develops OSP, which is described under the TS 101 321 specification. This method involves developing a *clearinghouse* provider to collect IP voice usage data. After a call is completed, OSP client software in both the originating and terminating gateways (or their controlling gatekeepers or SIP proxy servers) can report a tremendous variety of ETSI-specified usage data to the OSP server. This server, which is a third-party clearinghouse provider (such as ITXC, iBasis, and so on), typically controls, then exports, the OSP usage data or uses it to generate XML-based CDRs.

Originally developed to work with H.323 VoIP gateways, OSP is being enhanced to work with SIP. Besides facilitating billing settlements, the OSP specification defines the means to exchange interdomain pricing, routing, and authorization information. However, the OSP requires the clearinghouse to act as a trusted intermediary, and that implementation has been interoperability tested with many of those clearinghouses. Further, not all calls in the network can pass through the OSP server.

RADIUS-Based Approach

The Internet Engineering Task Force (IETF) has developed a RADIUS protocol that virtually all ISPs use to authenticate, authorize, and track the time used on dial-up Internet access. RADIUS accounting servers act as CDR archival-point VoIP softswitches and gateways. They can also be extended for vendor-proprietary RADIUS implementations to support additional data collection for VoIP, wireless, and prepaid (wireline/wireless) calling services. These servers must have ample disk memory and processing power to generate and save all the billing records and help in following an audit trail if needed.

VoIP gateways, softswitches, and intermediary servers have the information about the session and can provide information about the source and destination IP address, including port information, call duration, reason for disconnect, and so on.

SIP proxy servers, H.323 gatekeepers, and MGCP call agents in various VoIP networks pass the most common billing information.

IPDR-Based Approach

The Internet Protocol Detail Record (IPDR) Organization, an industry consortium, now offers a set of specifications for another usage record format—the Network Data Management-Usage specification Version 2.5 (NDM-U 2.5).

The intent behind these standards was to come up with a standard format for billing and mediation system vendors to use for VoIP CDRs. Although many IPDR participants have supported and endorsed the NDM-U, many vendors still have some proprietary modifications. IPDR members include vendors such as AceComm, ADC, Amdocs, Apogee, AP Engines, and Daleen Technologies.

The IPDR approach is more like packaging a traditional CDR in a more sophisticated way. It is based on XML and is readily extensible and convertible. IPDR formats enable a system to provide the billing-related information that other billing tools can transfer and process easily. Many systems prefer to use the IPDR format because it enables transforming data as needed by updating an XML schema.

Case Study: Cisco SIP Proxy Server and Billing

This case study is about a typical SIP-based VoIP network in which a Cisco SIP Proxy Server (SPS) sends to a RADIUS server Accounting-Request packets that correspond to the SIP transactions that the server processes. The Accounting-Request packets are Start and Stop records that contain a combination of standard RADIUS attributes and Cisco-defined VSAs.

Cisco SPS generates Accounting-Request packets for all branches of each INVITE and BYE transaction. This facilitates start and stop records being sent to a RADIUS server for all call attempts, including all branches of forked call-attempts, whether successful, unsuccessful, or canceled. All Accounting-Request packets for the same call contain the same Call ID, and the RADIUS server, or a billing server working with the RADIUS server, must be able to correlate Accounting-Request packets based on this Call ID. The high-level diagram in Figure 9-2 shows a SIP call from one SIP phone to another through Cisco SPS and the corresponding RADIUS Accounting-Request packet that Cisco SPS sends to the RADIUS server. In this example, the RADIUS server forms a CDR from the Accounting-Request packet and forwards the CDR to the billing server for correlation.

Figure 9-2 *Cisco SIP-Based VoIP Accounting Components*

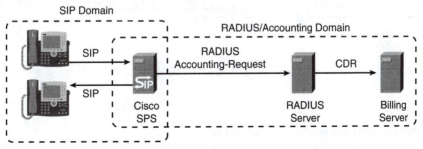

The configuration options in the Cisco SPS enable the customization of accounting triggers. To upstream entities, Cisco SPS appears as a server-side entity that handles requests. To downstream entities, Cisco SPS appears as a client-side entity that initiates requests. Configuration options enable accounting for call attempts on the server side or client side and for successful or unsuccessful call attempts.

The call flow in Figure 9-3 demonstrates the various accounting records that a call can generate.

Figure 9-3 *Typical SIP-based VoIP Accounting Call Flow*

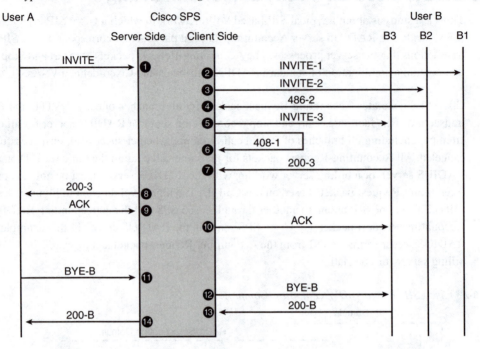

The following process describes the call-flow protocol outlined in Figure 9-3:

1. User A wants to call User B. User A sends an INVITE for User B to Cisco SPS.

2. User B has registered at both B1 and B2.

3. Cisco SPS sends the INVITE to both B1 and B2.

4. B2 is busy and returns 486. Cisco SPS sends client-side unsuccessful Stop.

5. User B has a Call Forward Busy contact set to B3, so Cisco SPS forwards INVITE to B3.

6. The INVITE to B1 times out. Cisco SPS generates an internal 408 and sends client-side unsuccessful Stop.

7. B3 answers the call and returns 200. Cisco SPS sends client-side Start.

8. Cisco SPS forwards 200 to User A and sends server-side Start.

9. User A sends an ACK.

10.   Cisco SPS forwards the ACK to User B.

11.   User A sends the BYE to Cisco SPS.

12.   Cisco SPS forwards the BYE to B3.

13.   Cisco SPS receives the 200 for the BYE from B3 and sends client-side successful Stop.

14.   Cisco SPS forwards the 200 for the BYE to User A and sends server-side successful Stop.

This completes the callflow steps in Cisco SPS client-side interface with the RADIUS server.

The RADIUS server accounting details are described next.

RADIUS Server Accounting

For a successful server-side call attempt, a Start record is sent when a 200 final response for the INVITE is returned upstream. A Stop record is sent when a final response is sent for the BYE.

RADIUS Interface for Cisco SPS

The Start record contains an **h323-start-time**, which is the time the INVITE was received, and an **h323-connect-time**, which is the time at which the 200 was sent. The **h323-call-origin** is set to answer, indicating that this is a server-side accounting record. The **sip-status-code** VSA is set to 200, which is the value of the final response for the INVITE. A text representation of the Start, complete with all standard RADIUS attributes and Cisco-defined VSAs, is as follows:

```
NAS-IP-Address = a.4.61.72
NAS-Port-Type = Virtual
User-Name = "1230"
Service-Type = Login-User
Acct-Status-Type = Start
Acct-Session-Id = "04fb5d3908f3bfbe24fabfbe24f9bfbe@a.4.61.70"
Called-Station-Id = "<sip:5670@a.4.61.72:5060>"
Calling-Station-Id = "<sip:1230@a.4.61.70:9090>"
Vendor-Specific-9-25 = "h323-setup-time=21:31:14.578 GMT Mon Apr 14 2003"
Vendor-Specific-9-28 = "h323-connect-time=21:31:24.692 GMT Mon Apr 14 2003"
Vendor-Specific-9-26 = "h323-call-origin=answer"
Vendor-Specific-9-27 = "h323-call-type=VoIP"
Vendor-Specific-9-1 = "sip-status-code=200"
Vendor-Specific-9-1 = "session-protocol=sip"
Vendor-Specific-9-1 = "call-id=04fb5d3908f3bfbe24fabfbe24f9bfbe@a.4.61.70"
Vendor-Specific-9-1 = "method=INVITE"
Vendor-Specific-9-1 = "prev-hop-via=SIP/2.0/UDP a.4.61.70:9090"
Vendor-Specific-9-1 = "prev-hop-ip=a.4.61.70:9090"
Vendor-Specific-9-1 = "incoming-req-uri=sip:5670@a.4.61.72:5060"
Vendor-Specific-9-1 = "outgoing-req-uri=sip:5670@a.4.106.19:5060"
Vendor-Specific-9-1 = "next-hop-ip=a.4.106.19:5060"
```

The Stop record contains an **h323-disconnect-time**, which is the time at which the BYE was received. The **h323-call-origin** is set to **answer**, indicating that this is a server-side accounting record. The **h323-disconnect-cause** is not used; instead, the **sip-status-code** VSA is added and set to the value of the final response for the BYE. For this reason, the Stop is not sent until the final response for the BYE has been sent. A text representation of the Stop, complete with all standard RADIUS attributes and Cisco-defined VSAs, is as follows:

```
NAS-IP-Address = a.4.61.72
NAS-Port-Type = Virtual
User-Name = "1230"
Service-Type = Login-User
Acct-Status-Type = Stop
Acct-Session-Id = "04fb5d3908f3bfbe24fabfbe24f9bfbe@a.4.61.70"
Called-Station-Id = "<sip:5670@a.4.61.72:5060>;tag=1F37F280-21AD"
Calling-Station-Id = "<sip:1230@a.4.61.70:9090>"
Vendor-Specific-9-29 = "h323-disconnect-time=21:31:44.770 GMT Mon Apr 14 2003"
Vendor-Specific-9-26 = "h323-call-origin=answer"
Vendor-Specific-9-27 = "h323-call-type=VoIP"
Vendor-Specific-9-1 = "sip-status-code=200"
Vendor-Specific-9-1 = "session-protocol=sip"
Vendor-Specific-9-1 = "call-id=04fb5d3908f3bfbe24fabfbe24f9bfbe@a.4.61.70"
Vendor-Specific-9-1 = "method=BYE"
Vendor-Specific-9-1 = "prev-hop-via=SIP/2.0/UDP a.4.61.70:9090"
Vendor-Specific-9-1 = "prev-hop-ip=a.4.61.70:9090"
Vendor-Specific-9-1 = "incoming-req-uri=sip:5670@a.4.61.72:5060"
Vendor-Specific-9-1 = "outgoing-req-uri=sip:5670@a.4.106.19:5060"
Vendor-Specific-9-1 = "next-hop-ip=a.4.106.19:5060"
```

An unsuccessful server-side call attempt has no Start record. A Stop record is sent when the best non-200 response for the INVITE is returned upstream, including the CANCEL scenario in which Cisco SPS waits for the 487 from the downstream and returns it upstream. The Stop record contains an **h323-start-time**, which is the time at which the INVITE message was received, and an **h323-disconnect-time**, which is the time at which the final response was sent. The **h323-call-origin** is set to **answer**, indicating that this is a server-side accounting record. The **sip-status-code** VSA is set to the value of the final response for the INVITE and is the most common attribute extension, as used in the networks.

Most of the Cisco VoIP network elements provide a RADIUS interface, acting as RADIUS clients for the support of the AAA functionality.

The AAA functionality corresponds to the authentication of the caller, the authorization of the call, and the accounting for the call. The authentication and authorization functions are used when subscriber billing is required or when the support of *whitelists* or *blacklists* is required. The accounting function is required for all types of billing—prepaid and postpaid billing and intercarrier settlements. Cisco VoIP-enabled network elements support the RADIUS Accounting Start, Accounting Stop, and Accounting Interim-Update messages, in addition to the Accounting-On and Accounting-Off messages.

Similarly, in today's H.323 VoIP implementation, the voice-enabled gateways send RADIUS accounting Start and Stop messages to a RADIUS server-based mediation or billing system. For the debit card application, the gateway interacts with the RADIUS server to obtain credit balance and time limit for the call (call authorization). Many commercial IP-based billing systems such as Digiquant and Mind have built-in RADIUS servers that can support billing for basic VoIP services without a mediation device. However, it is in the customer's best interest to use a separate mediation system if the services on offer are, or might become, more complex than a basic point-to-point call.

Cisco collaborates with mediation and billing partners, enabling customers to select the most appropriate level of functionality for their needs. Some Cisco partners perform mediation only, others perform mediation and billing in a tightly coupled fashion, and still others sell mediation and billing platforms independently or in an integrated fashion.

> **NOTE**   H.323 was the original protocol developed for VoIP on the Cisco VoIP gateways. That is why "h323" is present in the command names. However, because SIP and H.323 use a similar distributed call-processing and billing model, the same commands work for either H.323 or SIP as the VoIP protocol.

Prepaid and Postpaid Applications

Prepaid is one of the most common applications for billing. In prepaid applications, information access to user funds before the call is important so that you can see how much cash is available for the call to be made. When the call destination is known, a timer is started to disconnect the call when the prepaid funds have been consumed. A user-friendly approach might entail interrupting the call for clarity. Another important feature might be the ability to place the existing call on hold, ask the originating caller to add more funds to the card, collect the funds, and potentially resume the call.

Furthermore, these applications require an accurate way to apply the tariff to rate other calls. Other critical considerations include security and authenticating in scenarios when PINs are used and multiple calls are tried.

For postpaid applications, the call originator needs to be authorized. The call flow for such a service involves collecting the phone number of the person who originated the call (ANI) and sending it to the RADIUS server, essentially using it as an account number. An interactive voice response (IVR) system guides the caller throughout the application and enables him to use dual-tone multifrequency (DTMF) tones to traverse through the validation process.

Prepaid or postpaid, the cost of each call is an interesting issue to consider. The rating aspect becomes more important in VoIP because the caller location can be mobile and is not tied to a geographical coordinate. That is why you should assign negotiated rates for various combinations of locations or charge a flat rate.

The VoIP network generates CDRs that contain data about which extension made or received calls to or from which number and for how long. These records are generally stored in plain-text logfiles at the servers or even located in a PostgreSQL package or in MySQL databases with additional processing. The billing process starts only when the generation of rating procedures for CDRs has been defined well.

Challenges for VoIP Networks

The VoIP networks have evolved from proof-of-concept stages to mature services that drive revenues and cost savings. Over the years, the networks became a mix of many different call agents, proxy servers, VoIP gateways, and other elements that were added in evaluation phases with many different features. The providers now face two fundamental problems:

- Mixed usage and billing record formats

- Volume

All the different softswitches and services created a chaotic mix of usage and billing records in several different formats. The mix of formats became a problem in terms of interoperability and loss of data integrity.

With regard to volume, IP-related events typically produce far more records than traditional voice calls, and this is agnostic of the voice protocol in use at the softswitches. The VoIP records averaged nine events for normal calls and even more for special services or error cases. The data to be analyzed involves checking for the number of packets lost or delayed from the transmit side and the received side, checking for media packet inactivity between the source and destinations, and the usual call duration and calling/called number details. Furthermore, different records are generated by the ingress (incoming) than by the egress (outgoing) softswitches, requiring correlation of the records to provide a comprehensive view of the whole call. Even if the billing system could understand the VoIP services, the sheer number of records it would have to process would be a challenge in itself.

To address these challenges, a new group of *mediation* services companies have emerged to collect, correlate, and aggregate billing and accounting under one umbrella suite of services.

Mediation Services

A mediation system collects, correlates, and aggregates the accounting messages generated by the various VoIP-enabled network elements involved in a call. It converts these into standard or proprietary CDR formats, such that one and only one CDR is generated for each call. Mediation systems are usually required by service providers that already have a billing system and expect the output of the mediation system to be in a format that their existing billing system recognizes. Many mediation systems are able to support the commercial billing systems from various vendors such as Keenan, Amdocs, Portal, and Solect. Almost all VoIP deployments in Incumbent Local

Exchange Carriers (ILEC), Regional Bell Operating Companies (RBOC), and the more traditional U.S. and Canadian service providers with legacy billing systems expect CDRs to be presented in Belcore AMA Format (BAF).

However, VoIP also requires the billing system to know what is to be counted and analyzed. This information for analysis could be call duration, but it could also mean transferring megabytes of data (voice/video), fixing a price for video, or counting the instances of text-based messaging (SMS) or multimedia messaging service (MMS). A billing system has to rely on a mediation system that identifies what end users are doing with their configured calling plans and service-level agreements. The system can thus create an event-type record on which to rate the bill. As an end result, these systems provide the value addition to the billing systems to offer a comprehensive view of customer data and voice services.

Mediation Service vendors are now offering services that range from basic mediation (capture and aggregation of call events, generation of multiple CDR formats) to database-centric services such as reporting and analysis. Some also offer more sophistication via certain value-add modules for various rating methods and correlation services. Correlation will become a critical component in the coming days as we see VoIP calls being tied up with web access, audio/video conferencing, and telepresence in deployments.

Summary

Billing and mediation are important revenue-affecting pieces of any VoIP-based service. With so many VoIP protocols and small service providers and businesses launching VoIP, it is imperative that billing procedures are standardized and formats picked up prior to launch of service.

The global growth of VoIP-based systems presents several challenges to the service provider with regard to data capture, processing, and billing. Mediation software plays a key role in VoIP networks. It accepts data from various network elements (for example, softswitches, media servers, signaling gateways, and service development platforms) and transforms it into industry-standard billing data structures that can be used by virtually any billing system, including the legacy voice billing system of a service provider.

CHAPTER 10

Voice Security

This chapter provides an overview of typical security requirements in the context of Voice over IP (VoIP) service. You will learn about the various techniques to deploy to meet those requirements effectively and counter security threats.

Security Requirements

Before this chapter goes into the details of various techniques available to secure a VoIP network, you need to understand the problem and the set of requirements that must be met. This section outlines some of the typical security requirements. This is not an exhaustive listing. Specific VoIP services might have additional requirements:

- Integrity—The recipient should receive the packets that the originator sends without any change to their content. A third party should be unable to modify the packets in transit.

  This definition is strictly applied in the case of VoIP signaling. However, in the case of media, packet loss is usually tolerable.

- Privacy—A third party should not be able to read the data that is intended for the recipient.

- Authenticity—The sender and recipient of VoIP signaling or media messages need to be sure that the peer they are communicating with is in fact who it claims to be.

- Availability/protection from Denial-of-Service (DoS) attacks—The VoIP service should be available to the users at all times. Malicious or misbehaving users/devices should not be able to disrupt the service. Mitigation of DoS attacks requires taking measures to protect VoIP resources and to protect the underlying IP network.

Security Technologies

Given the security requirements for VoIP services, this section discusses some of the available technologies to ensure integrity, privacy, and authenticity. The technologies covered in this section are as follows:

- Shared-key

- Public-key cryptography

Shared-Key Approaches

One approach to authentication is a system in which the sender and the recipient share a secret password (sometimes referred to as a *shared-key*) that is unknown to a third party.

The sender calculates a hash of the message content and appends the hash value with the message. Upon receiving the message, the recipient also calculates the hash of the message with the shared password. Then it compares the calculated hash with the hash value that is appended to the message. If they match, the integrity of the message is assured, as is the authenticity of the sender.

You can use the shared password to encrypt the message content and transmit the encrypted data to the recipient. In this case, the privacy requirement is met because no third party that might sniff the data in transit can view the plaintext message content. The recipient runs the decryption algorithm with the shared password as one of the inputs and re-creates the plaintext message.

A system that has multiple data sources can meet the authenticity requirement by ensuring that each sender uses a unique key for the data sent.

In a shared-key approach, the administrator must provision the shared secret password. In a system that has numerous sender/recipient pairs, the provisioning overhead can be prohibitive.

In addition, if a shared-key is compromised (stolen/lost), all the devices using that shared-key need to be reprovisioned with the new shared-key.

Public-Key Cryptography

To alleviate the administrative overhead with shared-key approaches, you can use public-key cryptography.

The fundamental concepts in public-key cryptography are asymmetric keys and digital signatures, as discussed in the sections that follow.

Asymmetric Keys

Asymmetric key pairs are paired keys (usually of fixed length) referred to as the *public key* and the *private key* that are mathematically related to each other. They are usually represented in hexadecimal and have the following characteristics:

- Only the corresponding public key can decrypt data that is encrypted with a private key.

- Only the corresponding private key pair can decrypt data that is encrypted with a public key.

- There is one-to-one relationship between the keys.

The private key is kept a secret, and the public key is shared with all interested parties.

For authentication, a sender can use his own private key to encrypt the message. The message can be decrypted only with the corresponding public key. The recipient can decrypt the message as long as he has access to the public key of the sender. Because only the sender knows the private key, he must have encrypted the message.

For secure communication, a sender can encrypt the message content using public-key cryptography techniques. He does this using the public key of the recipient. The recipient can then decrypt the message with the corresponding private key. Because the intended recipient has the private key, he can decrypt the message. No other third party can decrypt this message, because no one else knows the private key of the recipient.

Notice that the sender must use his private key to encrypt the message for authentication purposes, whereas the recipient must use his public key to encrypt the message for secure communication. In the real world, the authentication phase comes first. After the sender and receiver authenticate each other, they switch to the *secure communication* phase.

Encryption using asymmetric keys is a slow and CPU-intensive process. Therefore, when a large amount of data is involved, people generally use public key cryptography to negotiate a unique shared secret per session. They employ symmetric key ciphers using this shared secret for the rest of the session.

Digital Signature

A digital signature is an attribute of the content of the message and the signer of the message. A digital signature serves a purpose similar to that of a signature in the real world—it is a tool for authenticating a message or some piece of data. Digital signatures use a set of complementary algorithms, one for signing and the other for verification.

First, a hash function is run over the content of the message. Then the hash result is transformed into a digital signature using the private key of the signer. A digital signature is typically appended to the message.

The recipient verifies the signature by running the verification algorithm over the original content of the message (excluding the signature itself) and the public key of the signer.

Digital signatures provide authentication. (The signer must have the private key.) Digital signatures also provide message integrity, because any change to the message content in transit results in a failure of the signature verification algorithm.

However, a digital signature does not provide privacy by itself. The signature is appended to the message, which is sent in clear-text and can be viewed in transit.

Certificates and Certificate Authority

Now, the question is how the public key is propagated to all possible recipients. Asymmetric key pairs are hard to maintain and configure. Certificates are meant as a solution to the public key distribution problem.

At the time of key generation, the public key of the entity (called the *subject*) is sent to the Certificate Authority (CA). The CA verifies the identity of the requestor (possibly by manual intervention) and issues a certificate that asserts the identity of the requestor and its public key.

This certificate that the CA issues includes information about the identity of the subject, among other things, and is signed by the CA.

Each device in the system is preprovisioned with the public key of the CA (if there are multiple CAs, the public key of each needs to be provisioned on each device) and trusts the certificates issued by that CA.

At the start of session establishment, the subject presents its certificate to its peer. The peer runs a signature verification algorithm to verify that a trusted CA has signed the certificate. If the signature is validated, the public key and the identity of the subject (called the *subject name*) are stored locally.

In summary, the public key of the trusted CA is preprovisioned on the devices. All other entities are authenticated by means of certificates and do not require manual provisioning. After the certificates (which contain the public keys) are propagated, the communication between entities in the system can be secured.

Public-Key-Based Protocols

This section looks at some of the security protocols that use public-key cryptography technology. These protocols are not restricted to VoIP usage. You can use them to secure other services.

TLS

The Transport Layer Security (TLS) protocol, specified in RFC 2246, evolved from Secure Socket Layer (SSL). TLS rides on top of underlying reliable transport protocols such as TCP. In the spirit of protocol layering, TLS is independent of the application layer that sits above TLS. Thus, you can use TLS with services other than VoIP. In VoIP context, TLS is typically used to secure signaling.

TLS is composed of two layers:

- Record protocol—The lower-level layer that provides connection security and is the workhorse. It provides privacy and integrity.

  The record protocol uses symmetric cryptography algorithms such as Data Encryption Standard (DES) and RC4 for data encryption. Another layer that sits on top of the record protocol layer negotiates the keys and algorithm to be used for a particular connection. You can use the record protocol layer without encryption.

  For integrity, each message includes a message integrity check using a keyed MAC. MAC computations use secured hash functions such as MD5 and Secure Hash Algorithm (SHA).

- Client layer—The higher-level layer that sits on top of the record protocol layer. Multiple protocols, such as the TLS handshake protocol, are defined at the client layer. The TLS handshake protocol is primarily engaged at the start of the data communication session. The TLS handshake protocol has two primary functions:

  — It authenticates the peer using symmetric or public-key cryptography techniques.

  — It optionally negotiates, on a per-connection basis, a shared-secret and symmetric encryption algorithm. The TLS handshake protocol then passes down to the record protocol layer the shared-secret and the negotiated encryption algorithm. The record protocol layer does the actual payload encryption.

  The other client layer protocols include the alert protocol, the change cipher specification protocol, and the application data protocol.

You can use TLS in server-auth mode or mutual authentication mode. In server-auth mode, the client authenticates the identity of the server via TLS. The server uses some other out-of-band means to authenticate the client. In mutual authentication mode, each entity authenticates its peer by verifying its certificate.

Figure 10-1 shows the flow of messages between a TLS client and TLS server in mutual authentication mode.

Figure 10-1 *Figure 10-1TLS Call Flow*

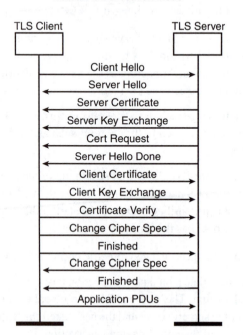

IPsec

IPsec

Whereas TLS operates above TCP, IPsec operates at the IP layer and provides security for the IP datagram using public-key cryptography techniques. IPsec uses two protocols to provide security—Authentication Header (AH) and Encapsulation Security Payload (ESP).

AH provides authentication and integrity. ESP provides privacy in addition to authentication and integrity by encrypting parts of the message. IPsec can operate in two different modes:

- Transport mode—An IPsec header is inserted between the IP header and the upper layer protocol (TCP/UDP) header. In this mode, only the payload of an IP datagram is protected.

- Tunnel mode—The entire IP packet is encapsulated in another IP datagram. An IPsec header is added between the outer and inner IP headers. In this mode, the entire IP packet is protected. This mode is typically used when a device that did not originate the packet provides security. This could occur over a Virtual Private Network (VPN) connection, for example.

Both IPsec protocols, AH and ESP, can operate in either transport mode or tunnel mode. The format of the AH or ESP header is the same regardless of whether tunnel or transport mode is used.

Figure 10-2 illustrates IPsec encapsulation in transport mode and tunnel mode.

Figure 10-2 *IPsec – Tunnel Mode and Transport Mode*

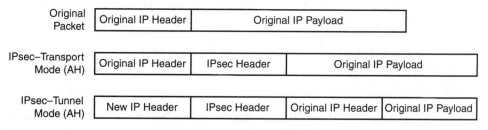

A separate key management protocol called Internet Key Exchange (IKE) is specified for management of security keys. IKE uses public-key cryptography techniques to negotiate an authentication key, security protocol (AH or ESP), hashing algorithm, and encryption algorithm.

SRTP

Secure Real-time Transport Protocol (SRTP), defined in RFC 3711, is a profile of the Real-time Transport Protocol (RTP). SRTP provides integrity, authenticity, and privacy protection to the RTP traffic and to the control traffic for RTP, RTCP (the Real-time Transport Control Protocol).

SRTP does not specify how the keys are exchanged between the sender and recipient. The key management systems are outside the scope of SRTP specification. In the case of VoIP, the signaling protocol can exchange keys before SRTP kicks in. If you use the signaling protocol for key exchange, you need to secure it by using TLS, IPsec, or similar means; otherwise, the keys that SRTP uses might be exposed to hackers.

Protecting Voice Devices

For availability of VoIP service, you need to protect the devices that source and terminate voice traffic against attacks, as described in further detail in the sections that follow.

Disabling Unused Ports/Services

Typically, you will find unused services or ports that are open on voice devices, making them vulnerable to hacker exploitation. Recommended practice is to disable these unused services or ports for VoIP devices and IP infrastructure devices (such as switches, routers, and so on). The following are some actions you should take:

■   Disable Telnet, Trivial File Transfer Protocol (TFTP), and similar services if they are not being used.

- If you are using Simple Network Management (SNMP) on a device only to gather data, set Simple Network Management (SNMP) to read-only mode.

- If you are using web-based administration, always use secure access with protocols such as Secure Socket Layer (SSL).

- Administratively disable any unused port on Layer 2 switches.

HIPS

You can use Host-based Intrusion Protection Systems (HIPS) to secure critical voice devices such as call processing elements. HIPS are typically software agents that collect information about usage of a wide variety of device resources such as CPU, login attempts, number of interrupts, and so on. This information is compared against a set of rules to determine if a security breach has taken place. Depending on the configured parameters, these systems can take preventive actions such as terminating the offending application, rate-limiting data from offending user/IP addresses, and so on.

Protecting IP Network Infrastructure

Because VoIP is a service that runs on an underlying IP network infrastructure, it is not enough to protect voice devices. It is imperative to protect the IP network so that it is available to carry voice traffic.

This chapter looks at the various technology challenges and potential exploits in an IP network infrastructure and the technologies available to counter those exploits. Because securing IP networks is a vast field in itself, this section presents only a flavor of the issues and is not intended to be exhaustive.

Segmentation

Typically characterized as a critical service, VoIP traffic should be separated from other traffic. Many segmentation strategies exist to accomplish this separation of traffic types.

You can apply some of these strategies, such as VLANs, at Layer 2. Place phone and other voice devices in a separate VLAN from other data devices.

At Layer 3, using separate IP address spaces (say 64.10.x.x for VoIP and 64.20.x.x space for data) enables easy filtering and recognition of VoIP traffic. Even within VoIP, recommended best practice advises separating the signaling traffic from media traffic.

If you are using DHCP, you should strongly consider having separate DHCP servers for VoIP.

Traffic Policing

Even with segmentation in place, a single VoIP device could consume all the bandwidth intended for VoIP, thus starving the other VoIP devices. To counter this, you need to implement traffic policing.

Most VoIP devices generate traffic that is bound by an upper limit. For example, phones using a g.711 codec generate traffic of not more than 64 kbps (plus packet overhead) for each direction of voice traffic. You can use this information to police the traffic coming from the devices.

IP infrastructure at the edge needs to implement appropriate queuing techniques (like priority queuing in Cisco IOS Software) to prevent a rogue device from clogging the bandwidth that is intended for voice.

802.1x Device Authentication

You need to block unauthorized users from accessing the network. Denying physical access to Layer 2 devices is the first line of defense. In wired Ethernet, you can do this by disabling unused ports and MAC address filtering. Filters are difficult to manage, however, and can be circumvented by programmable network interface cards (NIC). In a wireless environment, because no physical port exists, eavesdropping and MAC forgery are easier.

802.1x and Extensible Authentication Protocol (EAP) are standards for port-based access control for both wired and wireless access. 802.1x and EAP enforce authentication of a device before allowing access to a switch. EAP allows different underlying authentication mechanisms, such as RADIUS. Note that the client/host machine needs to support 802.1x. Although support for 802.1x is becoming available in more client operating systems, it might be disabled by default.

The client device is in an unauthorized state when it first contacts the wireless access point/wired switch. The client is permitted to send only 802.1x messages at this point. The client sends user credentials to the access point with EAP, and the access point forwards the request to an authentication server (for example, a RADIUS server) for verification. If the credentials are valid, the client requests credentials from the wireless access point/wired switch via 802.1x and EAP to verify the identity.

Figure 10-3 shows 802.1x message flow between a client device and switch.

Figure 10-3   *Figure 10-3802.1x Port Authentication*

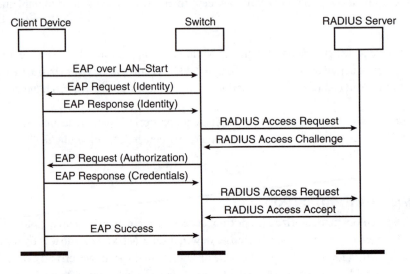

The client device is assigned an appropriate VLAN after it completes the authentication process.

Layer 2 Tools

This section discusses some of the tools available at Layer 2 to mitigate security risks. It assumes that you have a basic knowledge of the operation of Layer 2 devices and protocols. Each featured subsection has a short introduction of relevant Layer 2 technology. This is intended only as a refresher and not as a precise description of operation. The tools listed in this section are available in various Cisco Catalyst series products.

In the spirit of *security layering*, you should employ multiple technologies even if the security threats that these technologies are intended to address have some overlap.

DHCP Snooping

DHCP snooping provides network security by filtering malicious DHCP messages and by building a database of IP-to-MAC address mapping. DHCP snooping acts as a firewall between untrusted sources that send DHCP requests and the trusted DHCP server.

When the DHCP snooping feature is enabled on a Layer 2 device, it intercepts all DHCP messages to make sure that the DHCP responses are coming only from the trusted DHCP server. Any malformed or malicious (for example, DHCP response from an untrusted port) messages are dropped.

In addition, the Layer 2 switch builds a database of IP-to-MAC address mapping from the information in the DHCP messages. This mapping database is referred to as a *DHCP snooping binding database*.

IP Source Guard

IP Source Guard works in conjunction with DHCP snooping and takes it to the next level. With IP Source Guard, all IP traffic on an untrusted port is blocked except for DHCP messages. When the DHCP response is received and the *DHCP snooping binding database* is built, a per-port VLAN access control list (VACL) is installed on that port.

This VACL is applied to all subsequent IP traffic from that port, which restricts the device(s) on that port to using only those IP addresses that are legitimately obtained via DHCP. Traffic with a source IP address other than that in the DHCP snooping binding database is filtered out. This filtering limits the ability of a host to attack the network by claiming the IP address of a neighbor host.

Dynamic ARP Inspection

Devices use Address Resolution Protocol (ARP) to obtain a Layer 2 (typically MAC address) address of the intended recipient, given the Layer 3 (IP) address. On broadcast media, they do this by broadcasting an ARP request to all devices on that broadcast domain. The device whose IP address matches that of the ARP request is supposed to respond with an ARP response. All other devices are supposed to drop the ARP request.

The ARP specification does not include anything to prevent a malicious device on that broadcast domain from responding to the ARP request even if the address of the malicious device does not match that of the ARP request. A hacker can exploit this weakness by sending spurious ARP replies with its own MAC address embedded in the ARP reply. The ARP cache of the sender (and intermediate Layer 2 switch) is thus poisoned. All subsequent IP packets that are sent for the intended recipient are redirected to the malicious device. This is commonly referred to as a *man-in-the-middle attack*.

Dynamic ARP Inspection (DAI) is a Layer 2 technology that you can enable on a switch (or any device that performs Layer 2 functions) to mitigate this problem. DAI works in conjunction with DHCP snooping and uses the DHCP snooping binding database.

The DAI feature requires ports to be designated as trusted or untrusted. DAI inspects all ARP messages on untrusted ports and verifies that the ARP messages are not malicious by comparing the ARP messages against the DHCP snooping binding database. Finally, DAI drops any malicious ARP packets.

Additionally, you can configure a DAI feature to perform rate limiting of ARP requests to prevent flooding/DoS attacks.

CAM Overflow and Port Security

When powered up, Ethernet switches go through a *learning* stage. In this stage, the switch inspects the source MAC address of frames coming in each port. From this, the switch learns that a device with that source MAC address is connected to that port. The switch stores this mapping in Content Addressable Memory (CAM) as a table commonly referred to as *CAM table*. The Layer 2 switch uses this table to send a Layer 2 frame to the right destination port instead of flooding it to all ports. If the switch does not find a destination MAC address in the CAM table, it has no choice but to flood the frame to all non-source ports.

Malicious devices can exploit this behavior by *overflowing* the CAM table. They do this by flooding the switch with numerous frames, each with a different source MAC address. This results in the CAM table of the switch being full. The switch floods any subsequent Layer 2 frames that well-behaving hosts send because the source MAC address is not found in the CAM table. (The CAM table is already full.) The flooded packet reaches all nonsource ports, and the malicious device has access to the frames. This enables the malicious device to perform man-in-the-middle or DoS attacks.

The Cisco Port Security feature addresses this problem by configuring a maximum number of MAC addresses per port. If a particular port encounters this limit, the specified action is taken on that port. The offending port can be either shut down or placed in a restricted mode.

BPDU Guard and Root Guard

At Layer 2, typical topologies have physical loops for redundancy purposes. However, physical loops can result in broadcast loops (broadcast frames loop forever) and bridge table corruption. Switches run Spanning Tree Protocol (STP) to create a tree-like logical loop-free topology. At the root of this tree is a *root bridge*. The loop-free branches and leaves span the entire Layer 2 network.

The administrator assigns a priority to each switch. The switch that has the highest priority (the lowest number—a priority of 0 is better than a priority of 1) is elected as the root bridge. Per the STP algorithm, switches exchange bridge protocol data units (BPDU) to communicate this priority information and subsequent STP calculations. BPDUs do not have an inherent security mechanism. Thus, a malicious device can pretend to be a switch and make itself the root bridge.

Two Cisco features called Root Guard and BPDU Guard prevent malicious devices from sending BPDUs. BPDU Guard attempts to prevent malicious host devices from sending BPDUs. It disables a port upon BPDU reception if PortFast is enabled on the port.

The Root Guard feature is configured on a per-port basis and ensures that the port on which Root Guard is enabled is the designated port. If the switch receives superior STP BPDUs (with higher priority) on a Root Guard-enabled port, that port is moved to a root-inconsistent STP state. This root-inconsistent state is effectively equal to a listening state. Root Guard allows the device to participate in STP as long as the device does not try to become the root.

Circumventing VLANs

VLANs logically separate groups of devices that share a physical Layer 2 network. Typically, each port on a switch, except for trunk ports, is assigned to a particular VLAN. Trunks carry traffic of multiple VLANs between switches. On a trunk, each frame is encapsulated using 802.1Q or Inter-Switch Link (ISL) to identify the source VLAN. After the receiving switch receives the frame on a trunk, it strips the trunk encapsulation (802.1Q or ISL) and forwards it to the appropriate VLAN. Typically, the two switches negotiate whether trunking is enabled on a port and the VLANs carried on that port. This trunk negotiation is inherently insecure and can be exploited by malicious devices.

Malicious devices can negotiate trunking with switches. After the switch establishes trunking, it sends traffic for all the negotiated VLANs to the malicious device. This enables the malicious device to circumvent the VLAN separation and send/receive frames from other VLANs.

To counter this threat, you should disable negotiation of trunks on ports that are facing users.

NIPS

Network-based Intrusion Prevention Systems (NIPS) monitor and analyze network traffic to detect intrusion. NIPS have a management interface that can configure rules. NIPS throws alarms when encountering suspicious activity. Optionally, you can configure NIPS to perform actions such as resetting data connections, instructing a router to deny future traffic from an offending host, and so on.

You can deploy NIPS on that VoIP side and on the data side of the IP network. That is, you can configure NIPS to monitor voice traffic or data traffic for intrusion. Because the possible *flows* are limited in voice network, it is relatively easy to tune NIPS in a VoIP environment.

Layer 3 Tools

In addition to the Layer 2 tools described in the previous section, various tools are available at Layer 3 to mitigate security risks. This section assumes that you have a basic working knowledge of the operation of Layer 3 devices and protocols. Each featured subsection has a short introduction of relevant Layer 3 technology. This is intended only as a refresher and not as a precise description of operation.

Authentication of Routing Updates

Routing protocols operate by exchanging information between routers. By default, a router does not authenticate a sender of routing updates. A malicious device can pretend to be a router in the system and feed incorrect routing information. This can result in black-hole routing (DoS) or can enable man-in-the-middle attacks.

Routing protocols such as Open Shortest Path First (OSPF) and Border Gateway Protocol (BGP) support MD5 authentication of routing protocol messages. MD5 is based on a shared-secret approach, as discussed earlier. The routers in the system can be configured with shared-key(s). The sender does an MD5 hash of the message with the shared-key and appends the resulting hash to the message. The recipient performs a similar operation on receipt and verifies the authenticity of the sender and the integrity of the message. This process does not provide privacy.

RIPv1 does not support an inherent security mechanism. Older RIPv2 implementations support only plain-text authentication.

TCP Intercept

A TCP client sends a TCP-SYN message to initiate a connection to the server. The TCP server allocates resources (sockets, memory, and so on) to service this request and sends an SYN-ACK back to the client. The TCP server is said to have a *half-open connection* at this point. Per the TCP protocol, the server waits a certain amount of time (typically 30 seconds) to hear an ACK back from the client.

A malicious device can flood a TCP-based application server with a huge number of TCP-SYN messages. Because the server has to allocate resources and wait for each TCP connection request, it can quickly run out of resources to service additional requests. Malicious devices can aggravate this by sending TCP-SYNs with unreachable source addresses. This results in masking the identity of the attacker and routing the SYN-ACK from the server to a *black hole*.

The TCP intercept feature on routers (strictly speaking, this is a Layer 4 function) mitigates this SYN-flooding attacks by intercepting and validating SYN messages.

The TCP intercept feature can operate in *watch mode* or *intercept mode*. In watch mode, the Layer 3 device routes the SYN to the server normally and then waits a configurable period to see if the TCP connection has been established. If a connection has not been established within that time, the Layer 3 device sends an RST to the server to tear down the connection.

In intercept mode, the router answers the SYN coming from the client. This SYN does not reach the server. The router sends a SYN-ACK back to the client. If the client responds with an ACK, the router knows that this is a legitimate request. The router then sends the original SYN packet to the server and completes the three-way handshake with the server. The client and server then have a normal TCP connection.

Security Planning and Policies

As discussed throughout this chapter, various security threats exist, as do technologies to counter those threats. In terms of practicality, you cannot possibly deploy security technologies to counter *every* possible threat. You need to assess the security risks that are specific to your network and address the highest-priority risks first.

You need to design and document an operational plan, outlining critical applications, devices, and security risks in order of priority. This document should guide the security technologies that are deployed and prioritize future implementation. This operational plan should also include an incident response plan outlining specific initial steps to take in case of a security breach. The plan should document internal policies such as password policies, access control, and monitoring strategies and be communicated to the key people who will be implementing, enforcing, or resolving these security issues.

The sections that follow list some of the considerations that you need to take into account in formulating such a plan.

Transitive Trust

Transitive trust is trust that is transmitted through another party. For example, in a VoIP system with multiple server elements, a client can authenticate with *one* of the server elements. The other server elements do not need to authenticate the client again.

This trust model is common in many distributed systems. When you use this model, the server elements must align their security policies to guard against *weak links* that a malicious device can exploit.

VoIP Protocol-Specific Issues

The choice of specific VoIP technologies and services that are deployed play an important role in security planning. For example, *softphones* running on PCs complicate data-voice segmentation.

Complexity Tradeoffs

You also need to consider the complexity and the risk-reward ratio of implementing a certain technology. For example, public-key cryptography techniques involve an initial overhead with deploying infrastructure like certification authorities (CAs), certificates, and so on. On the plus side, a Public Key Infrastructure (PKI) infrastructure requires only minimal day-to-day maintenance.

NAT/Firewall Traversal

Firewalls that are VoIP-signaling-protocol aware typically work by inspecting the content of signaling messages. Based on the content of these signaling messages, they open up *pinholes* for the voice media to flow through. These voice application-aware firewalls are sometimes referred to as *Application-Layer Gateways* (ALG).

The firewall's capability to be VoIP-signaling-protocol aware breaks if signaling messages are encrypted. Because the intermediate firewalls cannot examine the content of signaling messages, the media might be blocked.

Therefore, it is advisable to use a private address space that is specific for VoIP instead of using Network Address Translation (NAT) within the VoIP address space.

Password and Access Control

Most devices come with default passwords that are easy to guess. As with all passwords, you should take the precaution of changing them and keeping them secret. For example, in a VoIP environment, you should keep administration and SNMP servers secure.

Also, devices might allow password resets if users have physical access to those devices (power-on password recovery on IOS devices). Remote management of devices is also common. Given this and a wide variety of other reasons, it is important to restrict physical access to devices and employ a restricted out-of-band management system.

Summary

Security is an important consideration in designing and implementing VoIP service. By its very nature, it encompasses almost every aspect of a network from Layer 2 devices to firewalls and Certificate Authorities.

A wide range of security technologies exist. Assessing the security risks and deploying technology that is appropriate for those risks is imperative to protecting VoIP services.

Part III: IP Signaling Protocols

CHAPTER 11

H.323

H.323 is an International Telecommunication Union Telecommunication Standardization Sector (ITU-T) specification for transmitting audio, video, and data across an Internet Protocol (IP) network, including the Internet. When compliant with H.323, vendors' products and applications can communicate and interoperate with each other. The H.323 standard addresses call signaling and control, multimedia transport and control, and bandwidth control for point-to-point and multipoint conferences. The *H* series of recommendations also specifies H.320 for Integrated Services Digital Network (ISDN) and H.324 for plain old telephone service (POTS) as transport mechanisms.

Currently, H.323v5 (version 5) is considered the latest version as ratified by ITU. The H.323 standard consists of the components and protocols outlined in Table 11-1.

Table 11-1   *H.323 ITU Drafts and Related Draft Annexes*

ITU Draft	Related Annex	Title
H.323		Packet-based multimedia communications systems
	Annex A	H.245 messages used by H.323 endpoints
	Annex B	Procedures for layered video codecs
	Annex C	H.323 on ATM
	Annex D	Real-time fax over H.323
	Annex E	Multiplexed Call Signaling over UDP
	Annex F	Audio Simple Endpoint Type
	Annex G	Text Simple Endpoint Type
	Annex J	Secure Simple Endpoint Type
	Annex K	HTTP-based Service Control
	Annex L	Stimulus Control Protocol
	Annex M.1	Tunneling of signaling protocols (QSIG) in H.323
	Annex M.2	Tunneling of signaling protocols (ISUP) in H.323
	Annex M.3	Tunneling of DSS1 through H.323
	Annex P	Transfer of Modem Signals over H.323

continues

Table 11-1 *H.323 ITU Drafts and Related Draft Annexes (Continued)*

ITU Draft	Related Annex	Title
	Annex Q	Far End Camera Control and H.281/H.224
	Annex R	Robustness Methods for H.323 Entities
H.225.0		Call signaling protocols and media stream packetization for packet-based multimedia communication systems
	Annex A	RTP/RTCP
	Annex B	RTP Profile
	Annex C	RTP Payload Format for H.261 video streams
	Annex D	RTP Payload Format for H.261A video streams
	Annex E	Video packetization
	Annex F	Audio and multiplexed packetization
	Annex G	Communication Between Administrative Domains
	Annex H	H.225.0 Message Syntax (ASN.1)
	Annex I	H.263+ Video Packetization
H.245		Control Protocol for multimedia communication
	Annex A	Messages: Syntax
	Annex B	Messages: Semantic Definition
	Annex C	Procedures
	Annex D	Object Identifier Assignments
	Annex E	ISO/IEC 14496-2 Capability Definitions
	Annex F	Logical Channel Bit Rate Management Capability Definitions
	Annex G	ISO/IEC 14496-1 Capability Definitions
	Annex H	ISO/IEC 14496-3 Capability Definitions
	Annex I	GSM Adaptive Multi Rate Capability Definitions
H.246		Interworking of H-Series multimedia terminals with H-Series multimedia terminals and voice/voiceband terminals on GSTN and ISDN
	Annex A	H.323-H.320 Interworking
	Annex C	ISUP/H.225.0 Interworking
	Annex E.1	MAP/H.225.0 Interworking
	Annex E.2	ANSI-41 MAP/H.225.0 Interworking
	Annex F	H.323-H.324 Interworking

Table 11-1   *H.323 ITU Drafts and Related Draft Annexes (Continued)*

ITU Draft	Related Annex	Title
H.235.0		Security framework for H-series (H.323 and other H.245-based) multimedia systems
H.235.1		Baseline Security Profile
H.235.2		Signature Security Profile
H.235.3		Hybrid Security Profile
H.235.4		Direct and Selective Routed Call Security
H.235.5		Framework for secure authentication in RAS using weak shared secrets
H.235.6		Voice encryption profile with native H.235/H.245 key management
H.235.7		Usage of the MIKEY Key Management Protocol for SRTP
H.235.8		Key Exchange for SRTP Using Secure Signaling Channels
H.235.9		Security Gateway Support for H.323
H.450.1		Generic functional protocol for the support of supplementary services in H.323
H.450.2		Call transfer supplementary service for H.323
H.450.3		Call diversion supplementary service for H.323
H.450.4		Call hold supplementary service for H.323
H.450.5		Call park and call pickup supplementary services for H.323
H.450.6		Call waiting supplementary service for H.323
H.450.7		Message waiting indication supplementary service for H.323
H.450.8		Name identification supplementary service for H.323
H.450.9		Call completion supplementary Services for H.323
H.450.10		Call offering supplementary services for H.323
H.450.11		Call intrusion supplementary services
H.450.12		Common information additional network feature for H.323
H.460.1		Guidelines for the use of the generic extensible framework
H.460.2		Number portability interworking between H.323 and SCN networks
H.460.3		Circuit status map
H.460.4		Call priority designation
H.460.5		Transport of Multiple Q.931 IEs

continues

Table 11-1 *H.323 ITU Drafts and Related Draft Annexes (Continued)*

ITU Draft	Related Annex	Title
H.460.6		Extended Fast Connect
H.460.7		Digit Maps
H.460.8		Querying for Alternate Routes
H.460.9		QoS Monitoring Reporting
H.460.10		Call Party Category
H.460.11		Delayed Call Establishment
H.460.12		Glare Control Indicator
H.460.13		Called User Release Control
H.460.14		Multi-Level Precedence and Preemption
H.460.15		Call Signaling Transport Channel Suspension and Redirection
H.460.16		Multiple-Message Release Sequence Capability
H.460.17		Tunneling RAS through H.225.0
H.460.18		Traversal of H.323 signaling across network address translators and firewalls
H.460.19		Traversal of H.323 media across network address translators and firewalls
H.460.20		Location Number for H.323
H.501		Protocol for mobility management and intra-/inter-domain communication in multimedia systems
H.510		Mobility for H.323 multimedia systems
H.530		Symmetric security procedures for H.510

The H.323 system is discussed in the following three sections:

- H.323 elements

- H.323 protocol suite

- H.323 call-flows

H.323 Elements

Figure 11-1 illustrates the elements of an H.323 system. These elements include terminals, gateways, gatekeepers, and multipoint control units (MCU).

Often referred to as endpoints, terminals provide point-to-point and multipoint conferencing for audio and, optionally, video and data. Gateways interconnect to Public Switched Telephone Network (PSTN) or ISDN networks for H.323 endpoint interworking. Gatekeepers provide admission control and address translation services for terminals or gateways. MCUs are devices that allow two or more terminals or gateways to conference with either audio and/or video sessions.

Figure 11-1   *Elements of H.323 Networking*

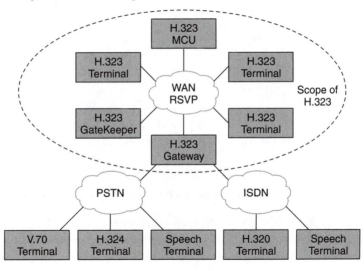

Terminal

The network element illustrated in Figure 11-2 is defined in H.323 as a *terminal*. H.323 terminals must have a system control unit, media transmission, audio codec, and packet-based network interface. Optional requirements include a video codec and user data applications.

Figure 11-2 *Relationships of H.323 Components*

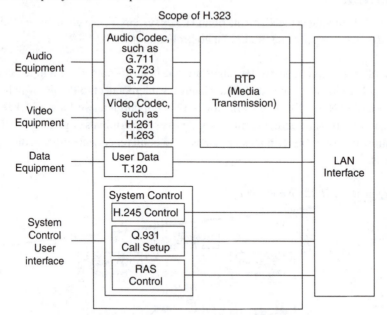

The following functions and capabilities are within the scope of the H.323 terminal:

■ System Control Unit—Provides H.225 and H.245 call control, capability exchange, messaging, and signaling of commands for proper operation of the terminal.

■ Media Transmission—Formats the transmitted audio, video, data, control streams, and messages onto network interface. Media transmission also receives the audio, video, data, control streams, and messages from the network interface.

■ Audio Codec—Encodes the signal from the audio equipment for transmission and decodes the incoming audio code. Required functions include encoding and decoding G.711 speech and transmitting and receiving a-law and μ-law formats. Optionally, G.722, G.723.1, G.728, and G.729 encoding and decoding can be supported.

■ Network Interface—A packet-based interface capable of end-to-end Transmission Control Protocol (TCP) and User Datagram Protocol (UDP) unicast and multicast services.

■ Video Codec—Optional, but if provided, must be capable of encoding and decoding video according to H.261/H.263 standards.

■ Data Channel—Supports applications such as database access, file transfer, and *audiographics conferencing* (the capability to modify a common image over multiple users' computers simultaneously), as specified in Recommendation T.120.

Gateway

The H.323 gateway reflects the characteristics of a Switched Circuit Network (SCN) endpoint and H.323 endpoint. It translates between audio, video, and data transmission formats as well as communication systems and protocols. This includes call setup and teardown on both the IP network and SCN.

Gateways are not needed unless interconnection with the SCN is required. Therefore, H.323 endpoints can communicate directly over the packet network without connecting to a gateway. The gateway acts as an H.323 terminal or MCU on the network and an SCN terminal or MCU on the SCN, as illustrated in Figure 11-3.

Figure 11-3 *Elements of an H.323 Gateway*

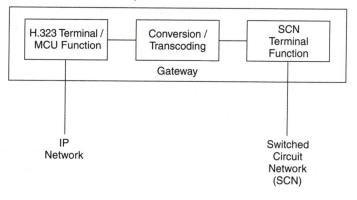

Gatekeeper

An optional function, the gatekeeper provides pre-call and call-level control services to H.323 endpoints. Gatekeepers are logically separated from the other network elements in H.323 environments. If more than one gatekeeper is implemented, inter-communication is accomplished in an unspecified manner.

The Gatekeeper can use a simple query/response sequence (Location Request [LRQ] or Location Confirmation [LCF]) to remotely locate users. New versions of H.323, such as H.323 versions 4 and 5 have attempted to recommend a gatekeeper inter-communication specification. With H.323 v3, Annex G/H.225.0 provides for "Communication between Administrative Domains." This new annex provides H.323 Gatekeepers with the ability to perform address resolution and pricing exchange in a scalable manner that facilitates the development of large-scale H.323-based networks.

Yet another protocol, the Open Settlements Protocol (OSP), also specified as European Telecommunication Standards Institute (ETSI) TS 101 321, is used largely for intra-domain interactions from both the gateway and gatekeepers. OSP provides the mechanism to permit the exchange of inter-domain pricing, authorization, and settlement information between Internet telephony operators.

If a gatekeeper is present in an H.323 system, it must perform the following:

■ Address Translation—Provides endpoint IP addresses from H.323 aliases (such as pc1@cisco.com) or E.164 addresses (standard phone numbers).

■ Admissions Control—Provides authorized access to H.323 using the Admission Request/ Admission Confirm/Admission Reject (ARQ/ACF/ARJ) messages, discussed in the "RAS Signaling" section later in this chapter.

■ Bandwidth Control—Consists of managing endpoint bandwidth requirements using Bandwidth Request/Bandwidth Confirm/Bandwidth Reject (BRQ/BCF/BRJ) messages, discussed in the "RAS Signaling" section later in this chapter.

■ Zone Management—Provided for registered terminals, gateways, and MCUs and discussed further in the "RAS Signaling" section later in this chapter.

Optionally, the gatekeeper can provide the following functionality:

■ Call Control Signaling—Uses the Gatekeeper Routed Call Signaling (GKRCS) model, reviewed in the "Call Control Signaling (H.225)" section later in this chapter.

■ Call Authorization—Enables the gatekeeper to restrict access to certain terminals and gateways or to restrict access based on time-of-day policies.

■ Bandwidth Management—Enables the gatekeeper to reject admission if the required bandwidth is not available.

■ Call Management—Services include maintaining an active call list that you can use to indicate that an endpoint is busy.

The MCU and Elements

The multipoint controller (MC) supports conferences between three or more endpoints in a multipoint conference. MCs transmit the capability set to each endpoint in the multipoint conference and can revise capabilities during the conference. The MC function can be resident in a terminal, gateway, gatekeeper, or MCU.

The multipoint processor (MP) receives audio, video, and/or data streams and distributes them to endpoints participating in a multipoint conference.

The MCU is an endpoint that supports multipoint conferences and, at a minimum, consists of an MC and one or more MPs. If it supports centralized multipoint conferences, a typical MCU consists of an MC and an audio, video, and data MP.

H.323 Proxy Server

An H.323 proxy server is a proxy specifically designed for the H.323 protocol. The proxy operates at the application layer and can examine packets between two communicating applications. Proxies can determine the destination of a call and perform the connection if desired. The proxy supports the following key functions:

- Terminals that don't support Resource Reservation Protocol (RSVP) can connect through access or local-area networks (LANs) with relatively good quality of service (QoS) to the proxy. Pairs of proxies can then negotiate adequate QoSs to tunnel across the IP network. Proxies can manage QoS with RSVP and/or IP precedence bits.

- Proxies support the routing of H.323 traffic separate from ordinary data traffic through application-specific routing (ASR).

- A proxy is compatible with network address translation, enabling H.323 nodes to be deployed in networks with private address space.

- A proxy deployed without a firewall or independently of a firewall provides security so that only H.323 traffic passes through it. A proxy deployed in conjunction with a firewall enables the firewall to be simply configured to pass all H.323 traffic by treating the proxy as a trusted node. This enables the firewall to provide data networking security and the proxy to provide H.323 security.

- An H.323 proxy in this mode is also called a *DUAL Gatekeeper* because it is performing the dual functions of an H.323 Gatekeeper and proxy server. More commonly, it allows H.323 clients such as NetMeeting to place multimedia calls on the Internet if they are within a private LAN or behind a firewall.

H.323 Protocol Suite

The H.323 protocol suite is based on several protocols, as illustrated in Figure 11-4. The protocol family supports call admissions, setup, status, teardown, media streams, and messages in H.323 systems. These protocols are supported by both reliable and unreliable packet delivery mechanisms over data networks.

Although most H.323 implementations today utilize TCP as the transport mechanism for signaling, H.323 version 2 does enable basic UDP transport. Also, other standards bodies are investigating the use of other reliable UDP mechanisms to create more scalable signaling methods.

Figure 11-4 *Layers of the H.323 Protocol Suite*

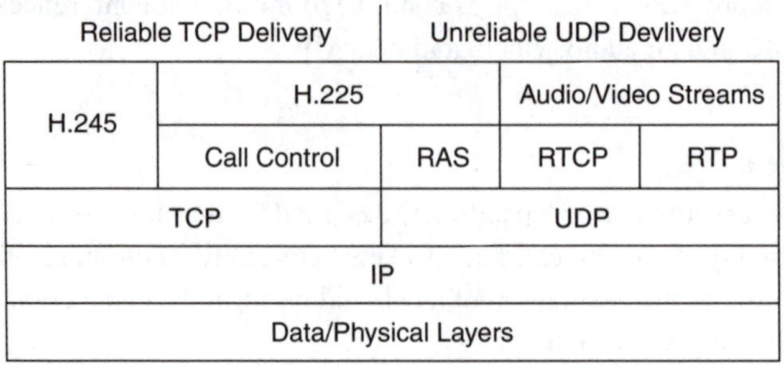

Reliable TCP Delivery		Unreliable UDP Devlivery		
H.245	H.225	Audio/Video Streams		
	Call Control	RAS	RTCP	RTP
TCP		UDP		
IP				
Data/Physical Layers				

The H.323 protocol suite is split into three main areas of control:

- Registration, Admissions, and Status (RAS) Signaling—Provides pre-call control in H.323 gatekeeper-based networks.

- Call Control Signaling—Used to connect, maintain, and disconnect calls between endpoints.

- Media Control and Transport—Provides the reliable H.245 channel that carries media control messages. The transport occurs with an unreliable UDP stream.

The remainder of this section focuses on these three key signaling functions.

RAS Signaling

RAS signaling provides pre-call control in H.323 networks where gatekeepers and a zone exist. The RAS channel is established between endpoints and gatekeepers across an IP network. The RAS channel is opened before any other channels are established and is independent of the call control signaling and media transport channels. This unreliable UDP connection carries the RAS messages that perform registration, admissions, bandwidth changes, status, and disengage procedures.

Gatekeeper Discovery

Gatekeeper discovery is a manual or automatic process endpoints use to identify which gatekeeper to register with. In the manual method, endpoints are configured with the gatekeeper's IP address and, therefore, can attempt registration immediately, but only with the predefined gatekeeper. The automatic method enables the relationship between endpoints and gatekeepers to change over time and requires a mechanism known as *auto discovery*.

Auto discovery enables an endpoint, which might not know its gatekeeper, to discover its gatekeeper through a multicast message. Because endpoints do not have to be statically configured or reconfigured for gatekeepers, this method has less administrative overhead. The gatekeeper discovery multicast address is 224.0.1.41, the gatekeeper UDP discovery port is 1718, and the gatekeeper UDP registration and status port is 1719. The following three RAS messages are used for H.323 gatekeeper auto discovery:

- Gatekeeper Request (GRQ)—A multicast message sent by an endpoint looking for the gatekeeper.

- Gatekeeper Confirm (GCF)—The reply to an endpoint GRQ indicating the transport address of the gatekeeper's RAS channel.

- Gatekeeper Reject (GRJ)—Advises the endpoint that the gatekeeper does not want to accept its registration. This is usually due to a configuration on the gateway or gatekeeper.

Figure 11-5 illustrates the messaging and sequencing processes for auto discovery.

Figure 11-5 *Gatekeeper Auto Discovery*

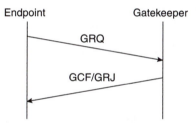

For redundancy purposes, the gatekeeper can identify alternative gatekeepers in GCF messages. You can use alternative gatekeepers when the primary gatekeeper fails.

Registration

Registration is the process that enables gateways, endpoints, and MCUs to join a zone and inform the gatekeeper of their IP and alias addresses. A necessary process, registration occurs after the discovery process, but before you can attempt any calls. You can use the following six messages to enable an endpoint to register and cancel registration:

- Registration Request (RRQ)—Sent from an endpoint to the gatekeeper RAS channel address

- Registration Confirm (RCF)—Sent by the gatekeeper and confirms an endpoint registration

- Registration Reject (RRJ)—Sent by the gatekeeper and rejects an endpoint registration

- Unregister Request (URQ)—Sent from an endpoint or gatekeeper to cancel a registration

- Unregister Confirm (UCF)—Sent from the endpoint or gatekeeper to confirm an unregistration

■ Unregister Reject (URJ)—Indicates that the endpoint was not preregistered with the gatekeeper

Figure 11-6 illustrates the messaging and sequencing processes for endpoint registering and endpoint and gatekeeper unregistering.

Figure 11-6 *Endpoint Registering and Endpoint and Gatekeeper Unregistering*

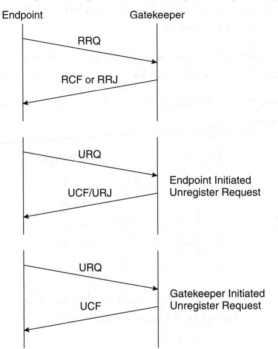

Endpoint Location

Endpoints and gatekeepers use *endpoint location* to obtain contact information when only alias information is available. Locate messages are sent to the gatekeeper's RAS channel address or are multicast to the gatekeeper's discovery multicast address. The gatekeeper responsible for the requested endpoint replies by indicating its own or the endpoint's contact information.

The endpoint or gatekeeper can include one or more E.164 addresses outside the zone in the request. You can use the following three messages to locate endpoints:

■ Location Request (LRQ)—Sent to request the endpoint or gatekeeper contact information for one or more E.164 addresses.

- Location Confirm (LCF)—Sent by the gatekeeper and contains the call signaling channel or RAS channel address of itself or the requested endpoint. It uses its own address when GKRCS is used and the requested endpoint's address when Directed Endpoint Call Signaling is used.

- Location Reject (LRJ)—Sent by gatekeepers that receive an LRQ for which the requested endpoint is not registered or has unavailable resources.

Admissions

Admission messages between endpoints and gatekeepers provide the basis for call admissions and bandwidth control. Gatekeepers authorize access to H.323 networks by confirming or rejecting an admission request. An admission request includes the requested bandwidth, which the gatekeeper can reduce in the confirmation. The following messages provide admissions control in H.323 networks:

- Admission Request (ARQ)—An attempt by an endpoint to initiate a call

- Admission Confirm (ACF)—An authorization by the gatekeeper to admit the call

- Admission Reject (ARJ)—Denies the endpoint's request to gain access to the network for this particular call

The ACF message contains the IP address of the terminating gateway or gatekeeper and enables the originating gateway to immediately initiate call control signaling procedures.

Status Information

The gatekeeper can use the RAS channel to obtain status information from an endpoint. You can use this message to monitor whether the endpoint is online and offline due to a failure condition. The typical polling period for status messages is 10 seconds. During the ACF, the gatekeeper also can request that the endpoint send periodic status messages during a call. You can use the following three messages to provide status on the RAS channel:

- Information Request (IRQ)—Sent from the gatekeeper to the endpoint requesting status.

- Information Request Response (IRR)—Sent from the endpoint to the gatekeeper in response to an IRQ. This message also is sent from an endpoint if the gatekeeper requests periodic status updates.

- Status Enquiry—Sent outside the RAS channel on the call signaling channel. An endpoint or gatekeeper can send Status Enquiry messages to another endpoint to verify call state. Gatekeepers typically use these messages to verify whether calls are still active.

Bandwidth Control

Bandwidth control is initially managed through the admissions exchange between an endpoint and the gatekeeper within the ARQ/ACF/ARJ sequence. The bandwidth can change during a call, however. You can use the following messages to change bandwidth:

■ Bandwidth Request (BRQ)—Sent by an endpoint to the gatekeeper requesting an increase or decrease in call bandwidth

■ Bandwidth Confirm (BCF)—Sent by the gatekeeper confirming acceptance of the bandwidth change request

■ Bandwidth Reject (BRJ)—Sent by the gatekeeper rejecting the bandwidth change request (sent if the requested bandwidth is not available)

> **NOTE**   Bandwidth control is limited in scope to only the gatekeeper and gateways and does not take into account the state of the network itself or the media capabilities (for example, codec type) of the endpoint. The gatekeeper currently looks only at its static bandwidth table to determine whether to accept or reject the bandwidth request.

Call Control Signaling (H.225)

In H.323 networks, call control procedures are based on International Telecommunication Union (ITU) Recommendation H.225, which specifies the use and support of Q.931 signaling messages. A reliable call control channel is created across an IP network on TCP port 1720. This port initiates the Q.931 call control messages between two endpoints for the purpose of connecting, maintaining, and disconnecting calls.

The actual call control and keepalive messages move to ephemeral ports (the ports that are temporarily assigned by a machine's IP stack for a specific use) after initial call setup. But 1720 is the well-known port for H.323 calls. H.225 also specifies the use of Q.932 messages for supplementary services. The following Q.931 and Q.932 messages are the most commonly used signaling messages in H.323 networks:

■ Setup—A forward message sent by the calling H.323 entity in an attempt to establish connection to the called H.323 entity. This message is sent on the well-known H.225 TCP port 1720.

■ Call Proceeding—A backward message sent from the called entity to the calling entity to advise that call establishment procedures were initiated.

■ Alerting—A backward message sent from the called entity to advise that called party ringing was initiated.

- Connect—A backward message sent from the called entity to the calling entity indicating that the called party answered the call. The connect message can contain the transport UDP/IP address for H.245 control signaling.

- Release Complete—Sent by the endpoint initiating the disconnect, which indicates that the call is being released. You can send this message only if the call signaling channel is open or active.

- Facility—A Q.932 message used to request or acknowledge supplementary services. It also is used to indicate whether a call should be directed or should go through a gatekeeper.

Figure 11-7 illustrates the signaling messages for call setup. Interaction with the gatekeeper is limited to RAS messages for call permission and, possibly, on status messages.

Figure 11-7 *Call Setup Signaling Messages*

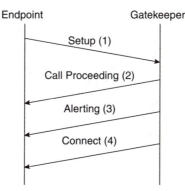

You can route the call signaling channel in an H.323 network in two ways:

- Direct Endpoint Call Signaling

- GKRCS

In the Direct Endpoint Call Signaling method, call signaling messages are sent directly between the two endpoints, as illustrated in Figure 11-8. This is more suitable to setups where a centrally controlled private dial plan is desired to work for endpoints. The endpoints supply the source information in many possible ways, such as with trunk group IDs, H.323-ID, trunk group (TG), and so on. Some GK applications/features that take advantage of this method are Least Call Routing (LCR), restriction lists, and so on as they receive all kinds of source information.

Figure 11-8 *Direct Endpoint Call Signaling*

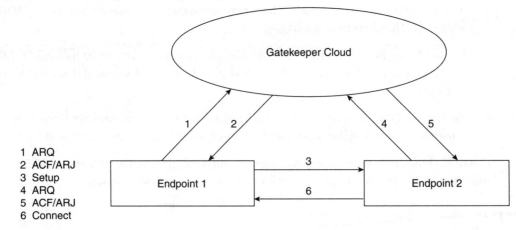

1 ARQ
2 ACF/ARJ
3 Setup
4 ARQ
5 ACF/ARJ
6 Connect

In the GKRCS method, call signaling messages between the endpoints are routed through the gatekeeper, as illustrated in Figure 11-9. Here, the endpoints supply the source information (for example, customer IDs) to route engines (RE) in the Gatekeeper to associate calls with different enterprises. The endpoints should, however, remove any customer IDs received from the REs to ensure proper caller ID display service.

Figure 11-9 *Gatekeeper Routed Call Signaling*

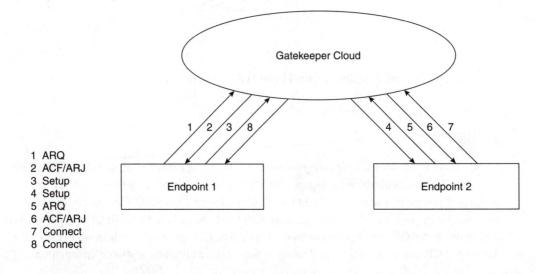

1 ARQ
2 ACF/ARJ
3 Setup
4 Setup
5 ARQ
6 ACF/ARJ
7 Connect
8 Connect

NOTE   In Figures 11-8 and 11-9, the Setup and Connect messages are call signaling channel messages, whereas the remaining messages are RAS channel messages.

You can offer supplementary services through the GKRCS method if the call signaling channel is left open during the call. Gatekeepers also can close the call signaling channel after call setup is complete. Some applications (for example, Wholesale VoIP) that require accurate call usage reporting and centralized provisioning of network elements prefer the GKRCS method. In other cases where the GW must not be a single point of failure and where the customer IDs and intelligent routing are important factors, applications prefer the direct endpoint signaling. A few applications that effectively use this method of defining are Least Cost Routing (LCR) and IP-based Contact Center.

Media Control and Transport (H.245 and RTP/RTCP)

H.245 handles end-to-end control messages between H.323 entities. H.245 procedures establish logical channels for transmission of audio, video, data, and control channel information. An endpoint establishes one H.245 channel for each call with the participating endpoint. The reliable control channel is created over IP using the dynamically assigned TCP port in the final call signaling message.

The exchange of capabilities, the opening and closing of logical channels, preference modes, and message control take place over this control channel. H.245 control also enables separate transmit and receive capability exchange as well as function negotiation, such as determining which codec to use.

If you use Gatekeeper Routed call signaling, you can control channel routing in two ways. You can use *Direct H.245 Control*, which occurs directly between two participating endpoints. Or, you can use *Gatekeeper Routed H.245 Control*, which occurs between each endpoint and its gatekeeper.

You can use the following procedures and messages to enable H.245 control operation:

■ Capability Exchange—Consists of messages that securely exchange the capabilities between two endpoints, also referred to as terminals. These messages indicate the terminal's transmit and receive capabilities for audio, video, and data to the participating terminal. For audio, capability exchange includes speech transcoding codecs such as G-series G.729 at 8 kbps, G.728 at 16 kbps, G.711 at 64 kbps, G.723 at 5.3 or 6.3 kbps, or G.722 at 48, 56, and 64 kbps. It also includes International Organization for Standardization (ISO) series IS.11172-3 with 32-, 44.1-, and 48 kHz sampling rates, and IS.13818-3 with 16-, 22.05-, 24-, 32-, 44.1-, and 48 kHz sampling rates; and GSM full-rate, half-rate, and enhanced full-rate speech audio codecs.

- Master-Slave Termination—Procedures used to determine which endpoint is master and which endpoint is slave for a particular call. The relationship is maintained for the duration of the call and is used to resolve conflicts between endpoints. Master-slave rules are used when both endpoints request similar actions at the same time.

- Round-Trip Delay—Procedures used to determine delay between the originating and terminating endpoints. The RoundTripDelayRequest message measures the delay and verifies whether the remote H.245 protocol entity is alive.

- Logical Channel Signaling—Opens and closes the logical channel that carries audio, video, and data information. The channel is set up before the actual transmission to ensure that the terminals are ready and capable of receiving and decoding information. The same signaling messages establish both uni-directional and bidirectional channels. After logical channel signaling is successfully established, the UDP port for the RTP media channel is passed from the terminating to the originating endpoint. Also, when using the Gatekeeper Call Routed model, this is the point at which the gatekeeper can divert the RTP streams by providing the actual UDP/IP address of the terminating endpoint.

Fast Connect Procedures

The two procedures available to establish media channels between endpoints are H.245 and Fast Connect. Fast Connect enables media connection establishment for basic point-to-point calls with one round-trip message exchange. These procedures dictate that the calling endpoint include the *faststart* element in the initial setup message.

The faststart portion consists of logical channel sequences, media channel capabilities, and the necessary parameters to open and begin media transmission. In response, the called endpoint returns an H.225 message (call proceeding, progress, alerting, or connect) containing a faststart element that selects the accepted terminal capabilities. At this point, both the calling and called endpoints can begin transmitting media if the setup sequence based on H.225 reached the connected state.

This method enables faster call setup times and is much simpler than executing the H.245 control messaging.

Tunneling H.245

You can encapsulate or tunnel H.245 messages within the H.225 call signaling channel instead of creating a separate H.245 control channel. This method improves call setup time and resource allocation, and it provides synchronization between call signaling and control. You can encapsulate multiple H.245 messages in any H.225 message. Also, at any time either endpoint can switch to a separate H.245 connection.

The fastStart method (also known as H.450.6 Extended Fast Connect [EFC]) is very useful in certain applications, such as where a network element in the middle of the network wants to play media to the calling endpoint before connecting the call (for example, to announce the amount of remaining credit or indicating that the call is progressing). Before the introduction of fastStart, the interior network element had to perform H.245 logical channel setup to transmit its message. The interior network element would then have to send an "Empty Capability Set" message to the calling endpoint, redirect the H.225.0 and H.245 signaling toward the called endpoint, and exchange a number of H.245 to reestablish media. With fastStart, the procedures are simplified and the call setup times are reduced.

Call Termination

Either endpoint participating in a call can initiate call termination procedures. First, the endpoint must cease media transmissions (such as audio, video, or data) and close all logical channels. Next, it must end the H.245 session and send a release complete message on the call signaling channel, if it's still open or active. At this point, if no gatekeeper is present, the call is terminated. When a gatekeeper is present, the following messages are used on the RAS channel to complete call termination:

- Disengage Request (DRQ)—Sent by an endpoint or gatekeeper to terminate a call

- Disengage Confirm (DCF)—Sent by an endpoint or gatekeeper confirming disconnection of the call

- Disengage Reject (DRJ)—Sent by the endpoint or gatekeeper rejecting call disconnection

Media Transport (RTP/RTCP)

RTP provides media transport in H.323. More specifically, RTP enables real-time, end-to-end delivery of interactive audio, video, and data over unicast or multicast networks. Packetization and transmission services include payload identification, sequencing, timestamping, and monitoring.

RTP relies on other mechanisms and lower layers to ensure on-time delivery, resource reservation, reliability, and QoS. RTCP monitors data delivery as well as controls and identifies services. The media channel is created using UDP, where RTP streams operate on an even port number and the corresponding RTCP stream operates on the next-higher (odd) port number.

H.323 Call-Flows

The call-flows outlined in this section demonstrate ways the H.323 family of protocols provides call setup between two endpoints. Assume these are speech calls and that all endpoints already completed registration with the appropriate gatekeeper. The call setup examples include two different gatekeeper implementations as well as two different call signaling methods.

The examples in Figures 11-10 and 11-11 detail call setup procedures for single gatekeeper implementations. Figure 11-10 illustrates call-flows using direct endpoint signaling between two endpoints sharing the gatekeeper.

Figure 11-10   *Direct Endpoint Signaling—Same Gatekeeper*

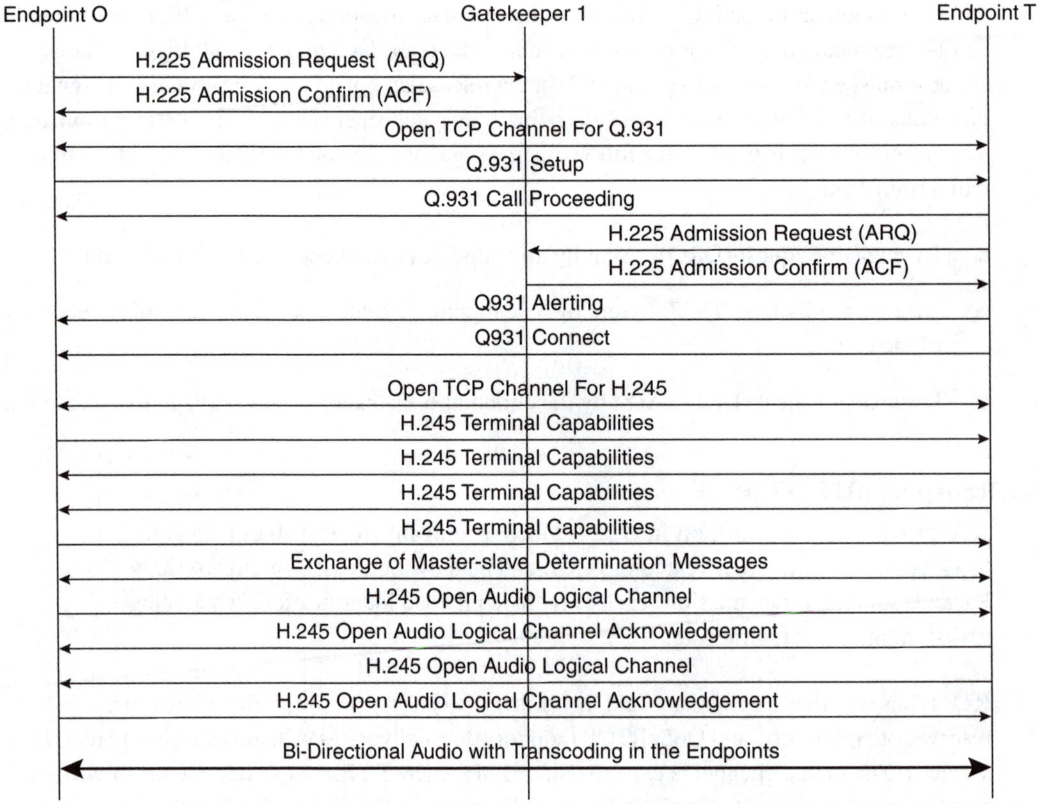

Figure 11-11 illustrates call-flows using gatekeeper call routed signaling between two endpoints sharing the gatekeeper. Note that the H.245 procedure is handled directly between the endpoints and is not gatekeeper-routed.

Figure 11-11   *Gatekeeper-Routed Call Signaling—Same Gatekeeper*

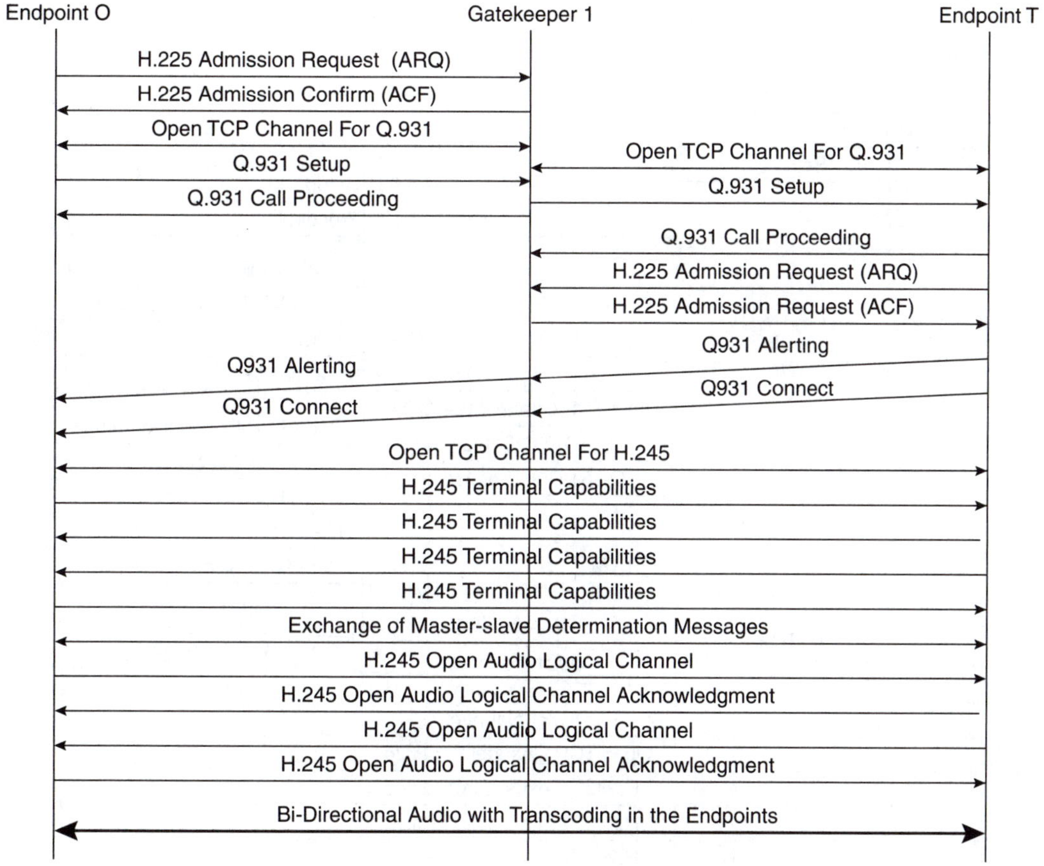

The examples in Figures 11-12 and 11-13 detail call setup procedures for dual-gatekeeper implementations. Specifically, Figure 11-12 illustrates call-flows using direct endpoint signaling between two endpoints that have different gatekeepers. The main difference between GKRCS and Directed Call Signaling is that in GKRCS the setup message is directed to the gatekeeper, and in Directed Call Signaling it is directed to the terminating endpoint.

Figure 11-12 *Direct Endpoint Signaling—Two Gatekeepers*

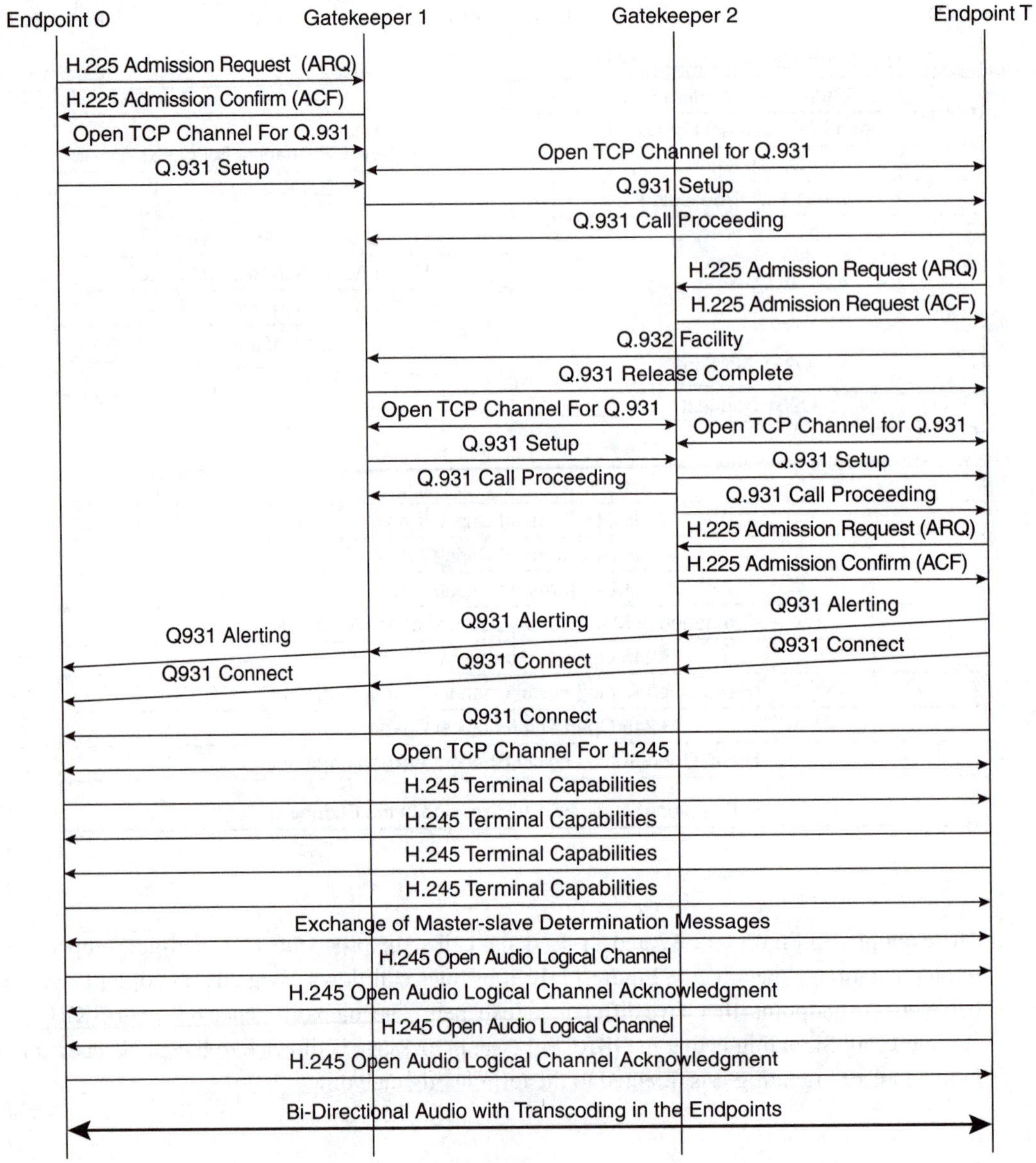

Endpoint O	Gatekeeper 1	Gatekeeper 2	Endpoint T

H.225 Admission Request (ARQ)

H.225 Admission Confirm (ACF)

Open TCP Channel For Q.931

Open TCP Channel for Q.931

Q.931 Setup

Q.931 Setup

Q.931 Call Proceeding

H.225 Admission Request (ARQ)

H.225 Admission Request (ACF)

Q.932 Facility

Q.931 Release Complete

Open TCP Channel For Q.931

Open TCP Channel for Q.931

Q.931 Setup

Q.931 Setup

Q.931 Call Proceeding

Q.931 Call Proceeding

H.225 Admission Request (ARQ)

H.225 Admission Confirm (ACF)

Q931 Alerting

Q931 Alerting

Q931 Alerting

Q931 Connect

Q931 Connect

Q931 Connect

Q931 Connect

Open TCP Channel For H.245

H.245 Terminal Capabilities

H.245 Terminal Capabilities

H.245 Terminal Capabilities

H.245 Terminal Capabilities

Exchange of Master-slave Determination Messages

H.245 Open Audio Logical Channel

H.245 Open Audio Logical Channel Acknowledgment

H.245 Open Audio Logical Channel

H.245 Open Audio Logical Channel Acknowledgment

Bi-Directional Audio with Transcoding in the Endpoints

The final H.323 call-flow example demonstrates call setup procedures for the GKRCS method, whereby each endpoint has a different gatekeeper. This enables LRQs and LCFs to be sent between the two gatekeepers, which enables control of billing records at the gatekeeper as all the setup and control messages pass through the gatekeeper.

Figure 11-13 *Gatekeeper Routed Call Signaling—Two Gatekeepers*

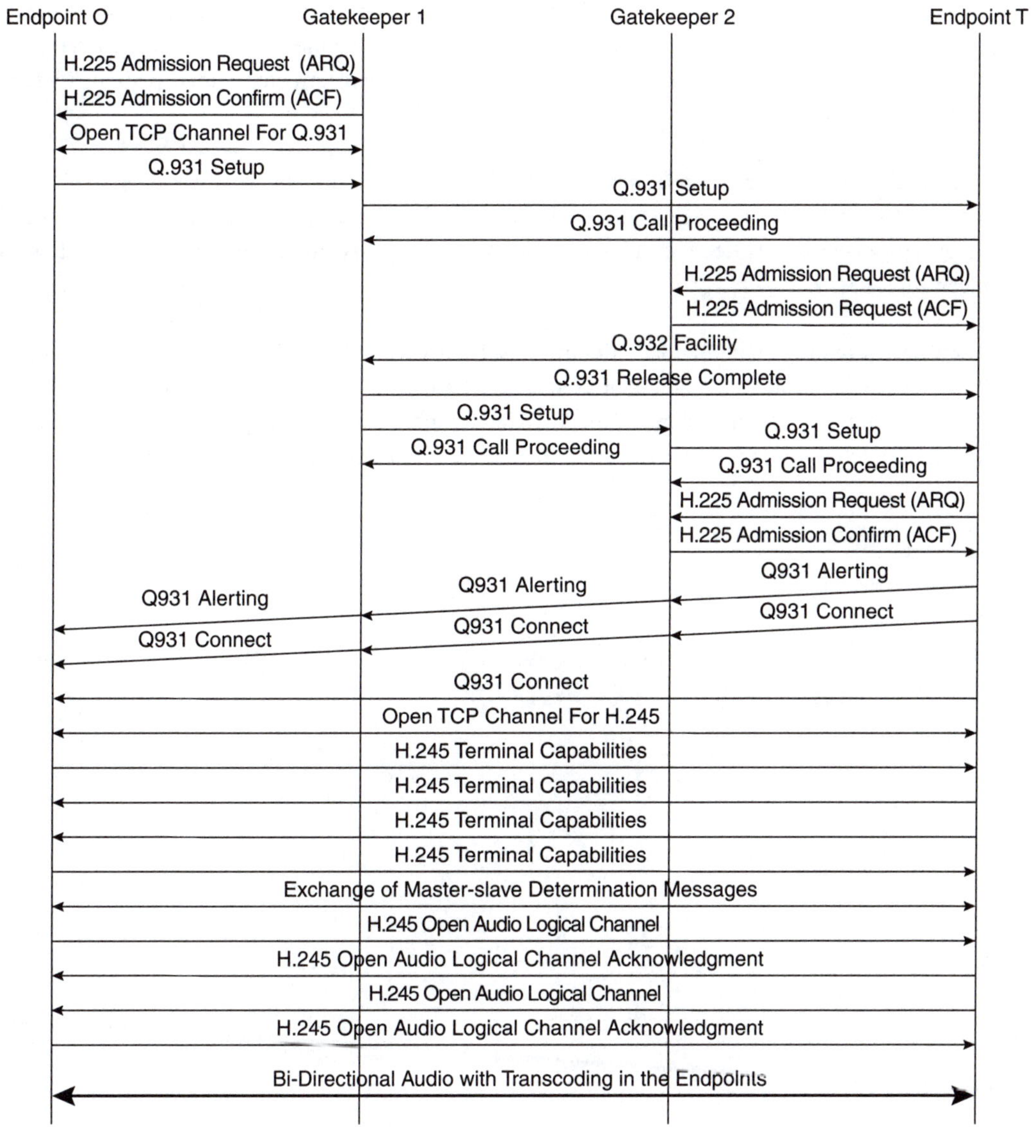

Summary

H.323 is a hybrid system constructed of centralized intelligent gatekeepers, MCUs, and less intelligent endpoints. Although the H.323 standard is more complete in recent revisions, issues have arisen, such as long call-setup times, overhead of a full-featured conferencing protocol, too many functions required in each gatekeeper, and scalability concerns for gatekeeper call-routed implementations.

When high-density gateways are needed for PSTN interconnection, alternatives such as Media Gateway Control Protocol (MGCP) and H.248 (MEGACO) are also considered. These call control systems provide a more effective and scalable solution for satisfying carrier-class implementations in certain cases.

Likewise, for intelligent endpoint configurations, SIP (Session Initiation Protocol) solves some of the problems found in H.323 and is offered as an alternative in many networks. However, H.323 still commands a substantial share of the VoIP deployments in the service provider voice market. Chapter 12, "Session Initiation Protocols," discusses SIP in more detail.

SIP

Session Initiation Protocol (SIP) is a signaling protocol that controls the initiation, modification, and termination of interactive multimedia sessions. The multimedia sessions could be as diverse as audio or video calls among two or more parties, chat sessions, or game sessions. SIP extensions have also been defined for instant messaging, presence, and event notifications. SIP is a text-based protocol that is similar to HTTP and Simple Mail Transfer Protocol (SMTP).

SIP is a peer-to-peer protocol, which means that network capabilities such as call routing and session management functions are distributed across all the nodes (including endpoints and network servers) within the SIP network. This is in contrast to the traditional telephony model, where the phones or end-user devices are completely dependent on centralized switches in the network for call session establishment and services.

SIP was defined in RFC 2543 (March 1999) by the Multiparty Multimedia Session Control (MMUSIC) Working group of the Internet Engineering Task Force (IETF). In June 2002, the IETF published a new SIP RFC (RFC 3261). IP telephony is still being developed and will require additional signaling capabilities in the future. The extensibility of SIP enables such development of incremental functionality. This chapter also describes some of the key extensions.

This chapter covers the following topics:

- SIP Overview—Covers function, network elements, and interaction with other protocols

- SIP Message Building Blocks—Covers SIP addressing, messages and headers, transactions, and dialogs

- Basic Operation of SIP—Provides a proxy, redirect server, and B2BUA server example

- SIP Procedures for Registration and Routing—Covers locating SIP servers, registering, and message routing

- SIP Extensions—Covers caller and callee preferences, Subscription-Notification, REFER, presence, and IM

SIP Overview

This section describes the key components of a SIP network, their function, and the interaction between them.

Functionality That SIP Provides

SIP provides the following capabilities for enabling multimedia sessions:

■ User location—SIP provides the capability to discover the location of the end user for the purpose of establishing a session or delivering a SIP request. User mobility is inherently supported in SIP.

■ User capabilities—SIP enables the determination of the media capabilities of the devices that are involved in the session.

■ User availability—SIP enables the determination of the willingness of the end user to engage in communication.

■ Session setup—SIP enables the establishment of session parameters for the parties who are involved in the session.

■ Session handling—SIP enables the modification, transfer, and termination of an active session.

SIP Network Elements

The SIP network typically comprises the following devices:

■ User agent—A user agent (UA) is a logical function in the SIP network that initiates or responds to SIP transactions. A UA can act as either the client or the server in a SIP transaction. A UA might or might not directly interact with a human user. A UA is stateful—that is, it maintains session or dialog state.

■ User agent client—A user agent client (UAC) is a logical function that initiates SIP requests and accepts SIP responses. Examples of UAC are a SIP phone initiating a call on behalf of a human user or a SIP Proxy forwarding a request on behalf of a UAC.

■ User agent server—A user agent server (UAS) is a logical function that accepts SIP requests and sends back SIP responses. A SIP phone accepting an INVITE request is one example.

■ Proxy—A proxy is an intermediate entity in the SIP network that is responsible for forwarding SIP requests to the target UAS or another proxy on behalf of the UAC. A proxy primarily provides the routing function in the SIP network. A proxy might also enforce policy in the network, such as authenticating a user before providing him with service. A proxy can be stateless, transaction stateful, or call stateful. Typically, proxies are transaction stateful—that is, they maintain state for the duration of a transaction (about 32 seconds).

- Redirect server—A redirect server is a UAS that generates 300 class SIP responses to requests it receives, directing the UAC to contact an alternate set of Uniform Resource Identifiers (URI).

- Registrar server—A registrar is a UAS that accepts SIP REGISTER requests and updates the information from the request message into a location database.

- Back-to-back user agent—A back-to-back user agent (B2BUA) is an intermediate entity that processes incoming SIP requests as a UAS. To answer the incoming SIP request, the B2BUA acts as a UAC, regenerates a SIP request, and sends it on the network. A B2BUA must maintain dialog state and participates in all transactions within the dialog.

Interaction with Other IETF Protocols

SIP by itself does not provide all the capabilities that are required to set up an interactive multimedia session. Instead, SIP is a protocol that is part of the framework of standard protocols that builds a multimedia architecture.

SIP agents or applications need other protocols for the following:

- To describe the characteristics of a session—The characteristics include whether a session is an audio or video session, what codecs are used, what the media source is, and what the destination addresses are.

- To handle media—These protocols control and transmit audio/video packets for a session.

- To support functions—Needs include AAA for authentication, authorization, and accounting; Resource Reservation Protocol (RSVP) for reserving network resources; Telephony Routing over IP (TRIP) for gateway selection and load balancing; Simple Traversal of UDP Through NAT (STUN)/Traversal Using Relay NAT (TURN)/Interactive Connectivity Establishment (ICE) protocols for firewall and NAT traversals; Domain Name System (DNS) for hostname-to-IP address resolution; and Transport Layer Security (TLS) for preventing eavesdropping, tampering, or message forgery.

Sessions that are established using SIP typically use the following IETF protocols:

- DNS—SIP session establishment might require the use of DNS to resolve host or domain names into routable IP addresses. DNS can also be used to load-share across multiple servers in a cluster identified by a hostname.

- Session Description Protocol (SDP)—SDP is used in a SIP message body to describe the parameters of the multimedia session. This information includes session type such as audio, video, or both and parameters such as codecs or ports needed to establish a media stream. RFC 2327 defines SDP.

■ Real-time Transport Protocol (RTP)—RTP, first defined in RFC 1889, transports real-time data such as audio or video packets to the endpoints that are involved in a session. Real-time Transport Control Protocol (RTCP), defined in RFC 1890, provides quality of service (QoS) feedback to the sender. RFC 3550 obsoletes RFC 1889.

■ RSVP—SIP can use RSVP to reserve network resources such as bandwidth prior to establishment of the media session. This ensures that the network resources are in place prior to the called party being alerted about an incoming call.

■ TLS—SIP recommends the use of TLS, defined in RFC 2246, to provide privacy and integrity of SIP signaling information over the network. TLS allows the client and server applications to authenticate each other, negotiate encryption algorithms, and establish cryptographic keys before sending the signaling information over the network.

■ STUN—SIP UACs can use the STUN protocol to discover the presence and type of Network Address Translation (NAT) between them and the public Internet. STUN also allows the client to discover the public IP address that is allocated to the NAT. This procedure works for most types of NAT except symmetric NAT. Symmetric NAT occurs when all requests from the same internal IP address and port to a specific destination IP address and port are mapped to the same external source IP address and port.

The preceding is by no means an exhaustive list of protocols that SIP uses. Depending on the signaling and application requirements, SIP might use other protocols.

SIP does not necessitate the use of the protocols in the preceding list. In the future, if newer or enhanced protocols perform similar functions, SIP will be able to use them with little or no change. Most of the information associated with these protocols is carried in the SIP message body. SIP treats the message body as an opaque container and transports it to the recipient. The SIP protocol layer does not interpret the message body.

SIP signaling is thus independent of the type of session being established. Therefore, from a SIP signaling perspective, the same set of messages is used regardless of whether an audio session, audio-video session, or some other type of session is established.

Message Flow in SIP Network

Figure 12-1 shows a basic SIP network comprising SIP proxies and user agents with connection to public switched telephone network (PSTN). The SIP UA, proxies, and SIP-PSTN gateway are located within an IP network. The SIP-PSTN gateway has SS7/PRI trunks going to a switch in the PSTN.

In Figure 12-1, solid lines represent SIP requests, and dotted lines indicate SIP responses.

Figure 12-1 *Path Taken by Request and Response Messages in a SIP Network*

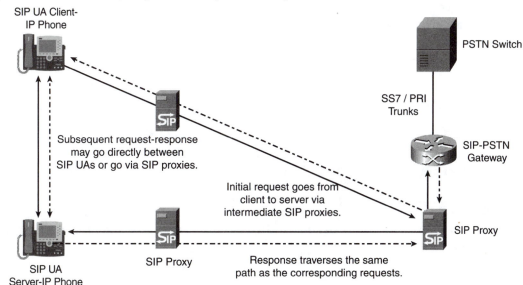

SIP Message Building Blocks

This section describes the structure of SIP messages, addressing schemes, and key header fields. Much of the SIP messages and header field syntax is identical to HTTP/1.1. Refer to RFC 3261 for an in-depth description.

> **NOTE**   You can find all RFCs online at http://www.ietf.org/rfc/rfcxxx.txt, where xxxx is the number of the RFC. If you do not know the number of the RFC, you can try searching by topic at http://www.rfc-editor.org/cgi-bin/rfcsearch.pl.

SIP Addressing

SIP addresses identify a user or a resource within a network domain. SIP addresses are typically referred to as *SIP URI*. A SIP URI is typically an e-mail-type address with a format such as one of the following:

        sip:user@domain:port
        sip:user@host:port

The user field identifies a user by name, such as john.doe, or by telephone number, such as 4081234567, within the context of a domain or a host. The port is an optional field. If no port is specified, the default port for a SIP URI is 5060. If a port is explicitly specified, you must use it. Examples of SIP URIs are as follows:

        sip:john.doe@company.com
        sip:4081234567@proxy1.company.com

The public SIP address of a user or a resource is referred to as an Address-of-Record (AOR). An AOR is a SIP URI that is globally routable and points to a domain whose location service can map the AOR to another SIP URI, where the user might be located.

RFC 3261 specifies a secure SIP URI format also known as a SIPS URI. The format of a SIPS URI is as follows:

> sips:user@domain:port

or

> sips:user@host:port

The default port for a SIPS URI is 5061.

SIP Messages

SIP messages can be broadly divided into SIP requests and responses, as further defined in the sections that follow.

SIP Requests

SIP requests are messages that are sent from client to server to invoke a SIP operation. RFC 3261 defines six SIP requests or methods that enable UA and proxy to locate users and initiate, modify, and tear down sessions:

■ INVITE—An INVITE method indicates that the recipient user or service is invited to participate in a session. You can also use this method to modify the characteristics of a previously established session. The INVITE message body might include the description of the media session being set up or modified, encoded per SDP. A successful response (200 OK response) to an INVITE indicates the willingness of the called party to participate in the resulting media session.

■ ACK—An ACK request confirms that the UAC has received the final response to an INVITE request. ACK is used only with INVITE requests. ACK is sent end to end for a 200 OK response. The previous hop proxy or UAC sends ACK for other final responses. The ACK request can include a message body with the final session description if the INVITE request did not contain a session description.

■ OPTIONS—A UA uses the OPTIONS request to query a UAS about its capabilities. If the UAS is capable of delivering a session to the user, it responds with the capability set of the UAS.

■ BYE—A UA uses BYE to request the termination of a previously established session.

■ CANCEL—The CANCEL request enables UACs and network servers to cancel an in-progress request, such as INVITE. This does not affect completed requests in which the UAS had already sent final responses.

■ REGISTER—A client uses a REGISTER request to register its current location information corresponding to the AOR of the user with SIP servers.

SIP Responses

A server sends a SIP response to a client to indicate the status of a SIP request that the client previously sent to the server. The UAS or proxy generates SIP responses in response to a SIP request that the UAC initiates. SIP responses are numbered from 100 to 699. SIP responses are grouped as 1xx, 2xx, and so on through 6xx. SIP responses are classified as *provisional* and *final*.

A provisional response indicates progress by the server but does not indicate the final outcome as a result of processing the SIP request. The 1xx class of SIP response indicates provisional status. A final response indicates the termination and the final status of a SIP request. All 2xx, 3xx, 4xx, 5xx, and 6xx class responses are final, specifically:

■ A 2xx class response indicates successful processing of the SIP request.

■ A 3xx class response indicates that the SIP request needs to be redirected to another UAS for processing.

■ A 4xx, 5xx, or 6xx class of response indicates failure in processing of the SIP request.

Table 12-1 lists the various SIP responses per RFC 3261.

Table 12-1   *SIP Response Table*

Class of Response	Status Code	Explanation
Informational	100	Trying
	180	Ringing
	181	Call is being forwarded
	182	Queued
	183	Session progress
Success	200	OK
Redirection	300	Multiple choices
	301	Moved permanently
	302	Moved temporarily
	305	Use proxy
	380	Alternative service

Table 12-1 *SIP Response Table (Continued)*

Class of Response	Status Code	Explanation
Client-Error	400	Bad request
	401	Unauthorized
	402	Payment required
	403	Forbidden
	404	Not found
	405	Method not allowed
	406	Not acceptable
	407	Proxy authentication required
	408	Request timeout
	410	Gone
	413	Request entity too large
	414	Requested URL too large
	415	Unsupported media type
	416	Unsupported URI scheme
	420	Bad extension
	421	Extension required
	423	Interval too brief
	480	Temporarily not available
	481	Call leg or transaction does not exist
	482	Loop detected
	483	Too many hops
	484	Address incomplete
	485	Ambiguous
	486	Busy here
	487	Request terminated
	488	Not acceptable here
	491	Request pending
	493	Undecipherable

Table 12-1   *SIP Response Table (Continued)*

Class of Response	Status Code	Explanation
Server-Error	500	Internal server error
	501	Not implemented
	502	Bad gateway
	503	Service unavailable
	504	Server timeout
	505	SIP version not supported
	513	Message too large
Global Failure	600	Busy everywhere
	603	Decline
	604	Does not exist anywhere
	606	Not acceptable

SIP Message Structure

A SIP message consists of the following:

- A start-line

- One or more header fields

- An empty line indicating the end of header fields

- An optional message body

You must terminate the start-line, each message-header line, and the empty line by a Carriage Return Line Feed (CRLF) sequence.

The start-line for a SIP request is a Request-Line. The start-line for a SIP response is a Status-line.

The Request-Line specifies the SIP method, the Request-URI, and the SIP version. The Status-line describes the SIP version, the SIP response code, and an optional reason phrase. The reason phrase is a textual description of the 3-digit SIP response code.

Table 12-2 shows the various components of a SIP request message.

Table 12-2   *SIP Request Components*

INVITE sip:bob@proxy.company.com SIP/2.0	Request Line
Via: SIP/2.0/UDP ph1.company.com:5060;branch=z9hG4bK83749.1 From: Alice <sip:alice@company.com>;tag=1234567 To: Bob <sip:bob@proxy.company.com> Call-ID: 12345601@ph1.company.com CSeq: 1 INVITE Contact: <sip:alice@ph1.company.com> Content-Type: application/sdp Content-Length: ...	SIP Message headers
	Blank line between SIP header fields and body
v=0 o=alice 2890844526 28908445456 IN IP4 172.18.193.102 s=Session SDP c=IN IP4 172.18.193.102 t=0 0 m=audio 49170 RTP/AVP 0 a=rtpmap:0 PCMU/8000	SDP body in SIP message

*The information in Table 12-2 is taken from RFC 3261.

Table 12-3 shows the structure of a SIP response message.

Table 12-3   *SIP Response Components*

SIP/2.0 200 OK	Status (Response) Line
Via: SIP/2.0/UDP ph1.company.com:5060;branch=z9hG4bK83749.1 From: Alice <sip:alice@company.com>;tag=1234567 To: Bob <sip:bob@proxy.company.com>;tag=9345678 Call-ID: 12345601@ph1.company.com CSeq: 1 INVITE Content-Length: …	SIP message headers
	Blank line between SIP header fields and body
v=0 o=bob 3800844316 3760844696 IN IP4 172.18.193.109 s=Session SDP c=IN IP4 172.18.193.109 t=0 0 m=audio 48140 RTP/AVP 0 a=rtpmap:0 PCMU/8000	SDP body in 200 OK response

*The information presented in Table 12-3 is taken from RFC 3261.

SIP Headers

A SIP message is composed of header fields (defined in RFC 3261) that convey the signaling and routing information for the SIP network entities. SIP follows the same format as defined for an HTTP header (RFC 2616). Each header field consists of a field name followed by a colon (:) and the field value.

Table 12-4 describes the functions of the key SIP headers

Table 12-4   *Key SIP Headers*

SIP Header	Explanation
From	This header indicates the identity of the initiator of a SIP request. The From header is usually the AOR of the sender. It consists of a SIP or SIPS URI and an optional display name.
To	This header indicates the desired recipient of a SIP request. The To header is usually the AOR of the recipient. The SIP request might not always be delivered to the "desired" recipient because of redirection or forwarding. The To header consists of a SIP or SIPS URI and an optional display name.
Call-ID	This header field identifies a series of SIP messages. Call-ID must be identical for all SIP requests and responses sent by either UA within a dialog.
Cseq	This header is composed of an integer value and method-name. This header identifies, orders, and sequences SIP requests within a dialog. The Cseq header also differentiates between message retransmissions and new messages.
Via	The Via header indicates the path taken by the request and identifies where the response needs to be sent.
Contact	This header identifies a SIP or SIPS URI where the UA wants to receive a new SIP request.
Allow	The Allow header lists the set of SIP methods supported by the UA that is generating the message.
Supported	This header lists all SIP extensions supported by the UA. SIP extensions are SIP RFCs other than RFC 3261. SIP extensions are represented as option tags such as 100rel defined in RFC 3262.
Require	This header has similar semantics to the Supported header, but the support of the SIP extension at the remote UA is a must for the transaction to be processed.
Content-Type	This header indicates the type of the message body that is attached to a SIP request or response. This header must be present if the SIP message has a body.
Content-Length	This header indicates the size of the message body (in decimal) in a SIP message. This header is a must when SIP messages are carried over stream-based protocols such as TCP.

SIP Transactions and Dialog

A SIP signaling session between two user agents might be comprised of one or more SIP transactions. A SIP transaction occurs between a UAC and a UAS, which might involve one or more intermediate SIP servers such as proxy or redirect. A SIP transaction comprises all messages that begin with the SIP request initiated from the UAC, until a final response (that is, a non-1xx response) is received from the UAS. A SIP transaction is identified by the Call-ID, via-branch, local tag, remote tag, and CSeq value. Figure 12-2 shows a SIP REGISTER transaction between a UAC and a registrar server. The SIP transaction comprises a SIP request message followed by one or more SIP response messages. In this case, the REGISTER message is a SIP request sent from the UAC to the registrar server. 100 Trying and 200 OK are SIP responses. The user agent server sends SIP responses to the UAC indicating the status of the SIP request.

Figure 12-2 *SIP REGISTER Transaction*

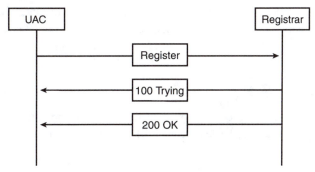

A SIP transaction can result in the establishment, modification, or termination of a media session. The establishment of a session also results in a SIP signaling relationship between the peers, known as a *dialog*. A dialog is defined as a peer-to-peer SIP relationship between two or more UAs that persists for the duration of the session. A dialog is the state identified by the Call-ID, the local tag, and the remote tag. Not all SIP transactions affect the state of a dialog. Multiple SIP transactions might take place within the context of a SIP dialog. Each SIP transaction within a dialog has a sequentially increasing integer value in the CSeq header.

A successful INVITE-200 OK transaction results in the establishment of a SIP dialog and an audio or video session between the participants. After the media session is established, you can exchange INVITE messages within the existing dialog context using the same Call-ID and tags to modify the media session parameters. Later, you can tear down the dialog using a BYE transaction or transfer it to another device using a REFER transaction, again within the dialog context.

A successful SUBSCRIBE-200 OK transaction results in the establishment of a dialog. The SUBSCRIBE request is discussed in the "SIP Extensions" section.

Dialog and transaction states are maintained at the SIP UAs or endpoints. SIP servers such as proxy and redirect typically maintain state for the duration of the transaction—that is, they maintain only the transaction state. The transaction state is held for at least 32 seconds per RFC 3261. SIP servers such as proxies and redirect servers maintain the transaction state, but not the dialog state, which enables them to serve many SIP endpoints. Because the network servers maintain only transaction state, a proxy that is going out of service within a cluster affects the transactions that are in progress but has no effect on established dialogs.

Transport Layer Protocols for SIP Signaling

SIP transactions use either connection-oriented transport layer protocols such as TCP or Stream Control Transmission Protocol (SCTP) or connectionless protocols such as UDP. For connectionless protocols, SIP specifies that the SIP application start retransmission timers to retry the SIP requests to guarantee end-to-end reliability.

SIP defines a SIPS URI, which indicates the need for securing the end-to-end SIP signaling information in a network. SIP RFC 3261 specifies the use of TLS or IPsec to encrypt the signaling information.

Basic Operation of SIP

SIP servers handle incoming requests in two ways. This basic operative is based on inviting a participant to a call. The three basic modes of SIP server operation described in this section are as follows:

■ Proxy servers

■ Redirect servers

■ B2BUA servers

Proxy Server Example

Figure 12-3 illustrates the communication exchange for the INVITE method using the proxy server.

Figure 12-3 *Proxy Mode of Operation*

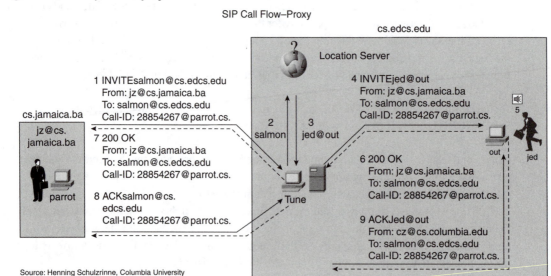

Source: Henning Schulzrinne, Columbia University

The operational steps in the proxy mode needed to bring a two-way call to succession are as follows:

1. The proxy server accepts the INVITE request from the client.

2. The proxy server contacts the location server to request the address of the called party UA.

3. The location server identifies the location of the called party and provides the address of the target server.

4. The INVITE request is forwarded to the address of the location that is returned. The proxy might add a Record-Route header to the INVITE message to ensure that all subsequent messages for that dialog are routed via the proxy. This might be needed for billing purposes or other applications that need to see the messaging for that dialog.

5. The called party UA alerts the user. The user answers the call.

6. The UAS returns a 200 OK indication to the requesting proxy server.

7. The 200 OK response is forwarded from the proxy server to the calling party UA.

8. The calling party UA confirms receipt of the 200 OK by issuing an ACK request, which is sent to the proxy (when the proxy inserts the Record-Route header in the INVITE message) or sent directly to the called party UA.

9. The proxy forwards the ACK to the called party UA.

Redirect Server Example

Figure 12-4 illustrates the protocol exchange for the INVITE request using the redirect server.

Figure 12-4 *Redirect Server Mode of Operation*

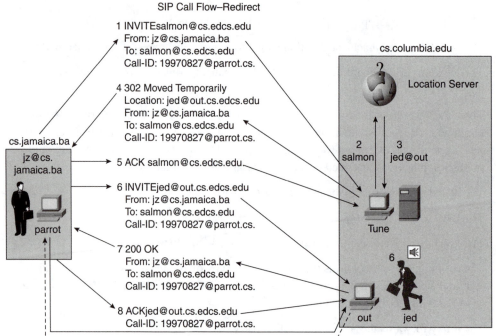

SIP Call Flow–Redirect

1 INVITEsalmon@cs.edcs.edu
From: jz@cs.jamaica.ba
To: salmon@cs.edcs.edu
Call-ID: 19970827@parrot.cs.

4 302 Moved Temporarily
Location: jed@out.cs.edcs.edu
From: jz@cs.jamaica.ba
To: salmon@cs.edcs.edu
Call-ID: 19970827@parrot.cs.

cs.jamaica.ba

jz@cs.
jamaica.ba

parrot

5 ACK salmon@cs.edcs.edu

6 INVITEjed@out.cs.edcs.edu
From: jz@cs.jamaica.ba
To: salmon@cs.edcs.edu
Call-ID: 19970827@parrot.cs.

7 200 OK
From: jz@cs.jamaica.ba
To: salmon@cs.edcs.edu
Call-ID: 19970827@parrot.cs.

8 ACKjed@out.cs.edcs.edu
Call-ID: 19970827@parrot.cs.

cs.columbia.edu

Location Server

2
salmon

3
jed@out

Tune

6

out   jed

Source: Henning Schulzrinne, Columbia University

The operational steps in the redirect mode to bring a two-way call to succession are as follows:

1. The redirect server accepts the INVITE request from the calling party UA.

2. The redirect server contacts location services to get the address of the called party UA.

3. Location services returns the address of the called party UA.

4. After the user is located, the redirect server returns the address directly to the calling party in a 3xx message, with an updated Contact: header pointing to the new destination(s). Unlike the proxy server, the redirect server does not forward an INVITE.

5. The UAC sends an ACK to the redirect server acknowledging the 3xx response.

6. The UAC sends an INVITE request directly to the Contact: address returned by the redirect server.

7. The called party UA alerts the user, and the user answers the call. The called party UA provides a success indication (200 OK) to the UAC.

8. The UAC sends an ACK to the UAS acknowledging the 200 OK response.

B2BUA Server Example

RFC 3261 does not define the B2BUA functionality. It describes it as concatenation of UAC and UAS. However, B2BUA forms an important element in providing centralized call control and feature management in SIP networks. Unlike a proxy, B2BUA can initiate new SIP calls and modify and terminate existing calls. SIP calls via a B2BUA server result in creation of two distinct dialogs, which enable it to modify one SIP session without affecting the other session.

B2BUA can act as a third-party call controller (3PCC) and can establish calls between two user agents. Figure 12-5 illustrates B2BUA acting as a 3PCC establishing calls between users A and B. RFC 3725 defines the best current practices for third-party call control in SIP. 3PCC modifies the session characteristics by modifying the Session Description Protocol (SDP) body. SDP is defined in RFC 2327.

Figure 12-5 illustrates the steps for call establishment in B2BUA server mode. This illustration is one of the four message flows described in RFC 3725.

Figure 12-5 *B2BUA Server Mode of Operation*

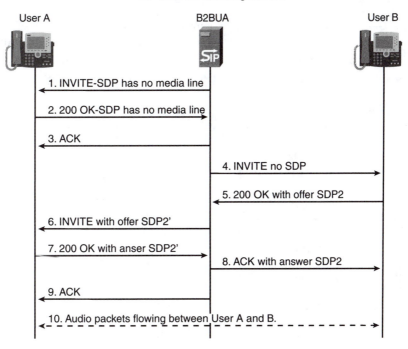

1. B2BUA sends an INVITE to user A. This INVITE contains an SDP body without media lines. This means that the media characteristics will be defined later by another INVITE.

2. User A is alerted. A 180 Ringing message will be sent from user A to B2BUA, but it is not shown explicitly in this message flow. When the call is answered, a 200 OK is sent to B2BUA. This 200 OK has an SDP body without media lines.

3. B2BUA sends an ACK to user A.

4. B2BUA sends an INVITE to user B. The INVITE message does not contain an SDP body.

5. User B is alerted and answers the call. 200 OK with offer SDP is sent back to the B2BUA.

6. B2BUA uses the SDP received in the 200 OK to create an INVITE with an SDP body and sends it to user A. The SDP body in the INVITE message is a modified version of the SDP body received in the 200 OK from user B. That is why it is labeled SDP2' in the message flow.

7. User A responds with a 200 OK with the answer SDP to B2BUA.

8. B2BUA sends an ACK with answer SDP to user B.

9. B2BUA sends an ACK to user A to acknowledge the 200 OK.

10. A call is established between user A and B. Audio packets are sent between user A and user B using RTP. There are two distinct SIP dialogs—one between user A and B2BUA, and the other between user B and B2BUA.

The B2BUA function also helps in protocol interworking between SIP devices with other protocols, such as H.323 and Media Gateway Control Protocol (MGCP). B2BUA allows transport layer interworking, such as TCP and User Datagram Protocol (UDP), IPv4/IPv6 address mapping, and topology or address hiding in SIP headers, such as Via, Contact, and Record-Route.

The products that leverage B2BUA functions include SIP-based IP-PBXs, softswitches, firewall/NAT traversal applications, call center applications, and conference servers.

SIP Procedures for Registration and Routing

This section describes the functional aspects of SIP as defined in RFC 3261 and the SIP extension RFCs. Registration and routing aspects covered are as follows:

- UA discovery of SIP servers in a network

- SIP registration and user mobility

- SIP message routing

- Routing of subsequent requests within a SIP dialog

- Signaling forking at the proxy

- Enhanced proxy routing

User Agent Discovering SIP Servers in a Network

The UA needs the IP address of the registrar or proxy server to register and provide SIP service. The UAC, however, might not have the IP address of a SIP proxy and might require mechanisms to discover the address of a SIP proxy server in its domain.

The UA gets the DNS server address during a DHCP procedure to acquire an IP address. The UA initiates a DNS procedure to discover the servers that provide SIP routing capabilities in its network. This allows the UA to reach peer user agents or services in the SIP network without explicit configuration.

The UAC can use DNS procedures (defined in RFC 3263) such as Naming Authority Pointer (NAPTR) to determine what services are supported in a domain. NAPTR records return a set of terminal DNS records, such as a Service Record (SRV) (defined in RFC 2782), to indicate the services and protocols that are supported within the domain. The UAC should filter those records that point to servers supporting SIP.

DNS SRV records help clients discover servers supporting an application protocol such as SIP by querying for a specific service and underlying transport protocol within a domain. To determine the address of SIP servers that support UDP transport in company.com domain, you need to query a query string **_sip_udp.company.com** with a DNS server. A DNS SRV query yields DNS A records, which then resolve to a SIP server IP address. The UA then sends the INVITE request to the resolved IP address.

SIP Registration and User Mobility

SIP endpoints register with a SIP registrar server. Typically, the registrar and proxy function are implemented within the same server. SIP endpoints involved in the registration process are typically end-user devices such as SIP IP phones or servers providing specialized functions such as voice mail and presence status.

SIP users and services typically have a well-known or public SIP or SIPS URI, also known as an AOR. An AOR should be a globally reachable address. The SIP AOR is just another way to reach a user, similar to a telephone number, and might be on the business card or the home page of a person.

The UA, upon activation, creates a time-limited binding between the user AOR and its current IP address at the proxy server. This process is called *registration*. The AOR of the user is typically configured on a UA such as an IP phone. The IP address of the phone could vary because it is typically provided via DHCP.

The UA sends a SIP REGISTER request to the registrar within the domain, providing its current address in the Contact header. The UA indicates its AOR in the To header of the REGISTER message. The registrar updates the location service database to bind the AOR of the user to his current address or location. The location of the user is also known as the *contact address* and is conveyed in the Contact header of the REGISTER message. The location database that the proxy or registrar server uses thus maps an AOR to zero or more contact addresses.

The Contact header has an expires parameter that indicates the duration for which this binding is valid. In the call flow illustrated in Figure 12-6, expires is set to 3600 seconds or an hour. The UA is expected to refresh the registration within the time specified in the expires header to keep this binding intact at the registrar. Therefore, the UA sends periodic registration messages to refresh this information. In the absence of refresh, the registrar deletes this binding.

The proxy uses the updated location database to route SIP requests that are addressed to the target SIP AOR.

This mechanism of registering the contact address with the registrar/location service enables SIP to inherently support user mobility. For example, an employee who has a SIP softphone on his laptop might travel to a different site within the company. When the SIP softphone or UA is turned on, it sends a REGISTER message to its configured SIP registrar and updates the location service with the current address at the visited site. The proxy can now seamlessly send calls for this user to the visited location based on the contact address in the location service database. This is also true if the user is traveling or telecommuting and logs on to the company network over a secure VPN connection. Figure 12-6 illustrates the SIP registration process and usage of associated headers.

Figure 12-6 *SIP Registration Process*

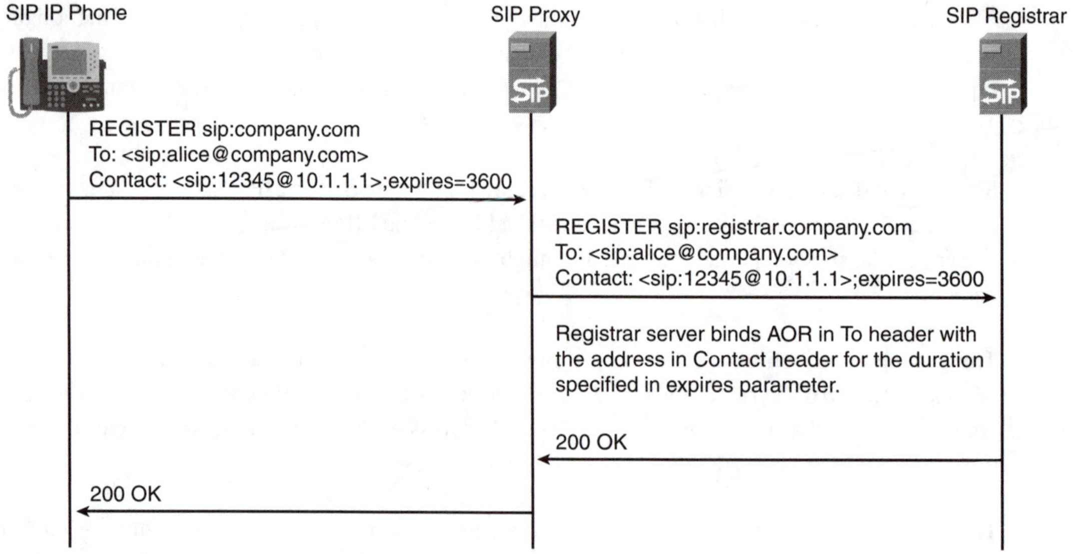

SIP Message Routing

A UAC that is acting on behalf of a user wants to establish an audio or audio-video session with another user. The INVITE request line has the SIP AOR of the called user for message routing. The UAC is now ready to send the INVITE to a SIP proxy server for routing the SIP message to the intended recipient.

After receiving a SIP request like INVITE, the proxy uses the AOR from the INVITE request line of the called user to look up the destination or next-hop address before forwarding the request.

SIP proxies are elements that route SIP requests to the UAS and SIP responses to the UAC. A request might traverse multiple proxies before it reaches the target UAS. Each proxy on the way makes routing decisions and modifies the request before forwarding the request to the next-hop device. A SIP proxy might rewrite the Request URI and add a Via header before forwarding the request message to the next-hop device. The proxy might insert additional headers like Record-Route in the request. SIP responses make their way through the same set of proxies as the request, but in the reverse order.

In practice, a SIP proxy is collocated with the SIP registrar server—that is, a proxy server usually implements the SIP registrar function. Thus, the proxy has access to the location database that is created during SIP registration. The UA routes the initial request such as INVITE or SUBSCRIBE to the local proxy in its domain. The proxy is then responsible for routing the SIP request based on its location database or static route information. Thus, the proxy serves as the rendezvous point for all SIP UAs and servers within the domain.

If the proxy is responsible for the domain in the request line, it looks up the location service database. This lookup provides zero or more addresses where the called user could be reached. Note that these contact addresses binding are available because of the registration procedure described previously or because of static configuration. If the contact address is a hostname, the procedure described in the previous section, such as using DNS SRV and A records for resolving the contact host-to-IP address, applies. The proxy then forwards the INVITE request to these locations.

If the proxy is not responsible for the domain in the request line, it forwards the request to the host that is specified in the request line.

To summarize, a SIP server such as a proxy or redirect server primarily performs the routing function—that is, it determines the next-hop device to where the SIP message needs to be forwarded. The next hop could be another proxy, redirect server, PSTN gateway, or UA. The SIP servers consult a location database to determine the next-hop address or the contact address of the user. Proxies can also have statically configured routes for devices like gateways into the PSTN or to another domain. A proxy can use DNS SRV or A records to route the message to the next hop.

Routing of Subsequent Requests Within a SIP Dialog

Subsequent SIP requests within a dialog usually do not traverse SIP proxies. UAs typically use the Contact header received in the dialog-creating transaction to send subsequent requests directly to their peer user agent. For example, the INVITE transaction might get routed to the UA of the called party via one or more proxies. This leads to the establishment of a SIP dialog and an active call. When one of the parties involved in a call hangs up, one UA usually sends the BYE request directly to the other UA. This enables the SIP proxies to scale up to provide service to an extremely large number of UAs.

SIP proxies, however, can indicate their willingness to be in the path of subsequent requests within a dialog by inserting a Record-Route header in the dialog establishing a request such as INVITE or SUBSCRIBE. In that case, following the establishment of a dialog, the UAs generate a Route header based on the combination of Record-Route and Contact headers. The UAs and intermediate proxies then use the Route header to route subsequent transactions.

This is useful if the proxy provides services in addition to routing. The proxy might be generating accounting records for calls such as timestamps, parties involved, and so on. In this case, the proxy wants to process not only the initial INVITE (that is, the establishment of the call) but also the BYE transaction (that is, when the call was terminated). This helps recording of the start time, connect time, and disconnect time of a call.

You can also use the proxy to enforce policies or checks at a central point in the network, in which case the proxy inserts a Record-Route header to ensure that all subsequent requests pass through it.

Figure 12-7 illustrates the message flow for a SIP call setup and termination involving the SIP proxy.

Figure 12-7   *SIP Call Setup and Teardown Involving the SIP Proxy*

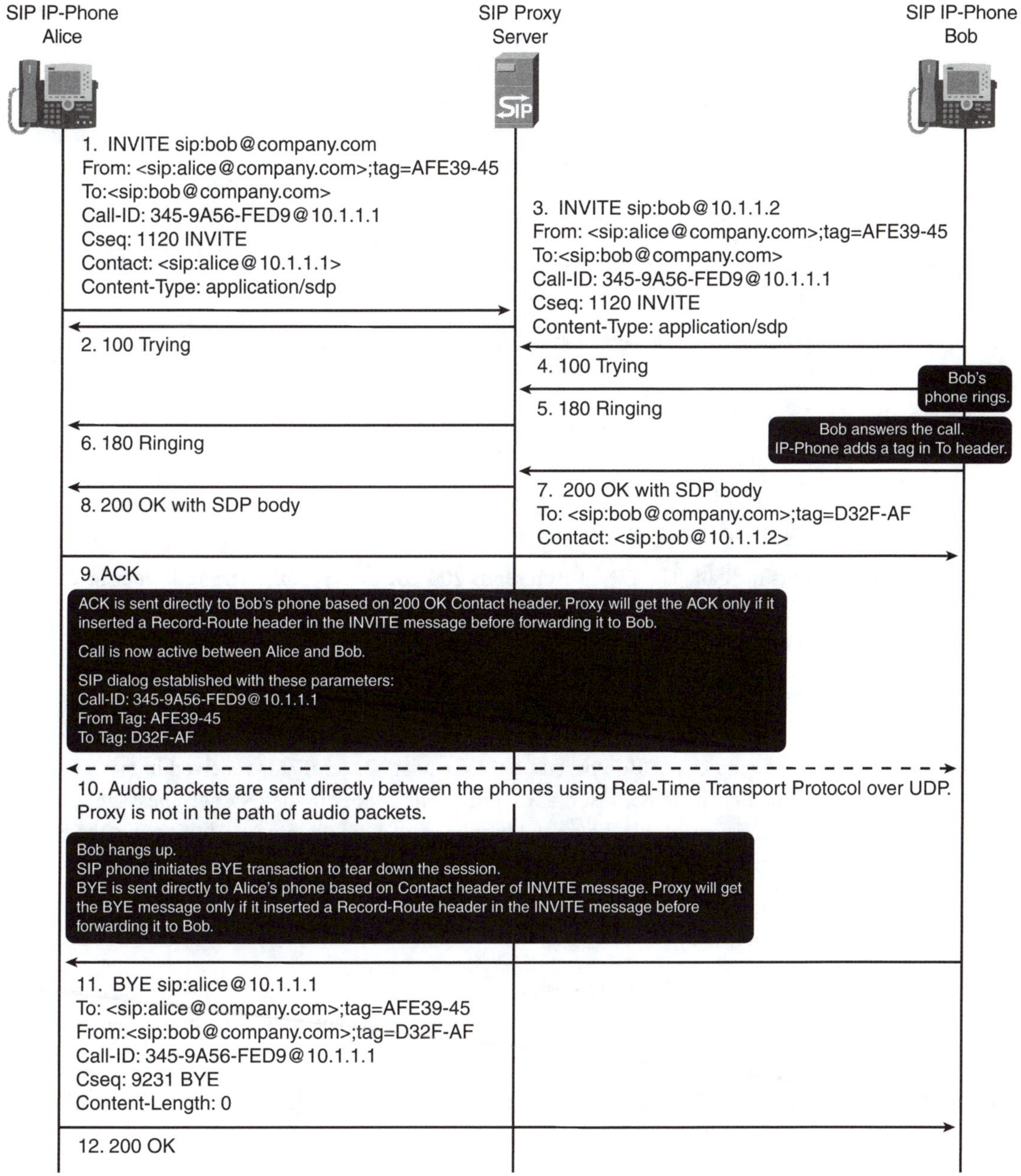

SIP IP-Phone
Alice

SIP Proxy
Server

SIP IP-Phone
Bob

1. INVITE sip:bob@company.com
From: <sip:alice@company.com>;tag=AFE39-45
To:<sip:bob@company.com>
Call-ID: 345-9A56-FED9@10.1.1.1
Cseq: 1120 INVITE
Contact: <sip:alice@10.1.1.1>
Content-Type: application/sdp

3. INVITE sip:bob@10.1.1.2
From: <sip:alice@company.com>;tag=AFE39-45
To:<sip:bob@company.com>
Call-ID: 345-9A56-FED9@10.1.1.1
Cseq: 1120 INVITE
Content-Type: application/sdp

2. 100 Trying

4. 100 Trying

Bob's
phone rings.

5. 180 Ringing

6. 180 Ringing

Bob answers the call.
IP-Phone adds a tag in To header.

8. 200 OK with SDP body

7. 200 OK with SDP body
To: <sip:bob@company.com>;tag=D32F-AF
Contact: <sip:bob@10.1.1.2>

9. ACK

ACK is sent directly to Bob's phone based on 200 OK Contact header. Proxy will get the ACK only if it
inserted a Record-Route header in the INVITE message before forwarding it to Bob.

Call is now active between Alice and Bob.

SIP dialog established with these parameters:
Call-ID: 345-9A56-FED9@10.1.1.1
From Tag: AFE39-45
To Tag: D32F-AF

10. Audio packets are sent directly between the phones using Real-Time Transport Protocol over UDP.
Proxy is not in the path of audio packets.

Bob hangs up.
SIP phone initiates BYE transaction to tear down the session.
BYE is sent directly to Alice's phone based on Contact header of INVITE message. Proxy will get
the BYE message only if it inserted a Record-Route header in the INVITE message before
forwarding it to Bob.

11. BYE sip:alice@10.1.1.1
To: <sip:alice@company.com>;tag=AFE39-45
From:<sip:bob@company.com>;tag=D32F-AF
Call-ID: 345-9A56-FED9@10.1.1.1
Cseq: 9231 BYE
Content-Length: 0

12. 200 OK

Figure 12-7 shows a SIP call setup from Alice to Bob via proxy. The SIP phones of Alice and Bob belong to the same enterprise, which is company.com. Both of their SIP IP phones are registered with the proxy server in the company.com domain.

1. The UA of Alice sends an INVITE with Request-URI sip:bob@company.com to the proxy server. The INVITE request has a unique Call-ID header and a From-Tag. The Contact header in the INVITE request has the address of the UA of Alice.

2. The proxy server accepts the INVITE and sends a 100 Trying back to the UA of Alice.

3. The proxy server looks up the location server database, gets the UA address of Bob, and forwards the INVITE to the user agent of Bob.

4. The phone that Bob has accepts the incoming INVITE request and sends back 100 Trying to the proxy.

5. The user agent of Bob starts ringing to alert the user about the incoming call. The UA of Bob sends 180 Ringing to the proxy to indicate the ringing state.

6. The proxy forwards the 180 Ringing to the UA of Alice. After the UA of Alice gets a 180, it starts playing a ringback tone to Alice.

7. Bob answers the call. The UA of Bob sends 200 OK to the proxy. The To header in 200 OK has a To-Tag that the UA of Bob generated. 200 OK has a Contact header that specifies the address of the UA of Bob.

8. The proxy forwards the 200 OK to the UA of Alice.

9. The UA of Alice acknowledges the 200 OK and sends an ACK directly to the UA of Bob. An ACK is sent to the UA of Bob based on the Contact header that is received in the 200 OK response. The proxy did not insert a Record-Route header in the INVITE message, so subsequent messages in this dialog will not be routed via the proxy. At this time, the SIP dialog is established. The dialog identifiers are Call-ID, From-Tag, and To-Tag.

10. Alice and Bob are conversing. Audio packets are sent directly between the phones using RTP over UDP.

11. Bob disconnects the call. His UA sends a BYE request directly to the UA of Alice using the Contact header received in the initial INVITE message. The flow of audio packets between the two phones is stopped.

12. The UA of Alice acknowledges the BYE transaction by sending 200 OK. Her phones also initiate call disconnection. The call is now terminated.

Signaling Forking at the Proxy

The proxy forwards the SIP request to one or more contact addresses either in parallel or in sequence. This feature in SIP is known as *forking*. During sequential forking, the proxy waits for the final response for the forwarded request before forwarding the request to the next location. During parallel forking, requests are forwarded to all the locations in parallel. In each case, the proxy forwards the best final response to the previous hop device, which is the UAC. For example, if the proxy gets 486 Busy and 200 OK from two forked legs, the 200 OK is forwarded to the UAC. The proxy can use the CANCEL request to cancel the forked legs for which it has not received the final response.

Sequential forking might be used in find-me, follow-me services, whereas parallel forking might be used for group-ringing applications. The find-me, follow-me service lets users have one phone number, which enables them to be contacted on multiple physical phones such as office, home, and mobile phone in a user-defined sequence. A group-ringing application involves all phones in the group ringing simultaneously for an incoming call.

Enhanced Proxy Routing

The SIP proxy can also provide enhanced routing capability based on local policy, application-defined scripts, or caller preferences. RFC 3841 is a SIP extension that enables a caller to express his preferences about request handling at the servers.

In the PSTN world, the caller does not have the authority or the capability to indicate how to route his calls or which features he prefers. SIP enables this via caller preference headers. These headers let the caller specify whether to route the call via proxy or redirect server, route the call only to the mobile phone of the called party, or reach the voicemail of the called party without ringing his phone.

Preference headers provide for a highly flexible and customizable call-routing application. This capability is discussed later in this chapter.

SIP Extensions

The IETF has defined extensions to the core SIP specifications to support protocol features for advanced services such as presence, application-specific routing, instant messaging, and call features. This section introduces the extensions for SIP Subscribe-Notify, Refer, and routing, based on caller preferences.

SIP Extension Negotiation Mechanism: Require, Supported, Allow Headers

SIP continues to evolve, and new capabilities are being proposed through IETF drafts and RFCs. These new RFCs are extensions to the core SIP RFC 3261. To maintain backward compatibility with baseline SIP implementations and facilitate inter-working with devices that do not support the newer extensions, SIP defines the extension negotiation mechanism. The extension negotiation is achieved using the Require and Supported headers.

SIP mandates that SIP entities that receive a SIP message ignore unknown headers. If the UAC insists that the UAS must understand the SIP extension to process a request, the UAC must indicate this using the Require header. The Require header contains option tags that are defined in the SIP extensions.

SIP extensions can define new header fields within existing methods that cannot be reasonably processed by the UAS or proxy that supports the only core SIP RFC. Thus, the SIP extensions need to define option tags. Option tags are populated in Require or Supported headers.

The Require header indicates that the UAC insists that the UAS must understand the extension for processing the request. If the UAS does not support an option tag in the Require header, it must reject the request with the Unsupported header containing the offending option tag. The UAC can resend the request without the extensions, or it can choose to terminate the transaction.

The Supported header is an indication to the UAS that the UAC understands a certain extension. It is up to the UAS to decide whether it wants to use that extension in the response messages. For example, option tag 100rel in the INVITE request indicates that the UAC supports RFC 3262. The UAS can choose to send 18x responses reliably by adding Require:100rel in the 18x responses. UAs that implement SIP extensions usually have configuration options that enable an administrator to control the enabling or disabling of the feature.

The Allow header field lists the set of methods supported by the UA that generated the SIP message. The addition of this header in dialog-initiating transactions such as INVITE or SUBSCRIBE enables the UAS to discover which SIP methods the UAC supports. Similarly, the UAS can send this header in the final responses such as 200 OK to indicate similar information to the UAC. For example, an INVITE request received with the Allow header that does not contain the REFER method might lead to the UAS disabling the "transfer" key on its user interface.

SIP UAs can also send an OPTIONS request to query the capabilities of remote devices such as proxy or UA. The OPTIONS requests include Allow (describes SIP methods), Accept (content-types), and Supported (SIP extensions) headers. The remote device sends back an OPTIONS response (200 OK) containing Allow, Accept, Accept-Language, Accept-Encoding, and Supported headers.

Caller and Callee Preferences

RFC 3841 is a SIP extension that enables a caller to express his preferences about request handling at the intermediate servers. This enables SIP servers to use additional information such as caller preferences for routing a SIP request. This includes matching the capability of the called user end devices with the caller preferences. For example, the caller might want to establish an audio and video session. In that case, the proxy should not route the INVITE request to those contacts that can perform only audio or IM sessions. Similarly, the caller might express an interest to reach the called party on his wireless IP phone only or directly leave a voice-mail message without talking to him.

The UAC indicates its preference in the INVITE or SUBSCRIBE request by adding the Accept-Contact, Reject-Contact, and Request-Disposition header (all defined in RFC 3841).

The Request-Disposition header field lets the caller specify preferences for the way a server should process a SIP request. The caller might indicate whether the server should proxy or redirect the SIP request. In the redirect server mode, all contact locations corresponding to the called party are returned to the UAC in a 3xx response in the Contact header. The UA of the caller can apply customized routing policies on the contact locations it receives from the redirect server.

The user can also specify whether the proxy should forward a request to all possible contact locations in parallel or go through them in sequence, contacting the next address when it has received a non-2xx or non-6xx final response for the previous address. For example:

```
Request-Disposition: proxy, parallel
```

During registration, the UA can indicate its capabilities such as support of SIP methods, audio, video, and IM to the proxy server. When a UA registers, it can choose to indicate a feature set associated with a registered contact. (See RFC 3840 for details.) During the message routing process, the proxy tries to match the caller preferences with the callee UA capabilities.

Some examples of usage of the headers added to INVITE or SUBSCRIBE requests are as follows:

- Accept-Contact: *; video;require;explicit—Forces the INVITE to be routed to an endpoint that supports video capability.

- Accept-Contact: *;msgserver;require;explicit—Indicates that the user wants to access the voice mail of the called party directly.

- Accept-Contact:*;mobility="mobile";require;explicit—Sends the call only to the wireless phone of the called user.

- Request-Disposition: proxy, parallel—Indicates that the server should proxy the request and use parallel fork if multiple contacts are present.

- Reject-Contact: *;msgserver—Indicates that the caller wants to avoid voice mail of the called party. In this case, the proxy shall not include contact that has "msgserver" tag while routing the INVITE transaction. As a result, the caller is not routed to the voice-mail server of the called party.

SIP Event Notification Framework: Subscription and Notifications

RFC 3265 describes the SIP extensions that enable SIP UAs to subscribe for notification from another SIP device when certain events take place. This is a framework by which SIP nodes can request notification from remote peers when monitored events take place. Notifications are generated for network events. Examples of network events include a user registering with or unregistering from the network, a voice mail being deposited in the mailbox of a user or a voice mail being retrieved from the mailbox, or a user changing his online status from idle to busy or away. This is essentially a mechanism to share state information in a distributed system, such as a SIP network. The framework is independent of the events that are being monitored. That is why you can adapt it so easily to a broad range of applications.

For example, a SIP phone might subscribe to the voice-mail status of its user from a SIP-based messaging system. The duration of the subscription is defined by the Expires header in the SUBSCRIBE request.

SUBSCRIBE and NOTIFY Methods

RFC 3265 defines the subscription and notification framework for SIP using two new SIP methods: SUBSCRIBE and NOTIFY.

A SIP entity acts as a subscriber when it sends a SUBSCRIBE for a specific event type, such as message-summary, to a SIP entity that the Request URI identifies. A new header "Event" defines the event type or the class of event types. The Event header is mandatory for SUBSCRIBE requests. The duration of the subscription is indicated in the Expires header.

The Request URI of a SUBSCRIBE request contains enough information to route the request to the appropriate entity per the request routing procedures that SIP outlines. The Request URI of a SUBSCRIBE request also contains enough information to identify the resource for which the event notification is desired, but not necessarily enough information to uniquely identify the nature of the event. The Event header defines the exact state for which the subscription is requested. For example, **Event: presence** refers to the presence state of the user, whereas **Event: reg** refers to the registration status of the SIP entity.

The UAS that is processing the SUBSCRIBE request acts as the notifier; it sends a NOTIFY request back to the subscriber whenever a state change takes place, while the subscription is active. For example, when a voice mail is deposited, the SIP-based messaging system sends a NOTIFY to the subscribing SIP phone. NOTIFY requests must contain a *Subscription-State* header that indicates whether a subscription is active, pending, or terminated.

If the Subscription-State value is pending in the NOTIFY request, the notifier has received the subscription but not authorized it. This might happen when the notifier is waiting for the end-user input to determine whether to accept a subscription from this subscriber.

If the "Subscription-State" value is active, the notifier has accepted and authorized the subscription. A Subscription-State value of **terminated** indicates that the notifier has terminated the subscription.

You can also send SUBSCRIBE messages within a preexisting dialog. If you send them outside of the dialog, SUBSCRIBE might cause the establishment of a new dialog. Subsequent NOTIFY messages are sent within the dialog that the SUBSCRIBE message creates. The subscriber can refresh the subscription by sending a new SUBSCRIBE with an Expires value.

Most common uses of this mechanism are for providing voice-mail status notifications, monitoring registration, and showing the presence status of users. You can also use this mechanism to emulate PBX features, which require shared state between devices, such as shared line appearance.

Monitoring Registration State Using the Subscription-Notification Framework

A registration represents a dynamic state that the registrar maintains in the network. Registration state changes when a user registers or unregisters from the network. Applications might be interested in monitoring the registration or online state of users.

For example, the application server subscribes to the registration state of Alice with the registrar. Initially, Alice is not registered, and the registrar indicates that in the initial NOTIFY. Later Alice comes online and registers. The registrar sends a NOTIFY to the application to indicate the new state.

The registration status is carried in the body of the NOTIFY request. It is represented using an XML document in the NOTIFY body. RFC 3680 defines the format of the XML body for the registration state.

Figure 12-8 illustrates the use of subscription to monitor registration status.

Figure 12-8 *Monitoring Registration State Using the Subscribe-Notify Framework*

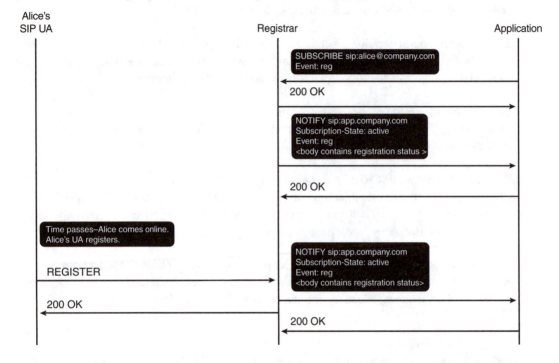

SIP REFER Request

RFC 3515 is a SIP extension that defines a new SIP request called REFER. REFER asks the recipient (identified by the REFER Request-URI) to access the resource described in the Refer-To header. The recipient of the REFER method is also required to send notifications to the sender about the progress made in accessing the resource. The notifications are sent using the NOTIFY method. This RFC also describes a new event package "refer" that is used in the notification messages for REFER. Thus, REFER causes an implicit subscription to be established at the recipient.

You can send REFER within an established dialog, such as within an INVITE dialog to trigger call transfer. In this case, the Refer-To header specifies the SIP URI of the transfer target.

If you send REFER outside of an established dialog, it leads to the establishment of a dialog. An application that can possibly use out-of-dialog REFER is the click-to-dial service. In this case, a user clicks on an online directory that causes his phone to call the desired party. The application server for the click-to-dial feature sends a REFER message to the phone of the initiator with a Refer-To pointing to the remote party. After the phone receives the REFER, it alerts its user (initiator of click-to-dial service) and then places a call by sending an INVITE request to the URI provided in the Refer-To header.

You can add third-party participants in a conference by using REFER. A client can send REFER to the participant, asking him to send an INVITE request to the conference URI. In addition, the client can send a REFER request to the conference controller, asking it to send an INVITE to the participant, requesting him to join the conference bridge. These are some sample usages of the REFER request. REFER is a flexible and powerful concept that you can use for a variety of applications.

Presence and Instant Messaging Overview

Presence describes the willingness, availability, and ability of a person to communicate with another. Presence service enables users to publish their availability status and display messages or icons as a form of self-expression. Instant Messaging (IM) refers to the transfer of text messages between users in near real-time.

IM provides the capability of real-time, text-based communication, but it is useful only if the recipient can participate. Presence provides the ability to subscribe to the online status of a person to determine his willingness to engage in IM sessions and calls. When user presence is integrated within the communication infrastructure, it becomes easy to determine the best possible way to reach the target. For example, a busy executive might be in a conference call and might not be available for another call. However, he might be open for an IM session. Similarly, a missed call list on the SIP phone might indicate the current availability status of callers. This enables the user to prioritize the order in which he return the calls.

The presence status of a person is the aggregation of the status from various devices such as desk phone, calendar application, IM client on computer, and cell phone. Presence service collects this information and provides a unified view. This aggregation determines not only the availability of a person, but also the best way to reach him. Presence thus increases the likelihood of success in a call attempt.

A basic presence service enables users to publish and share their information with others to make the communication experience more personalized and productive. The presence service enables users to control who gets access to their presence state and the degree to which information is shared. The presence service can provide a default (also known as *polite blocking*) status such as unavailable to those subscribers who are denied access.

SIP Extensions for IM and Presence

SIP for Instant Messaging and Presence Leveraging Extensions (SIMPLE) is an IETF group that works on using SIP and proposing SIP extensions for interoperability across IM and presence services. RFC 3856 defines a presence event package for SIP.

You use the SUBSCRIBE method to subscribe to the presence state of another user. Although you can send subscribes directly to another user, typically you use a presence server to handle presence subscription requests and publish presence status on behalf of a user.

A *presence server* is a SIP network server that handles presence requests on behalf of the target end users and publishes presence information on behalf of a user. The presence server has an advantage over the peer-to-peer infrastructure because polling is not required to monitor when a remote party has come online. In addition, the server enables the implementation of network-based policy such as security and privacy control.

A UA sends a SUBSCRIBE with a presence event package to subscribe to the presence status of another user. The target user or resource whose presence information is being tracked is known as *presentity*. Presentity is defined in RFC 2778, which provides a model for presence and instant messaging. A SIP URI typically identifies the *presentity*.

The SIP proxy routes this SIP request to the presence server in the network. The presence server subscribes to the presentity of the target user or presence status on behalf of the subscriber. The SIP UA or endpoint device of the target user accepts the subscription for presence. This UA is also referred to as the *presence agent* (PA).

When the target user changes status, the PA notifies the presence server of a presence status change. The SIP NOTIFY request provides the notification, with the presence status contained in an XML body. The presence server subsequently notifies all remote parties subscribing to this presence information.

Because the presence server controls the distribution of sensitive presence information, the presence server must seek permission of the target user whenever a remote party requests subscription to its presence information. If the presence server has a predefined policy, the server uses that to allow or deny the subscription of the presence status. If the server has no such policy, it sends a request to the local user to authorize the subscription or use the default system-wide policy to handle the subscription.

RFC 3428 extends SIP and defines a new SIP request MESSAGE that enables the transfer of instant messages. MESSAGE requests carry the message content in the form of MIME body parts. Similarly, RFC 3903 defines a new SIP request: PUBLISH for publishing event states such as presence state.

Summary

SIP is an IETF signaling protocol for multimedia applications involving one or more participants. The IETF approach is to create a layered and functional architecture in which highly optimized protocols realize specific features and functionality. SIP is a flexible protocol that supports extensions for new applications and services.

SIP is distributed in nature, enabling better scalability at the network servers. SIP dialog state is maintained at the endpoints. SIP network servers are either stateless or maintain transaction state information for at least 32 seconds.

This chapter provides an overview of SIP and its operation. Refer to the appropriate SIP RFC for further details.

CHAPTER 13

Gateway Control Protocols

This chapter covers two Internet Engineering Task Force (IETF) gateway control protocols that control Voice over IP (VoIP) gateways from external call-control elements: Media Gateway Control Protocol (MGCP) and H.248/MEGACO. These gateway control protocols are designed to support VoIP architecture, where the media functions are separated from call-signaling functions. Therefore, their use is prevalent in large trunking gateways and residential gateways. MGCP is widely deployed and is the focus of this chapter. H.248/MEGACO is another contending protocol, and it is briefly explained at the end of this chapter. MEGACO stands for media gateway control, but do not confuse it with MGCP.

MGCP Overview

MGCP is a protocol used by media gateway controllers (MGC, also known as call agents) to control media gateways (MG). MGCP is based on a master/slave paradigm in which MGC is the master that issues commands to the MG (slave). The MG acknowledges the command, executes it, and notifies the MGC of the outcome (successful or not). In this architecture, the MG handles the media functions, such as conversion of time-division multiplexing (TDM)/ analog signals into Real-time Transport Protocol (RTP)/Real-time Transport Control Protocol (RTCP) streams. MGC handles the call-signaling functions.

In this model, the call-control intelligence resides in the MGC, and the MG is a "dumb" entity that acts on the commands of the MGC.

MGCP messages are carried over User Datagram Protocol (UDP). Because UDP does not guarantee message delivery, messages are retransmitted, if needed.

MGCP has its historic roots in two other earlier protocols: Simple Gateway Control Protocol (SGCP) and Internet Protocol Device Control (IPDC). This chapter covers MGCP version 1.0 as described in RFC 2705 and does not go into the details of SGCP, IPDC, or earlier versions of MGCP.

MGCP uses Session Description Protocol (SDP) to describe the media sessions. SDP describes session parameters of the media flow between the MGs such as IP addresses, the UDP port, RTP profiles, and multimedia conference capabilities. MGCP follows the conventions of SDP as defined in RFC 2327, and implementations are expected to conform. The SDP specification defines several media types; MGCP, however, limits the usage of SDP to two media types: audio circuits and data access circuits.

Call agents use the following SDP parameters to provision telephony gateways:

- IP addresses—Use remote gateway, local gateway, or multicast audio conference addresses to exchange RTP packets

- UDP port—Indicates the transport port used to receive RTP packets from the remote gateway

- Audio media—Specify audio media, including codec

MGCP Model

The MGCP assumes a connection model in which the basic constructs are endpoints and connections (see Figure 13-1). Connections are grouped in calls. One or more connections can belong to one call. Connections and calls are set up at the initiative of the MGC. Before going into the details of MGCP, the sections that follow describe endpoints and connections in further detail.

Figure 13-1   *MGCP Connection Model*

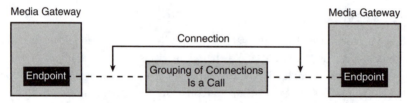

Endpoints

Endpoints are sources or sinks of data. They are either physical or logical entities that exist in an MG.

One example of a physical endpoint is an interface on an MG that terminates a circuit originating from a public switched telephone network (PSTN) switch.

An example of a logical endpoint is an announcement server endpoint that plays/streams the announcement based on a command from the call agent.

Physical endpoints typically require hardware installation, whereas creation of logical endpoints can be performed in software.

Each endpoint is identified by an endpoint-identifier that has two components:

- The domain name of the MG that contains the endpoints

- A local name or identifier within that gateway

Connections

Connections can be either point-to-point or multipoint. A point–to-point connection is an association between two endpoints with the purpose of transmitting data between them. You establish a multipoint connection by connecting the endpoint to a multipoint session.

Create a connection on each endpoint that will be involved in a call. Each connection is designated locally by a connection ID and is characterized by a set of connection attributes.

The endpoints that are involved in a connection could be in separate gateways or in the same one.

Calls

A group of connections composes a *call*. Call agents assign call identifiers, which are unique for each call and are globally unique throughout the system. A unique call identifier links all connections that are associated with a call. This identifier enables accounting or billing mediation to occur for calls.

MGCP Commands and Messages

MGCP implements the media gateway control interface as a set of transactions. The transactions are composed of a command and a mandatory response.

All MGCP commands consist of a command line, followed by a set of parameter lines, and optionally followed by a session description. The command line has the following format:

<Command name> <Transaction-ID> <Endpoint-ID> <MGCP ver>

Each parameter line, in turn, consists of a parameter code followed by a parameter value.

All responses consist of a response header followed by an optional session description.

Although RFC 2705 has no formal classification, for ease of understanding, you can classify MGCP commands into three categories:

■ Basic call control commands—These are used in almost every call interaction. They are as follows:

— CreateConnection (CRCX)

— ModifyConnection (MDCX)

— DeleteConnection (DLCX)

■ Advanced call control commands—MGC might need to know about the occurrence of certain call-related events in an endpoint. Typical examples of these events are dual-tone multifrequency (DTMF) digits, fax tones, off-hook/on-hook events, and so on. MGCP provides an interface for the MGC to request the gateway to watch for certain events on the endpoints and report their occurrence to it. The MGC uses the NotificationRequest (RQNT) command to request the gateway to report the occurrence of certain events. The gateway reports the occurrence of these events to the MGC using the Notification (NTFY) command.

■ Management commands—These are not directly related to call control, but the MGC and the gateway exchange them to inform each other about certain non-call-related events. For example, a gateway might experience a hardware problem on some of its endpoints and need to inform the MGC about this. MGCP provides four different commands for management purposes:

— AuditConnection (AUCX)

— AuditEndpoint (AUEP)

— RestartIn-Progress (RSIP)

— EndpointConfiguration (EPCF)

The sections that follow describe each of the more commonly used MGCP commands and briefly explain the commonly used parameters that can appear in the particular command. Each parameter code is provided in parentheses. This is not an exhaustive listing. Refer to RFC 2705 for an exhaustive listing of the parameters (http://www.ietf.org/rfc/rfc2705.txt).

CreateConnection (CRCX)

As its name indicates, this command creates a connection between two endpoints. The parameters for the CreateConnection command provide the necessary information to the gateway (GW) to build a connection:

■ Call ID —This is a globally unique parameter that the MCC assigns. All connections that are related to a call share this identifier.

■ Notified Entity (N)—This optional parameter specifies where to send notifications.

■ Local Connection Options (L)—This parameter describes data communication characteristics that are used to execute the *CreateConnection* command. The fields in this parameter include encoding method, packetization period, bandwidth, type of service (ToS), and use of echo cancellation. By default, echo cancellation is always performed.

■ Mode (M)—This parameter dictates the mode of operation for the connection. The options are full duplex, receive only, send only, inactive, and loopback.

■ Remote Connection Descriptor (RC)—This parameter indicates the connection descriptor for the remote side of the connection, typically on the other side of the IP network. This parameter might have a null value if the information for the remote end is not yet known.

ModifyConnection (MDCX)

The *ModifyConnection* command changes the characteristics of the gateway view of a connection or call. The allowed parameters and fields in *ModifyConnection* are the same as those in the *CreateConnection* request, with the addition of the *Connection ID* parameter. The Connection ID parameter uniquely identifies the connection at the endpoint. You can change the following connection parameters by using the *ModifyConnection* command: encoding scheme, packetization period, echo cancellation, and connections to activate or deactivate.

DeleteConnection (DLCX)

A call agent or a gateway uses the *DeleteConnection* command to terminate a connection. Call agents use this request to terminate a connection between two endpoints or to clear all connections that terminate on a given endpoint. The gateway might issue this command to clear connections if it detects that an endpoint can no longer send or receive audio. If the gateway clears a connection, a reason code is included in the message indicating the cause.

After connections are terminated, gateways should place the endpoint into inactive mode, thus making it available for a subsequent session. A valuable attribute of the *DeleteConnection* command is that it distributes statistics regarding a call. Table 13-1 lists the statistical data contained in the *DeleteConnection* message.

Table 13-1   *Statistical Information from the DeleteConnection Message*

Data	Explanation
Packets sent	Number of packets sent on the connection
Octets sent	Number of octets sent on the connection
Packets received	Number of packets received on the connection
Octets received	Number of octets received on the connection
Packets lost	Number of packets lost as indicated by sequence numbers
Jitter	Average interpacket delay in milliseconds
Latency	Average latency in milliseconds

NotificationRequest (RQNT)

The MGC uses the *NotificationRequest* command to request the gateway to send notifications upon the occurrence of specified events in an endpoint. The two important parameters used in this command are the Requested Events parameter, identified by the parameter code **R**, and the Signal Requests parameter, identified by the parameter code **S**. Before this chapter goes in to the details of other parameters, it is important to understand the R and S parameters.

The Requested Events (**R**) parameter contains the list of events that the gateway is requested to detect and report on to the call agent. Possible events in the list include fax and modem tones, continuity tone and detection, on-hook and off-hook transition, flash hook, channel-associated signaling (CAS), wink, and DTMF (or pulse digits). In addition, a requested action can qualify each event. The actions, when specified, are encoded as a list of keywords, enclosed in parentheses, and separated by commas. Table 13-2 lists the codes for various actions.

Table 13-2   *MGCP Event Action Codes*

Action	Code
Notify immediately	N
Accumulate	A
Treat according to digit map	D
Swap	S
Ignore	I
Keep signal(s) active	K
Embedded notification request	E

When no action is explicitly specified, the default is to notify the event to the MGC. The following is an example of the "requested events" parameter line:

```
R: hu(N)
```

In this example, the gateway is requested to look for the **hu** (hang-up/on-hook event) and notify immediately (denoted by action code **N**) when that event occurs.

The Signal Requests(**S**) parameter specifies a set of signals that the gateway is asked to apply to the endpoint. The commonly used signals include ringing and distinctive ringing, ring back, dial, intercept, busy, answer, call waiting, off-hook warning, and continuity tones. Signals are split into three different types depending on their behavior:

- On/Off (OO)—These signals are applied until they are turned off.

- Time-Out (TO)—After these signals are applied, they remain until they are turned off or until a time-out occurs based on a signal-specific time period.

- Brief (BR)—This signal duration is short and stops on its own.

Table 13-3 lists the common events and signals. For the signals, the type of event is also specified. Note that the same event can have a different duration based on the *package* it is part of.

Table 13-3 *Events and Signals*

Event Symbol	Definition	Duration
Hd	Off-hook transition	OO
Hu	On-hook transition	OO
Dl	Dial tone	Handset emulation package -TO (120 s)
Rg	Ringing	Handset emulation package -TO (30 s)
Hf	Flash hook	BR
Bz	Busy tone	Handset emulation package - OO
Aw	Answer tone	OO
Wt	Call-waiting tone	TO (30 s)
ci(string)	Caller ID	BR
Mt	Modem tone detected	-
Ft	Fax tone detected	-
Cg	Network congestion tone	TO
It	Intercept tone	OO
Wk	Wink	BR
Wko	Wink off	BR
dtmf 8	DTMF digit 8	BR
mf 9	MF digit 9	BR
Ann	Play an announcement	TO (var.)
Java	Load a Java script	TO (var.)

Other parameters that are typically present in NotificationRequest are as follows:

- Notified Entity (N)—If present, this specifies where to send notification. If absent, it indicates that notification should be sent to the originator.

- Request Identifier (X)—This correlates the NotificationRequest command with the notification that it triggers.

Notification (NTFY)

The gateway sends a *Notification* based on requested events in the notification request and on the occurrence of these observed events. The *Notification* command contains the following parameters:

- Notified Entity (N)—If present, this parameter specifies where to send notification. If absent, this parameter indicates that notification should be sent to the originator.

- Requested Identifier (X)—This parameter is equal to the "request identifier" in the NotificationRequest. It correlates the request to the notification.

- Observed Events (O)—This parameter contains a list of events that the gateway detected based on the requested event parameter in an earlier NotificationRequest command from the MGC.

AuditEndpoint (AUEP)

The call agent can use the *AuditEndpoint* command to determine the status of an endpoint. This is typically done at initialization of the call agent to find the status of all the endpoints it controls. This request contains an Endpoint ID parameter that identifies the endpoint being audited and a Requested Information parameter containing the following subparameters:

- Endpoint List—This identifies the endpoint that is being audited. You can use a wildcard to indicate all endpoints that match the wildcard.

- Notified Entity (N)—This is the notified entity for active notification requests.

- Requested Events (R)—This is a list of currently requested events.

- Digit Map —Endpoint currently uses this. *Digit maps* are described in the later section titled "Advanced MGCP Features."

- Signal Requests (S)—This is a list of signal requests that are currently applied to an endpoint.

- Request Identifier (X)—This is an identifier for the last "NotificationRequest" received by an endpoint.

- Connection Identifiers (I)—This is a list of the current connections that exist for the specified endpoint.

- Detect Events (T)—This is a list of events that are currently being detected in quarantine mode.

- Local Connection Options (L)—This is a list of all current values, such as codec and packetization period. You can use this parameter to request the current event packages that are supported on the specified endpoint.

The response from the gateways for the AUEP will include information about each of the items for which auditing information was requested.

AuditConnection (AUCX)

Call agents use the *AuditConnection* command to retrieve information about connections. This command contains the Endpoint ID and Connection ID indicating the location and connection that are being audited. The Requested Information subparameters contain the following information:

- Call ID —This is the unique identifier of the call to which the Audited connection belongs.

- Notified Entity (N)—This is the currently notified entity for the connection.

- Local Connection Options (L)—These are the options that are currently being applied for this connection.

- Mode (M)—This is the current mode of connection.

- Remote Connection Descriptor (RC)—This is the remote SDP that is being used for the connection.

- Local Connection Descriptor (LC)—This is the gateway used for the connection.

- Connection Parameters (P)—This is the current value of the parameter at the Audited connection.

RestartIn-Progress (RSIP)

The gateway uses the *RestartIn-Progress* command to inform the call agent that an endpoint or group of endpoints was taken out of service or is back in service. The *RestartIn-Progress* command contains the following parameters:

- Endpoint id—This identifies the endpoint that is taken in or out of service.

- Restart Method (RM)—This specifies one of the following different types of restarts:

  — The *graceful* restart method indicates that specified endpoints will be taken out of service after a specified time and that the call agent should not attempt to establish new connections.

  — The *forced* restart method indicates that endpoints were abruptly taken out of service and that connections were lost.

  — The *restart* method indicates when endpoints that have no existing connections will be put back in service.

  — A *disconnected* method indicates that the endpoint has become disconnected and is trying to establish connectivity.

- Restart Delay (RD)—This is used to express delay in number of seconds.

EndpointConfiguration (EPCF)

The EndpointConfiguration command enables the call agent to specify the encoding of signals that the endpoint receives. This is particularly useful in international circumstances that use both μ-law and A-law encoding techniques. This command passes the encoding information to the gateway with the Bearer Information (B) parameter, which identifies the coding technique for the data received on the line side of the endpoint it identifies. Currently, the only subparameters that are defined are A-law and μ-law.

MGCP Response Messages

All MGCP commands are acknowledged. The acknowledgment carries a return code, which indicates the status of the command. The return code is an integer number for which four ranges of values have been defined:

■ Values between 100 and 199 indicate a provisional response.

■ Values between 200 and 299 indicate a successful completion.

■ Values between 400 and 499 indicate a transient error.

■ Values between 500 and 599 indicate a permanent error.

Table 13-4 lists the return codes and an explanation for each code.

Table 13-4 *MGCP Return Codes*

Return Code	Explanation
100	Command is currently being executed. Final response to follow.
200	Normal transaction execution.
250	Connection was deleted.
400	Unable to execute transaction because of transient error.
401	Telephone is already off-hook.
402	Telephone is already on-hook.
500	Unable to execute transaction because endpoint is unknown.
501	Unable to execute transaction because endpoint is unready.
502	Unable to execute transaction because of insufficient endpoint resources.
510	Unable to execute transaction because of protocol error detection.
511	Unable to execute transaction because of request containing unrecognized extension.
512	Unable to execute transaction because of gateway being unable to detect one of the requested events.

Table 13-4   *MGCP Return Codes (Continued)*

Return Code	Explanation
513	Unable to execute transaction because of gateway being unable to generate one of the requested signals.
514	Unable to execute transaction because of gateway being unable to send the specified announcement.
515	Transaction refers to an incorrect Connection ID.
516	Transaction refers to an unknown Call ID.
517	Unsupported mode.
518	Unsupported event package.
519	Gateway does not have a digit map.
520	Unable to complete transaction because of endpoint restarting.
522	No such event or signal.
523	Unknown action or combination of actions.
524	Inconsistent with local connection options.

MGCP Call Flows

This section illustrates a few typical call flows with an explanation of the semantics of each message. The call flows are presented in order of increasing complexity. Note that the call flows presented here are shown as an example for illustration purposes. An implementation for a particular vendor of MGCP might follow a different call flow.

Basic MGCP Call Flow

A simple point-to-point call is set up using two different commands: CreateConnection and ModifyConnection.

Figure 13-2 shows a call flow for a call setup between two endpoints. The endpoints are assumed to be on different gateways, and the MGC controls both the gateways. Only the relevant portions of the messages are shown in the figure. The originating side and a terminating side of this two-party call are labeled with suffixes *Orig* and *Term*, respectively. Messages in the figure are labeled numerically, and the corresponding label is referenced in the explanation that follows. Of course, the labels are not part of the MGCP messages.

Figure 13-2 *Basic MGCP Call Flow*

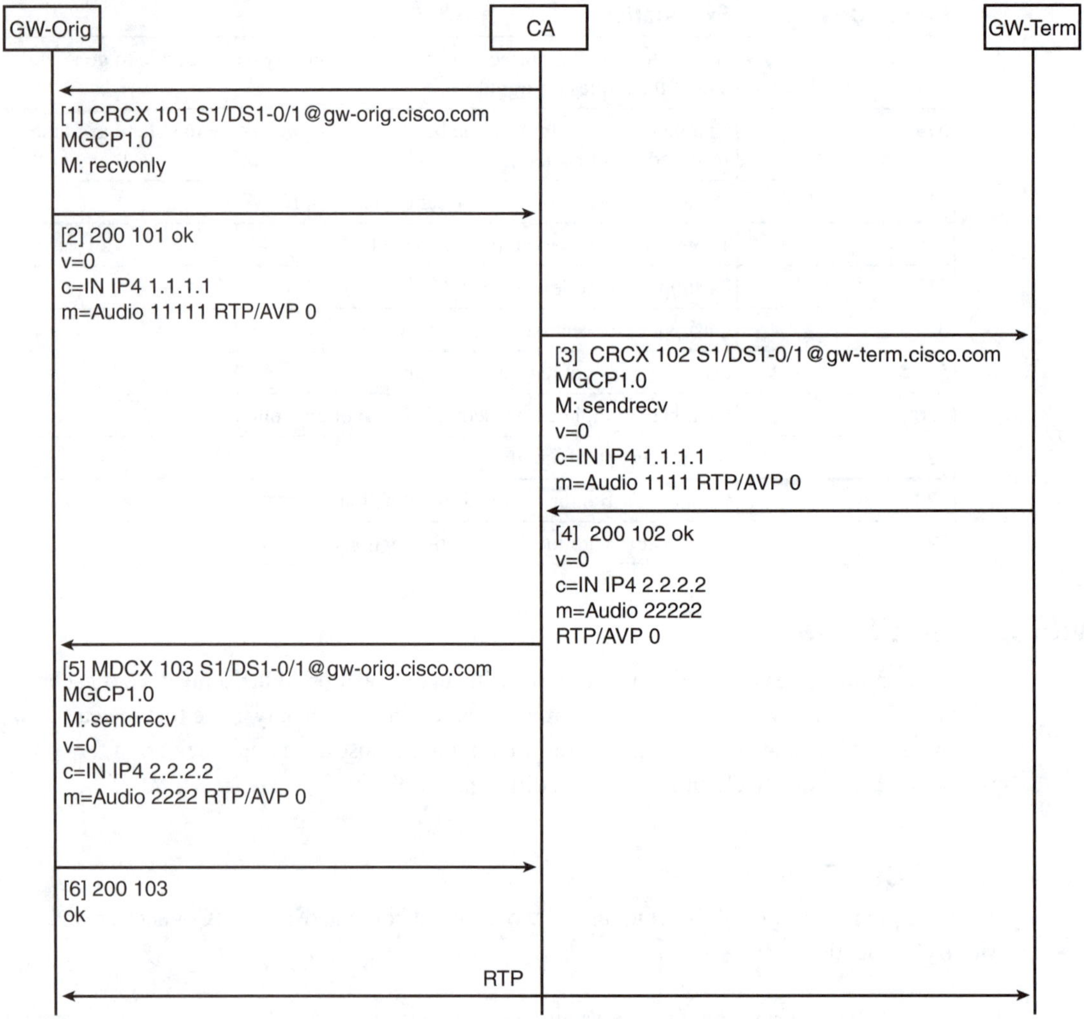

1. The call agent sends an initial CRCX to the GW-Orig and specifies endpoint S1/DS1-0/1. The connection mode is set to recvonly. This setting indicates to the GW-Orig that the endpoint should receive media from the IP network but not send media to the IP network. This is necessary because the call agent has not set up the connection on GW-Term and hence does not know the session description at that end.

2. GW-Orig responds with a 200/OK indicating that the connection was created successfully and providing a local session description (encoded per SDP specification). This session description includes the local IP and port (1.1.1.1 and 11111) that the gateway has opened to receive RTP streams. SDP also indicates that the codec being used is G.711μ-law (denoted by RTP/AVP 0).

3. The call agent then sends a CRCX to endpoint S1/DS1-0/1 on GW-Term. The session description received from GW-Orig is included in the RemoteConnectionDescriptor of this CRCX, and the mode is set to sendrecv.

4. GW-Term responds with a 200/OK and includes its own session description in the response.

5. The call agent passes the SDP of GW-Term to GW-Orig in a MDCX command and changes the connection mode to sendrecv.

6. After GW-Orig executes the MDCX command and responds with 200/OK, call setup is complete and RTP streams flow between GW-Orig and GW-Term.

Trunking GW-to-Trunking GW Call Flow

The call flow discussed in the preceding section showed you that setting up connections using MGCP is fairly straightforward. However, the call flow does not tell you how and why the call agent decided to set up the connection between those two endpoints. In real life, the call agent learns about this from external signaling. A typical example is an SS7 trunk terminating on the call agent. In such a case, the SS7 messages trigger the actions of the call agent.

Figure 13-3 shows the interaction between SS7 messages and MGCP.

Figure 13-3 *Trunking GW-to-Trunking GW Call Flow*

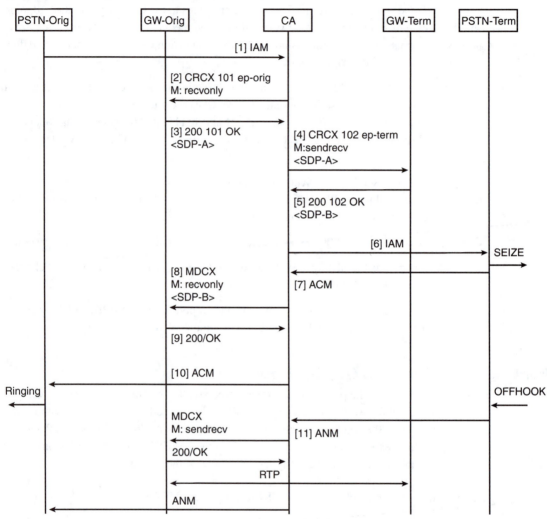

An initial address message (IAM) [1] comes in to the call agent on an SS7 trunk. This action triggers the call agent to analyze the IAM and decide how to handle it by consulting its local configuration. The local configuration (or an external database lookup) tells the call agent to set up a call between the two endpoints ep-orig and ep-term on the gateways GW-Orig and GW-Term.

The call agent sends two CreateConnection messages [2] and [4] that are similar to the call flow illustrated in Figure 13-2. After PSTN-term seizes the line, it sends an SS7 ACM [7] message to the call agent. Then the call agent sends an MDCX [8] to GW-Orig. Notice that the ConnectionMode is now set to recvonly. This is because, at this point, only the ringing tone needs to flow back to the originating side. The originating side cannot send audio yet.

After the terminating phone is picked up, PSTN-Term sends an ANM [11] message to the call agent. This triggers the call agent to send an MDCX to GW-Orig setting the mode to sendrecv. This completes the setup of gateways for two-way audio.

Advanced MGCP Features

This section outlines some of the advanced features of MGCP, including the following:

- Events and event packages

- Digit maps

- Embedded notification requests

- Non-IP bearer networks

Events and Event Packages

The concept of events and signals is central to MGCP. A call agent can ask an MG (via a RQNT message) to be notified about certain events occurring in an endpoint (such as off-hook events), and a call agent can request certain signals (such as dial-tones) to be applied to an endpoint.

Events and signals are grouped in packages within which they share the same namespace. A particular endpoint might support one or more packages. Table 13-5 lists the ten basic packages defined in MGCP. Note that additional event names and packages can be defined by implementers and registered with Internet Assigned Numbers Authority (IANA).

Table 13-5   *Basic Packages in MGCP*

Package	Name
Generic Media Package	G
DTMF Package	D
MF Package	M
Trunk Package	T
Line Package	L
Handset Package	H
RTP Package	R
Network Access Server Package	N
Announcement Server Package	A
Script Package	Script

RFC 2705 has specific recommendations for which event packages should be implemented on certain endpoint types. This is done to enable interoperability between multivendor gateways and call agents. Table 13-6 lists the basic endpoint types, their profiles, and their supported packages.

Table 13-6 *Endpoint Types and Supported Packages*

Gateway	Supported Packages
Trunk gateway (ISUP)	G, D, T, R
Trunk gateway (MF)	G, M, D, T, R
Network Access Server (NAS)	G, M, T, N
NAS/VoIP gateway	G, M, D, T, N, R
Access gateway (VoIP)	G, D, M, R
Access gateway (VoIP, NAS)	G, D, M, R
Residential gateway	G, D, L, R
Announcement server	A, R

Digit Maps

In many cases, the MGC needs to collect digit events that occur at the endpoint. Residential gateways typically use this system to collect the numbers that a user dials. Trunking gateways can use digit maps to collect access codes and other things. One approach is for the gateway to notify the MGC of dialed digits as soon as they are dialed. This digit-by-digit approach results in numerous RQNT and NTFY message exchanges between gateway and MGC.

The alternative approach to using digit maps is for the MGC to load the GW with a list of possible matches for dialed digits and to notify the MGC when a match is made. The digit map is expressed using a syntax derived from the UNIX **egrep** command.

Embedded Notification Requests

You can apply only one RQNT command to a media gateway at a given time. After the event that is specified in the RQNT occurs at the endpoint, the media gateway sends a NTFY to the MGC informing it of the occurrence. Only then can the MGC send a new RQNT with a new set of *Requested Events*. This gives rise to the possibility of a race condition in which some of the interesting events might occur at the endpoint while the gateway has sent a NTFY for the older RQNT but has not yet received the new RQNT from the MGC.

To alleviate this problem, MGCP introduced the concept of *embedded notification request*. Using this construct, the MGC can embed one notification request within another. The media GW applies the embedded notification request as soon as a Requested Event occurs without waiting for further instruction from the MGC. The embedded NotificationRequest can include a new list of Requested

Events, Signal Requests, and a new digit map. An embedded NotificationRequest is specified by using action code **E** in the Requested event list. Following is an example of an embedded NotificationRequest in a Requested Events (R) parameter line:

R: hd(E(R[0-9]))

This tells the gateway to look for the **hd** event. As soon as the **hd** event occurs, the gateway should apply **[0-9]** as the requested event.

Non-IP Bearer Networks

MGCP is typically used when IP is the bearer network for carrying media. However, MGCP enables a connection to be established over several other types of bearer networks. This includes audio transmission over an ATM network using ATM adaptation Layer 2 (AAL2) and TDM-to-TDM connections (hairpinning) where a call originating from a PSTN network is sent back into the PSTN network.

H.248/MEGACO

H.248 (as it is known in the ITU world) or MEGACO (as it is known in the IETF world) is similar to MGCP in terms of architecture and purpose. This section provides a brief description of H.248 constructs without going into the details.

The main constructs in the H.248 connection model are terminations, contexts, and commands.

Termination is the source or sink of one or more media streams. A *context* is an association between a collection of terminations. A termination can be in only one context at any given time. A special type of context, the *null context*, contains all terminations that are not in another context. For instance, in an access gateway, all idle lines are represented by terminations in the null context.

You use commands to manipulate terminations and contexts. The **Add** command adds a termination to a context. The **Subtract** command removes a termination from a context and might result in the context being released if no terminations remain. The **Move** command moves a termination from one context to another. The **Modify** command changes the state of the termination.

You can see that, in MGCP, a termination resembles an endpoint and a context resembles a call. Also, the **Add** command is similar to the CRCX command, and the **Subtract** command is similar to the DLCX command.

One of the important differences is that H.248 is connection-centric, whereas MGCP is endpoint-centric.

Summary

MGCP is a vital component for a distributed architecture based on a separation of media and signaling functions. It will continue to play an important role in the transition from a legacy network, where the components are in one monolithic platform to a network whose components are distributed.

Because this is a new and evolving industry, MGCP and H.248 have to develop over time to suit industry needs.

MGCP is a fairly simple protocol at its core and will be continue to play a vital part in packet-based voice networks for many years to come.

Part IV: VoIP Applications and Services

CHAPTER 14

PSTN and VoIP Interworking

The previous chapters described public switched telephone network (PSTN) and various Voice over IP (VoIP) technologies in isolation from one another. In real-world carrier networks, VoIP and PSTN technologies coexist and will continue to do so for some years to come. This chapter describes alternatives for interworking between VoIP and PSTN.

Cisco Packet Telephony

The Cisco Packet Telephony architecture is based on the creation of three logical planes: connection control, call control, and services. Each plane represents a different functional aspect of a voice service and interacts with the other logical planes through well-defined open interfaces. The three planes are organized into a hierarchy, with connection control at the lowest level, call control above connection control, and services above call control. Figure 14-1 illustrates the functional composition of the Cisco packet telephony architecture.

Figure 14-1 *Cisco Packet Telephony Architecture*

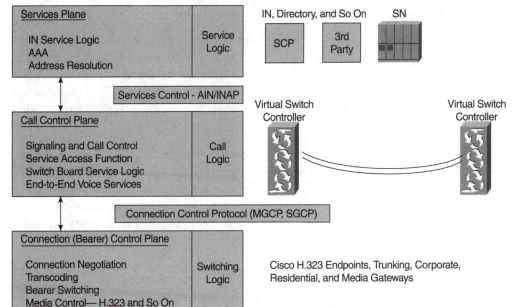

The softswitch provides the following call control plane functions in the Cisco Packet Telephony architecture:

■ The connection or bearer control plane encompasses the functionality that is necessary to set up, maintain, and tear down voice paths through the packet network. The Cisco AS5850, MGX8850, 2600, 3600, and 3810 are examples of media gateways (MG) that perform bearer control functions. The bearer control plane communicates with the call control plane using an industry-standard control protocol such as Media Gateway Control Protocol (MGCP).

■ The call control plane comprises the functionality that is necessary to signal, process, and route voice and data calls over the packet network. Functions within this layer are close to those found in the call-processing logic of an existing time-division multiplexing (TDM) switch. Typical call control plane functions include Signaling System 7 (SS7) protocol processing, digit analysis and manipulation, route selection, hunting, switch-based features, and interfacing with external service logic programs.

The call control plane communicates with the connection control plane using MGCP, Session Initiation Protocol (SIP), H.323, or MEGACO. The architectural intent of this interface is to cleanly separate the connection control from the call control in such a way that the call control plane is independent (and unknowing) of the underlying voice packet transport. This enables the same call control plane to be used with either a Layer 3 (IP) or Layer 2 (Asynchronous Transfer Mode/Frame Relay [ATM/FR])-oriented MG.

The call control plane can also communicate with the service plane to provide flexible, enhanced services. This interface is typically a standards-based Intelligent Network (IN) protocol running over SS7 transaction capabilities application part (TCAP), although many additional vendor-proprietary variants and extensions exist.

■ The service plane encompasses the logic that is necessary to provide enhanced nonswitch-resident services. You can accomplish such functions with Service Control Points (SCP) or service nodes. When you use SCPs, the call control plane signals the SCP using the Advanced Intelligent Network (AIN) or IN protocol over SS7 TCAP. Typical SCP applications include number translation (800#), account code authentication, credit card validation, and Virtual Private Network (VPN).

When using service nodes, a call control node typically routes a call to the service node for processing. The service node then applies its own feature-specific treatment to the voice or data stream and completes call routing to the intended destination. Depending on the feature, the service node can either remain in the path of the call or give control of the call back to the call control node. Typical service node applications include voice mail, debit card, and voice-activated dialing.

A particular product might encompass the capabilities of one or more of the logical planes from the preceding list. For example, an H.323 gateway might include the bearer control and call control planes.

Packet Voice Network Overview

A call agent such as the PGW2200 provides call control capability for the next-generation network. It controls how narrowband TDM voice traffic is consolidated over the packet infrastructure and ways in which you can apply services to those calls. You can use the virtual switch controller (VSC) in a variety of applications to provide call control functions. Examples of applications that are enabled on the packet voice network architecture include the following:

- Packet voice Interexchange Carrier (IXC) tandem applications

- Packet voice Local Exchange Carrier (LEC) Class 4 relief applications

- Endpoint client multimedia applications

- Corporate voice on-net and off-net services

- VoIP local/end office applications on cable infrastructure

Figure 14-2 depicts a generic packet voice application and illustrates various architectural components and how they fit and interact with each other.

Network Elements

This section reviews each network element that is identified in Figure 14-2. These elements include the following:

- Call agent (PGW2200)

- MG

- Service Control Point (SCP)

- Service node

- Cable headend

- Residential gateway

- H.323/SIP endpoint/client

Figure 14-2 *Packet Voice Network Architecture*

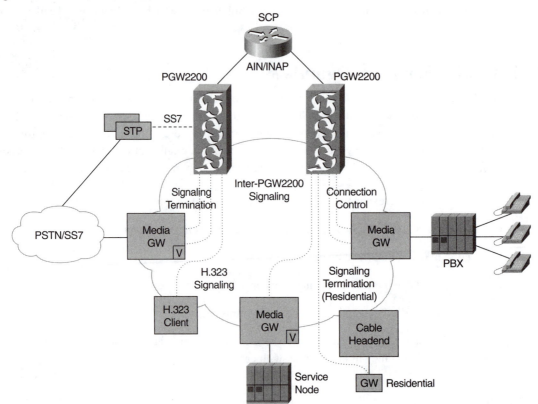

Call Agent: PGW2200

The Cisco PGW2200 is a carrier-class call agent that performs the signaling and call control tasks (such as digit analysis, routing, circuit selection, and more) within the PSTN gateway infrastructure. Taking advantage of a vast SS7 protocol library and supporting industry-standard control protocols, including MGCP, H.323, and SIP, the Cisco PGW2200 gives service providers the capability to seamlessly route voice and data calls between the PSTN and packet networks.

The Cisco PGW2200 consists of the following three required elements:

- Cisco media gateway controller (MGC) software, running on Sun Microsystems general computing platforms

- Cisco Signaling Link Terminals (SLT)

- LAN switch for IP interconnectivity of Cisco PGW2200 elements

The following are the optional elements:

- H.323 Signaling Interface (HSI) adjunct processor

- Management products, including the Cisco MGC Node Manager, Cisco Voice Services Provisioning Tool (VSPT), and Cisco Billing and Measurement Server (BAMS)

The following PSTN gateway applications are enabled by the Cisco PGW2200:

- VoIP transit

- Primary Rate Interface (PRI) Grooming and TDM Offload

- SIP PSTN gateway

- H.323 PSTN gateway

At a high level, the PGW2200 provides the following core capabilities:

- Call-signal processing, including ISDN Level 3 (Q.931), SS7 Level 4 (ISDN User Part [ISUP]), H.323, Multi-Frequency/channel-associated signaling (MF/CAS), and call signaling toward devices located at residential gateways connected through cable or digital subscriber line (DSL) Customer Premise Equipment (CPE). It also includes the capability to translate between different signaling types on different call legs.

- Address resolution, call routing, resource management, connection control, and call detail record (CDR) generation.

- Service access functions for accessing services that execute on external server platforms (such as SCP or Service node).

- Management interfaces using Simple Network Management Protocol (SNMP) for faults, performance, and configuration. Used as a web-based configuration tool and element management system.

Media Gateway

The MG performs the following high-level functions:

- Physical T1/E1 TDM facility termination from the PSTN or private branch exchanges (PBX)

- Echo cancellation into the circuit-switched network

- Balance of the jitter buffers

- Voice activity detection (VAD), such as silence suppression and comfort noise regeneration

- Voice compression using International Telecommunication Union (ITU) recommendations such as G.711, G.723.1, and G.729

- Tone generation, which generates dial, busy, ring-back, and congestion tones

- Dual-tone multifrequency (DTMF) transport, which enables use of touch tones for voice-mail applications with codecs that support DTMF detection/transport

- μ-law and a-law transcoding when required

- Quality of service (QoS) support

Service Control Point

The SCP provides the execution environment for service logic. It is responsible for processing transaction requests and returning a response. A typical transaction request in the voice world is a number translation.

Examples of this service include 800 (toll-free) service and Local Number Portability (LNP). A toll-free application that is running on the SCP, for example, has a sophisticated logic that enables the end user to control how incoming calls are routed. You can base toll-free call routing on dialed number, time of day, day of week, geographic point of origination, and even on how busy a terminating automatic call distribution (ACD) might be at a given moment. Customers or the service provider (SP) can own the SCP.

Cable Headend

The Universal Broadband Router is an integrated cable modem termination system (CMTS) and Cisco 7200 series router that uses radio frequency (RF) line cards.

The Universal Broadband Router provides a single integrated solution with CMTS functionality, the capability to terminate the Data-over-Cable Service Interface Specifications (DOCSIS) protocol, and the capability to perform all the required data routing functions. Instantiation of this component also includes a digital subscriber line access multiplexer (DSLAM).

Residential Gateway

The residential gateway is a voice/data CPE device that provides from two to four ports of plain old telephone service (POTS) capability. The device runs the DOCSIS protocol to provide packet data and telephony services over the hybrid fiber-coaxial (HFC) cable to the CMTS. Another example of this component is a DSL modem.

H.323/SIP Endpoint/Client

The H.323/SIP client represents a broad range of voice/multimedia applications that are hosted natively on the IP network and are run by the endpoints that support SIP or H.323 as their VoIP protocol. These endpoints might have multimedia capabilities besides voice.

Network Interfaces

The four main network interfaces for the PGW2200 call agent are signaling termination, inter-call agent signaling, connection control, and services control, as illustrated in Figure 14-3.

Figure 14-3 *Network Interfaces*

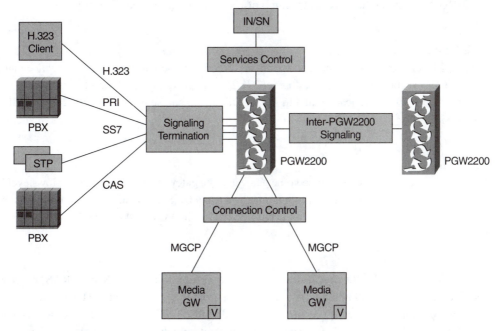

Each PGW2200 network interface is discussed in the following sections.

Signaling Termination

The signaling termination capability enables PGW2200 to mediate between many signaling variants, such as SS7, PRI, CAS, and H.323, to name a few.

SS7 Links

Several mechanisms are available to terminate SS7 signaling traffic on the PGW2200:

■ Nonassociated signaling (A-links)—These are terminated directly on the PGW2200 using either a V.35 or T1/E1 physical interface. Optionally, to increase reliability characteristics, you can configure a set of Signaling Link Terminals (SLT) to handle the lower layers of SS7. The SLTs are implemented using Cisco 2600 series routers fronting Sun servers that host the PGW2200 application.

■ Fully associated signaling (F-links)—These carry bearer traffic and are terminated on the packet gateway. The packet gateway is responsible for executing Message Transfer Parts (MTPs) 1 and 2, encapsulating MTP Layer 3 (MTP L3) protocol data units, and sending them to the PGW2200 for MTP L3 and ISDN User Part (ISUP) processing. The transport between the packet gateway and the PGW2200 is carried out using Reliable User Data Protocol (RUDP), a thin reliability layer on top of User Datagram Protocol (UDP).

PRI Links

The PRI links carry a D channel and terminate directly on the voice gateway. The voice gateway peripherals execute Level 1 (L1) and Level 2 (L2)—the lower layers of the PRI interface (Q.921). Layer 3 (L3; Q.931) is encapsulated in the RUDP packet and sent to the PGW2200 for call processing.

CAS Links

CAS links terminate directly on the voice gateway. The gateway periphery handles low-level CAS protocols, such as line and address signaling. You use a CAS application programming interface (API) to backhaul the call-processing events over IP to the PGW2200 for call handling.

H.323

The PGW2200 handles the precall-level Registration, Admissions, and Status (RAS) requests in addition to call-level Q.931 requests that originate from the H.323 clients. This signaling termination follows delivery procedures described in the H.323 standard. In other words, the PGW2200 has H.225 RAS/Q.931 capabilities, but it does not have H.323 gatekeeper functionality.

Inter-PGW2200 Signaling

The PGW2200-to-PGW2200 protocol scales the network by distributing control over multiple PGW2200 platforms. A modified ISUP protocol called Enhanced ISUP (E-ISUP) exchanges call-control information between the PGW2200s over an IP network using RUDP. MTP information is not required, so it is not transported.

The E-ISUP messages also carry Session Description Protocol (SDP) elements in ISUP generic digits information elements, which the PGW2200 uses to specify connection attributes in MGCP.

> **NOTE**   The industry is moving toward using SIP or a variant of SIP, known as SIP-T, for an inter-MGC communication protocol.

Connection Control: MGCP

You can establish end-to-end voice connections in the packet network by using MGCP, an open mechanism to set up connections in IP networks. MGCP is a TCP/UDP-based transaction protocol that permits manipulation of the connections represented by physical or logical endpoints. The connections are described using attributes such as IP addresses, codecs, and so on. MGCP manages call setup requests and connections from phones that are connected to gateways, such as cable or DSL modems.

Services Control

Access to service can follow two paths:

- IN (AIN/INAP/convergence sublayer-1 [CS-1]) platforms such as SCPs interface initially over standards-based AIN/INAP interfaces that are transported over the SS7 network, with future migration to IP-based transport.

- Service node services (such as calling cards and voice mail) initially connect over TDM PRI interfaces. In the future, the service node platforms will transition to IP networks to avoid unnecessary TDM/IP interworking.

Figure 14-4 clarifies the interworking with PGW2200 in the network.

Figure 14-4   *Call Agent Transformation*

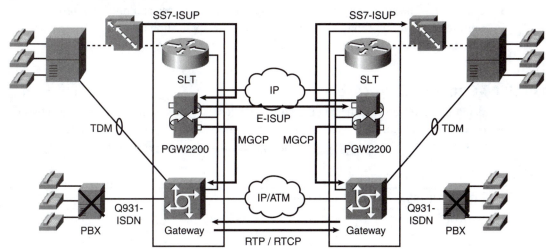

PGW2200 Architecture and Operations

Figure 14-5 depicts the major functional blocks internal to the Cisco PGW2200 platform.

Figure 14-5 *Functional Components of the PGW2200*

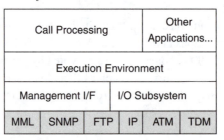

The Cisco PGW2200 is an open platform that is built to host third-party developed applications through a set of powerful application/protocol building tools and associated APIs.

These tools include the following:

■ Application Toolkit—The PGW2200 Application Toolkit enables users to customize protocols and their interworking features. The toolkit also provides powerful language tools and an API to develop state- and event-driven applications that reside on the PGW2200 platform.

■ Conversion Analyzer—The Conversion Analyzer generates output reports using traces in the interworking engine. Information in the report includes message input, conversion, and output.

■ Simulator—The simulator enables users to create message sets and run them through a mirrored interworking engine to determine/diagnose application or protocol errors. Detailed reports include message input, conversion, and output.

PGW2200-Supported Protocols

A great PGW2200 feature is the fact that its architecture supports multiple access and network protocols. New protocols and variations of existing protocols continue to be added to the library. Table 14-1 provides a comprehensive list of protocols.

Table 14-1 *SC-Supported Protocols*

ANSI ISUP (SS7)	ITU Q.931 PRI	Belgian Q761 ISUP
BTNUP	ETSI ISUP V2	Alcatel 4400 PRI
BTNUP NRC	ETSI Q.SIG	NI-2 (Bell-1268)

Table 14-1   *SC-Supported Protocols (Continued)*

China TUP	ITU Q.767 ISUP	NI-2+ (Bell-1268-C3)
DNPSS	French ISUP	Polish ISUP
Dutch ISUP	German ISUP	Finland Q761 ISUP
ETSI PRI	Hong Kong Q761 ISUP	Australian Q761 ISUP

Execution Environment

The Execution Environment (XE) provides common services to application programs that are running on the signaling host. The major goals of the XE are the following:

- Provide application programs with a flexible, stable, and consistent infrastructure

- Enable new applications to be more easily integrated with existing applications that are running on the same platform

- Minimize the amount of work that application developers must do to create a new application

- Provide a simplified interface to operating system services so that third parties can develop custom applications that can run in a process on the PGW2200

Services provided by the XE include the following:

- Process management—Enables the XE to manage processes. This includes orderly startup, shutdown, and monitoring of process health. Process management also is used to implement the cut-over to a new version of a process with minimal interruption of service.

- Alarms—Enable processes to register, set, and clear alarms. Alarm sets and clears are automatically reported to processes that request this service. You can use this capability to report alarms to attached management interfaces, enabling such processes to implement necessary recovery action.

- Logs—Enable a process to log messages to shared log files, based on a facility and logging severity level.

- Statistics—Enable a process to update shared counters that are used for reporting and alarms. Alarms based on shared counters are automatically generated on behalf of all processes on the platform. Measurement reports are automatically generated at periodic intervals.

- Command management—Enables processes to exchange commands and responses. This service also is used to provide a unified interface to the protocol conversion engine or to external systems that control or monitor the XE platform through a management interface (such as TransPath Man-Machine Language [MML]).

- Configuration management—Enables a process to be notified when configuration data changes. It coordinates dynamic reconfiguration across all processes on the platform.

- Access control—Ensures that platform services are provided only to those processes that are authorized to use them.

- Process shell—Provides a framework that processes use to interface with the services that are provided under the XE. It features a uniform event dispatching mechanism, support for interprocess communication (IPC), timers, signals, and a set of foundation classes for applications development.

- IPC—Enables processes within the platform to exchange messages.

- Signal handling—Provides an interface for conditions that are signaled through the operating system.

North American Numbering Plan

The PGW2200 can handle the North American Numbering Plan (NANP) as presented to an access tandem or IXC network:

- Operator services (0-, 0+, 00) with or without 10XXX or 101XXXX routed to either a North American number (NXX-XXXX or NPA-NXX-XXXX) or an international number (CC+NN).

- Normal calls with or without 10XXX or 101XXXX routed to either a North American number (NXX-XXXX or NPA-NXX-XXXX) or an international number (CC+NN).

- Support for # end of number indicator. This enables callers to press # to prompt the switch to stop waiting for another digit before processing the number dialed.

- Cut-through call to carriers (10XXX+# or 101XXXX+#).

- Support for 950-XXXX format numbers (both nature of addresses [NOAs]).

- Conversion of NXX-XXXX numbers to NPA-NXX-XXXX numbers.

- Support for IN triggers (toll free, premium service, and LNP).

Route Analysis

PGW2200 call routing routes a call from the ingress MG to the appropriate egress MG. Call routing does not refer to the routing of packets within the packet cloud; the connection control layer handles this. If the same PGW2200 controls the originating and terminating MGs, the call routing takes place in one step within the PGW2200.

If a different PGW2200 controls the egress gateway, both an originating and terminating PGW2200 are involved in call routing. The originating PGW2200 analyzes the call request message, such as SS7 initial address message (IAM), and selects a route to reach the egress gateway or terminating PGW2200 that serves the egress gateway. The route analysis selects one of the following:

- A "hop-off" or egress gateway that is connected to the selected trunk group

- The IP address of the terminating PGW2200 that determines the egress gateway

- The residential gateway

- A hair-pinned connection in the ingress gateway back out to the originating network

If two PGW2200s are needed, the originating PGW2200 uses E-ISUP to communicate with the terminating PGW2200s to perform call setup. Figure 14-6 illustrates the primary, secondary, and congestion overflow options, as determined by the route selection process.

Figure 14-6 *Route Selection Process*

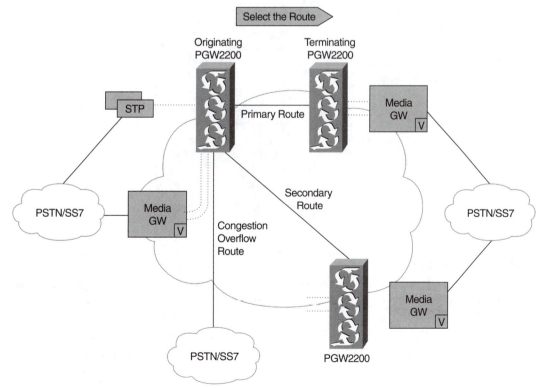

Digit Analysis

The PGW2200 performs a digit analysis and screening function against A or B numbers (LNP and AIN/INAP triggers). The dialed or translated number selects the route, and the terminating PGW2200 is responsible for selecting the egress gateway. First the selection is carried out by digit analysis and selection of "preferred" hop-off gateways (such as trunk groups). Then it is carried out by performing busy/idle handling on the terminating gateway resources, selecting an outgoing circuit on the TDM interface, and, finally, invoking appropriate signaling procedures (ISUP IAM) toward the terminating PSTN switches. Figure 14-7 illustrates the egress gateway selection process.

Figure 14-7 *Egress Gateway Selection*

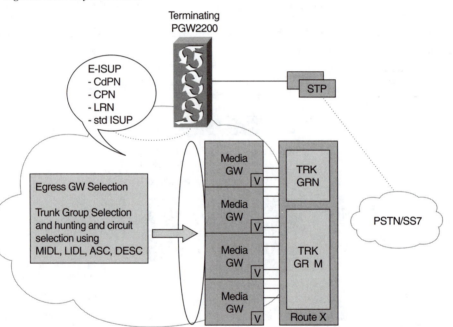

Reroute on Congestion

The PGW2200 contains the status of trunks that are connected to the egress gateways (a busy/idle map) that the PGW2200 controls. If an egress gateway cannot complete a call because of an internal resource error, an explicit indication is sent back to the PGW2200 with an MGCP negative acknowledge. The PGW2200 can then choose another route to attempt the call. If two PGW2200s are involved, the terminating PGW2200 informs the originating PGW2200 using E-ISUP (Release [REL] with congestion), and a call reroute is attempted if alternate routes were provisioned.

PGW2200 Implementation

The PGW2200 can provide a high level of availability that is equal to or better than a traditional switch. The system, as illustrated in Figure 14-8, is based on fault-tolerant platforms consisting of an active and standby unit and a separate set of SLTs that terminate SS7 traffic.

Figure 14-8 *PGW2200 Implementation*

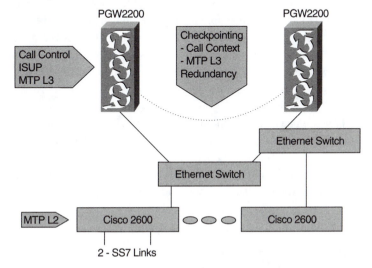

Call state information is copied from the active unit to the standby unit. This process also is called *check-pointing* and ensures that stable calls are not lost in a switchover from active to standby PGW2200. The SLTs terminate the MTP L2 traffic and send the MTP L3 information to the active unit. Preliminary analysis indicates combined system availability of 0.9999985 or 0.782 minutes of downtime per year.

To maximize PGW2200 fault tolerance, MTP L2 traffic is terminated on separate hardware platforms, and MTP L3 traffic is transmitted across dual Ethernet switches. This level of redundancy enables the active and standby systems to share the SS7 links and LANs/WANs.

The Cisco 2600 is the first router to support SLT functionality. You can remove, add, or service an SLT without disrupting the SS7 network. The Cisco 2600 SLT supports two SS7 link ports, whereby each port can handle an aggregate of two erlangs of traffic. (An *erlang* is the number of calls multiplied by the average handle time [AHT] of the call divided by 3600.) SLTs are connected through standard Ethernet and deliver MTP L3 information to the PGW2200 through RUDP across the LAN/WAN.

Application Check-Pointing

Check-pointing occurs between PGW2200s and ensures that in-progress calls are preserved in the event of a failover. The call-processing engine sends checkpoint events to the local checkpoint process during the call setup and call release phases.

During the call setup phase, the first checkpoint event is generated when the resource manager secures the physical circuit resource from the packet gateway. The event contains enough information to enable the remote resource manager to update the logical state of the assigned circuit. The second checkpoint event is generated when the call is answered. The event data stored in the remote resource manager contains only enough information for the remote call-processing engine to maintain the call until it is released. Therefore, in the event of a failover, calls are kept in service, but no service features are supported.

During the call release phase, a checkpoint is generated when the resource manager receives an acknowledgment from the packet gateway that is associated with the call release request.

Check-pointing also is applied to protocol supervisory messages in case logical state changes of bearer circuits occur between initial call setup and release. These messages include the following:

- Blocking and unblocking messages and commands

- Circuit reset messages and commands

MGC Node Manager

The MGC Node Manager (MNM) is a Telecommunication Management Network (TMN)-based solution for the end-to-end management of networks providing SS7-enabled services. MNM provides consolidated management of the Cisco network elements (NEs), thus enabling the virtual switch system to be treated as a single managed element. MNM responsibilities consist of the physical network elements that comprise the voice and signaling portions of the virtual switch, including these:

- PGW2200

- Voice-encoding units

- Voice traffic within the virtual switch domain

- Intraswitch and inter-virtual switch signaling traffic

- Signaling traffic between the PSTN or PBX and the virtual switch network as seen by the PGW2200

MNM responsibilities exclude the following:

■ External voice network elements (telephone switches)

■ Data or TDM networks providing voice or signaling transmission to the virtual switch

■ Signaling traffic to and from the PSTN and the virtual switch domain

The MNM domain encompasses signaling and traffic voice elements, as illustrated in Figure 14-9.

Figure 14-9 *MGC Node Manager Domain*

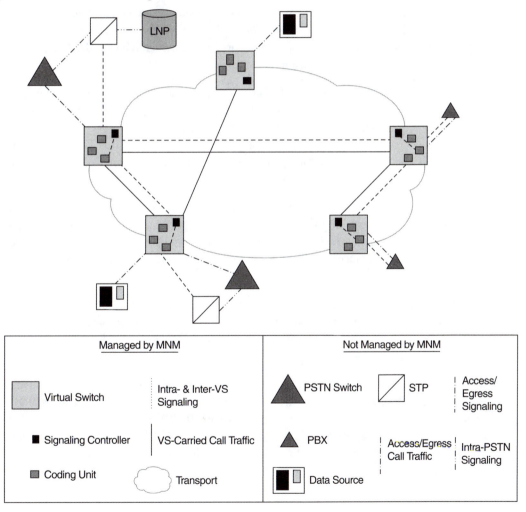

In this domain, the MNM provides traditional FCAPS functionality for fault, configuration, performance, and security management. Accounting services, however, are provided by CDRs that the PGW2200 generates. The MNM directly manages the PGW2200 and interoperates through SNMP and other interfaces to external Element Management Systems (EMS).

The external EMSs actually manage the NEs that compose the remaining part of the virtual switch. MNM functionality for fault, configuration, performance, and security within the domain is as follows:

- Fault Management—Displays a graphical representation of domain-specific alarm information and severity level. Also supports sophisticated event correlation, problem isolation, and state information, summarized at the component level. The fault management browser supports point-and-click navigation through alarm hierarchies and network topology maps for simple element identification.

- Configuration Management—Provides both graphical and text-based utilities and graphical user interface (GUI) support for all NEs within the domain. In some cases, the MNM integrates or interfaces with existing Cisco element managers to leverage the robust line of management products that is currently deployed in Cisco customer sites. You access element-specific management utilities through a point-and-click interface from the network topology map.

- Performance Management—The MNM collects traffic and performance data from relevant elements and archives them in a central database. The MNM provides basic reporting and graphics applications for reviewing the collected data. An open-database Structured Query Language (SQL) interface is provided for offline and customer-specific reporting and analysis tools.

- Security Management—The MNM supports role-based access to various management functions and NEs. You can define user groups to simplify user administration; standard user-ID and password functionality is supported. Standard SNMP community string security governs SNMP access.

The MNM also provides SNMP, TL1, and SQL (nonreal-time) interfaces for propagating alarms to the upper network management layer. Apart from these interfaces, the MNM can provide standards-based interfaces to Operations Support System (OSS) network management systems, including Common Management Information Protocol/Q2 (CMIP/Q2) and Common Object Request Broker Architecture (CORBA). The MNM provides a GUI that enables users to control the EMS directly.

The MNM architecture takes into consideration the following key SP requirements:

- Separates configuration, accounting, performance, fault, and security per the TMN specification

- Provides a layered management architecture, with the capability to integrate either with legacy network management systems or planned future systems

- Uses a recursive layered network object model

- Adopts CORBA as a strategic direction for interfaces

- Provides flow-through provisioning

- Manages network traffic performance

- Correlates alarms

- Provides standards-based interfaces

Accounting

Every call that the PGW2200 handles produces call detail information. The amount of detail generated is comprehensive; each CDR contains the following information:

- Called and calling number

- Answer time, disconnect time, and call completion codes

- Route information, originating trunk group and member, and terminating trunk group and member

- ISUP information

- ISDN service information and extensions

- Account codes and pins

Along with this information, more than 80 additional elements are available for custom CDR configuration in flexible user-defined formats. If a data or usage element is not available, the TransPath Message Definition Language (MDL) can generate separate fields in a special array marked "custom" for future CDR requirements. These arrays are set to both ITU and American National Standards Institute (ANSI) standards.

CDRs are written to a spool file that is automatically closed at customer-definable intervals or when the file exceeds a specified size. You can retrieve closed files or send them to downstream processing systems, such as Automatic Messaging Accounting (AMA) formatting or billing mediation devices, as needed. Customers also can generate midcall CDR information that logs data from up to eight event points in a call.

PSTN Signaling Over IP

In a softswitch architecture, one of the requirements for carriers to move to an IP-based infrastructure is a transition technology to transport PSTN signaling over IP.

VoIP signaling protocols such as SIP and H.323 have been specifically designed assuming IP as the underlying transport. Legacy PSTN signaling protocols such as SS7 and ISDN have stringent performance and functional requirements that IP does not readily meet.

To meet these requirements, additional protocol layers are needed on top of IP. The SIGTRAN working group of Internet Engineering Task Force (IETF) defined a set of encapsulation methods and end-to-end protocol mechanisms to support the functional and performance requirements of PSTN signaling. SIGTRAN architecture consists of the following:

- An adaptation layer for each PSTN signaling protocol (such as MTP3, ISDN, and so on) to support the services expected by a particular PSTN signaling protocol from its underlying protocol layer. Examples of these adaptation layers are MTP3-User Adaptation Layer (M3UA), ISDN Q.921-User Adaptation Layer (IUA), and so on.

- Stream Control Transmission Protocol (SCTP) as the transport protocol that supports a common set of functions for signaling transport.

To meet the reliability and performance requirements for carrier-grade networks, SIGTRAN specifications introduced the concepts of Application Server (AS) and Application Server Process (ASP).

AS is defined as a logical entity that serves a specific application instance. An example of an AS is an MGC handling the Q.931. Practically speaking, an AS is modeled at the SG as an ordered list of one or more related ASPs (for example, primary, secondary, and tertiary).

ASP is a process instance of an AS. Examples of ASPs are primary or backup MGC instances.

The sections that follow describe SCTP and IUA specified by the SIGTRAN working group.

SCTP

TCP is the most common reliable transport protocol used in IP networks. However, it is deemed unsuitable for carrying PSTN signaling for the following reasons:

- Head-of-line blocking occurs, in which a lost packet causes undue delay of delivery of subsequent packets to the application.

- The stream-oriented nature of TCP is unsuitable for the message-oriented nature of PSTN signaling. Message delimiters and explicit "push" operations are needed to meet latency requirements.

- TCP has no native support for multihomed hosts. For applications with high availability, this support is a requirement of PSTN signaling.

- TCP is relatively vulnerable to denial-of-service (DoS) attacks.

Because of these limitations with TCP, the SIGTRAN working group specified SCTP in RFC 2960. SCTP has the following features:

- Message orientation.

- Acknowledged error-free nonduplicated transfer of user data.

- Sequenced delivery of user messages with optional out-of-order delivery to avoid head-of-line blocking.

- Piggybacking, in which multiple user messages can be bundled and sent as one SCTP packet across the network. This provides efficiency.

- Support for multihoming by introducing the concept of an association between endpoints. At startup, each SCTP endpoint can provide its peer with a list of transport addresses (multiple IP addresses) through which it can be reached and from which it originates packets. SCTP association spans data transfer over all possible source/destination combinations in a manner that is transparent to the user application.

- Resistance to some DoS attacks.

IUA

As mentioned previously, in softswitch architecture, the media functions are separated from call control functions. The media functions are part of MG, and call control functions are part of MGC or call agent.

ISDN, as an in-band signaling mechanism, arrives along with the media at the MG. The ISDN signaling information needs to be transported (also known as backhaul) to the MGC for call processing. In the IUA specification, the GW terminates Q.921 and backhauls Q.931 to MGC.

RFC 3057 specifies IUA, which Figure 14-10 illustrates.

Figure 14-10   *ISDN User Adaptation Layer Architecture*

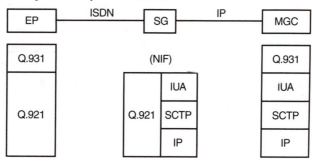

IUA provides the following services to the upper layer:

- Support for transport of Q.921/Q.931 boundary primitives. In the backhaul scenario, the Q.921/Q.931 boundary primitives are exposed. The IUA layer needs to support all the primitives of this boundary to successfully backhaul Q.931.

- Support for communication between Layer Management modules on SG and MGC. This is to help Layer Management modules manage the SCTP association(s) between the SG and MGC. For example, the Layer Management modules can instruct the IUA layer to establish an SCTP association to a peer IUA node.

- Support for management of active associations between signaling gateway (SG) and MGC. The IUA layer at the SG maintains the availability and active/inactive state of all ASPs. It manages the SCTP associations and the traffic between the SG and ASPs.

Changing Landscape of PSTN-IP Interworking

As the focus changes from getting basic VoIP in networks to interworking across different islands of VoIP, the service providers and carriers face new challenges in setting up the networks by supporting different protocols and network elements. If you add the issues related to billing and security to this scenario, the complexity increases further. Some of the trends as seen by deployments by VoIP providers have shown that topology hiding in the network that is run with multiple interconnected IP domains is now a common feature everywhere. Table 14-2 shows the most common trends in the momentum to drive VoIP forward.

Table 14-2 *New VoIP Interconnect Trends*

Moving From	Moving To
Flat bandwidth billing	Usage billing
Best effort	Service-level agreements (SLA) and QoS
Open network connections	Topology hiding
TDM interconnects	IP interconnects, signaling protocol interoperability
Same codec interconnects	Transcoding
Assumed trust	Security
Simple IP domain	Interconnected IP domains
Lawful intercept (LI) ability—optional	LI required

When VoIP carriers and providers connect to other carriers, they do interworking using one of the following approaches:

■ Colocate with the carrier and pull the data connections

■ Increase the data connection lease capacity from the local carrier

■ Use a gateway or an *intermediary box* to connect into the TDM network of an incumbent carrier

For the most cost-effective solution, the carriers use the third option and allow peering as an important tool to connect different H.323 or SIP networks across geographies, as Figure 14-11 illustrates.

Figure 14-11 *PSTN-IP Networking*

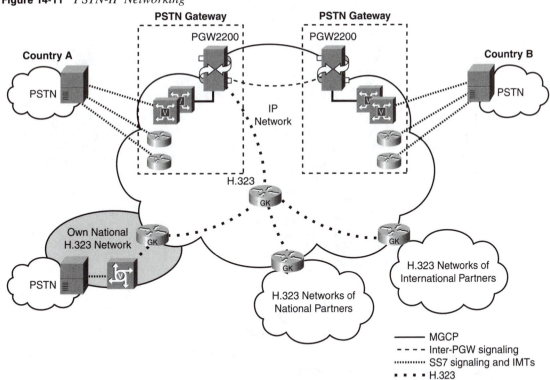

Using this intermediary box approach enables the following applications and services:

■ International transit

■ International and national termination of H.323 VoIP traffic

■ Network interconnect for H.323 VoIP operators

This approach uses the following technologies/devices:

- PGW2200 for call control and CDR collection in central and remote zones

- Carrier-class VoIP gateways MGX8230 with VISM-PR cards, AS5300 voice gateways, and AS5000 universal gateways

With SIP being used in many VoIP networks, Figure 14-12 gives a more realistic picture of SIP and H.323 network terminations that the PGW2200 handles.

Figure 14-12 *PSTN-IP Networking*

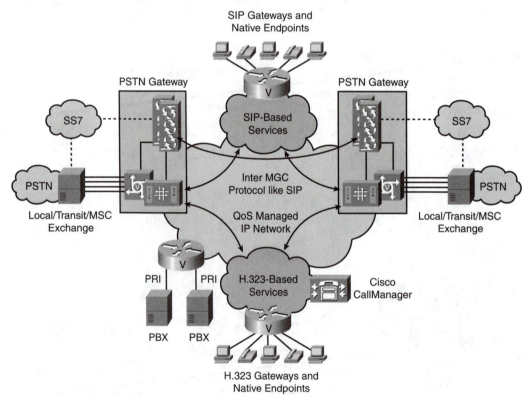

Session Border Controller (SBC)

VoIP peering and connectivity for two or more networks is now becoming an important task for large deployments.

This enables service providers and enterprises to interconnect VoIP networks directly without the need to have calls going from one VoIP network to another to travel over the PSTN. The providers can further reduce operational expenses because of lower costs in fees and taxes, less regulation, and so on. Therefore, it is logical for some vendors to conceptualize a session border controller (SBC) that not only serves as a useful peering point but also solves the interoperability issues between islands of VoIP traffic. Although there are various interpretations of what an SBC can do or should do in a network, SBCs are conceived with the following interworking functions (IWF) for each of these areas, as shown in Figure 14-13:

■ IP address and port translations

■ Billing and CDR normalization

■ VoIP security (NAT traversal, LI, Authentication, and so on)

■ Media interworking to resolve codec, DTMF-RELAY, and FAX issues

■ QoS and bandwidth management

■ Rich signaling and application interworking

■ Consistency with VoIP protocols

Figure 14-13 *SBC Components*

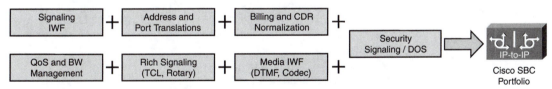

The interoperability issues that you see when connecting with different networks are addressed through these IWFs.

You can find SBC functionality in the following classes of devices:

■ Standalone SBC

■ Routing devices

■ Media gateways

■ Security devices

Many industry vendors have implemented one or more of these functions and have used the SBC effectively in network peering. In the past two years, standalone devices have gained popularity and have created a niche market segment by providing varying levels of functionality that are appealing to service providers and VoIP carriers.

SBCs give the value addition that a provider needs to interconnect with disparate networks. Figure 14-14 illustrates how an SBC helps an SP in various interconnect scenarios.

Figure 14-14 *Where VoIP Networks Interconnect*

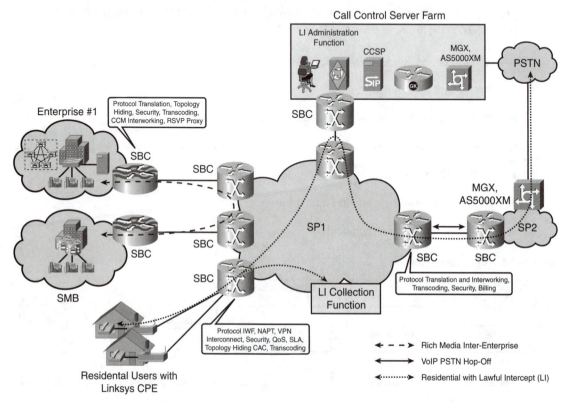

The SP1 as shown is connected to another SP network called SP2 and also talks to other VoIP islands—namely ones owned by Enterprise#1, some Small and Medium Business (SMB), or a residential VoIP network owned by another provider. These individual networks might have their own VoIP management systems, but because traffic from all of them needs to traverse through the large provider SP1, the SBC at each peering point provides the normalization and much-needed interoperability.

Summary

The Cisco Packet Telephony architecture enables you to separate application, call control, and bearer planes. The call agent is a major component of this architecture, because it helps to bridge applications to bearer planes. The PGW2200 is the Cisco instantiation of a call agent. As this architecture implies, the PGW2200 enables customers to use different vendors in each component of the architecture (application, call control, and bearers). This enables you to use Cisco MGs with call agents of other vendors and with the PGW2200.

Building a call agent for an SP customer requires you to pay attention to many details. Route selection, call control, and reliability are just a few of the issues covered when building this piece of the Cisco Packet Telephony architecture.

Besides call agent, SBC offers another valuable component in VoIP networks. Currently, SIP, H.323, and MGCP are clear choices for VoIP networks carrying a bulk of VoIP traffic. SBCs act as the connecting devices between two VoIP providers. Each provider uses an SBC to connect to multiple peer networks and helps him reduce the operational expenses to offer massive deployments of VoIP traffic.

CHAPTER 15

Service Provider VoIP Applications and Services

Chapter 14 showed how enterprise businesses are trying to more effectively manage their communications using Voice over IP (VoIP) in their business. The enterprises clearly see VoIP as a tool to remain competitive and improve the quality of their customer service. The service provider (SP) view of telephony service relies on the offering of consistent service to mass markets with a well-defined set of benchmarks on service offering, pricing, and quality of service (QoS).

At the end of 2004, In-Stat, a telecom research firm, estimated there to be 1.3 million broadband IP lines in use in the United States, with growth reaching to 3.9 million lines by the end of 2005. Most providers around the globe acknowledge that IP has won the transport layer for the network, and voice, along with data, video, and value-added services carried over the IP network, are cumulatively the key driving force in the telecommunications marketplace. The global market for consumer VoIP services has arrived, with total VoIP subscribers worldwide at 16 million in 2005 and projected to grow to more than 55 million in 2009, reports In-Stat.

Service providers traditionally have been categorized as cable companies, telco companies, and broadband and wireless companies that own the underlying network to some extent. With VoIP and advanced service offerings, a new breed of providers uses the network infrastructure of the traditional providers and offers value-added services. Namely, those providers include AOL, Vonage, Yahoo! Broadband, Skype, and Google. With IP as the common foundation for transport, these companies are now competing against each other for a share of the VoIP marketplace. Overlaps exist in the service offerings, however, and the highest priority for providers is to devise a resolution for the dilemma of how to drive revenue growth while keeping the operational expenses in control.

The Service Provider Dilemma

One key dilemma that the service providers face today is that, with more services over VoIP and with the advent of new technologies such as Session Initiation Protocol (SIP), service providers have gradually devalued the call control plane for the services. At one point, the core call control of the network was the critical piece, and the handsets/endpoints were of little importance. With consumers asking for more intelligence in their hands, a whole suite of consumer premise equipment (CPE) and small office-home office (SOHO) products is driving subscriber features.

The call control switch residing in the provider network is now distributed geographically, and many different servers share the functionality. Current technology reduces the obstacles that VoIP offerings face, and the SPs find that revenue derived strictly from voice-only traffic is a difficult market unless VoIP applications offer the next paradigm shift. The dilemma that SPs face is which applications based on VoIP will make money.

It is not just about who can provide VoIP services. It is about what those services can offer in terms of revenue and what role they take after integration with existing and new communication services that run over an IP backbone. Clearly, consumers and small and medium enterprises are fueling the demand for these new services and applications. The trend so far has been to drive the applications that put more control in the hands of the end user and integrate the multiple communication methods available today (voice, e-mail, instant messaging [IM], conferencing, Short Message Service [SMS], Multimedia Messaging Service [MMS], and so on).

The providers have little choice but to partner with multiple vendors to ensure that the VoIP network traverses through many servers while offering revenue margins.

SPs need the following:

- Carrier-class reliability and scalability

- A shared platform for all subscribers—multitenancy

- Reduction of operational expenses

Subscriber needs are as follows:

- Robust feature functionality

- Multimedia, predictive dialing, speech recognition, automatic call distribution (ACD), recording, and so on

- Full administrative control of their own virtual call center/home network

- Rapid deployment

- Powerful integration with CPE

This chapter reviews the way that SPs are trying to develop new applications that fulfill the subscriber needs and help them achieve the desired results. It also covers some of the emerging technologies and deployments that are evolving out of VoIP and IP packet-based service as a fundamental premise that has helped with synergies in different market spaces, whether wireline, cable, or simple data networks. Providers often refer to these synergies as "triple play" of providing data, voice, and video services to consumers such that they can optimize revenue-per-subscriber ratios and fuel business growth. They can now consolidate these packet-based services into a single switching and transport network. If they add wireless mobility to triple-play, it becomes a *quad-play* offering.

Service Provider Applications and Benefits

When enterprise businesses think about consolidating their voice and data networks into a single multiservice network, the initial application they usually consider is *toll-bypass.* Toll-bypass enables businesses to send their intraoffice voice and fax calls over their existing TCP/IP network. By moving this traffic off the public switched telephone network (PSTN), businesses can immediately save on long-distance charges by using extra bandwidth on their data network without losing existing functionality.

You can immediately quantify the savings gleaned with toll-bypass. In fact, some businesses that have plenty of intraoffice calling—both domestic and international—have seen a Return On Investment (ROI) in as little as three to six months.

As enterprise businesses become more comfortable with VoIP and toll-bypass, the next applications they usually consider are those they can apply to customer service, interactive project groups, and distance-based training. The following are some examples of applications that you can apply to these areas:

- Microsoft Communicator—Communicator 2005 is an integrated communications client, enabling information workers to communicate in real time. As the recommended client for Microsoft Office Live Communications Server (LCS) 2005, Communicator 2005 integrates with Microsoft Office System applications and enterprise telephony infrastructure.

  Microsoft also launched Microsoft Office Communicator Mobile. Based on the user interface of the Microsoft Office Communicator 2005 desktop client, Communicator Mobile is being launched as a unified communications client that provides information workers with a premier mobile collaboration experience through native integration of mobile applications with enterprise-grade, real-time communications tools. The client goes beyond simple voice services, incorporating connected communication modes such as security-enhanced IM, presence awareness, and integrated VoIP telephony.

- Microsoft NetMeeting—Prior to the Microsoft LCS launch, NetMeeting was the commonly known VoIP client of the company. It is still used in some networks where it provides integration between traditional phone services with application-sharing and H.323-based video-conferencing. This integration of services enables employees in different locations to easily collaborate on projects and reduce expenses by consolidating equipment and data/voice networks.

- Cisco IP Phone—This provides the look and feel of a traditional handset, with the added functionality of IP connectivity. Instead of relying on an existing private branch exchange (PBX) for functionality, such as dial tone, an IP Phone works in conjunction with newer IP-based PBXs. These IP-PBXs not only provide the same functionality that traditional PBXs do (dial tone, voice mail, and conferencing), but they also take advantage of all IP-based services that are available in the network to offer new features. Because it is an IP device, the IP Phone can use not only VoIP services, but also any other IP-based multiservice application that is available on the network.

- PC-based softphone—This extends the handset functionality onto the PC with a graphical user interface (GUI) that provides the same functionality as the handset and integrates with other multiservice applications such as web browsing, NetMeeting, or directory services based on Lightweight Directory Access Protocol (LDAP). It also eliminates the need to have an additional device (the handset) on each desktop, because the softphone uses headsets and speakers, which are common on most standard PCs.

- VoIP Integrated IM clients—With the onset of VoIP softphones, there is a need to integrate IM and presence-based applications with transport of voice. GoogleTalk, Skype, Yahoo!, Gizmo, and AOL are just a few of the latest software applications that achieve this functionality and have drawn attention lately. Although the current solutions are tied to their own IM application, the trend is toward IM-agnostic solutions. (For example, the Google IM application should be able to talk to Yahoo or Skype, and so on.)

All the services that have been discussed so far are considered first-generation, standards-based services. Just as TCP/IP data services rapidly evolved, second-generation VoIP and integrated data/voice services based on TCP/IP will also quickly evolve. These services will be driven by increased competition between businesses; open-standard application programming interfaces (API); protocols such as H.323, LDAP, Telephone Application Programming Interface (TAPI) and Java Telephony API (JTAPI); and the creativity of enterprise network managers and programmers.

Service Provider VoIP Deployment: Vonage

Vonage, a New Jersey-based U.S. company, is a leading provider of broadband connection-based telephony. It has 1.2 million customers and is the largest national provider of phone service that sends calls over Internet. It has clearly demonstrated the wide-scale real-world deployment of VoIP. Some of the Vonage facts, taken from http://www.vonage.com, are as follows:

- Vonage leads the industry with more than 5 percent market share in VoIP service.

- As of March 2006, Vonage claims to have completed 1.8 billion+ VoIP calls with 1.5 million active lines.

- It has set up more than 2000 active rate centers in more than 150 global markets.

- It is now available in more than 5000 retail locations.

- Vonage has distribution agreements with Local Exchange Carriers (LECs) and multiple service operator (MSO) ISPs.

The Vonage deployment of VoIP as a service provider offers residential and business voice services to end users at competitive rates, thereby challenging the legacy providers. Vonage uses SIP as the session protocol for call establishment and services and is agnostic about the Internet connections at the consumer premises because they could be any of the following:

- DSL

- Wi-Fi

- Cable modem

- Broadband-over-powerline (BPL)

In terms of PSTN interconnectivity, the Vonage SIP-based VoIP applications take on two distinct forms: IP-to-IP and IP-to-PSTN. This enables backward compatibility with the PSTN and enables communication with the next-generation wireless or peering IP networks.

The successful deployments of Vonage all over the globe have transformed the VoIP perception of a value-add technology into a revenue-generating service. Recently, many other companies, such as SS8, Lingo, B2, Packet8, and RocketVoip, have also successfully deployed VoIP services.

VoIP Operational Advantages

Changing requirements in the business and residential telephony markets mandate that the new telecom features and capabilities are added into the TDM infrastructure in the most efficient way, with minimal delays and low overhead operational costs. VoIP offers the following advantages that enable the providers to reconsider their investments in the existing TDM infrastructure:

- Equipment use and call control capacity are dynamic.

- The distribution of call control logic and intelligence is more transparent and easy to manage.

- The use of signaling resources is efficient.

- Device provisioning and updates are done in a production environment and are simpler than similar work in PSTN.

- Adding new features and applications over time is easy.

- Remote management and third-party control are simpler because network resources are shared across applications.

Service Provider Case Study: Prepaid Calling Card

The following case study discusses a service that enables service providers to handle prepaid and debit calling cards. With this new service, service providers can use their existing VoIP network, gateways, and gatekeepers. They also can differentiate themselves from other VoIP service providers by offering bundled services and realizing greater profits that they can use to fund network expansions or reduce toll-bypass costs. A sample case study with BOWIE.net is presented next. It could also be used in the Vonage deployment with the same service infrastructure as described.

BOWIE.net Multiservice Networks

BOWIE.net is a regional Internet service provider (ISP) with 60 points of presence (POP) throughout the Southeast and along the East coast of the United States. It has a Cisco-powered network and currently provides residential and business access to the Internet, managed network services, and web hosting.

BOWIE.net began offering 4¢/minute long-distance VoIP services throughout its 60 POPs. It focused this service primarily to its existing business and residential customers, who were usually temporary workers and had short-term usage needs. Most did not have mobile phones with bargained monthly service plans or even a long-distance call service provider.

As competition in the residential market space grew, BOWIE.net sought alternative ways to differentiate itself from its competitors. One initiative it explored was offering prepaid or debit card services with its VoIP network.

Because BOWIE.net already used AS5400s for VoIP access, it was a natural fit to use the prepaid calling card feature added in the Cisco IOS system software. The service would not only provide BOWIE.net with prepaid revenue, but it also could be offered at a premium price because of its flexibility.

BOWIE.net worked with Cisco Systems and its partners to implement the prepaid calling card service. The partners provided the billing applications, and Cisco provided the VoIP infrastructure. Because of these partnerships, BOWIE.net was able to determine which partner could meet its technology and cost needs without concern that the solution would not interoperate.

BOWIE.net implemented the prepaid calling card solution with minimal configuration changes and equipment additions. The biggest pieces it had to add were the servers that hosted the billing applications. BOWIE.net used its existing RADIUS authentication servers and Trivial File Transfer Protocol (TFTP) servers for the implementation. It used the RADIUS servers for account number and pin number verification and the TFTP servers to store the prompts played to the subscribers when they entered the service. In addition, it used its existing AS5400s and 3640s for VoIP gateways and SIP proxy servers. In some trial runs, it even used H.323 gatekeepers and offered an H.323-based VoIP network.

Figure 15-1 shows a simplified topology of the BOWIE.net network. The key points to notice are that the billing, TFTP, and RADIUS servers can reside anywhere in the IP network, and that the existing IP backbone and VoIP gateways are being used.

Figure 15-1 *BOWIE.net SIP Network Components*

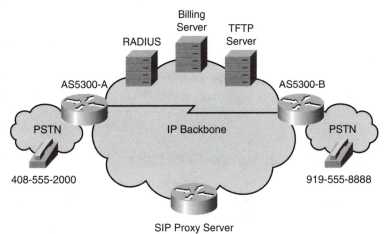

A typical prepaid calling card call proceeds as follows:

1. A subscriber purchases a prepaid calling card from BOWIE.net in $10, $20, $50, or $100 increments. The card is activated, and the account and pin numbers are defined in the RADIUS server and billing system.

2. When a subscriber wants to place a call, he dials in to the BOWIE.net VoIP network through a 1-800 access number.

3. The AS5400 receives the call from the PSTN, and the subscriber is prompted with a greeting from BOWIE.net. The subscriber is asked to choose whether he wants the remaining prompts to be played in English or another language, such as Spanish or Mandarin Chinese.

4. The subscriber is then asked to enter the account and pin numbers from his calling card. At this point, the RADIUS/billing server authenticates the subscriber information. After the subscriber is authenticated, he is asked to enter the destination phone number. Based on the called party number, the billing server determines the billing rate, and the subscriber is prompted with his remaining time and currency balance for that account.

5. After the subscriber enters the called number, the billing server starts the call detail record (CDR) for both originating and terminating gateways.

6. When the account balance of the subscriber reaches a low-water threshold, he is prompted that the balance is about to terminate. If the subscriber continues to talk past the allowed account balance, the call is terminated automatically. At this point, the subscriber has the option to extend the balance on this calling card or purchase a new card from BOWIE.net.

7. After the call is terminated, the billing server completes the call detect records (CDRs) for that specific call.

The TFTP server stores the prompts (in .au format) that the AS5400 VoIP gateways play for greetings, balance status, currency status, and time remaining. These files require more space than the AS5400 Flash memory allows, so the subscriber must download them from the TFTP server. You can obtain these prompts from Cisco.com, or BOWIE.net can create them using any .au format-capable tool.

Session Border Control: Value Addition

The session border controller (SBC) concept adds a new dimension to service provider applications because it enables the providers to quickly adapt their VoIP network to a reliable interface using VoIP services available in other carrier networks. Differences in vendor implementations of VoIP signaling, SIP RFC/draft interpretations, T.38 fax support, VoIP codec, and DTMF transport variations hinder new deployment of next-generation networks with VoIP. An SBC box can resolve this vendor incompatibility by developing and designing interworking functions (IWF). Depending on the vendor and application, these IWFs can be grouped together to perform a set of desired tasks for the deployment. The following two examples are of interest for a typical SP deployment:

■ SP-Enterprise/Residential edge for service-level agreement (SLA), signaling, and media normalization:

Signaling IWF + QoS/BW + Media IWF + Billing/CDR

■ SP-SP edge to exchange VoIP traffic:

Signaling IWF + Address/Port Translation + Billing/CDR + Rich Signaling

With these IWFs, the SBC deployments can manage multimedia flows across peering carriers and further enable the processing and manipulation of media. The SBC application server is deployed at the edge of the network and operates alone or in conjunction with any call control engine. As you learned in Chapter 9, "Billing and Mediation Services," a common complaint of SPs is that of lost or unaccounted revenues from billing. A stateful call control server (such as SIP B2BUA or MGCP call agent) can provide centralized collection of CDRs and can work with the IWF offered by the SBC to collectively control and manage the CDR-related information. This information enables carriers to recover revenues associated with lost CDRs/billing data, thereby boosting the possible revenues and margins.

In addition, the sophisticated routing engine of the Multiprotocol Signaling Switch (MSW) maximizes route revenue and enforces agreed-upon business terms to deliver the highest possible revenues and margins.

VoIP Peering: Top Priority for the Service Providers

Although VoIP as a technology has witnessed explosive growth in different parts of the world (VoIP market at $190.7 billion by 2007 per Insight Research), the stage is now set for Internet telephony service providers (ITSPs and VoBBs), VoIP carriers, and applications service providers to form some common standards or understanding on connecting different VoIP islands. These island networks need to resolve settlements (related to billing/charging for bulk minutes) from connections and handover of calls from one VoIP network to another. The providers are also interested in reducing or fully eliminating the costs of commercial peering through PSTN termination in these networks. VoIP peering and interconnectivity with VoIP has emerged as the top priority for all providers.

Many companies are looking into solutions for these problems. SBCs, as described in the previous section, are helping in this regard but have not resolved all the issues, especially in providing for a globally distributed VoIP peering network that can seamlessly offer a plug-and-play approach to connecting the diverse networks. The providers struggle when multilateral exchange of VoIP traffic is met with issues like these:

- Resolving numbering/dialing plan issues

- Interoperability issues on protocol standards and implementations

- Privacy and security issues with caller identity and validation, caller-ID spoofing, voice spams, and so on

The providers are working hard to resolve these issues, which have come up from a recent push for deploying end-to-end VoIP. It is interesting to note that IP network operators who are managing gigabits of data traffic across borders will now have to think about newer strategies as the VoIP transition adds more load and challenges to their IP networks. In addition, the wireless providers are also looking at leveraging VoIP in the context of convergence of fixed and mobile networks in an all-IP world.

Service Provider VoIP and Consumer Fixed Mobile Convergence

Just like an SBC, Consumer Fixed Mobile Convergence (FMC) complements and extends the voice/wireless solutions for a provider. MSOs are always looking for innovative ways to offer enhancements to existing cellular service. With consumer FMC, they can allow all calls made within proximity of the Wi-Fi router to connect over the MSO network using VoIP, whereas calls placed from the same wireless client device are completed over the partnering cellular carrier network.

This service can also be considered for deployment in enterprise environments, where it is more likely that a corporate employee would adopt the idea of carrying a single instrument that works over the corporate Wi-Fi and with the corporate-offered cellular service.

Many vendors are deploying portable Wi-Fi-only handsets. They intend to untether consumers from their traditional fixed-line telephones while offering an alternative to a cell phone. That would enable them to make VoIP calls from anywhere that their carrier is offering a Wi-Fi hot spot (at home, work, school, around town, airports, coffee shops, hotels, and even internationally). However, this Wi-Fi-only approach leads to lots of no-coverage areas where the handset is out of reach of an available Wi-Fi signal. The value-add demonstrated in the Consumer FMC is the ability of the subscriber to roam onto a cellular network, when drifting away from the signal of the Wi-Fi radio, while maintaining a service bundle with the MSO (triple-play with mobility).

Figure 15-2 illustrates the idea behind offering smooth handover of calls across different voice networks.

Figure 15-2 *Foundation for Fixed Mobile Convergence*

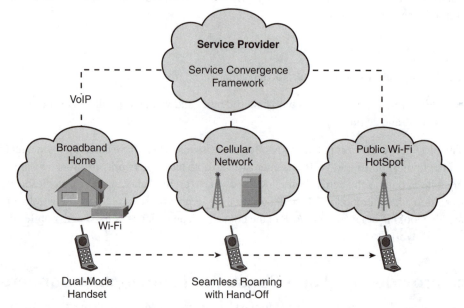

Table 15-1 outlines the benefits of fixed mobile convergence to both the service provider and the subscriber.

Table 15-1   *Service Provider and Subscriber Benefits of Fixed Mobile Convergence*

Service Provider Benefits	Subscriber Benefits
Customer loyalty	Single phone—at home, road, and work
Increased average revenue per user (ARPU)	Ability to save valuable mobile minutes
Expanded footprint/coverage	Triple-play service on the move
Optimized wireless spectrum by offloading calls to Wi-Fi	

Consumer FMC offers a huge potential for service providers to extend VoIP-related services from wireline to wireless domains, thereby saving the end user money on his phone use. With seamless merging of fixed-line service benefits and the convenience of cellular handsets, the carriers and providers can reclaim migrated traffic and protect core infrastructure revenue.

Summary

In SP markets, IP as a means of transport for networks is the driving force. The data-voice-video combined in a wired or wireless world (also referred to as *convergence*) is built on the foundation of VoIP fundamentals. However, new revenue-driven applications and the ability to reduce operational expenses via this IP convergence are what the providers are looking forward to. The traditional SP VoIP applications that are related to toll bypass, debit card, and so on are evolving into newer applications that are built on the use of IM, text messaging, video on demand, advanced CPE that allows seamless transitions from wired to wireless networks, and so on. The SP perspective/mission has been to prove that VoIP has the potential to offer better service than traditional telephone landline service.

This chapter also reviewed the importance of SBC functionality that aims to fix the interworking issues between disparate VoIP networks and the way this forms a critical piece in driving some of these applications. Similarly, FMC is another shift in extending VoIP to new levels of convergence of services.

CHAPTER 16

Enterprise Voice over IP Applications and Services

As enterprise businesses enter the 21st century, they are faced with constant demands to create more goods and services, improve the quality of their customer service, and reduce expenses in an effort to remain competitive. In addition, they are discovering that, not only is their data network a mission-critical piece of their business, but if they use it properly, it can be a competitive advantage for obtaining and retaining customer loyalty.

For many years, businesses have been building networks based on Transmission Control Protocol/Internet Protocol (TCP/IP) to take advantage of the power of TCP/IP networking and the many services it can provide. These services include ubiquitous Internet access for remote users, easy-to-use web browsers, internal corporate intranets and web servers, Java applications, and extranets with trading partners and suppliers. All these services make it easier for enterprise businesses to build new business applications, enable web-browser access to information databases, and provide new services to both internal and external customers.

Enterprise Voice over IP (VoIP) applications include business voice services and features, site-to-site voice calls over IP networks, Public Switched Telephone network (PSTN) access, unified messaging, and advanced IP services such as instant messaging and presence-enabled networks.

The enterprise requirements are evolving as more workers telecommute or are on the road. People are increasingly working across geographically dispersed sites. It is also imperative for the enterprise to extend the corporate infrastructure to the remote offices or homes to overcome geographic barriers and drive productivity. This includes the capability to make or receive calls, access messaging services, and indicate availability for communication, irrespective of the access device, such as a regular phone, a softphone running on a PC, or a cell phone.

Migrating to VoIP Architecture

The adoption of IP communication typically involves phased migration. The first step might consist of moving the time-division multiplexing (TDM) trunks from a legacy enterprise private branch exchange (PBX) to a voice gateway. Voice gateways provide interworking between the legacy TDM networks and IP networks. Voice gateways use an IP network to transport voice calls between the legacy PBXs located at the various sites across the enterprise. The users continue to get the various call features from the traditional PBX, while the enterprise realizes cost savings by using a converged network for voice and data.

When the customer is ready to implement an IP-based communication infrastructure, the next step might involve the use of hybrid TDM IP PBX or an IP PBX. The IP PBX handles on-net (intra-enterprise) calls as well as off-net (PSTN) call routing support. In both models, a VoIP client is implemented as a desktop IP phone or runs as a client on the personal computer. Calls made from the VoIP clients are serviced by the IP PBX, which provides call routing services and features like a legacy PBX. Connectivity to PSTN is provided using voice gateways that support channel associated signaling (CAS), primary rate interface (PRI), and Signaling System 7 (SS7) signaling.

The enterprise network is also engineered to provide the necessary quality of service (QoS) for prioritizing voice traffic, network security, availability, and fault tolerance.

Cisco CallManager (CCM) is an IP PBX and is a key component of the Cisco IP Telephony solution. CCM extends enterprise telephony features and services to packet telephony network devices. CCM provides call processing, signaling, and connection services to configured services including IP phones, softphones, VoIP gateways, and messaging servers. It uses standard protocols such as H.323 and Session Initiation Protocol (SIP) for call signaling with other IP PBXs, IP phones, and voice gateways.

Enterprise Voice Applications and Benefits

When enterprise businesses begin thinking about consolidating their voice and data networks into a single multiservice network, the initial application they usually consider is *toll-bypass*. Toll-bypass enables businesses to send their intraoffice voice and fax calls over their existing TCP/IP network. By moving this intraoffice traffic off the public switched telephone network (PSTN), businesses can immediately save on long-distance charges by using extra bandwidth on their data network without losing existing functionality.

> **NOTE**   Before implementing VoIP-based toll-bypass service, ensure that the use of VoIP technology in general, and use of toll-bypass in particular, is not in violation of prevailing laws or practices in the country or region of operation.

Businesses can immediately quantify the savings gleaned with toll-bypass. In fact, some businesses with a large amount of intraoffice calling, both domestic and international, have seen a return on investment (ROI) in as little as three to six months.

As enterprise businesses become more comfortable with VoIP and toll-bypass, the next applications they usually consider are ones they can apply to customer service, interactive project groups, and distance-based training. The following are some examples of applications that you can apply to these areas:

- Click-2-Call enables businesses to put a link on their websites that automatically places a call from a customer service representative to a customer.

- Microsoft Netmeeting provides integration between traditional phone services with application-sharing and H.323-based video conferencing. This integration of services enables employees in different locations to easily collaborate on projects and reduce expenses by consolidating equipment and data/voice networks.

- A Cisco IP Phone provides the look and feel of a traditional handset, with the added functionality of IP connectivity. Instead of relying on an existing PBX for functionality, such as dial tone, an IP phone works in conjunction with newer IP-based PBXs. These IP PBXs not only provide the same functionality as traditional PBXs (dial tone, voice mail, and conferencing), but they also take advantage of all IP-based services available in the network to offer new features. Because it is an IP device, the IP Phone can use not only VoIP services, but also any other IP-based multiservice application available on the network.

- The Cisco PC-based SoftPhone extends the handset functionality onto the PC with a graphical user interface that provides the same functionality as the handset and integrates with other multiservice applications such as web browsing, Microsoft Netmeeting, or directory services based on Lightweight Directory Access Protocol (LDAP). It also eliminates the need to have an additional device (the handset) on each desktop because the SoftPhone uses headsets and speakers, which are commonplace on most standard PCs.

All the services discussed so far are considered first-generation, standards-based services. Just as TCP/IP data services rapidly evolved, second-generation VoIP and integrated data/voice services based on TCP/IP will quickly evolve as well. These services will be driven by increased competition between businesses, open-standard application programming interfaces (API), protocols such as SIP, LDAP, Telephone Application Programming Interface (TAPI), Java Telephony API (JTAPI), Linux, and the creativity of enterprise network managers and programmers.

Advanced Enterprise Applications

The use of VoIP for toll-bypass and the resulting cost savings was the first step the enterprises took toward adopting a converged voice and data infrastructure. The enterprise customers were able to successfully roll out telephony services over corporate IP networks across their headquarters, branch offices, and home offices. This resulted in significant cost savings for the intraenterprise calls.

The use of IP telephony also helped employees get ubiquitous access to their corporate resources such as intranet and communication infrastructure. Employees are able to use VPN to get access to the corporate network and communicate using a softphone running on a PC using their enterprise extension numbers. With VoIP, a person working from his home or a hotel room can originate and receive calls made to his office number. He can also use other features such as hold, transfer, and conferencing from his softphone. He has access to his voice mailbox and email using unified messaging systems.

Thus, IP communication has enabled employees to be connected to their offices while being on the road and at home. The increasing mobile and geographically dispersed workforce brings new challenges for achieving collaboration, reachability, and effectiveness in communication. Enterprises are now looking at driving productivity by using a range of advanced services such as video communication, collaboration tools, and presence-aware services.

Web-Based Collaboration and Conference

Enterprises are increasingly using voice and video conference applications, document sharing, and collaboration tools to cut down on travel time and cost. These applications increase productivity by providing tools that make the meetings close to the experience of being in the same room. Document sharing and collaboration enables real-time review and modification of documents in a highly interactive manner. This interactive experience significantly reduces the time needed to reach decisions, helps drive the convergence of ideas, and reduces time spent in e-mail and travel. All this drives up employee productivity and has a direct effect on the profitability of companies.

Cisco MeetingPlace—part of the Cisco IP Communications system—is a rich-media conferencing solution that integrates voice, video, and web-conferencing facilities that make remote meetings as natural and effective as face-to-face meetings. Cisco MeetingPlace is deployed on the enterprise network and integrates with the organization's security, voice, and data infrastructure. The conference attendees require a phone and browser to participate. It can also be extended to external affiliates of the company. The use of the company network as the transport network for voice and video traffic results in significant cost savings.

Cisco MeetingPlace integrates on the user desktop. It provides an easy-to-use, intuitive web-based interface to

- Set up and manage meetings

- Join and leave meetings

- Customize the tones and announcements when attendees join and leave conferences

Cisco MeetingPlace integrates with web browsers, Cisco IP Phones, IM clients, and calendar systems such as Microsoft Outlook.

During a conference session, participants use a browser-based interface to

- View a list of participants who are sharing data and speaking—updated in real time

- Share and review documents, such as presentations and spreadsheets

- Allow text messaging (IM) sessions among the participants

- Provide security via attendee authentication and secure transport for media sessions

- Record, store, and play back conferences

- Collaborate on any application or document and pass control to other participants

Video integration with MeetingPlace requires additional video conferencing hardware, such as multipoint control unit, enhanced media processor card, and gateway with video capabilities. Customers will also need video endpoints or cameras on their desktops as part of video-conferencing deployment.

The Need for Presence Information

Most of the calls that fail to reach the called party end up in voice mail. The called party might not be at his or her desk—they might be traveling, in a meeting, or working from a remote location. As a result, the caller and called parties might make multiple attempts to reach each other—the result is a delay in making crucial business decisions.

The key issue is that the caller might not be sure when and how to reach the called party. Most people would not call their friend or colleague if they had an indication that the person was either busy or unavailable. If the caller knows in advance the availability of the called party, the chances of making a productive call increases significantly. Presence provides this crucial piece of information.

Presence describes the willingness and ability of a person to communicate. Instant messaging systems enable an end user to recognize the online or offline status of a friend before sending a message. This concept has been extended to monitoring a variety of end-user device states such as traditional phones, wireless phones, and IP clients running on laptops and PDAs. The integration of an end-user's calendar also feeds in to the presence state of a person.

Presence enables a person to project their readiness to communicate to the rest of the users in the network. The availability of presence information enables friends and colleagues to select the most appropriate time and channel of communication. Presence state can be diverse, such as

- Logged in/logged out

- Busy/Idle

- Registered/Unregistered

- In a meeting

- Out of office

- On vacation

- Do not disturb

The availability of this information to others reduces the chances of a person being interrupted during an important business meeting with a client. It also lets the caller use a less disruptive means of communication, such as instant messaging instead of trying the person's cell phone.

Presence information is primarily based on the following:

- Device state

- User state

Networks and associated devices report end-user device states, such as registration information for mobile and IP phones. The states reported are the idle, busy, and logged-out statuses. The devices can also report whether they support audio, video, IM, and so on. This provides information about the endpoints at which the user can be reached.

In addition to the device state, a person can set the user state on his device to something such as do not disturb, and can provide a useful message such as, "In a meeting till 4PM." Similarly, a user might indicate that she is available for instant messaging sessions even though she is in a meeting.

The presence state of a user is therefore an aggregation of the device and user-provided state.

Presence-Aware Services

The integration of presence information within the enterprise communication infrastructure opens up the possibility for enhanced services and productivity gains. The following are examples of the enhanced services that use presence information:

- Buddy list on the phone—Users can create a contact list or an address book on the IP phone system that is similar to the buddy list on IM systems. When the communication network is enabled for presence, the address book can be enhanced to show the presence or availability state of the users. The address book displays the device and user state indication of the contacts at a glance and gets updated in real time. The caller can place a call to the contacts in the list based on the availability status. This feature combines a speed-dial feature with availability information.

- Call routing using availability and features—An enterprise user can be reached via multiple devices, such as his desk phone, softphone on his laptop, Wi-Fi–enabled IP phone, PDA, and so on. The use of presence information such as login status, registration status, and busy/idle status for call routing can increase the chances of reaching the person and avoid the voice mail system. For example, if the user is not logged in at his desk but the Wi-Fi phone is registered with the enterprise PBX, the call can be directly routed to the Wi-Fi phone.

- Enhanced missed call list—The missed call list shows the calls that were not answered when the user was away. Presence information could be coupled with these phone numbers to show the device and user statuses of the callers and the best way to reach them. The user can attempt to return calls to the callers whose statuses show up as available.

- Availability of users for ad-hoc conference—A user trying to invite others for an impromptu conference call can check the device and user status of others as well as their availability for voice/video communication before calling them to join the conference call.

- Camp-on service—When a user wants to reach a number that is currently in busy or in logged-out state, the user can invoke the camp-on service. The enterprise PBX continues to monitor the status of the number that is currently in busy state. When the target phone and the requestor of camp-on service are both in idle state, the PBX places a call first to the requestor of the camp-on service. When the requestor answers the call, the PBX extends the call to the target phone number.

- Click-to-dial applications—Presence information is increasingly getting integrated with the e-mail clients such as Microsoft Outlook and corporate directory information. Enterprise users can see the presence state of a person in the corporate directory or against the sender in their inbox. They can use a click-to-dial application to initiate a call or an IM session if the party is available.

- Enhanced contact center applications—Presence information can be leveraged in contact centers to route calls across agents located in different geographic locations. With the use of open and standards-based protocols to distribute presence information, all the agents in the contact center are no longer tied to the same PBX system or vendor. This allows the application servers to gather agent status from various locations and distribute calls seamlessly across multiple contact centers. The availability of presence and IM also helps the agents contact the domain or subject matter experts in real time to resolve customer queries faster and more effectively.

Wi-Fi–Enabled Phones

The use of Wi-Fi–enabled (compatible with 802.11a/b/g/n standards) IP phones in the enterprise enables users to be connected from anywhere within the enterprise, from public hotspots, and from their home offices. The use of Wi-Fi phones affords all the productivity gains as well as better audio quality than cellular systems. Wi-Fi phones enable users within an enterprise to receive calls made to their extensions, without being tied to their desks.

Some of the Wi-Fi phones can also allow users to switch between VoIP and cellular phone networks. A person may initiate a VoIP call using his phone at the office. As he walks out of the office, the call gets seamlessly switched over to a cellular network. When he comes back within the enterprise network, the call gets moved back to the enterprise VoIP network.

The advantage is much greater flexibility in mobile communication as well as a potential cost savings by shifting the call minutes from a cellular network to an enterprise network.

Better Voice Quality Using Wideband Codecs

The initial VoIP implementations tried to meet the standards set by the legacy PSTN. Legacy PSTN switches and PBX have a limited bandwidth of 4 kHz, which allows sampling of audio frequencies between 300 Hz–3400 Hz. While the PSTN is restricted to narrowband frequencies, VoIP permits the use of wideband codecs. Wideband codecs sample at 16 kHz, allowing transmission of frequencies up to 8 kHz. These codecs offer much better sound clarity without a high demand on network bandwidth.

G722.2 is a wideband codec defined by ITU. G722.2 is an adaptive multirate codec with a bit rate between 6 and 23.85 kbps. iSAC from Global IP Sound is another wideband codec with a variable transmission rate between 10 and 32 kbps. iSAC is also robust against packet loss. Both of these codecs sample at 16 kHz.

These codecs are useful for VoIP applications such as distance learning, on-demand training, conferencing, and multimedia sessions such as online gaming. These codecs help improve the user experience by providing more realistic sound quality.

Summary

Businesses initially used VoIP to consolidate their voice and data networks. As the initial cost benefits of a converged network was realized, enterprise businesses have started using the converged network for a range of new applications to drive up productivity. Enterprises are using VoIP to improve collaboration across their global sites. VoIP provides new tools, such as presence and instant messaging, for the workers to collaborate with their peers halfway around the world. The availability of high-quality audio using wideband codecs, video conferencing, and document sharing enables more effective and pleasant communication.

The overall benefit is that enterprise VoIP helps improve the productivity of the employees by improving collaboration and communication.

Symbols

Numerics

A

CISCO SYSTEMS

Cisco Press

3 STEPS TO LEARNING

STEP 1   **STEP 2**   **STEP 3**

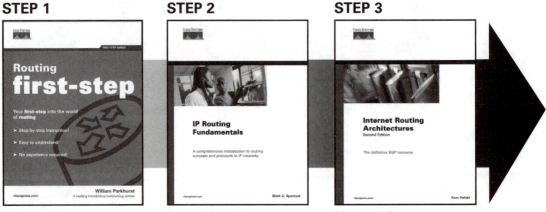

First-Step   **Fundamentals**   **Networking
Technology Guides**

STEP 1 **First-Step**—Benefit from easy-to-grasp explanations.
No experience required!

STEP 2 **Fundamentals**—Understand the purpose, application,
and management of technology.

STEP 3 **Networking Technology Guides**—Gain the knowledge
to master the challenge of the network.

NETWORK BUSINESS SERIES

The Network Business series helps professionals tackle the business issues surrounding the network. Whether you are a seasoned IT professional or a business manager with minimal technical expertise, this series will help you understand the business case for technologies.

Justify Your Network Investment.

Look for Cisco Press titles at your favorite bookseller today.

Visit **www.ciscopress.com/series** for details on each of these book series.

CISCO SYSTEMS

Cisco Press

Your **first-step** to networking starts here

Are you new to the world of networking? Whether you are beginning your networking career or simply need a better understanding of a specific technology to have more meaningful discussions with networking experts, Cisco Press First-Step books are right for you.

➤ **No experience required**

➤ **Includes clear and easily understood explanations**

➤ **Makes learning easy**

Check out each of these First-Step books that cover key networking topics

Computer Networking First-Step
ISBN: 1-58720-101-1

LAN Switching First-Step
ISBN: 1-58720-100-3

Network Security First-Step
ISBN: 1-58720-099-6

TCP/IP First-Step
ISBN: 1-58720-108-9

Voice over IP First-Step
ISBN: 1-58720-156-9

Routing First-Step
ISBN: 1-58720-122-4

Wireless Networks First-Step
ISBN: 1-58720-111-9

Visit **www.ciscopress.com/firststep** to learn more.

What's your next step?

Eager to dig deeper into networking technology? Cisco Press has the books that will help you move to the next level. Learn more at **www.ciscopress.com/series**.

ciscopress.com   **Learning begins with a first step.**

Cisco SYSTEMS

Cisco Press

FUND MENTALS SERIES
ESSENTIAL EXPLANATIONS AND SOLUTIONS

Voice over IP Fundamentals

A systematic approach to understanding the basics of Voice over IP

Jonathan Davidson, CCIE® No. 2500
James Peters

1-57870-168-6

When you need an authoritative introduction to a key networking topic, **reach for a Cisco Press Fundamentals book**. Learn about network topologies, deployment concepts, protocols, and management techniques and **master essential networking concepts and solutions**.

Look for Fundamentals titles at your favorite bookseller

802.11 Wireless LAN Fundamentals
ISBN: 1-58705-077-3

**Cisco CallManager Fundamentals:
A Cisco AVVID Solution**
ISBN: 1-58705-008-0

Cisco LAN Switching Fundamentals
ISBN: 1-58705-089-7

Cisco Unity Fundamentals
ISBN: 1-58705-098-6

Data Center Fundamentals
ISBN: 1-58705-023-4

IP Addressing Fundamentals
ISBN: 1-58705-067-6

IP Routing Fundamentals
ISBN: 1-57870-071-X

Network Security Fundamentals
ISBN: 1-58705-167-2

Storage Networking Fundamentals
ISBN: 1-58705-162-1

Voice over IP Fundamentals
ISBN: 1-57870-168-6

Coming in Fall 2005
**Cisco CallManager Fundamentals:
A Cisco AVVID Solution**, Second Edition
ISBN: 1-58705-192-3

Visit **www.ciscopress.com/series** for details about the Fundamentals series and a complete list of titles.

CISCO SYSTEMS

Cisco Press

NETWORKING TECHNOLOGY GUIDES

MASTER THE NETWORK

Turn to Networking Technology Guides whenever you need **in-depth knowledge of complex networking technologies**. Written by leading networking authorities, these guides offer theoretical and practical knowledge for **real-world networking applications and solutions**.

Look for Networking Technology Guides at your favorite bookseller

**Cisco CallManager Best Practices:
A Cisco AVVID Solution**
ISBN: 1-58705-139-7

**Cisco IP Telephony: Planning, Design,
Implementation, Operation, and Optimization**
ISBN: 1-58705-157-5

Cisco PIX Firewall and ASA Handbook
ISBN: 1-58705-158-3

Cisco Wireless LAN Security
ISBN: 1-58705-154-0

**End-to-End QoS Network Design:
Quality of Service in LANs, WANs, and VPNs**
ISBN: 1-58705-176-1

Network Security Architectures
ISBN: 1-58705-115-X

Optimal Routing Design
ISBN: 1-58705-187-7

Top-Down Network Design, Second Edition
ISBN: 1-58705-152-4

CISCO SYSTEMS

A Cisco AVVID Solution
**Cisco CallManager
Best Practices**

Delivers the proven solutions that make a difference
in your Cisco® IP Telephony deployment

Salvatore Collora, CCIE® No. 4321
Ed Leonhardt, CCIE No. 3264
Anne Smith

ciscopress.com

1-58705-139-7

Visit **www.ciscopress.com/series** for details about Networking Technology Guides and a complete list of titles.

Learning is serious business.
Invest wisely.

Cisco Press

CISCO CERTIFICATION SELF-STUDY

#1 BEST-SELLING TITLES FROM CCNA® TO CCIE®

Look for Cisco Press Certification Self-Study resources at your favorite bookseller

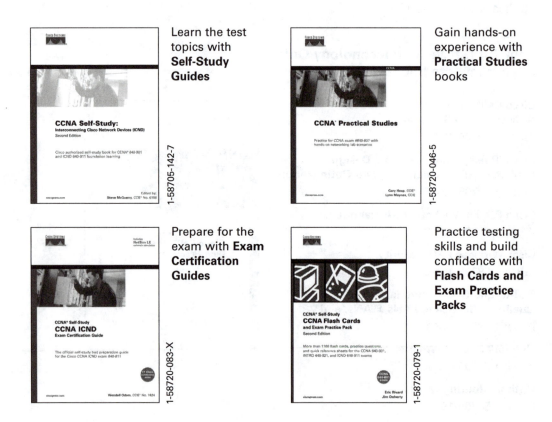

Learn the test topics with **Self-Study Guides**

Gain hands-on experience with **Practical Studies** books

Prepare for the exam with **Exam Certification Guides**

Practice testing skills and build confidence with **Flash Cards and Exam Practice Packs**

Visit **www.ciscopress.com/series** to learn more about the Certification Self-Study product family and associated series.

Learning is serious business.
Invest wisely.

Cisco Press

CCIE PROFESSIONAL DEVELOPMENT
RESOURCES FROM EXPERTS IN THE FIELD

CCIE Professional Development books are the **ultimate resource for advanced networking professionals**, providing practical insights for effective network design, deployment, and management. **Expert perspectives, in-depth technology discussions, and real-world implementation advice** also make these titles essential for anyone preparing for a CCIE® exam.

Look for CCIE Professional Development titles at your favorite bookseller

Cisco BGP-4 Command and Configuration Handbook
ISBN: 1-58705-017-X

Cisco OSPF Command and Configuration Handbook
ISBN: 1-58705-071-4

Inside Cisco IOS® Software Architecture
ISBN: 1-57870-181-3

Network Security Principles and Practices
ISBN: 1-58705-025-0

Routing TCP/IP, Volume I
ISBN: 1-57870-041-8

Troubleshooting IP Routing Protocols
ISBN: 1-58705-019-6

Troubleshooting Remote Access Networks
ISBN: 1-58705-076-5

Coming in Fall 2005
Cisco LAN Switching, Volume I, Second Edition
ISBN: 1-58705-216-4

Routing TCP/IP, Volume I, Second Edition
ISBN: 1-58705-202-4

Visit **www.ciscopress.com/series** for details about the CCIE Professional Development series and a complete list of titles.

Learning is serious business.
Invest wisely.

CISCO SYSTEMS

Cisco Press

NETWORK BUSINESS SERIES

JUSTIFY YOUR NETWORK INVESTMENT

Understand the business case for technologies with Network Business books from Cisco Press. Designed to support anyone **searching for optimal network systems,** Network Business titles help you justify your network investments.

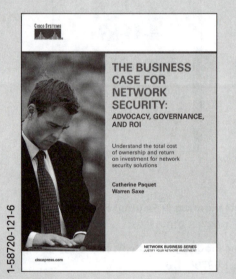

1-58720-121-6

Look for Network Business titles at your favorite bookseller

The Business Case for E-Learning
Kelly / Nanjiani • ISBN: 1-58720-086-4

The Business Case for Network Security
Paquet / Saxe • ISBN: 1-58720-121-6

The Business Case for Storage Networks
Williams • ISBN: 1-58720-118-6

The Case for Virtual Business Processes
Young / Jude • ISBN: 1-58720-087-2

IP Telephony Unveiled
Brown • ISBN: 1-58720-075-9

Power Up Your Small-Medium Business
Aber • ISBN: 1-58705-135-4

The Road to IP Telephony
Carhee • ISBN: 1-58720-088-0

Taking Charge of Your VoIP Project
Walker / Hicks • ISBN: 1-58720-092-9

Coming in Fall 2005

The Business Case for Enterprise-Class Wireless LANs
Castaneda / Alasdair / Vinckier • ISBN: 1-58720-125-9

MPLS for Decision Makers
Sayeed / Morrow • ISBN: 1-58720-120-8

Network Business Series.   **Justify Your Network Investment.**

Visit **www.ciscopress.com/netbus** for details about the Network Business series and a complete list of titles.

Cisco Press

SAVE UP TO 30%

Become a member and save at **ciscopress.com**!

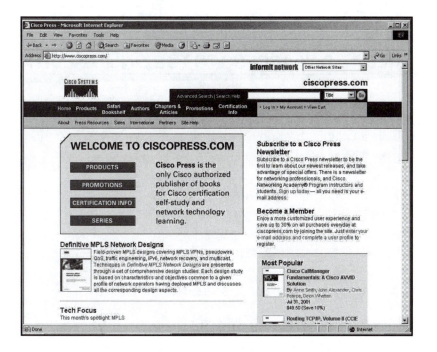

Complete a **user profile** at ciscopress.com today to become a member and benefit from **discounts up to 30% on every purchase** at ciscopress.com, as well as a more customized user experience. Your membership will also allow you access to the entire Informit network of sites.

Don't forget to subscribe to the monthly Cisco Press newsletter to be the first to learn about new releases and special promotions. You can also sign up to get your first **30 days FREE on Safari Bookshelf** and preview Cisco Press content. Safari Bookshelf lets you access Cisco Press books online and build your own customized, searchable electronic reference library.

Visit **www.ciscopress.com/register** to sign up and start saving today!

The profile information we collect is used in aggregate to provide us with better insight into your technology interests and to create a better user experience for you. You must be logged into ciscopress.com to receive your discount. Discount is on Cisco Press products only; shipping and handling are not included.

Learning is serious business.
Invest wisely.

THIS BOOK IS SAFARI ENABLED

INCLUDES FREE 45-DAY ACCESS TO THE ONLINE EDITION

The Safari® Enabled icon on the cover of your favorite technology book means the book is available through Safari Bookshelf. When you buy this book, you get free access to the online edition for 45 days.

Safari Bookshelf is an electronic reference library that lets you easily search thousands of technical books, find code samples, download chapters, and access technical information whenever and wherever you need it.

TO GAIN 45-DAY SAFARI ENABLED ACCESS TO THIS BOOK:

- Go to **http://www.ciscopress.com/safarienabled**

- Complete the brief registration form

- Enter the coupon code found in the front of this book before the "Contents at a Glance" page

If you have difficulty registering on Safari Bookshelf or accessing the online edition, please e-mail customer-service@safaribooksonline.com.